Broken Timelines - Books 1-3: Egypt, Mesopotamia, the Indo-Europeans and Harappans

Jack Stornoway

Published by Digital Ink Productions, 2019.

While every precaution has been taken in the preparation of this book, the publisher assumes no responsibility for errors or omissions, or for damages resulting from the use of the information contained herein.

BROKEN TIMELINES - BOOKS 1-3: EGYPT, MESOPOTAMIA, THE INDO-EUROPEANS AND HARAPPANS

First edition. December 26, 2019.

Copyright © 2019 Jack Stornoway.

ISBN: 978-1989852972

Written by Jack Stornoway.

Table of Contents

Introduction 1

Section 1: Dynastic Egypt 6

Conventional View of Ancient Egypt 8

Early Egyptology 10

Ancient Egyptology 12

Dark Age Egyptology 17

The First Egyptian Short Timeline 19

Ancient Kingdoms and Dark Ages 20

Second Egyptian Dark Age 22

Egyptian Middle Kingdom 29

First Egyptian Dark Age 32

Egyptian Old Kingdom 35

Foundations of Egypt 42

Christian Timeline 43

Islamic Timeline 46

The Even More Christian Timeline 48

Carbon Dating 49

Section 2: Dynastic Mesopotamia 53

Sumero-Akkadian Timeline 55

Babylonian Timeline 76

Assyrian Timeline 79

Hittite Timeline 82

Kassite-Mitanni-Hyksos Timeline 84

Dynastic Mesopotamia in the CMT 95

Dynastic Mesopotamia in the ULT 97

Section 3: Indo-European and Harappan Historic Era 99

The Vedas 101

The Iron Ages 104

Dating the Vedas 107

The Avesta 112

The Greco-Aryans 122

The West-Europeans 130

The Balto-Slavs 133

The Hattians and Hittites 136

The Kassites, Mitanni and Hyksos 139

The Harappans 143

Brahmi and Kharosthi 157

Dating the Harappans 173

The Minoans 178

Section 4: Pre-Dynastic Egypt 182

Zep Tepi 183

Rule of Spirits of the Dead and Demigods 189

The 10 Kings of Thinis 190

The 30 Kings of Memphis	192
1817-Year-Line of Kings	216
Reign of the Demigods	217
Spirits and Followers of Horus	219
Reign of the Gods	220
Section 5: Pre-Dynastic Mesopotamia	228
Kish Civilization	229
Antediluvian Shuruppak	233
Ziusudra, Utnapishtim, and Atrahasis	235
Dynastic Shuruppak	238
Shuruppaki Genetics	240
Antediluvian Zimbir	242
Axis-Mundi	244
Laschamp Event	247
Zimbari Genetics	249
Antediluvian Larak	250
Laraki Genetics	252
Antediluvian Bad-tibira	259
Dumuzid the Shepherd	261
The Shepherd and the Smith	263
The Mountain in the Steppes	265
Jewish Antediluvian Bloodlines	272

Recent Out of Africa Theory? 276

The Underworld in the Mountain 279

The Dumuzid Saga 282

Ishtar and Tammuz, and Zababa 287

Adonis, Attis, Atunis, Tithonus, and Osiris 291

Dionysus, Disonuso, Diwonijo, and Bacchus 296

Panthers and Lions 310

Yemo the Shepherd 314

The Queen of Heaven 318

Antediluvian Eridu 324

Section 6: Indo-Aryan and Harappan Mythic Era 328

Yima, Yama, Yami, and Ymir 329

The Rama Epics 340

Rama and Ra 346

The Monkey-God 348

The Sha and the Enusha 351

The Werelions and Werejaguars 354

The Bird-Man 357

The Snake-People 360

The Elephant-Man 362

The Bull-Man 364

Conclusion 366

References... 368

Available Formats... 390

Introduction

Modern Eurasian cultures, and by extension all modern cultures, can be traced back to just a few ancient civilizations, which handed down to us: language, writing, mathematics, engineering, architecture, agriculture, the foundation of scientific understanding, and a plethora of religions. These preeminent cultures were Egypt, Sumer, Akkad, the Indus Valley Civilization, and China. Additionally, several ancient texts survive that have unclear origins, including the Vedas and the Avesta, both being early Indo-European works.

Today, Indo-European languages dominate global politics and finance, accompanied by Chinese and Semitic languages. Of the UN's six working languages, four are Indo-European (English, French, Russian, and Spanish), one is Chinese (Mandarin dialect), and one is Semitic (Arabic). Other major Indo-European languages include German, Italian, Portuguese, and Hindi. Most official national languages are Indo-European, either the aforementioned, or: Dutch, Gaelic, Danish, Swedish, Norwegian, Icelandic, Greek, Polish, Czech, Slovak, Lithuanian, Latvian, Slovene, Croatian, Bosnian, Serbian, Albanian, Macedonian, Bulgarian, Romanian, Ukrainian, Belarusian, Armenian, Farsi, Urdu, Bengali, Nepalese, or Sinhala. Additionally, within South Asia, several regional languages have more than 10 million speakers, most of which are Indo-European. Chinese is the only surviving Chinese language, although some linguists view it as a language family in itself, with its dialects more properly viewed as languages. Arabic is the most wide-spread of the Semitic languages, although, again, some linguists prefer to view it as a language group composed of several regional forms of Arabic. Hebrew, Amharic, and Tigrinya have also survived as official national languages within the Semitic language group. As the Indo-European languages are all believed to be derived from a common source, that culture and its descendant cultures played a major role in the development of the modern world. Likewise, the ancient Chinese and Semitic cultures have impacted the modern world, however, none of the major modern cultures are derived from the Egyptians, Sumerians, or

Harappans. We are at best their adopted children, and at worst cultures that have pillaged their remains to establish ourselves.

The earliest major Semitic culture was the Akkadians, who conquered the Sumerians. Later, their cultural descendants, the Babylonians, and Assyrians conquered the Egyptians. Meanwhile, the Harappans were either conquered or colonized by the Indo-Aryan off-shoot of the Indo-Europeans, who eventually gave rise to the majority of modern South Asian cultures. Other Indo-European cultures settled across Europe and Central Asia, giving rise to the Medians, Persians, Greeks, and Romans, who each took turns dominating the nations around them until the rise of the Arabs under Mohamed allowed the Semites to become dominant again in the Middle East. In China, the slow relentless expansion of the Chinese culture dislodged the Turks and Mongols, who managed to seize Central Asia and Anatolia from the Indo-Europeans. The Indo-Europeans responded to the rise of the Arabs, Turks, and Mongols, by expanding westward across the Atlantic, and then around the world, ultimately subjugating almost the entire globe, before turning on themselves and fighting two world wars and a cold-war that threatened to end all life on Earth.

All of this 'progress' would not have been possible without the foundational cultures of the ancient world: Egypt, Sumer, and the Indus Valley Civilization, and yet, after hundreds of years of studying them, we refuse to accept that they knew their own history. Instead, we have simply made up histories for them, histories that do not fit any of the surviving evidence. Based on the current 'conventional' timelines, found in any history book printed since the 1950s, the Hyksos simply appeared at the border of the Egyptian Empire and conquered them. Later, they were driven out of Egypt and simply disappeared again. They did not pass through the Hittite, Assyrian, or Babylonian Empires, and were never mentioned by those cultures, something hard to imagine, as the Hyksos that were driven out of Egypt amounted to 480,000 warriors, plus their families and slaves. You'd think someone would have noticed a horde of millions passing through their land.

BROKEN TIMELINES - BOOKS 1-3: EGYPT, MESOPOTAMIA, THE INDO-EUROPEANS AND HARAPPANS

In the conventional timelines, the Egyptians were a thousand years behind the Sumerians in technology during the Old and Middle Kingdom periods. The Sumerians had horses and wagons before the Egyptians began building pyramids, and even though the two cultures were major trading partners, no horses or wagons even entered Egypt. They must have had their border-guards telling everyone to leave their wagon at the border and just carry everything on their backs. Not only did the Egyptians build the great pyramids without the horse, or wagon, or even the wheel, because, you know, they were all parked at the border, but then the Old Kingdom collapsed, and the Middle Kingdom that immerged after the dark age also didn't want any of this newfangled, no, wait, oldfangled technology, but they chose to dig the canal linking the Nile and Fayum without any vehicles to carry away the unwanted debris. Then, because they wanted to prove they could really do something virtually impossible, and in the hardest way imaginable, the terraced the Fayum depression, creating a lake the size of Lake Ontario, all by hand, and without any vehicles or beast of burden. Seriously? Yes, look it up in any history book. The almighty Egyptologists have spoken!

The conventional timelines continued to baffle the mind as one looks at the Sumerian civilization, which, since the two cultures were trading from the earliest point in Egyptian history, is now subject to the historical-fictional passed off by Egyptologists. Because these cultures were around at the same time, the Sumerians are forced to have existed circa 3500 to 1900 BC, an impossibly late-date, as their cities would have had to be built in swamp-land. They would have had no local access to rock and would have had to import the rocks for the lower levels of their cities from the Zagros Mountains. While transporting the rocks would not have been hard, one has to wonder why they would sail a barge out into the middle of a swamp, and dive down into the muck to lay the foundations of a city. Why could artificial islands if they knew were there was land? Why try to raise cattle inside of cities? Seriously! That is what Assyriologists would have us all believe! On the other hand, the Sumerians recorded that the cities were founded long before the water level rose, meaning the foundations of the cities would have been the original cities' walls and buildings. Of course, both the ancient Sumerians and modern paleo-climatologists agree that this was thousands of years before Egyptologists have determined the Old Kingdom existed, so the Sumerians must have been wrong, Egyptologists certainly can't be wrong, they have tenure! The ancient Egyptians and Sumerians didn't even have a Bachelor's degree.

This bizarre timeline of Sumer, then forces the Indus Valley Civilization to have existed as recently as 3500 to 1300 BC. This means that this major culture of ancient South Asia, which spanned almost all of Pakistan, and a large swath of north and west India, a civilization larger that the combined are of the Egyptian and Sumerian civilizations, somehow existed in between two iron age civilizations, and yet was a bronze age civilization. The ancient Harappans traded as far north as the Aral Sea in Central Asia, and yet never noticed the iron-working Yaz civilization, in the area of modern Uzbekistan. They also didn't notice the various iron-working cultures across India which have been dated back as far as 2400 BC. So, for over a thousand years, they traded widely across the region, but apparently not with anyone actually living there. Seriously? Yes, although unlike the Egyptologists and Assyriologists, Indologists will generally snicker when they're asked to defend this nonsense, as most don't actually believe it themselves, but repeating random nonsense is how you get tenure, so here goes, 'Once upon a time...'

While Manetho and modern Egyptologists do agree on the general outline of Egyptian history, there are some striking differences, modern Egyptologists have removed over a hundred kings from Manetho's timeline, compressing Egyptian history from a dynastic period that should have started in 5510 BC, to a dynastic period that starts in 3100 BC. There are also ongoing efforts to change the foundation date of the 1st Dynasty of Egypt to 3000 BC (Ian Shaw) or 2770 BC (David Rohl). These ongoing attempts to revise Egyptian 'history' create more and more fictional history, as dynasties are either forced to coexist or erases them entirely from the timeline. Manetho's 7th Dynasty is now considered fictitious by Egyptologists,[1] even though it was mentioned in the Turin King List, and the names of the kings were recorded in the Abydos King Lists, both lists dating from the New Kingdom era.

What the ancient Egyptians actually recorded was that their civilization was founded circa 5500 BC, not 3100 BC, and using this timeline most of the archaeological evidence within Egypt makes sense. There are ruins in Egypt which have to date back to much earlier periods, such as the Osireion, and the Labyrinth, both of which are built well below the waterline. As the waterline has been lower since the Aswan Dam was built in the 1960s than any other time in Dynastic or post-Dynastic history, these ruins must date back at least 15,000 years, when paleo-climatologists have found the Nile almost dried out due to the expansion of the glaciers in the Ethiopian Highlands. The ancient Egyptians had records of this, not the expanding glaciers, but the societies that existed in near Abydos and Memphis around 15,000 years ago, meaning that their records must have been fairly accurate for a very long time. Unfortunately, no one seems to care what the Egyptians actually recorded, after all, it wasn't written in English, it was in one of those weird foreign languages, and so Egyptologist have been able to make up complete nonsense for a century now, inventing entire civil wars to explain how there could have been so many kings and even dynasties around at the same time!

Section 1: Dynastic Egypt

The purpose of this work is to demonstrate that the original Egyptian timeline, as recorded by Manetho and the ancient Egyptian King Lists, and as documented by the foremost Egyptologist of the British Empire, Sir W. M. Flinders Petrie, actually makes far more sense than the CET. The original timeline is herein called the Unified Long Timeline (ULT) as it also takes into account the dynastic records of Mesopotamia, and the various lines of scientific evidence amassed in the past century such as dendrochronology, paleoclimatology, and carbon-dating.

The dates used in the ULT are taken from Petrie's Researches In Sinai from 1906, and should not be misconstrued as exact dates. Petrie himself states that the earlier dates could be up to a century off, due to the limited amounts of records and artifacts dating to the Old and Middle Kingdoms. Likewise, the CET used herein is the 'Middle Chronology' of Egyptology. Egyptologists have worked out several variations of the short timeline, with each generation seeming to want to distinguish itself by erasing more of Egypt's ancient history. And it is history, it was written down. There were Kings and Queens recorded, yet the way Egyptologists are going, by the year 3000, the Great Pyramids of Giza will probably have been designed by Archimedes and built by Cleopatra. The various versions of the CET proposed the past century can deviate by up to 630 years for the foundation of the 1st Dynasty, therefore the CET dates given should also be considered relative. The following is a comparison between the two timelines:

BROKEN TIMELINES - BOOKS 1-3: EGYPT, MESOPOTAMIA, THE INDO-EUROPEANS AND HARAPPANS

Dynastic Egyptian Timelines

Period	Dynasty	CET	ULT
Early Dynastic Period	1st	3100 BC to 2890 BC	5510 BC to 5247 BC
Early Dynastic Period	2nd	2890 BC to 2686 BC	5247 BC to 4945 BC
Old Kingdom	3rd	2686 BC to 2613 BC	4945 BC to 4731 BC
Old Kingdom	4th	2613 BC to 2498 BC	4731 BC to 4454 BC
Old Kingdom	5th	2498 BC to 2384 BC	4454 BC to 4206 BC
Old Kingdom	6th	2384 BC to 2181 BC	4206 BC to 4003 BC
First Egyptian Dark Age (First Intermediate Period)	7th		4003 BC to 3933 BC
First Egyptian Dark Age (First Intermediate Period)	8th	2181 BC to 2160 BC	3933 BC to 3787 BC
First Egyptian Dark Age (First Intermediate Period)	9th	2160 BC to 2130 BC	3787 BC to 3687 BC
First Egyptian Dark Age (First Intermediate Period)	10th	2130 BC to 2040 BC	3687 BC to 3502 BC
Middle Kingdom	11th	2061 BC to 1991 BC	3502 BC to 3459 BC
Middle Kingdom	12th	1991 BC to 1803 BC	3459 BC to 3246 BC
Second Egyptian Dark Age (Second Intermediate Period)	13th	1803 BC to 1649 BC	3246 BC to 2793 BC
Second Egyptian Dark Age (Second Intermediate Period)	14th	1705 BC to 1690 BC	2793 BC to 2533 BC
Second Egyptian Dark Age (Second Intermediate Period)	15th	1674 BC to 1535 BC	2533 BC to 2249 BC
Second Egyptian Dark Age (Second Intermediate Period)	16th	1660 BC to 1600 BC	2249 BC to 1731 BC
Second Egyptian Dark Age (Second Intermediate Period)	Abydos	1650 BC to 1600 BC	
Second Egyptian Dark Age (Second Intermediate Period)	17th	1580 BC to 1549 BC	1731 BC to 1580 BC
New Kingdom	18th	1549 BC to 1292 BC	1580 BC to 1322 BC
New Kingdom	19th	1292 BC to 1189 BC	1322 BC to 1202 BC
New Kingdom	20th	1189 BC to 1077 BC	1202 BC to 1102 BC
Third Egyptian Dark Age (Third Intermediate Period)	21st	1069 BC to 945 BC	1102 BC to 952 BC
Third Egyptian Dark Age (Third Intermediate Period)	22nd	945 BC to 720 BC	952 BC to 755 BC
Third Egyptian Dark Age (Third Intermediate Period)	23rd	837 BC to 728 BC	755 BC to 721 BC
Third Egyptian Dark Age (Third Intermediate Period)	24th	732 BC to 720 BC	721 BC to 715 BC
Third Egyptian Dark Age (Third Intermediate Period)	25th	732 BC to 653 BC	715 BC to 664 BC
Late Period	26th	672 BC to 525 BC	664 BC to 525 BC
Late Period	27th	525 BC to 404 BC	525 BC to 404 BC
Late Period	28th	404 BC to 398 BC	404 BC to 398 BC
Late Period	29th	398 BC to 380 BC	398 BC to 380 BC
Late Period	30th	380 BC to 343 BC	380 BC to 343 BC
Late Period	31st	343 BC to 332 BC	343 BC to 332 BC
Greek Period	Argead	332 BC to 310 BC	332 BC to 310 BC
Greek Period	Ptolemaic	310 BC to 30 BC	310 BC to 30 BC

Conventional View of Ancient Egypt

Open any history book today and turn to the Egyptian civilization and you'll see pretty much the same thing: the Kingdom of Egypt was founded around 3100 BC. If you go one step further and open a book on Egyptology you'll see scholarly debates about when it was exactly, with some radical Egyptologists claiming it was as early as 3400 BC, or as recent as 2770 BC. The way Egyptian history is presented it would seem that around 5000 years ago the Egyptian civilization was founded by nomadic tribes that suddenly decided to settle down somewhere.

These settlers built pens for their livestock and started farming the local grains. They then built some mud huts, and eventually through some inspired genius, invented writing, first as simple pictures, and then as more and more highly complex hieroglyphs. This no doubt led to discovering mathematics, geometry, and as their mud huts got bigger, architecture and engineering. Finally, some egotistical king decided he needed a private mountain to be buried in and worked thousands of slaves to death building the first pyramid.

Other kings decided they needed bigger and bigger pyramids, working more and more slaves to death until some slaves rebelled. Jews, Christians, and Muslims have holy books that describe a rebel from the house of Pharaoh named Moses, who unleashed ten plagues upon Egypt, causing widespread death and destruction to the point that the king let the slaves go. Then the Egyptians stopped building pyramids, probably because they didn't have enough slaves, and their civilization slowly withered until Alexander the Great invaded. After that, the Egyptian civilization ceased to exist, as the country was ruled by a series of foreign cultures starting with the Greeks, and then the Romans, Arabs, Turks, and British, before emerging as the country it is today.

While the history from the conquest of Alexander onward is essentially correct, almost everything described in the two paragraphs above before Alexander is fundamentally wrong. Egyptologists reading the above paragraphs might be surprised that anyone could believe such nonsense, yet many intelligent and educated people believe what is stated above. The above description of Egyptian history is so widespread, that when paleo-climatologists discovered proof of the 5.9 Kiloyear Event, it was suggested that this was what caused the nomadic tribes to settle in the Nile region. The 5.9 Kiloyear Event was an intense period of atmospheric drying and the expansion of deserts across North Africa. Before this event, much of what is today the Sahara Desert was grasslands and forests. The event happened around 5900 years ago and is linked to many human migrations that happened at the time. Naturally one of these migrations would have been out of the Sahara into the Nile River valley.

As Egyptologists all seem to agree that Egyptian civilization was founded sometime after 5900 years ago the concept has begun to gain acceptance within the Egyptology community. The idea that the 5.9 Kiloyear Event is what forced the nomadic tribes to settle in the Nile and become farmers certainly seems valid unless one asks why the virtually identical 8.2 Kiloyear Event didn't do the same thing 2300 years earlier? The answer, of course, is the circular logic that Egyptian civilization developed after the 5.9 Kiloyear Event because Egypt appears in the archaeological record starting sometime between 5400 and 4770 years ago. But did it?

Early Egyptology

This idea that Egypt was founded around 3100 BC is a fairly new idea, it has only been around for about a century. The founders of Egyptology generally claimed that Egypt was thousands of years older. Modern Egyptology began in the early 1800s when Jean-François Champollion first deciphered Egyptian hieroglyphs and set off a period of Egyptomania in Post-Napoleonic Europe. Champollion and another linguist and founder of Egyptology, Ippolito Rosellini, organized the Franco-Tuscan Expedition to Egypt of 1828-29, which greatly expanded the number of ancient Egyptian records Europeans had to study. Champollion was convinced from his translations of the ancient dynastic records, that Egypt was founded in 5867 BC.

Many early Egyptologists studying the ancient Egyptian dynastic records came to similar dates, such as Georg Friedrich Unger who in 1867 published the date of 5613 BC for the foundation of Egypt.[2] In 1904 Eduard Meyer discovered the Sothic Cycle of Heliacal Risings of Sirius, which forms the bases for the traditional timeline of Egypt, and placed the foundation date for Egypt at no later than 3315 BC. Meyer revolutionized the way Egyptologists were dating ancient Egyptian events by introducing so-called 'approximate dates,' which dealt with the gaps in Egyptian history by grouping together events that were known to have happened in relation to each other, and then dating them to the latest possible point they could have taken place according to the ancient Egyptian use of the Sothic calendar. This meant that events could have happened earlier than Meyer's dates, but not later.

Sir Flinders Petrie, who was the first chair of Egyptology in the United Kingdom, placed the foundation of Egypt at 5510 BC in his 1906 book *Researches In Sinai*. Petrie was a pioneer of systematic methodology in archaeology, the preservation of artifacts, and led many excavations of the most important archaeological sites in Egypt. Until his death in 1933, Petrie continued to be an advocate for the long timeline of Egyptian history, even as the world of Egyptology slowly shifted towards the now ubiquitous short timeline. In Petrie's own words:

> "*If any one wishes to abandon these dates, they must also abandon the greater part of the information that we have, cast Manetho and the Turin papyrus aside, ignore the evidence of Cretan archaeology, and treat history as a mere matter of arbitrary will, regardless of all records. As against this general position of dates there is nothing to be set in favour of any very different schemes, nothing — except the weightiest thing of all - prepossessions.*"[3]

So what happened?

Ancient Egyptology

The question 'How old is Egypt?' is not a new question. The oldest known archaeological digs in Egypt actually date back to the time of ancient Egypt. King Thutmose IV, who reigned around 1400 BC was famous for the restoration of the Sphinx at Giza, and then erecting the Dream Stele, between the two paws of the Sphinx. Around 1250 BC King Ramesses II's son Khaemweset, famously excavated and restored many historic buildings, tombs, temples, and pyramids. Prince Khaemweset is often described as 'the First Egyptologist' due to his efforts in discovering and restoring historic buildings. Restoration texts from Khaemweset have been found associated with the pyramid of Unas at Saqqara, the tomb of Shepseskaf called the Mastabat al-Fir'aun, the Sun-Temple of Nyuserre Ini, the Pyramid of Sahure, the Pyramid of Djoser, and the Pyramid of Userkaf.

For someone who has never studied the history of Egypt, the idea that the ancient Egyptians were discovering and restoring the ruins of ancient Egypt might seem strange. It is important to remember that whenever Egypt was founded, it was around for a very long time. King Thutmose IV and Prince Khaemweset lived during the period of Egyptian history known as the New Kingdom, while the buildings they were discovering and restoring dated back at least a thousand years earlier to the Old Kingdom.

Both the ULT and CET agree that the New Kingdom existed between approximately 1580 to 1102 BC ULT or 1549 to 1077 BC CET. The two timelines disagree over what happened before the New Kingdom. The generally accepted CET places the Old Kingdom between 2686 and 2181 BC, while the ULT places the Old Kingdom between 4945 and 4003 BC. Specific versions of both timelines may differ by several hundred years when discussing the Old Kingdom.

Regardless of the timeline used, King Thutmose II and Prince Khaemweset lived at least a thousand years after the buildings they were discovering and restoring were originally built, and possibly several thousand years. It seems likely that the two ancient Egyptologists would have believed it had been several thousand years, and not just one thousand years, as the Abydos King List was created at approximately the same period, and matches closely to the timeline worked out by Manetho over a thousand years later. The Abydos King List is a list of the names of seventy-six kings of ancient Egypt, found on a wall of the Temple of Seti I at Abydos, and dated to around 1270 BC.

The ancient Egyptians kept many lists of their kings, however, each list reflects the bias of whoever wrote it. For example, the Abydos King List omits kings the priests of Abydos found heretical, such as Akhenaten, and the entire Hyksos Dynasty. This abundance of lists that only partially agree with each other is what has caused the multitude of variations of both the long and short-timelines. This plethora of histories was discovered by the Greeks when they ruled Egypt and was tackled by the Egyptian historian Manetho around 300 BC when he complied and published *Aegyptiaca*. *Aegyptiaca*, which means 'History of Egypt' in Greek was the seminal work on Egyptian history during the Greco-Roman period.

The influence of Manetho on Egyptology cannot be understated. For two thousand years, historians and Egyptologists believed that Manetho had been the first to organize the ancient kings and queens of Egypt into the dynasties we still use today. Unfortunately, the late Roman era was fraught religious controversy, one of which was the age of the world, as the early Christians believed that humanity was only created in 5509 BC, while the Rabbinical Jews believed it was in 3750 BC, and the Samaritans believed it happened around 4400 BC. Yet the Egyptians and Babylonians both claimed their civilizations were older than any of those dates. Early Christian theologians attacked the works of ancient historians like Manetho and Berossos, claiming that both Egypt and Babylonia had to date to after the Great Flood of Noah, which happened circa 3000 BC according to the original Greek translation of the Old Testament called the Septuagint.

Eusebius, the 'Father of Church History' wrote the following first draft of the short timeline around 300 AD, quoting and then deconstructing Manetho's Aegyptiaca in order to prove the 'Hebrew timeline':

"Excerpted from the Eusebius' Chronica

BOOK I.

Reign of Spirits and Followers of Horus

Dynasties of Gods, Demigods, and Spirits of the Dead.

From the Egyptian History of Manetho, who composed his account in three books. These deal with the Gods, the Demigods, the Spirits of the Dead, and the mortal kings who ruled Egypt down to Darius, king of the Persians.

1. The first man [or god] in Egypt is Hephaestus [Ptah], who is also renowned among the Egyptians as the discoverer of fire. His son, Helios [Ra], was succeeded by Sosis [Shu]: then follow, in turn, Cronos [Geb], Osiris, Typhon [Set], brother of Osiris, and lastly Orus [Horus], son of Osiris and Isis, These were the first to hold sway in Egypt. Thereafter, the kingship passed from one to another in unbroken succession down to Bydis through 13,900 years. The year I take, however, to be a lunar one, consisting, that is, of 30 days : what we now call a month the Egyptians used formerly to style a year.

2. After the Gods, Demigods reigned for 1255 years, and again another line of kings held sway for 1817 years: then came thirty more kings of Memphis, reigning for 1790 years; and then again ten kings of This [Thinis], reigning for 350 years.

3. There followed the rule of Spirits of the Dead and Demigods, for 5813 years.

4. The total [of the last five groups] amounts to 11,000 years, these however being lunar periods, or months. But, in truth, the whole rule of which the Egyptians tell - the rule of Gods, Demigods, and Spirits of the Dead - is reckoned to have comprised in all 24,900 lunar years, which make 2206 solar years.

5. Now, if you care to compare these figures with Hebrew timeline, you will find that they are in perfect harmony. Egypt is called Mestraim by the Hebrews; and Mestraim lived not long after the Flood. For after the Flood, Cham (or Ham), son of Noah, begat Aegyptus or Mestraim, who was the first to set out to establish himself in Egypt, at the time when the tribes began to disperse this way and that. Now the whole time from Adam to the Flood was, according to the Hebrews, 2242 years.

6. But, since the Egyptians claim by a sort of prerogative of antiquity that they have, before the Flood, a line of Gods, Demigods, and Spirits of the Dead, who reigned for more than 20,000 years, it clearly follows that these years should be reckoned as the same number of months as the years recorded by the Hebrews: that is, that all the months contained in the Hebrew record of years, should be reckoned as so many lunar years of the Egyptian calculation, in accordance with the total length of time reckoned from the creation of man in the beginning down to Mestraim. Mestraim was indeed the founder of the Egyptian race; and from him the first Egyptian dynasty must be held to spring.

7. But if the number of years is still in excess, it must be supposed that perhaps several Egyptian kings ruled at one and the same time; for they say that the rulers were kings of This, of Memphis, of Sals, of Ethiopia, and of other places at the same time. It seems, moreover, that different kings held sway in different regions, and that each dynasty was confined to its own nome : thus it was not a succession of kings occupying the throne one after the other, but several kings reigning at the same time in different regions. Hence arose the great total number of years. But let us leave this question and take up in detail the timeline of Egyptian history."

Clearly, early Christian Egyptologists learned the lesson of Eusebius and passed it on to their secular descendants: If you don't like what the Egyptians recorded, just make up something!

Modern Egyptologists entirely reject the idea that the Egyptians didn't know the difference between months and years, the idea is so preposterous it is surprising that anyone would have bothered writing it down. It supposes that most of the ancient kings of Egypt ruled for less than a year. It's as if Eusebius had no idea how babies are made.

...but if that first idea doesn't work, no worries, maybe all the kings were around at the same time. Maybe every little village had a king. Why not? It's not like the Egyptians built anything that would require a unified government, drawing resources from across the country. This multiple concurrent dynasties hypothesis would enter Egyptology in the early 1800s, be thoroughly debunked by 1900, and then return to dominate Egyptology by the 1950s.

Dark Age Egyptology

During the European Dark Ages that followed the fall of Rome, the question became mute as few Europeans could read, and most of the books from the pre-Christian era had been burnt. The Great Pyramids of Giza were believed by Medieval Christians to be grain solos erected by the Jewish patriarch Joseph while he was enslaved in Egypt. This strange idea of a solid stone grain solo still finds believers among Christian fundamentalists today.

In Egypt and the greater Islamic world, interest in the ancient Egyptians continued unabated. Most of the ancient Greek and Roman books that survived the Christian book burnings, only survived because copies of them survived in Persia and Arabia. Egyptian historians wrote extensively about the ancient Egyptian civilization, including Abdul Latif al-Baghdadi, a teacher at Cairo's Al-Azhar University around 1200 AD, and Al-Maqrizi an Egyptian historian around 1400 AD. Unfortunately, after centuries of occupation by the Nubians, Assyrians, Persians, Greeks, Romans, and Arabs, the Egyptians had lost the ability to translate hieroglyphs and hieratic. Around 900 AD the alchemist Ibn Wahshiyyah managed to partially decipher the ancient Egyptian scripts, however, it wasn't until Champollion's work in the early-1800s AD that the full translation of ancient Egyptian text became possible.

As Europe passed through the Renaissance classical Greek and Roman works began to circulate again in Europe, and historians began to question the idea that the Pyramids of the Giza plateau were used to store grain. Napoleon's invasion of Egypt inspired the imagination of Europeans, and less than a decade after Napoleon's defeat, Jean-François Champollion announced he had deciphered the ancient Egyptian hieroglyphs. For the first time in over 1000 years, humanity could read what the ancient Egyptians had written down. Expeditions were mounted to Egypt to recover as many texts and artifacts as possible. Europe had entered the age of Egyptomania, and the Rape of Egypt had begun.

Champollion's translation of the ancient hieroglyphs that supported Manetho's ancient timeline re-sparked the old animosity between bible literalists and the early European Egyptologists. The conflicting dates had become even more problematic because the Bibles in Europe had been changed by the 1500s, and now the world was only 6000 years old, meaning Champollion was stating that Egypt was founded over 1800 years before God made the world!

The changes in the Bible were caused by the decision to switch from the dating used in the old Greek Septuagint to the dating used in the Masoretic Text found in the Rabbinical Jewish Tanakh. The Greek Septuagint is a translation of the ancient Hebrew scriptures that became the Old Testament of the Bible, made around 300 BC when Judea was part of the Greek world. The Masoretic Texts was a version of the same Jewish scriptures that were used by a group of Rabbis between 600 and 1000 AD, that had a different dating for the lives of the ancient patriarchs than the Septuagint. The Masoretic Texts were copied from older texts by a group of Jewish scribes called the Masoretes, and date to sometime before 400 AD, as a fragment of one was found in 1970 dating to between 210 and 390 AD.

The three competing calendars and ages of the Earth were noted by the Early Christians, who adopted the Greek Septuagint over the Rabbinical Jewish texts or Samaritan texts. Starting around 800 AD some Christian leaders began to switch to the Masoretic Text, believing they were more accurate copies of the ancient Hebrew scriptures. While this had at first been heretical, by 1500 AD almost all Old Testaments in Europe were based on translations of the Masoretic Text. During the Renaissance and Reformation, and into the Age of Enlightenment the idea that the world was created around 4000 BC was accepted as fact by almost everyone in Europe. Sir Isaac Newton, Johannes Kepler, and Martin Luther each published dates for the age of the world, ranging between 4004 and 3961 BC.

The First Egyptian Short Timeline

The second school of thought quickly developed within Egyptology, based on the premise that the Egyptians couldn't have founded their civilization before God made the world, and therefore Egyptian history could not date back further than 4004 BC. The problem was that the ancient Egyptians had records of their kings. The king lists might have been incomplete, but the combined length of the reigns the Egyptologists knew about added up to over 5000 years, ending when Alexander conquered Egypt in 332 BC. The early advocates of the short timeline decided to follow Eusebius' advice, and promote the idea of multiple concurrent dynasties. The reason there were so many kings, was because multiple kings were ruling at the same time. In this theory, there would have been different kings ruling from different capitals, at the same time.

The advocates of this new short timeline decided that some of the dynasties in the Old and Middle Kingdoms were just Provincial governors that Manetho had intentionally added to his king lists to make the Egyptian Civilization seem older than it was. One of the leading promoters of this idea in the mid-1800s was Chevalier Bunsen, a German scholar and diplomat. Using the multiple concurrent dynasties approach Bunsen calculated the foundation of Egypt as being in 3643 BC after God made the world, but before He destroyed it with the Great Deluge. Proponents of this theory believed that the Old Kingdom was a pre-flood civilization, while the Middle and New Kingdoms were post-flood. This first version of the short-timeline was disproved by Auguste Mariette, who pointed out that dynasties often erected monuments in cities other than their capitals, including the capitals from other dynasties. If they were competing dynasties, this could not have happened. Additionally, the Turin and Abydos King Lists were discovered proving that Manetho had faithfully compiled a king list that matched what the New Kingdom era Egyptians had believed a thousand years before him. Egyptologists universally turned back to the long timeline.

Ancient Kingdoms and Dark Ages

The reason there are so many options when dating Egyptian history is due to its complexity. Ancient Egypt wasn't a kingdom that built a bunch of pyramids and was then conquered by the Greeks. What we today call Ancient Egypt was, in fact, a series of kingdoms that rose and fell in the Nile region over several thousand years. They are called the Old, Middle, and New Kingdoms by Egyptologists. Separating these kingdoms were dark ages, which Egyptologists call the First, Second, and Third Intermediate Periods. Following the Third Intermediate Period, or Third Egyptian Dark Age, was the Late Period when Egypt attempted to rebuild for the fourth time, but then fell under the control of foreigners.

Followers of both the short and long timelines agreed when the New Kingdom was founded, and pretty much everything that happened afterward. The New Kingdom was founded approximately 1580 BC ULT (1549 BC CET) and is the Kingdom of Egypt referenced in the Tanakh (Bible's Old Testament), where the Jews were apparently enslaved for some time. It is also the Egypt of Greek mythology, where Helen had apparently been during the Battle of Troy, according to Herodotus and later writers. This was also the Egypt that fought the Hittites for control of Canaan, and can, therefore, be found in Hittite and Babylonian records from that period. Additionally, radiocarbon dating has firmly placed the beginning of the New Kingdom between 1570 and 1544 BC.[4] The dating of this kingdom is simply not in doubt, other than a few decades one way or the other.

The New Kingdom collapsed around 1102 BC ULT (1077 BC CET) primarily due to environmental factors. The dendro-timeline, which is the timeline of Earth's ecological history for the past few thousand years worked out by studying tree rings, shows that around 1160 to 1140 BC the world became dark for a couple of decades, and there was very little plant growth. This is believed to have been a major factor in the collapse of several civilizations in the following century. The period of darkness is believed to have been caused by the eruption of the Hekla 3 volcano in Iceland, which would have filled the atmosphere with ash, blocking sunlight. This is believed to be where the term 'dark age' is derived, as the Greek Dark Age began then, and recorded massive migrations and invasions at the onset. In the case of Egypt, there were additional droughts caused by low rainfalls in Ethiopia, which is the source of most of the Nile's water. The kingdom fractured and ultimately fell to invading armies from Nubia to the south, and Assyria to the northeast.

Second Egyptian Dark Age

While there is a general agreement on what happened after the New Kingdom, there is a great deal of disagreement over what happened before. The reason for the disagreements over the pre-New Kingdom dates stems from the fact that there are gaps in the Egyptian records for the First and Second Egyptian Dark Ages. The Third Egyptian Dark Age, also called the Greek Dark Age, lasted just over 400 years, while the Western Dark Age, from the Fall of Rome to the Renaissance lasted approximately 1000 years. It is the question of "How long were those dark ages?" that drives the debate over the age of Egypt.

The Second Egyptian Dark Age saw the collapse of the Middle Kingdom, widespread famine, the invasion of Egypt by the Hyksos from the Middle East, and the invasion of Egypt by the Nubians from the south. This was followed by a period of time during which the country was divided under the rule of these two foreign peoples, and ultimately a series of wars in which the native Egyptians drove out the foreigners. It is generally agreed that the Second Egyptian Dark Age comprises the 13th through Seventeenth Dynasties.

The exact reason for the collapse of the Middle Kingdom is unclear, however, what is known is that there was a prolonged famine, and the last pharaoh of the 12th Dynasty, Queen Sobekneferu, had no heirs. It is believed by some Egyptologists that the first pharaoh of the 13th Dynasty was Sobekneferu's nephew, however, there is no clear evidence of this. In fact, Egyptologists disagree over who the first pharaoh of the 13th Dynasty was, some stating Sekhemre Khutawy Sobekhotep I, and others stating Khutawyre Wegaf. The reason forth this disagreement is caused by the fact that there are multiple ancient incomplete and conflicting king lists for this dynasty. Nevertheless, whoever it was, the transition from Sobekneferu to this new pharaoh was peaceful, indicating that he was likely related to Sobekneferu.

The 13th Dynasty is usually described as an era of chaos and disorder. The dynasty was undoubtedly characterized by decline, with a large number of kings with short reigns and only a few references to them found in the ruins of Egypt. It is clear that they were not from a single family line, and some of them were born commoners. The true timeline of this dynasty is difficult to determine as few monuments are dating from the period. Many of the kings' names are only known from odd fragmentary inscriptions.

During the 13th Dynasty the Egyptian economy faltered, and Egypt began withdrawing its armies from the southern fortresses built during the Middle Kingdom. These fortresses were deep in Nubian territory, which Egypt had been colonizing during the Middle Kingdom. As the Egyptian power waned during the Second Egyptian Dark Age, Nubian power grew united under the rule of the Kingdom of Kush, and ultimately Nubia invaded and then occupied southern Egypt.

One of the primary ways that the CET and ULT differ is that the CET has multiple dynasties coexisting during the dark ages, while the ULT has them generally in sequence. The difference reflects how the 14th Dynasty is interpreted. In the CET, the 14th Dynasty is a regional kingdom that broke away from Egypt sometime in the 12th Dynasty and ruled the Nile Delta for somewhere between 75 and 155 years. In the ULT, the 14th Dynasty followed the 13th Dynasty and ruled all of Egypt.

The exact borders of the 14th Dynasty are not known due to the general scarcity of monuments left by this dynasty. Seals attributable to the 14th Dynasty have been found throughout Egypt, including territory that advocates of the CET claim were under the rule of the 13th Dynasty. Additionally, 14th Dynasty seals have been found as far south as Dongola, deep in Nubia, and as far north as Tel Kabri, deep in Canaan. This indicates that the 14th Dynasty still had extensive control of, or at least influence over, the territories of the Middle Kingdom, and strongly supports the ULT.

In the CET, the Nubian Kingdom of Kush invaded southern Egypt in the 13th and Fourteenth Dynasties, which were happening concurrently, and then both dynasties were invaded by people from the northeast called the Hyksos. In the ULT, the 14th Dynasty, which followed the 13th Dynasty, was invaded by Kush to the south, and then the Hyksos to the northeast.

The origin and nature of the Hyksos are also unclear, what is known is that they invaded from the Middle East. The term 'Hyksos' derives from the Egyptian expression 'heqau khaswet' which translates as 'rulers of foreign lands,' and was in use for centuries before the so-called Hyksos invasion to refer to any foreign government. This invasion was historically described as violent, but after a century of excavations into Second Egyptian Dark Age ruins, it is now believed to have been a peaceful migration. It is known that there was both famine and plague in Egypt at the time, and so these immigrants were probably settling in virtually empty towns.

According to the ancient Egyptians before occupying Egypt, the Hyksos had conquered the Amorites and Canaanites, which on the CET should have happened shortly before the invasion of Egypt circa 1674 BC. According to Assyriologists, using the Conventional Mesopotamian Timeline (CMT) this was during the reign of King Abi-eshuh of the First Babylonian Empire, and the reign of King Bazaya of the Old Assyrian Empire. Yet neither the Babylonians nor Assyrians noticed an army of Semites, Hurrians, and Indo-Aryans sneaking through their territory, and conquering their trading partners: the Amorites and Canaanites, before launching an invasion of their greatest rival: Egypt.

On the ULT the Hyksos invasion of Egypt happened during the Babylonian Dark Age, and the Hyksos were the Mitanni. In the ULT the Hittite Empire sacked Babylon circa 3038 BC, and the Babylonian Empire was left in disarray. The Mittani-Aryan and Kassites from the Zagros Mountains migrated into Babylonia approximately 25 years later circa 3013 BC. This group was not unified at the time, comprising a confederation or horde. In either timeline, the early Kassite rule of Babylonia was poorly documented, and there are large gaps in the historical records for the Babylonian Dark Age. In the ULT a faction of Kassites and Indo-Aryans invaded and conquered the Amorites and Canaanites forming the Mitanni Kingdom shortly after occupying Babylonia. This so-called 'empire' was also a confederation throughout its existence, as proven by the Battle of Meggido, where Thutmose III's armies fought an alliance of 330 Mitanni princes supporting the city of Kadesh circa 1457 BC. After defeating the combined armies of the 330 Mitanni princes at Meggido, Thutmose III's army was able to launch an invasion of the Mittani Empire a few years later, capturing the king without facing any defending army.

Centuries after the occupation of Babylonia and the establishment of the Mitanni Kingdom, the Kassite-Mittani invaded Egypt in circa 2533 BC ULT, or, shortly after conquering the Amorites and Canaanites, the mysterious and sneaky Hyksos invaded Egypt in 1674 BC CET without the Babylonian or Assyrian empires noticing. Either way, the Hyksos formed the 15th Dynasty, which did for some time control all of Egypt north of Nubia. The following 16th Dynasty is hotly debated by Egyptologists, with some CET proponents stating it was a vassal kingdom of the 15th Dynasty, and other CET proponents claiming it was an independent kingdom, while in the ULT it was an Egyptianized-Hyksos dynasty that ruled northern Egypt after the 15th Dynasty. Very little is known of this dynasty, even the number of kings is debated.

One of the reasons for the lack of information regarding these dynasties is that an insurgent dynasty called the Abydos Dynasty rose up as an Egyptian nationalist faction that spent three decades driving the Hyksos out of Egypt, in the process vilifying them, and then destroying all references to them. The Abydos Dynasty, and the 17th Dynasty they subsequently established would, however, lay the foundation of the New Kingdom that rose up around 1580 BC ULT (1549 BC CET).

The Abydos Dynasty was not listed by Manetho and so doesn't have a dynastic number until after they had driven the Hyksos from Egypt when they became the 17th Dynasty. The information we have on the Abydos Dynasty today is drawn entirely from Egyptology, however, it does not add any years to either timeline as the Abydos and Sixteenth Dynasties were definitely concurrent.

So, how long did the Second Egyptian Dark Age last? How long did the 13th through Seventeenth dynasties last? The collapse of the Middle Kingdom, the invasion of the Nubians, the immigration of the Hyksos, the century-long Hyksos dynasty, the 30-year war to drive them out of Egypt, and reign of the 17th Dynasty that started the Egyptian economic recovery? According to the ULT: 1666 years, according to the CET: 206 years!

This situation was under heavy debate early in the 20th century when Sir W. M. Flinders Petrie summed it up:

> "Setting aside altogether for the present the details of the list of Manetho, let us look only to the monuments, and the Turin papyrus of kings, which was written with full materials concerning this age, with a long list of kings, and only two or three centuries later than the period in question. On the monuments we have the names of 17 kings of the XIIIth dynasty. In the Turin papyrus there are the lengths of reigns of 9 kings, amounting to 67 years, or 7 years each on an average. If we apply this average length of reign to only the 17 kings whose reigns are proved by monuments, we must allow them 120 years ; leaving out of account entirely about 40 kings in the Turin papyrus, as being not yet known on monuments. Of the Hyksos kings we know of the monuments of three certainly ; and without here adopting the long reigns stated by Manetho, we must yet allow at least 30 years for these kings. And in the XVIIth dynasty there are at least the reigns of Karnes and Sekhent nebra, which cover probably 10 years. Hence for those kings whose actual contemporary monuments are known there is required:
>
> XIIIth dynasty . . 120 years
>
> Hyksos at least 30 [years]
>
> XVIIth dynasty . . 10 [years]
>
> *160 [years]*
>
> This leaves us but 46 years, out of the 206 years, to contain 120 kings named by the Turin papyrus, and all the Hyksos conquest and domination, excepting 30 years named above.

> *This is apparently an impossible state of affairs ; and those who advocate this shorter interval are even compelled to throw over the Turin papyrus altogether, and to say that within two or three centuries of the events an entirely false account of the period was adopted as the state history of the Egyptians."*[5]

Manetho calculated the age of Egypt by adding together the number of years each pharaoh ruled, believing they ruled one after another and skipped the Abydos dynasty as they were concurrent with the 16th Dynasty. Conversely, the proponents of the CET have multiple dynasties ruling at the same time, and even have the 15th Dynasty starting before the 14th Dynasty, and the 12th Dynasty starting before the 13th Dynasty in order to make the numbers fit. As most of the records from the period were destroyed by the Seventeenth and Eighteenth Dynasties, there is little evidence one way or the other.

There is however the question of the collapse of the Middle Kingdom, which was caused by famine. If the CET is correct then the collapse happened around 1803 BC, a time that shows no evidence of significant climatic issues in the geologic records. If the ULT is correct, this happened around 3246 BC, in a period referred to as Great Shock of 3250 BC. This is the point in time that the world's climate changed significantly into a neo-glacial period that lasted until around 1500 BC. There are several pieces of evidence supporting the existence of this Great Shock of 3250 BC.

During this time the world's weather became stormier, and there was far more rain, which would have caused significant flooding along the Nile, and in the Fayum, as well as along other rivers throughout the world.[6] The GISP2 ice core samples from Greenland show there was a spike in atmospheric sulfate at 3250 BC, believed to have been from an increasing number of polynyas in the Arctic, caused by an expansion of oceanic surface ice.[7] The GRIP ice core sample from Greenland shows the 3250 BC point as being at a low point in atmospheric methane, followed by a rapid increase over the next 200 years, which is attributed to an abrupt increase in global wetlands.[8]

Ice core samples from the Huascaran glacier in Peru, show an abrupt cooling at about 3250 BC.[9]

So there are two options:

1) the CET which states the Middle Kingdom collapsed around 1803 BC, for unknown reasons. It was followed by multiple concurrent dynasties, that fought multiple wars against foreign powers, ultimately being occupied, and then fought another war for their independence, all of which happened in around 200 years.

2) the ULT which states the Middle Kingdom collapsed around 3246 years ago during the global climatic change called the Great Shock of 3250 BC. It was followed by a series of dynasties that fought a series of losing wars against invaders, ultimately being occupied, and then fought a war for their independence, which took place over 1600 years.

Egyptian Middle Kingdom

To consider the collapse of the Middle Kingdom, and how long the Second Egyptian Dark Age lasted one needs to consider the nature of the Middle Kingdom, as well as the differences between the Middle Kingdom and the New Kingdom. The Middle Kingdom emerged from the First Egyptian Dark Age and built on the ruins of the Old Kingdom. The Middle Kingdom lasted around 350 years, spanning the 11th and 12th dynasties. Both the ULT and CET generally agree about the length of the Middle Kingdom's history. The Middle Kingdom was also highly militant occupying most of Nubia to the south, and parts of Canaan to the northeast.

The major building projects of the Middle Kingdom were focused on waterworks and unlike the Old Kingdom, they only built small pyramids. This kingdom created the 15 km long Great Canal in the Bahr Yussef, that ran from the Nile to the Fayum. The Fayum is a natural depression west of Giza that was filled with water after the Grand Canal opened, creating Lake Moeris which was comparable in size to Lake Ontario in North America. The land around Lake Moeris became the breadbasket of Egypt and would remain so throughout the rest of Egyptian history until the Greek Period.

The Egyptians of the Middle and New Kingdoms did not speak the same language, although the languages were similar, like comparing ancient Latin to modern Italian. The language of the Middle Kingdom is called Middle-Egyptian by Egyptologists, while the language of the New Kingdom and later periods is called Late-Egyptian. Middle-Egyptian was standardized during the 11th dynasty and then evolved into Late-Egyptian during the Second Egyptian Dark Age, which was ultimately standardized during the 18th Dynasty. Middle-Egyptian continued to be used as a literary language alongside Late-Egyptian much as Latin continues to be used as a clerical and academic language alongside Italian and other modern languages. Nevertheless, during the 400-year-long Third Egyptian Dark Age, the language did not change noticeably, yet according to CET proponents during the 200-year-long Second Egyptian Dark Age, the language went through significant changes. This is clear evidence supporting the ULT, as significant changes, such as those that allowed Latin to morph into Italian take long periods of time.

The dominant religion of the Middle Kingdom was the Cult of Amen, who had been part of the Hermopolitan Ogdoad during the Old Kingdom. During the Second Egyptian Dark Age, the Cult of Amen merged with the Cult of Ra, becoming the Cult of Amen-Ra, which was generally the dominant cult throughout the New Kingdom. Amen was originally a mystery god whose name meant something like 'the invisible one,' while Ra was the Sun-god by the beginning of the Second Egyptian Dark Age, after originally being a creator god in the Old Kingdom.

Another major development during the Second Egyptian Dark Age was the development of the Book of the Dead. During the Middle Kingdom, the dominant religious texts were the Coffin Texts, which was a precursor to the Book of the Dead. The focus of the Coffin Texts was Osiris, and the spirit's journey to the Duat, or afterlife, while the later Book of the Dead was focused on Osiris' death, and the struggle of his son Horus against his brother Set.

Egyptologists believe the Book of the Dead developed as a propaganda piece used by nationalists to help turn the people against the Hyksos 16th Dynasty whose kings were associated with the god Set. According to the CET, this new religious text developed over a thirty-year period between 1580 to 1549 BC. This is a very short period for a new religion to develop and be taught to the common people that needed to be turned against the Hyksos. Meanwhile, the ULT allows hundreds of years for the development of this religion and its adoption by the populous, which seems more likely given the centuries that Christianity and Buddhism took to develop and become adopted by a significant portion of the population.

The development of the Cult of Amen during the Middle Kingdom either dates to 2061 to 1803 BC CET or 3502 to 3246 BC ULT. The Cult of Amen included the blue-skinned god Amen as part of the Theban Triad. This triad included his wife Mut, which meant 'mother,' and his son Khonsu, which meant 'traveler.' While Amen was depicted as blue-skinned, Mut was depicted as light-skinned, and Khonsu was depicted as brown-skinned.

The Theban Triad is very iconically similar to the Puri Triad from India, which includes the blue-skinned Krishna, the brown-skinned Subhadra, and the light-skinned Balarama. The life of Krishna is dated by various ancient Indian sources to between approximately 3227 to 3102 BC, during the Harappan Civilization. According to the Mahabharata, Krishna died in a fortress on an island off the coast of India near the city of Dwarka. After he died the fortress was reported to have sunk into the sea, which is believed by Hindus to have happened in 3102 BC. The remains of a large sunken structure have been discovered in waters off the coast of Dwarka, which does at least make the traditional dating for Krishna's life plausible. If the Puri Triad dates to around 3227 to 3102 BC, and the two triads have a common source, it seems far more likely the Theban Triad dates to sometime around 3502 to 3246 BC than sometime around 1500 years later.

While this might seem like a non-sequitur, the Egyptians were trading with the Harappans at the time, and the ULT examines not only the evidence in Egypt but also their trading partners. The timeline of the Sumerian and Harappan Civilizations are both impacted by the use of the ULT in Egypt, as both cultures not only can but must exist earlier than currently documented by Assyriologists and Indologists. Fortunately, both cultures have both ruins and written records of earlier periods of their own civilizations, which no longer need to be dismissed as fiction. In the case of the Harappan Civilization, there are the Ramayana, Mahabharata, and other ancient Indian epics that tell of an ancient civilization that once existed in South Asia. A civilization which was described as being in the same lands as the Harappan civilization, and at the same time. As the Harappans were actively trading with the Sumerians prior to going into decline circa 3250 BC, and both cultures were trading with the Egyptians, it seems illogical to assume that the two iconically identical triads formed independently.

First Egyptian Dark Age

Before the Middle Kingdom, was the dark age known as the First Intermediate Period. Again this period of time is subject to a great deal of debate as again the written records of the time period are fragmentary. This time period spans the Seventh through Tenth Dynasties, which either took around 125 years according to the CET or around 500 years according to the ULT. In the CET, the First Egyptian Dark Age took place between approximately 2181 and 2040 BC, while in the ULT it took place between approximately 4003 and 3502 years ago.

If the Old Kingdom collapsed around 2181 BC, there are no clear reasons why it collapsed. Several reasons are listed by Egyptologists, primarily focused on the long reign of Pepi II, the last major pharaoh of the 6th Dynasty. Pepi II ruled for over seven decades, which according to Egyptologists caused the collapse of the Old Kingdom because he outlived his immediate successors. This long-lived king apparently caused the destabilization of the kingdom, unlike other long-lived monarchs throughout human history, which generally created stability.

Another theory that has been proposed is the so-called 4.2 Kiloyear Event. This event is theorized to have happened, largely based on the fact that Egypt supposedly collapsed at this time. The Akkadian civilization also collapsed around this point, however, the dating of the Akkadian empire is also unclear as there were three dark ages after the fall of the Akkadian Empire, correlating to the Egyptian dark ages. The earliest clear correlations between the Mesopotamian civilizations and Egyptian civilizations date to the 13th Dynasty in the Middle Kingdom.

Unlike most environmental events throughout the past few thousand years, the so-called 4.2 Kiloyear Event is not known from traditional environmental indicators such as ice-core-samples. The 4.2 Kiloyear Event was theorized because there appears to have been a drying period at the end of the Old Kingdom, which CET proponents place around 2181 BC. Conversely, if the Old Kingdom collapsed around 4003 BC, it correlates to the 5.9 Kiloyear Event, which took place between 4200 and 3900 BC. The 5.9 Kiloyear Event is known from multiple physical sources, and ties into the rapid drying in Tadrart Acacus of southwestern Libya.

The First Egyptian Dark Age was a time of chaos, and virtually nothing is known of the 7th Dynasty. Many Egyptologists believe the dynasty may not have happened at all. The source for the dynasty is Manetho's Aegyptiaca, which unfortunately no longer exists, and the quotes of Aegyptiaca do not agree on what the 7th Dynasty was. Africanus' quote from around 200 AD lists 70 kings in 70 days, while Eusebius' quote from around 300 AD lists 5 kings in 75 days. Whatever caused the collapse of the Old Kingdom seems to have been complete, leaving nothing but chaos in the aftermath.

The 8th Dynasty is generally accepted by Egyptologists and is also interpreted as a time of chaos by Egyptologists. Africanus' and Eusebius' quotes of Manetho also disagree, with Africanus quoting the 8th Dynasty as lasting 27 kings who reigned for 146 years, and Eusebius quoting 5 kings who reigned for 100 years. There is virtually no archaeological evidence for the Seventh or Eighth Dynasties, and as a result, modern Egyptologists only assign around 25 years for both dynasties, while the ULT accepts the idea that these dynasties took place over 100 to 150 years.

There is also very little archaeological evidence for the Ninth and Tenth Dynasties, however, Egyptologists do generally agree that the dynasties existed. The Turin King List from the New Kingdom listed 18 kings for the 9th Dynasty, although the names are lost. As there is little archaeological evidence, modern Egyptologists allow for the 18 kings to have reigned for only 30 years between 2160 and 2130 BC. This means that each king ruled an average of fewer than 2 years. As there is more evidence for the 10th Dynasty Egyptologists recognize 5 pharaohs who reigned for 90 years between 2130 and 2040 BC, which averages 18 years per king. Conversely, the ULT accepts 285 years for the two dynasties between 3787 and 3502 BC, which averages around 12 years per king.

Unfortunately, as there is very little evidence remaining from the First Egyptian Dark Age, meaning that is it unlikely to be proven when exactly the period was. Nevertheless, the collapse of the Old Kingdom at the proven 5.9 Kiloyear Event makes more sense than at a hypothetical 4.2 Kiloyear event that lacks all paleo-climatological evidence. If the Old Kingdom ended around 2181 BC in the CET, then it would have been founded around 2686 BC. On the other hand, if the Old Kingdom ended around 4003 BC in the ULT, then it would have begun around 4945 BC.

Egyptian Old Kingdom

The Old Kingdom spanned the Third through Sixth Dynasties and was the time when the ancient Egyptians are believed to have built the great pyramids, Sphinx, and ancient megalithic temples near the Sphinx. The Old Kingdom was preceded by the Early Dynastic era which covered the 1st and 2nd Dynasties. The Early Dynastic era is not clearly understood due to limited and conflicting information from the period. By the beginning of the Old Kingdom, enough information remains for us to have a relatively complete understanding of the next few centuries.

The first king of the Old Kingdom was Djoser of the 3rd Dynasty, who ordered the construction of the step pyramid in Saqqara, near Memphis. Like the later Middle and New Kingdoms, the Old Kingdom had a distinct form of spoken Egyptian, which is now known as Old-Egyptian. Old-Egyptian was written similar to Middle-Egyptian, however, it was a different spoken dialect. There were some minor differences between the hieroglyphs used in the Old Kingdom to those used in the Middle and New Kingdoms, however, they remained largely unchanged throughout Egyptian history until the adoption of the Coptic script during the Greek Era. Hieroglyphs themselves date back to the pre-Dynastic period, although pre-Dynastic Hieroglyphs are generally untranslatable, and the Archaic-Egyptian of the first two dynasties is scarce.

Throughout the Old, Middle, and New Kingdoms, the more common script used was the hieratic script, which is considered to be a simplified form of hieroglyphs. During the Third Egyptian Dark Age, which coincides with the Greek Dark Age, the Egyptians developed the Demotic Script, which seems to have been influenced by Aramaic, and was used alongside hieroglyphs until the Christian era, when the Greek-influenced Coptic Script was developed.

The fact that the Old Kingdom had a different dialect of spoken Egyptian is extremely significant, as it seems highly unlikely that a new dialect would have developed and become dominant in the 125 years allotted by the CET, however, it is plausible in the 500 years allotted by the ULT. This is re-enforced by the fact that both dialects used the same written scripts, and there are no signs of invasions by foreigners.

The question of 'when was the Old Kingdom?' is essential to understanding the physical evidence found from that period, and the nature of the kingdom itself. Regardless of when it was, most Egyptologists agree that during the Old Kingdom all the large pyramids were built, the Sphinx was carved, and the megalithic temples were built. There have been consistent dissenters throughout the past two centuries regarding the Sphinx, megalithic temples, and Osireion, which some Egyptologists, as well as other researchers, believe might be from an earlier unknown period of civilization due to their unusual and unique construction techniques. Some believe the Great Pyramid of Khufu must have been built before the mastabas that surround it. The mastabas date to the 3rd Dynasty, whereas the Pyramid of Khufu is believed to have been built in the 4th Dynasty. Nevertheless, the accepted history has the Great Pyramids of Giza, and maybe the Sphinx and megalithic temples near the Sphinx were built in the 4th Dynasty.

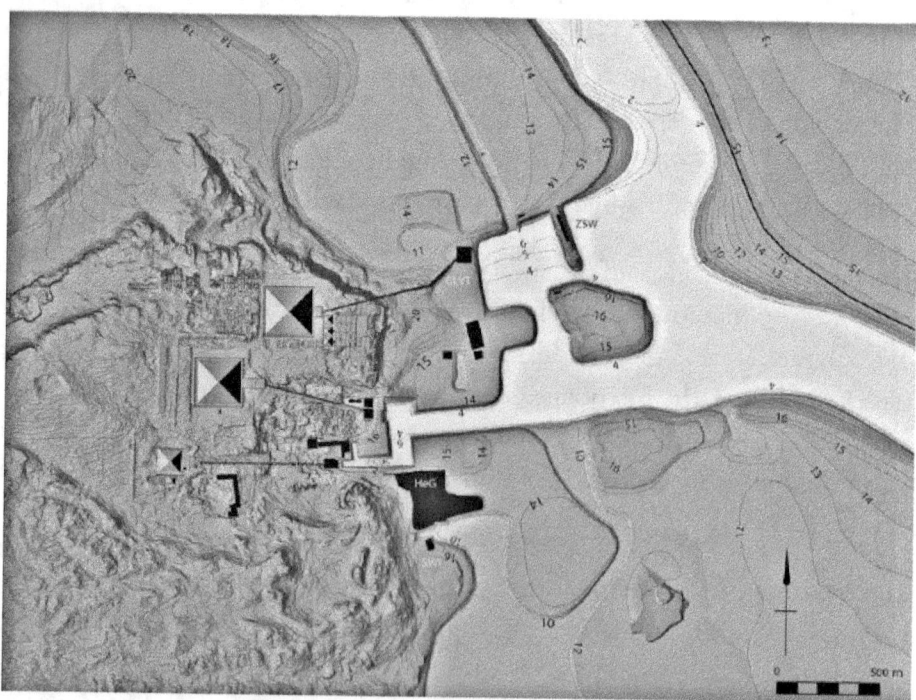

If this kingdom existed between 2686 and 2181 BC, as claimed in the CET it existed entirely within the dry period that began with the 5.9 Kiloyear Event. On the other hand, if the Old Kingdom existed between 4945 and 4003 BC, it existed during the African Humid Period and collapsed during the 5.9 Kiloyear Event. The African Humid Period is well documented by samples taken from multiple dried lakes and rivers across the modern Sahara Desert. Between 14,000 and 4,000 BC the Sahara was a fertile land of rain-forests and savannas like equatorial Africa is today. During this time the Nile would have received much higher water flow year-round than after the 5.9 Kiloyear Event, as not only were the Blue and White Nile Rivers receiving more in-flow, but at least three additional tributaries were flowing in from the west in modern Sudan. These other rivers dried up during the 5.9 Kiloyear Event. On the previous page is an image showing the Nile during the Old Kingdom era circa 2686 to 2181 BC CET, and below is the same image with the water level of the Old Kingdom in 4945 to 4003 BC ULT.

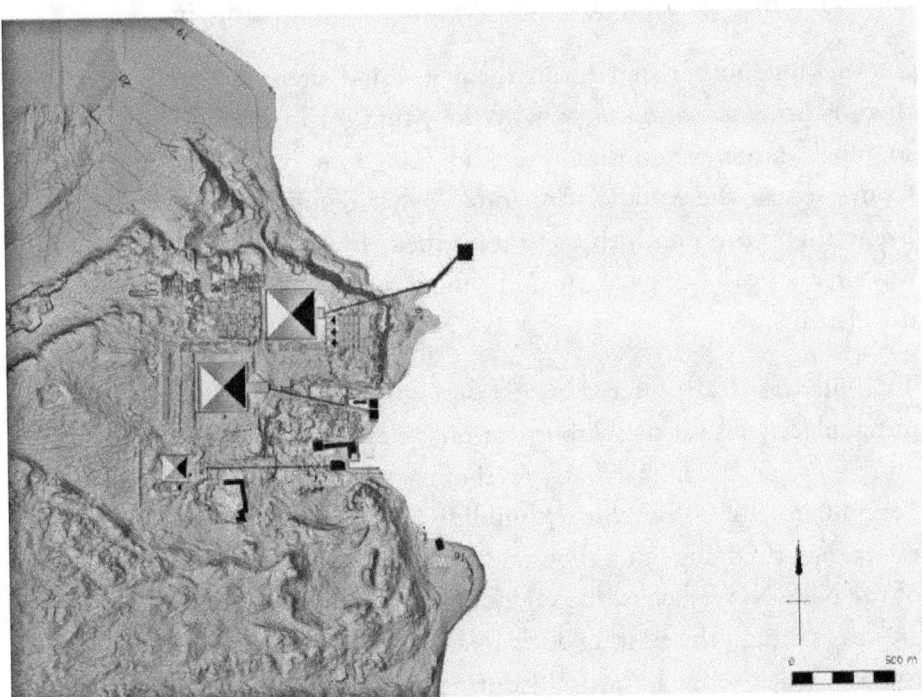

Given that the Giza Plateau has causeways reaching out towards the Nile, with docks at the end for ships to unload their stone blocks, there must have been water present at the docks during the Old Kingdom. Furthermore, given that the Sphinx enclosure shows signs of significant water damage, it seems clear that there was water in the area of the Sphinx enclosure after the Sphinx was created. If the Old Kingdom existed between 2686 and 2181 BC, there is no explanation for this water. If the Old Kingdom existed between 4945 and 4003 BC, the source of the water is explained by the annual Nile river floods, which would have been much higher than they were after the 5.9 Kiloyear Event. This would also explain why the major construction efforts of the Middle Kingdom were geared towards water conservation and agricultural expansion. During the African Humid Period, rainwater and Nile overflow would have naturally collected in the Fayum depression forming a natural Lake Moeris, however, by the Middle Kingdom, the Grand Canal had to be dug connecting the depression to the lower level of the Nile. On the previous page, and below, are two comparative views of the Giza harbor area, the above one set circa 2500 BC, and the below one set circa 4500 BC just before the Nile water-levels began dropping.

If both kingdoms existed during the dry period after the 5.9 Kiloyear Event there is no explanation as to why the Middle Kingdom felt they needed so much more water than the Old Kingdom had apparently needed. Conversely, if the Middle Kingdom is what rebuilt after the 5.9 Kiloyear Event, their obsession with water if justified. The entire harbor area for Giza was altered by the kings of the Old Kingdom so they could get their ships to the plateau.

The Nile was clearly altered greatly during the Old Kingdom, however, the initial placement for the harbors for both Khafre and Menkure make much more sense on the higher water level of the Nile during the Humid African Period before 4000 BC. Surely building longer causeways would have been easier than dredging out a thousand times as much mud to change the path of the Nile. Nevertheless, the Old Kingdom did dredge out the vast harbor area to maintain the existing dock area. The only logical explanation for this that the Nile dropped drastically during the Old Kingdom, which it should have if it was in the last few centuries of the African Humid Period. Evidence of this drastic drop between the 4th Dynasty when the Giza Pyramids were built, and the 6th Dynasty when the Old Kingdom ended, can be found right behind the Sphinx enclosure.

During the 6th Dynasty, the so-called Osiris Shaft was dug. This shaft started on the surface about halfway between the Sphinx and the Pyramid of Khafre, north of the causeway, which was partially taken apart to dig a well 30 meters (~90 feet) deep. The name Osiris Shaft, or Tomb of Osiris, is derived from the Egyptian Egyptologist Zahi Hawass' observation that the tomb at the bottom of the shaft seems iconically similar to the Osireion. It is also called Campbell's Tomb, named after the British Consul to Egypt at the time when it was rediscovered in 1830 AD by Howard Vyse and Giovanni Caviglia. Vyse and Caviglia had the sand cleared out to a depth of 30 meters, and removed a basalt sarcophagus that now resides at the British Museum. The next major excavation wasn't until 1933-34 by the Egyptian Egyptologist Selim Hassan who described it in Antiquity in 1944:

> *"Upon the surface of the causeway they first built a platform in the shape of a mastaba, using stones taken from the ruins of the covered corridor of the causeway. In the centre of this superstructure they sank a shaft, which passed through the roof and floor of the subway running under the causeway to a depth of about 9.00 m. At the bottom of this shaft is a rectangular chamber, in the floor of the eastern side of which is another shaft. This descends about 14.00 m. and terminates in a spacious hall surrounded by seven burial-chambers, in each of which is a sarcophagus. Two of these sarcophagi, which are of basalt and are monolithic, are so enormous that at first we wondered if they contained the bodies of sacred bulls.*
>
> *In the eastern side of this hall is yet another shaft, about 10.00 m. deep, but unfortunately it is flooded. Through the clear water we can see that it ends in a colonnaded hall, also having side-chambers containing sarcophagi. We tried in vain to pump out the water, but it seems that a spring must have broken through the rock, for continual daily pumping over a period of four years was unable to reduce the*

> *water-level. I may add that I had this water analysed and finding it pure utilized it for drinking purposes"*[10]

The water level that stopped Hassan's team had dropped enough by the 1990s that Zahi Hawass was able to excavate the lower level in 1999. Hawass was the first to associate the tomb at the bottom of the shaft with the description by Herodotus in The Histories circa 450 BC of the tomb of Khufu. Herodotus' description of the Tomb of Khufu was generally considered fiction by Egyptologists before Hawass noted the similarities. Hawass team also recovered pottery fragments at the lowest level dating to the 6th Dynasty, the last dynasty of the Old Kingdom, although also noted the burial chambers were added later during the Late Period. Presumably, the tomb was open circa 450 BC if Herodotus was able to describe it. Hawass' description of the Tomb of Osiris at the bottom of the shaft was published in 2007 on his blog at drhawass.com:

> *"The channel surrounding the emplacement in the lowest level seems to have been deliberately designed so that groundwater would fill it, making the emplacement in the centre into a sort of island. This configuration could represent the primeval waters of Nun, which covered the world at the time of creation, with the island in the center representing the first mound of earth to emerge. The water further symbolizes the connection of Osiris to fertility and rebirth. The emplacement with a large sarcophagus in the centre and a pillar at each corner (perhaps representing the four sacred legs of the god as described in later texts) is very similar to the configuration of the Osireion of Seti I at Abydos*
>
> *We were surprised to find that there was also some red polished pottery with traces of white paint, which probably dates to the 6th Dynasty. the earliest artefacts found inside date to Dynasty 6.*
>
> *I believe that the Osiris Shaft is what the Greek author Herodotus, the "father of history," was talking about when he said that Khufu*

was buried on an island in an underground chamber, located in the shadow of the Great Pyramid and fed by a canal from the Nile."

The fact that the water level dropped by up to 30 meters between the 4th Dynasty and the 6th Dynasty is further proof that the CET is impossible, as a significant drop of the Nile level during the second millennium BC did not happen. If it had, the Nile at Giza would have been significantly below the sea level of the Mediterranean. This drop could only have happened at an earlier point when the African Humid Period was ending, circa 4000 BC.

Foundations of Egypt

The 1st and 2nd Dynasties are very poorly understood, as Egyptologists cannot seem to find anything dating to the right time. This is dismissed as being due to the Early Dynastic period being very long ago, and very very chaotic. Both those points are valid, however, in the CET the 1st Dynasty began circa 3100 BC, yet we've uncovered the ruins of cities dating back to 5000 to 5300 BC that seems fairly intact, so where are the early dynastic cities? In 2015, the remains of an unknown village were discovered in the Nile delta's Dakahlia governorate. As there was nothing that associated the village with any specific dynasty, carbon-dating was used to date the village, which showed it was approximately 7000 years old.[11] In 2016 another unknown village was found, this one in the vicinity of Abydos, and dated to around 5,316 BC using carbon dating. This 7300-year-old village was described by Egyptian archaeologist as:

> *"The size of the graves discovered in the cemetery is larger in some instances than royal graves in Abydos dating back to the 1st Dynasty, which proves the importance of the people buried there and their high social standing during this early era of ancient Egyptian history."*[12]

These discoveries essentially prove the existence of dynastic Egypt at approximately 5300 to 5000 BC, however, they are not interpreted that way by Egyptologists, who claim they are pre-dynastic. If Egyptologists accepted the ULT, the village found in the vicinity of Abydos would no doubt be accepted as the lost town of Thinis, where King Menes, also called Narmer, was from. Unfortunately, they cannot accept the ULT without admitting they've been wrong about the Egyptian timeline for the past century, so, they will likely never find Thinis, and they'll need to make up a new name for the village discovered in 2016. They'll also need to make up some more fiction explaining how these people were, who built exactly like the 1st Dynasty people in the Abydos region and coincidentally lived in the Abydos region, but a couple of thousand years earlier.

Christian Timeline

So if the ULT fits the geological and paleoclimatological evidence far better than the CET, why has the CET become ubiquitous in Egyptology? In a word: Christianity.

Egyptologists were divided into two camps during the late-1800s, some supporting the long timeline, and some supporting the short timeline. The long timeline proponents based their views of Egyptian history on the ancient records of Egypt, while the short timeline proponents based their view of Egyptian history on the version of the Bible they were using at the time. The pattern was identical for Iraqi, Indian, and Chinese history, where the dates of the ancient Mesopotamian, Harappan, and the early Chinese civilizations were all simply moved to after the Great Flood.

The Great Flood is a story from Jewish folklore in which a massive global flood was once sent by one of the ancient Jewish gods to massacre all of humanity and some rebellious angels that were living on the planet at that time, along with a group of giants the angels had made by impregnating human women. There are dozens of known versions and variations of the story found in the early Christian, Jewish, Gnostic, and Mandaeism texts, however, one was adopted into the Christian Bible, and so Christian fundamentalists need for all of history to conform to the Biblical timeline, or accept that the writers of the Bible weren't omniscient.

This rewriting of history across the world was so complete that even the current Chinese culture accepts the dating for the life of the Yellow Emperor at around 2,700 to 2,600 BC, a date invented by the Jesuit missionary Martino Martini in the 1600s. The fact is, China does have ancient records that predate the Jesuit mission to China, and which places the life of the Yellow Emperor approximately 6,200 to 6,100 BC, but they are ignored by the modern Chinese. In India and Pakistan, ruins have been excavated that are part of the Harappan Civilization, yet date to 7000 BC, which Indian archaeologists recognize as part of a long term civilization. Western archaeologists ignore the ruins entirely, leaving the established date for the Harappan Civilization at 3300 to 1300 BC after God made the world.

Ironically, almost all western scholars reject the flood myth entirely, yet cling to the dating established by the earlier generations of historians and archaeologists, who insisted on dating ancient civilizations according to the biblical timeline. The shift to the CET that is so ubiquitous today, began with James Henry Breasted in the early 1900s. Brested is widely considered the father of American Egyptology having been the first American to obtain a Ph.D. in Egyptology, which he had earned from the University of Berlin in 1894. Shortly after receiving his Ph.D., he joined the faculty at the University of Chicago, where, in 1901 he became director of the Haskell Oriental Museum, and in 1905 was promoted to full professor, holding the first chair in Egyptology and Oriental History in the United States.

Between 1899 to 1908 Brested conducted multiple fieldwork expeditions to Egypt, which established his reputation. He also published numerous articles and monographs, including his 'History of Egypt from the Earliest Times Down to the Persian Conquest.' That he was a leading Egyptologist in his day is not doubted, however, modern Egyptologists generally ignore the fact that he was also a Christian fundamentalist. Brested began his post-secondary education at North-Western College, now known as North Central College, which was then, and continues to be affiliated with the United Methodist Church. From there he went on to attend the Chicago Theological Seminary which is a Christian ecumenical American seminary located in Chicago and was at the time affiliated with the United Church of Christ. Brested had been working on becoming a congregational minister, however, found his faith shaken by the idea that biblical timeline might not be accurate.[13] Ultimately he transferred to Yale, where he received his master's degree before continuing to the University of Berlin.

While he had been educated in the then ubiquitous long timeline, he ultimately reformulated the then discredited short timeline, claiming the 1st Dynasty of Egypt was founded circa 3400 BC. While he did not mention the Biblical creation and great flood narratives, it is worth noting that his new dating places the Old Kingdom back where the earlier short timeline proponents placed it, before the flood, but after the creation of the world. This idea is not new, nor invented by Christians, in fact, Muslims scholars came to the same conclusions centuries earlier.

Islamic Timeline

Medieval Muslims believed that the Islamic prophet Idris was the Jewish patriarch Enoch that lived before Noah's flood. The prophet Idris founded Egypt after leaving Babylon because the people there were being bad Muslims. This is a chronologically confusing sentence, however, is consistent with medieval Islamic teachings, which some Muslims continue to believe today. The prophet Idris was also believed by some early Islamic scholars to be Hermes Trismegistus, who was the builder of the Great Pyramid of Khufu (Cheops) in Hermetic thought, while his brother Agathodaemon was the builder of the Pyramid of Khafre (Chephren) a thousand years earlier. This belief was documented by Al-Maqrizi around 1200 AD:

> "One of these pyramids is the tomb of A'adimun (Agathodaemon) and the other of Hermes. Between these two figures there are nearly a thousand years, A'adimun being the older of the two. The inhabitants of Egypt, that is to say the Copts, argue that these two characters were two prophets who appeared before the coming of Christianity."

Around a century earlier the Islamic scholar Al-Shahrastani wrote in the *Kitab al–Milal wa al-Nihal* that:

> "They (the Sabeans) say that Adsimun (Agathodaemon) and Hermes were Seth and Enoch respectively."

To a medieval Muslim, this would mean that the Pyramids pre-dated the flood, as both the Islamic prophets Seth and Idris (Enoch) were prophets from before the time of Nuh (Noah). These Islamic prophets are also considered the Jewish and Christian pre-flood patriarchs Seth and Enoch, and the Gnostic enlighted beings Agathodaemon and Hermes Trismegistus, which lived before the flood. Naturally, Brested didn't mention any of this, as other historians and archaeologists would have thought him quite mad.

Although modern Egyptologists like to ignore the para-biblical timeline proposed by Brested or claim it is simply coincidence, it is a very strange coincidence that he placed the First Egyptian Dark Age at the time of the Great Flood. According to the then accepted translations of the Bible, the Great Flood happened in 2348 BC, while in Brested's short timeline the First Egyptian Dark Age happened between 2475 and 2160 BC.

This 'coincidence' did make Egyptian 'history' more palatable to Christians, who at the time dominated American and European politics and controlled the amount of money flowing into Egyptological research. Brested and those that followed his CET received far more funding than the heretics trying to disprove the correctness of the Holy Bible, and therefore Brested's CET slowly became dominant over the following decades.

The Even More Christian Timeline

In 1995 an even more Christian timeline was proposed by self-declared agnostic David Rohl in his work *A Test of Time: The Bible - from Myth to History*. Rohl's goal was to synchronize the Egyptian timeline with the Biblical timeline, an odd thing for an agnostic to do. One would expect an agnostic to try to synchronize the Biblical timeline with the Egyptian timeline, not the opposite, if an agnostic bothered to look into it all.

To synchronize the Egyptian timeline to the Biblical timeline, Rohl proposes removing another 350 years from the CET, placing the foundation of the 1st Dynasty in 2770 BC. Rohl's proposed changes focus on the Third Egyptian Dark Age, which Rohl wants to synchronize with the Tanakh. The current version of the Egyptian Timeline, the Biblical King Shihsaq of Egypt is identified with King Shoshenq I, however, Rohl has suggested changing this to King Ramesses II, who lived hundreds of years later. To compress the timeline, Rohl has proposed that the 21st and 22nd Dynasty were contemporary.

This even more Christian timeline forces the Aegean and Mesopotamian timelines to be even more compressed than they already are. This means that the Mediterranean and Mesopotamian Iron Age would have started in the 800s BC, almost 1000 years after the Indian Iron Age, and 700 years after the Yaz Iron Age in Central Asia. This timeline is generally rejected by Egyptologists, however, there is a growing number of Egyptologists seriously considering it.

Carbon Dating

Of course, we are no longer living in that age, so what about modern scientific dating systems? Surely the Egyptologists have used carbon dating the prove when these kingdoms existed. Well, yes they have, and no they haven't. As the land of Egypt has been occupied for thousands of years, and only biologic materials can be carbon dated, and biological materials don't generally survive the passage of time, the situation is murky.

Early carbon dating tests showed the Old Kingdom to be thousands of years older than Egyptologists said it was,[14] so the Egyptologists rejected the science. More recent radiocarbon studies are very close to what the Egyptologists state using the CET, however, these results are found by systematically ignoring any results that deviate from the CET by more than one thousand years. Therefore the tests cannot prove that the Old Kingdom is 1500 years older than the CET demands because those results are systematically excluded.

The way these carbon dating tests are shaped by the CET and end up confirming the CET is simple to demonstrate. If the Old Kingdom was founded around 7500 years ago when the ULT indicates, there would have still been people living in Egypt around 5100 years ago when the CET indicates. In order to conduct tests scientists need pieces of biological artifacts from the time period they want to test, which they have to get from Egyptologists, who state when they believe the artifacts date from. This means that the scientists already have a date that their tests need to confirm, which means that the outcome shaping has already begun.

Egyptologists have always rejected carbon dating results that deviate greatly from the CET using one of several reasons. If the artifact isn't something that can be definitively dated to a specific dynasty, perhaps by an inscription on it, then the results can be dismissed by claiming the artifact was sent in error and must date from a different dynasty, or is predynastic. As carbon dating destroys the object tested, most artifacts sent to scientists are unimportant pieces of debris that don't include inscriptions. On the other hand, if the artifact can be positively linked to a specific dynasty yet the carbon dating is off by centuries or millennia, Egyptologists either claim the test was faulty or simply ignore the test results entirely.

There is of course also the scientific rebuttal of carbon dating for ancient times which some Egyptologists engaged in if pushed to explain away a carbon-date. The way carbon dating works is by comparing the amount of carbon to carbon-14 in an object. Carbon is found in three forms on Earth, carbon-12, carbon-13, and carbon-14, and while carbon-12 and carbon-13 are both stable and relatively common, carbon 14 is both unstable and rare. Carbon-14 is a radioisotope with a half-life of 5,730±40 years. This means that it is possible to figure out how long an organism has been dead by comparing the amount of carbon to carbon-14 in the body. The longer the organism has been dead, the less carbon-14 it will have, and therefore a calculation of the estimated time of death can be made. At least in theory.

The carbon-dating method depends on knowing how much carbon the organism was exposed to while alive, and what percentage of that carbon was carbon-14. If the amount of carbon in the atmosphere was stable, and if there were no new sources of carbon-14 being introduced, then the method would work exactly as envisioned, however, neither of those conditions are met on Earth. Every time a major volcanic eruption occurs massive amounts of carbon is spewed into the atmosphere. This carbon is believed to be almost entirely carbon-12, meaning that the percentage of carbon-14 in an organism that died after the eruption would be skewed by the extra carbon-12, and the organism may appear to had died decades earlier than a creature that died shortly before the eruption.

An additional variable is introduced when more carbon-14 is introduced to the environment. Carbon-12 and carbon-13 are converted into carbon-14 when it is hit by high energy particles, such as during a nuclear blast. Therefore an organism that died shortly before humanity started exploding nuclear warheads will appear to had died long after any organism that has died since we started exploding them. Naturally, while this may be confusing to our distance descendants, it does not impact Egyptology, however, there are other sources of high energy particles that occasionally cause spikes in the amount of carbon-14 in our atmosphere. One of these sources is cosmic rays, which are believed to be the main ongoing source of new carbon-14, however, for some reason the volume of cosmic rays occasionally spikes, causing spikes in the amount of carbon-14 in the atmosphere.

Scientists have been examining very old trees since the 1970s in an attempt to calibrate carbon-testing. Tree-rings have been used for centuries to work out the ancient environment of the planet, as trees grow better in warm and moist years, leaving thicker rings for those years. Because some species of trees can live for thousands of years, continuous tree-ring timelines have been worked out going back to 12,460 years ago.[15] By carbon-dating samples from these tree-ring scientists have found points in the time when major volcanic eruptions have happened, and more recently when major spikes in carbon-14 have happened. In 2012 a cosmic-ray spike was found in tree-ring samples from 774-775 AD,[16] another was found in 2017 from 3372-3371 BC,[17] and another was also found in 2017 from 5480 BC.[18] Each time one of these cosmic-ray spikes is found it requires the calibration curve to be adjusted and therefore all carbon-dates from before the cosmic-ray spike need to be updated. This constantly fluctuating dendro-timeline is the reason why most Egyptologists haven't embraced carbon-dating.

Additionally, as people have lived in Egypt throughout all of Egyptian history, and people have been obsessed with old artifacts throughout all of human history, older artifacts have been routinely dug up and then deposited with later debris. This means that when artifacts are found they cannot be definitively dated by debris they are found with. It also means that it is easy for Egyptologists to dismiss any radiocarbon dating results that deviate from the CET. The views of Egyptologists regarding scientific methods, such as carbon dating were well stated by Felix Höflmayer of the Austrian Academy of Sciences, Institute for Oriental and European Archaeology in 2016:

> "The historical timeline of Egypt is a political timeline, and as such it is a priori independent from archaeological phases and sites'

stratigraphies, material culture such as pottery, or scientific dating approaches, that is, radiocarbon dating."[19]

Political history, independent from science or facts? Ah yes: fiction, that explains the time-traveling Hyksos.

Section 2: Dynastic Mesopotamia

Mesopotamian Archaeological Timeline

Period	CMT			ULT		
Ubaid 0	6500 BC	to	5400 BC	8331 BC	to	7231 BC
Ubaid 1	5400 BC	to	4800 BC	7231 BC	to	6631 BC
Ubaid 2	4800 BC	to	4500 BC	6631 BC	to	6331 BC
Late Ubaid	4500 BC	to	4000 BC	6331 BC	to	5831 BC
Early Uruk	4000 BC	to	3800 BC	5831 BC	to	5631 BC
Middle Uruk	3800 BC	to	3400 BC	5631 BC	to	5231 BC
Late Uruk	3400 BC	to	3100 BC	5231 BC	to	4931 BC
Jemdet Nasr	3100 BC	to	2900 BC	4931 BC	to	4731 BC
Site(s)	Carbon-Dated Timeline					
Natufian	13,050 BC		to			7505 BC
Qaramel	13,000 BC		to			6783 BC
Jericho	9500 BC		to			1400 BC
Göbekli Tepe	9130 BC		to			7370 BC
Byblos	8800 BC		Continuously Inhabited			
Aswad	8700 BC		to			7500 BC
Nevalı Çori	8400 BC		to			8100 BC
Hassuna	7750 BC		to			6780 BC
Çatalhöyük	7500 BC		to			5700 BC

The Conventional Mesopotamian Timeline is largely based on correlations with James Henry Breasted's short timeline of Dynastic Egyptian history, which was designed to make Egyptian history fit into the Biblical Timeline. Breasted funded expeditions to Iraq in the 1920s through his position at the Oriental Institute, which among other things cemented his para-biblical timeline within Assyriology. This timeline was originally considered proven by the layer of alluvium found in the ruins of southern Iraq that were seen as proof of the biblical global flood. This layer of alluvium ultimately proved to be from many river floods, which happened over several thousand years through the Ubaid-era. As a result, the original Ubaid, Uruk, and Jemdet Nasr periods have been extended back from 4000 to 2900 BC, to 6500 to 2900 BC.

This extended Conventional Mesopotamian Timeline is based on the comparison of different levels of cultural development at the times of the floods, and not a carbon-dated timeline. While this timeline does allow the

Mesopotamian civilization to have developed over several thousand years, instead of suddenly appearing around 4000 BC, it still leaves the Mesopotamian civilization springing up around 6500 BC, after most of the carbon-dated ruins in the Middle East had been abandoned. The Natufian ruins in the Levant have been carbon-dated to between 13,050 to 7505 BC. The ruins of Qaramel in Syria have been carbon-dated to 13,000 to 6783 BC. The ruins of Göbekli Tepe in southeast Turkey have been carbon-dated to between 9130 and 7370 BC. The ruins of Tell Aswad in Syria have been carbon-dated to between 8700 and 7500 BC. The ruins of Nevalı Çori near Göbekli Tepe on the Middle Euphrates have been carbon-dated to between 8400 and 8100 BC. The ruins of Tell Hassuna on the Tigris river in Northern Iraq have been carbon-dated to between 7750 and 6780 BC. This naturally leads to the question of why people were building cities in the Levant and Northern Mesopotamia, but nothing in Southern Mesopotamia, even though the region was more climatically stable then, than during the apparently later Sumerian civilization.

If the history of the Egyptian civilization is returned to the longer timeline used by historians and Egyptologists for thousands of years, then the early dynastic period of Sumer would date to circa 7500 BC. This allows both the Sumerian dynastic records to correlate with the Ubaid era ruins and both to coexist with the later periods of neighboring civilizations to the north and west.

Sumero-Akkadian Timeline

Sumero-Akkadian Dynastic Timeline

Dynasty	CMT			ULT		
1st Kish	2900 ? BC	to	2800 ? BC	25,179 BC	to	7698 BC
1st Uruk	2800 ? BC	to	2700 ? BC	9868 BC	to	7558 BC
1st Ur	2700 ? BC	to	2600 ? BC	7558 BC	to	7381 BC
Awan	2700 ? BC	to	2600 ? BC	7381 BC	to	7025 BC
2nd Kish	2700 ? BC	to	2600 ? BC	7025 BC	to	4998 BC
Hamazi	2600 ? BC	to	2500 ? BC	4998 BC	to	4638 BC
2nd Uruk	2500 ? BC	to	2400 ? BC	4638 BC	to	4451 BC
2nd Ur	2500 ? BC	to	2400 ? BC	4451 BC	to	4283 BC
Adab	2500 ? BC	to	2400 ? BC	4283 BC	to	4193 BC
Mari	2500 ? BC	to	2400 ? BC	4193 BC	to	4057 BC
3rd Kish	2500 ? BC	to	2400 ? BC	4057 BC	to	3957 BC
Akshak	2500 ? BC	to	2300 ? BC	3957 BC	to	3864 BC
4th Kish	2500 ? BC	to	2359 BC	3864 BC	to	3765 BC
3rd Uruk	2359 BC	to	2334 BC	3910 BC	to	3885 BC
Akkad	2334 BC	to	2154 BC	3885 BC	to	3700 BC
4th Uruk	2244 BC	to	2195 BC	3700 BC	to	3651 BC
Gutian	2195 BC	to	2119 BC	3651 BC	to	3575 BC
5th Uruk	2119 BC	to	2112 BC	3575 BC	to	3568 BC
3rd Ur	2112 BC	to	2004 BC	3568 BC	to	3462 BC
Isin	2017 BC	to	1788 BC	3462 BC	to	3227 BC

The fundamental problem with changing the timeline of Egypt is that Egypt is the only ancient civilization that has a long history that is generally understood, in many cases down to the decade. Therefore, Egypt is used as the metric against which other ancient civilizations are dated. If we didn't have Egypt, other ancient civilizations would exist at unclear points in time, at least in theory. With carbon dating, dendrochronology, and paleoclimatology, we could establish a timeline without Egypt, unfortunately, we have Egypt. Unfortunate, because the existence of the Egyptian timeline forces every other civilization into specific points in time, that generally do not fit the scientific evidence.

While there are many possible mentions of Egypt in Sumerian and Akkadian literature in the earliest periods, none mention anyone specific until the 13th

Dynasty of Egypt. During the 13th Dynasty, a stela of Governor Yantinu of Byblos indicates that King Neferhotep I was contemporary with kings Zimri-Lim of the city-state of Mari, and Hammurabi of the Old Babylonian Empire. As the CET places the 13th Dynasty's existence between approximately 1803 to 1649 BC, with Neferhotep I reigning sometime around 1747 to 1736 BC,[20] then both Zimri-Lim and Hammurabi must have reigned around that time.

There is significant physical evidence for the conventional dates being very wrong, and it isn't new. In 1980 Henry Wright published a paper called *Problems of absolute timeline in protohistoric Mesopotamia* that dealt with this issue. The paper's introduction began with the eloquent statement:

> *"Though scholars are seeking to answer increasingly precise questions about ancient Mesopotamian economic and political developments the chronological frame of reference which they must use is not significantly more precise than it was forty years ago. This dilemma has been recently emphasized by James Mellaart. He begins his argument with reconsiderations of the evidence and reasoning supporting both the Egyptian and Mesopotamian earlier dynastic timelines proposing that for both sequences much earlier datings are defensible He then considers the carbon 14 age determinations corrected to approximate actual calendrical dates from Mesopotamia Anatolia Egypt and the Levant These datings he argues also support much older absolute timeline for protohistoric south west Asia proposal will be criticized by many specialists It is my purpose here to look critically at the archaeological use of carbon 14 age determinations from greater Mesopotamian sites of the early fourth to early third millennia BC in an effort to suggest ways of improving our absolute timeline from this limited region."*

Wright ultimately concluded that there were not enough carbon-dated artifacts from Egypt and Mesopotamia to reconstruct a timeline independent from the historic method used by Egyptologists and Assyriologists in his time. Unfortunately, the situation has not changed much since 1980. There have been multiple attempts to create an Egyptian timeline based on carbon-dating, however, any attempts by non-Egyptologists to alter the conventional timeline by more than a century or two have been completely ignored. Nevertheless, Wright did point out that there were many inconsistencies known even back in 1980. The paper by James Mallaart that Wright referenced was published a year earlier: *Egyptian and Near Eastern timeline: A dilemma?*[21] It began with the following introduction:

> *"There exists a widespread belief among historians that radiocarbon dating is incompatible with the historical timelines of Egypt and Mesopotamia. In this article the author, lecturer in Anatolian archaeology at the Institute of Archaeology, University of London, attempts to show that a high historical timeline is required by re-interpretation of the Uruk and Jemdet Nasr sequences and their links with Egypt. A comparison with dendrochronology-corrected radiocarbon dating suggests that it is compatible with a high historical timeline. By combining these two independent forms of dating it becomes possible to reconstruct a uniform time scale."*

In the 1980s and 1990s, there were many attempts to correct the dating of the earlier dynastic periods of Egypt to a long-timeline, however, Egyptologists provided a large number of reasons to dismiss the scientist's findings. One of the best arguments against accepting the older dates that carbon-14 was indicating was that the Egyptians reused materials when they built newer buildings. Therefore, just because a piece of wood used to build a temple might be centuries older than when the temple is believed to have been built by Egyptologists using the CET, these Egyptologists can dismiss the data, as the Egyptians probably built all their temples with wood that had been lying around for centuries. It is a claim that cannot be disproved scientifically.

The problem with changing the Egyptian timeline to ULT is that all other cultures that traded with Egypt need to fit into the ULT. If the Old Kingdom was circa 4945 to 4003 BC, then the Sumerian Civilization would have to date to around the same time, as we know they traded with each other. The city of Uruk should specifically show the earlier dating, as it is generally regarded as being the first major city in Sumer. Until the time of Saddam Hussein, the southern region of Iraq was a marshland, where ancient cities rose above the surrounding waters on what appear to be either terraced hills or artificial mounds. This meant that land was always scarce in the ancient Sumerian cities, and as result buildings were routinely rebuilt.

Above is a photograph of an Iraqi marshland town taken in the 1970s. The mound that Uruk was built on, has 13 known distinct periods of construction, each one earlier than the previous as we dig deeper into the mound. Assyriologists date the buildings from Uruk 13 period to circa 5000 BC CMT. Clearly, the earliest Urukians could not have been trading with the Egyptians if the 1st Dynasty of Egypt wasn't founded until 3100 BC CET, yet the earliest Urukians were building flat-topped ziggurats, virtually identical to the mastabas of the 1st and 2nd Dynasties in Egypt.

Ubaid	Sumerian	Akkadian	Old Babylonian	Neo-Babylonian	
					god, heaven, star, An (Anu)
					Earth, earth, land
					man
					woman
					mountain
					female slave
					head
					mouth
					bread

One of the main reasons that Assyriologists and Egyptologists believe that Sumer and Egypt were in contact from the earliest periods of their respective histories, is due to the similarity of their scripts. Both the Egyptian hieroglyphs and Sumerian cuneiform combine logographic, syllabic, and alphabetic elements in the same way that few other systems have. Sumerian cuneiform emerged in Sumer during the Late Uruk period between 3400 and 3100 BC CMT (5231 to 4931 BC ULT). An earlier phase of proto-writing has been discovered dating from at least the Late Ubaid period circa 4500 to 4000 BC CMT (6331 to 5831 BC ULT), which appears to have evolved into cuneiform. This earlier proto-writing period used the same pictographic symbols as early Sumerian, vaguely similar to hieroglyphics. Unfortunately, few examples have been found, and it has not been translated.

Meanwhile, hieroglyphics had been under development in Egypt beginning as a pictographic script starting in the pre-dynastic era, in a time period called Naqada III circa 3200 to 3100 BC CET (5610 to 5510 BC ULT), which directly preceded the 1st Dynasty. The earliest hieroglyphics sentence to have been deciphered dates to the 2nd Dynasty, from between 2890 and 2686 BC CET, (5149 to 4945 BC ULT). In the 1900s when the original Egyptian long-timeline was in use, the fact that the earliest Sumerian script looked like the primitive Egyptian hieroglyphs wasn't a problem, the Egyptians had influenced the development of Sumerian cuneiform.

Once the CET became dominant the situation becomes confusing, as now Sumerian Cuneiform influenced the formation of Egyptian Hieroglyphs, yet the Egyptians decided to copy the older no-longer-used pictographic script instead of Cuneiform as the basis of their Hieroglyphs. Below are a series of pre-Dynastic tokens from the tomb of U-j at Abydos, Egypt, dated to the Amratian period between 4000 and 3500 BC CET (6410 to 5910 BC ULT).

Another reason that the earliest phases of both Sumerian and Egyptian history are believed to have influenced each other is that both cultures built large stone platforms, called mastabas in Egypt, and flat-topped ziggurats in Sumer. In both cultures, the stone platforms evolved into pyramid-like structures, pyramids in Egypt, and ziggurats in Sumer. The oldest known mastabas in Egypt date to the pre-historic era, however, they were far simpler than those of the dynastic period. During the 1st Dynasty, the construction of mastabas copied the basic house plan and consisted of several rooms. During the 2nd and 3rd Dynasties, the stairway mastaba became common. These mastabas had a sunken burial chamber and a stairway that allowed access to the top of the mastaba. Below is a photograph of a mastaba from Saqqara, Egypt, dating from circa 2686 to 2613 BC CET (5247 to 4945 ULT).

By the 3rd Dynasty, the kings of Egypt had transitioned from building mastabas to pyramids, however, mastabas continued to be used by commoners until the end of the 3rd Dynasty. Hundreds of mastabas were built on the Giza Plateau for nobility and commoners during the 3rd

Dynasty, surrounding where the Pyramid of Khufu would later be built. The fact the Western Mastaba Field and Eastern Mastaba Field are built in alignment with the Pyramid of Khufu, which would not be built until the next dynasty has been used by some to suggest that the Pyramid of Khufu was already built by the 3rd Dynasty, and Khufu was at best repairing or rebuilding an older pyramid or mastaba.

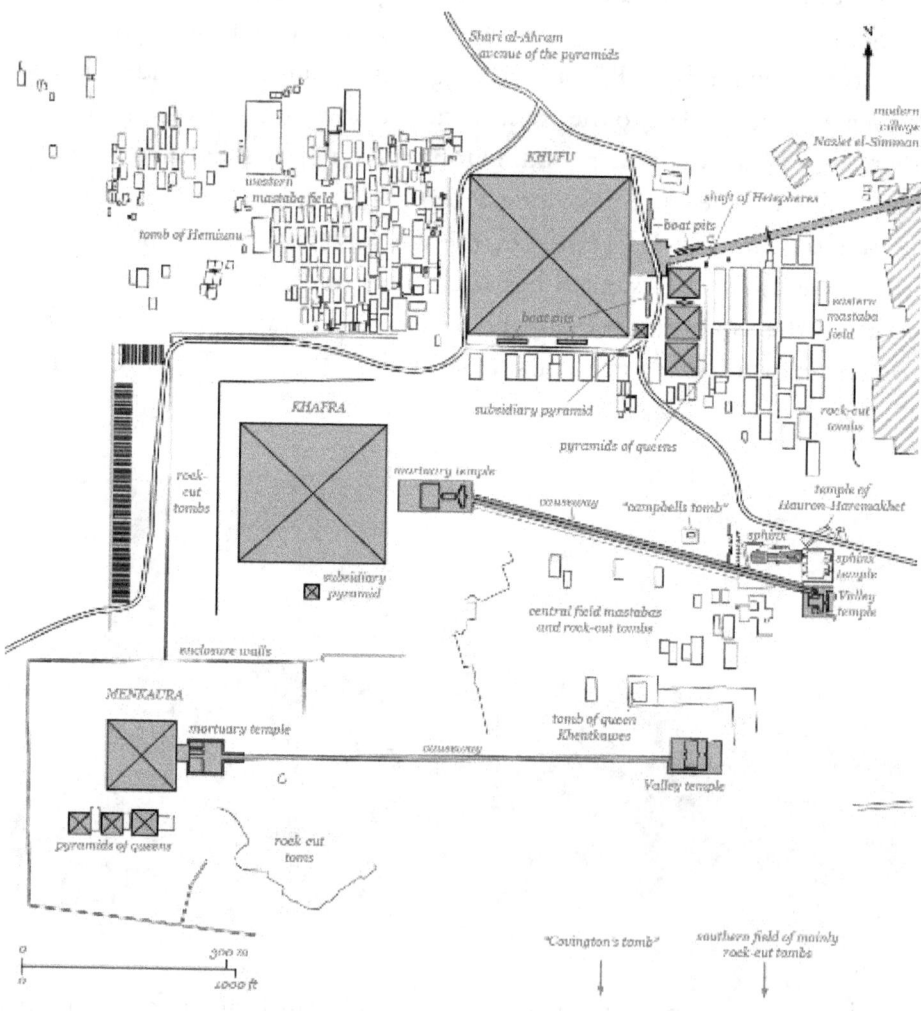

Above is a map of the Giza Plateau in Egypt, which shows the Mastaba fields of the 3rd Dynasty build around the 4th Dynasty Pyramid of Khufu. By the 4th Dynasty, the kings were building larger pyramids, reaching a zenith with the Pyramids of Khufu and Khafra on the Giza Plateau, while the nobles and commoners were either building small pyramids or tombs cut into rock cliffs. This means that the mastabas were built from the late pre-dynastic period to the end of the 3rd Dynasty, circa 3200 to 2613 BC CET (or 5610 to 4731 BC ULT).

In Mesopotamia, the oldest known flat-topped ziggurats date back to the Ubaid period between 6500 and 4000 BC CMT (8331 to 5831 BC ULT). By 3000 BC, the Mesopotamian and Iranian Plateau ziggurats were being built in a pyramidal shape, as evidenced by the ziggurat of Tepe Sialk, in the modern city of Kashan, Iran. It's unclear when the Sumerians transitioned to building pyramidal ziggurats from flat-topped ziggurats, as the humid conditions of southern Iraq and the fact that the Sumerians had limited land, caused the Sumerian ziggurats to be repeatedly rebuilt. Below is a photo of the ruins of Tepe Sialk in Iran, the oldest known surviving pyramidal ziggurat.

Therefore, the time period when Mesopotamians were building flat-topped pyramids ranged sometime between 6500 and 3000 BC CMT or 9510 to

3000 BC ULT, while the Egyptians were building mastabas between either 3200 and 2613 BC CET or 5610 and 4731 BC ULT. This means that the Mesopotamians were either shifting from flat-topped to pyramidal ziggurats around the time that the Egyptians started to build mastabas according to the conventional timelines, or the two civilizations were building raised platforms and then pyramidal structures around the same time using the ULT.

The Egyptians and Sumerians also began building with the same niched facades during the pre-Dynastic era. In Egypt, niched facade construction began during the Amratian Culture circa 4000 to 3500 BC CET (6410 to 5910 BC ULT), and was discontinued by the end of the Third Dynasty, circa 2686 to 2613 BC CET (4945 to 4731 BC ULT). In Mesopotamia, niched facade construction began during the Late Uruk period circa 3400 to 3100 BC CMT, and was discontinued during the Jamdet Nasr period circa 3100 to 2900 BC CMT.

As there are no clear parallels between the archaeological and dynastic periods, or delineation between the dynastic and pre-dynastic period in Sumer like there are in Egypt, correlating the two timelines using the prevalence of niched facade construction seems valid. If both cultures were building with niched facades at the same time and stopped around the same time, then the end of the 3rd Dynasty circa 4731 BC ULT would date the end of the Jemdet Nasr period to circa 4731 BC ULT. Using the conventional timelines, the niched facade construction design was used in Egypt between 4000 and 2613 BC, and in Sumer between 3400 to 2900 BC. While in ULT, the niched facade construction design was used in Egypt between 6410 and 4731 BC, and in Sumer between 5231 to 4731 BC.

Below is a photograph of the ruins of Shunet El-Zebib, in Abydos, Egypt, dated to the 2nd Dynasty, dated to between 2890 and 2686 BC CET (5247 to 4945 BC ULT), which shows the surviving lowest level's niched facade. Fortunately, the lowest level was buried in sand for thousands of years, allowing the original facade to survive the passage of time. The upper levels have been heavily damaged by sandstorms since the original construction.

On the next page is a photo of the surviving niched facade on the lower level of the Uruk Ziggurat.

Generally, the ULT does correlate well with the Ubaid and Sumerian periods of Mesopotamian history. However, there is the question of the correlation of Egypt's King Neferhotep I and King Zimri-Lim of Mari, and King Hammurabi of Babylon. The CET places the reign of Neferhotep I sometime between 1747 to 1736 BC and 1705 to 1694 BC[22] depending on the version of the CET used. King Zimri-Lim of Mari's reign is dated to circa 1775 to 1761 BC, as this correlates with the life of King Neferhotep I. King Hammurabi's reign is dated to somewhere between 1933 and 1890 BC to 1696 and 1654 BC depending on the version of the CMT used. In both timelines, there are various different versions compiled by different historians. The five dominant chronologies of the CMT are known as the Ultra-Long, Long, Medium, Short, and Ultra-Short timelines. These timelines allow for up to a 250-year fluctuation of the dating of Mesopotamian history. The Middle Chronology is used for the CMT dates herein.

Dating the life of King Neferhotep I using the ULT means placing the life of Neferhotep I significantly earlier, between 3246 and 3092 BC. This means that the lives of King Zimri-Lim of Mari and King Hammurabi of

Babylon also needs to be moved back to an earlier period. This also means that Mari and Babylon need to have existed at the time. The dating of the Mesopotamian civilization, like the Egyptian Civilization, is subject to gaps where dark ages interrupted civilization. As the Egyptian history was compiled before the Sumerian civilization was even discovered, Assyriologists have traditionally used the Egyptian timeline as a baseline to set the dating for the Sumerian and Akkadian dynasties.

The Mesopotamian timeline is divided into four distinct time periods: the Sumerian, Akkadian, Babylonian, and Late eras. The oldest era is the Sumerian era, which Assyriologists date to between approximately 2900 to 2334 BC CET. These dates were invented to correlate the Sumerian civilization with the Egyptian Early and Old Kingdom eras, as the two cultures were clearly trading extensively at the time. In order to fit the over 21,000 years of recorded Sumerian civilization into the less than 600 years allotted by Assyriologists most of it has to be ignored. Like the Egyptians, the Sumerians recorded a series of dynasties that ruled from different cities, with the kingship passing between the cities as the dynasties changed. In order to try to force the Sumerian civilization into a period of less than 600-years, Assyriologists have had to dismiss the Sumerian claims that the dynasties were in sequence, and assume that they were all happening at the same time. While this may work for most of the dynasties, three of them are more than 600 years long: the 1st Kish Dynasty, the 1st Uruk Dynasty, and the 2nd Kish Dynasty. Therefore these dynasties are simply assumed to be exaggerated by Assyriologists.

The idea that we should dismiss the recorded histories of the Sumerians, Assyrians, Armenians, and other Mesopotamian peoples came from the same source as the idea that we should ignore thousands of years of Egyptian history: James Henry Breasted. Above is a photograph from 1920 of Breasted at the ruins of the Ziggurat of Ur, built by the Neo-Sumerian King Ur-Namma, whose live is dated to circa 2112 to 2092 BC CMT (3568 to 3550 BC ULT). While Breasted is considered an Egyptologist, and not an Assyriologist, he is the source of the CET, and used his position as the founder and first head of the Oriental Institute to push the CET chronology into Assyriology and Indology through the 1920s.

The Oriental Institute was established by Breasted in 1919 with funding from John D. Rockefeller Jr. and the University of Chicago. In the early 1920s, the Oriental Institute funded expeditions to Egypt, Iraq, Syria, Palestine (Israel), and India. In 1923, Breasted became the first archaeologist to be elected to membership in the National Academy of Sciences, and as of 1926, he served as the president of the History of Science Society. That he was influential in the development of Archaeology as an academic field in America cannot be doubted, however, he was also a Christian fundamentalist that insisted on dating civilizations according to the Biblical timeline. He was the source of the currently ubiquitous conventional Egyptian timeline, which he resurrected after it had previously been proposed and disproved in Europe during the 1800s. Unfortunately, the records of the Egyptians and Sumerians do not fit into the Biblical timeline in which the world was created circa 4000 BC, and therefore those ancient human historical records have been both dismissed and even discredited by so-called Egyptologists and Assyriologists.

As the Sumerians rebuilt their cities repeatedly, and the Akkadians and Babylonians that later lived in them rebuilt them as well, very little remains from the Sumerian era, making dismissing the *Sumerian King List* fairly easy. The situation is further complicated by the fact that most of the work done into Mesopotamian history took place during the Ottoman, British, and Ba'athist rules' of Iraq, which were punctuated by World War 1, World War 2, the Republican Revolution, the Iran-Iraq War, the Desert Storm Wars, the US-led Sanctions, the 2003 Invasion of Iraq, and subsequent occupation of Iraq.

Regardless of when the Sumerian civilization existed, the ruins in Iraq are far older than 2900 BC. Assyriologists classify the earlier eras as the Ubaid, Uruk, and Jamdet Nasr eras, and date them to between 6500 BC CMT and the beginning of the dynastic era. If the Egyptian Old Kingdom wasn't dated to circa 2686 to 2181 BC CET, these earlier periods of Iraqi ruins would be considered Sumerian. These ruins are in the same cities that the Sumerians later lived in, including Uruk, Ur, and Eridu, yet these ruins cannot be dated to the Sumerian civilization, as the Sumerians were trading with the Egyptians early in their civilization.

If the ULT is used for the Egyptian civilization, and the end of the Jemdet Nasr era is synchronized with the end of the Egyptian 3rd Dynasty, then the Ubaid, Uruk, and Jemdet Nasr eras would span the period of circa 8331 to 4731 BC, permitting almost all of the dynasties after the first dynasty to exist within known ruins. The second dynasty on the Sumerian King Lists was the 1st Uruk Dynasty which would span the time period of 9868 to 7558 BC ULT. The first dynasty was the 1st Kish Dynasty, which spanned the time period of 25,179 to 7698 BC ULT. Nothing survives from the 1st Kish Dynasty, even the location of Kish is unknown, however, it is believed to be somewhere in the region of Babylon. As the 1st Kish Dynasty cannot be proven to have existed by any currently known archaeological evidence, it is best to deal with it as a pre-Dynastic period, along with the Antediluvian period on the Sumerian King Lists.

Before 7000 BC, most of southern Iraq would have been dry land, however by 6000 BC the region was beginning to flood as the water level in the region rose after the Persian Gulf flooded. Throughout most of the Last Glacial Period, the Persian Gulf was exposed land, as the region only averages around 35 meters below modern sea level, and the oceans fell to as low as 135 meters below modern sea level. The Persian Gulf flooded between 10,000 and 7000 BC, following which the southern region of Iraq began flooding, creating the wetland that Sumer was built in.

The fact that Sumer was built in a wetland should itself point to the civilization being older than the wetland, as civilizations aren't generally built in swamps. The oldest phases of construction in Uruk, from before the Uruk 5 period, includes the use of large amounts of limestone and bitumen, while after Uruk 5 the Sumerians switched to building with abode bricks. Building with adobe in a wetland makes some sense, as they would have had access to mud, however, the limestone is a mystery, as the Sumerians did not have a local source of stone, which was one of their major imported commodities. Importing enough stone to build the base of a ziggurat is a hopelessly illogical concept, yet it is a requisite of the CMT. Clearly, the earliest Urukians had access to locally sourced limestone, which would mean they were quarrying in the region prior to the water level rising after 7000 BC.

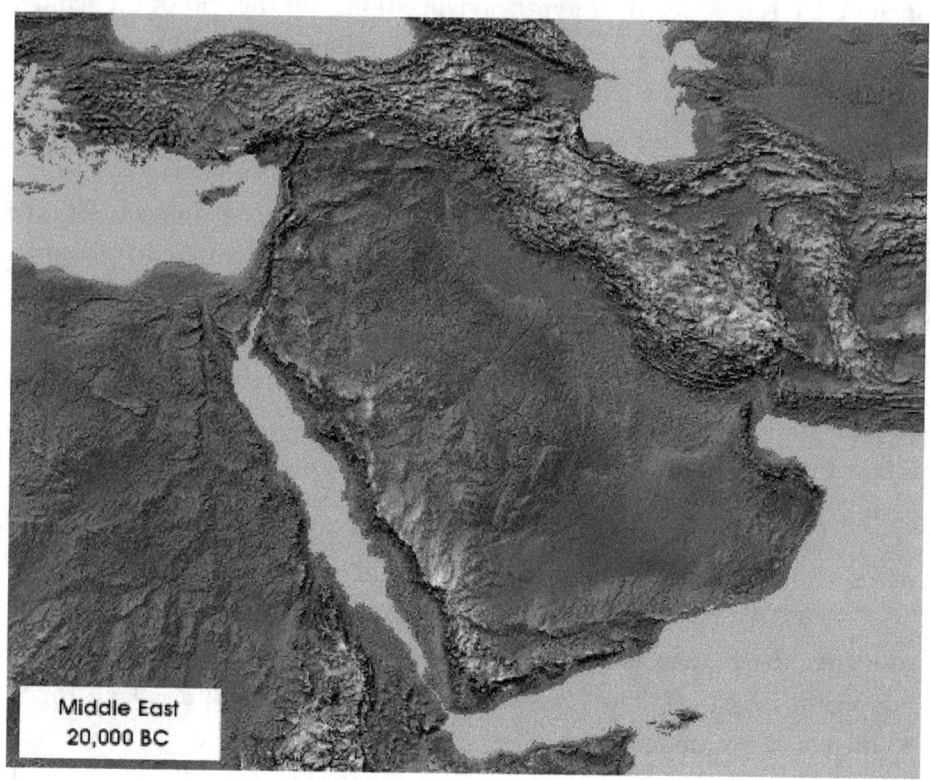

Middle East 20,000 BC

Using this longer timeline for the Sumerian civilization also allows the Sumerian King Lists to make sense, as they claimed that King Gilgamesh reigned around 3900 years before King Sargon, who is traditionally dated to around 2300 BC CET, however, would date to approximately 3850 BC ULT. One problem with allowing the Sumerian civilization to span the length of the Ubaid period is that we have no clay tablets from the Ubaid period that show signs of writing, however, that does not mean that they were not writing.

The invention of the clay tablet as a form of record may have been a late invention and would have naturally led to the use of a standardized impression tool, and ultimately a new writing system, which we call cuneiform. For the Sumerians, the invention of the clay tablet would have been as revolutionary as the invention of movable type was to the Europeans in the 1400s. Movable type standardized calligraphy and enforced the use of the Latin alphabet across western Europe. Over the following centuries, cultures that did not use the Latin alphabet slowly fell behind technologically and socially, as ideas could not move as freely in those cultures.

Above is an Ubaid era seal imprint depicting the water-god Enki (center) and the two-faced messenger-god Isinu (right). The pictographs on the Ubaid era imprint indicates that the seal dates to at least the Late Ubaid era, circa 4500 to 4000 BC CMT (6331 to 5831 BC ULT). On the next page is a similar imprint from the Akkadian era showing Ea, the Akkadian Enki (center), and Usumu, the Akkadian Isinu, (right). The Akkadian era seal dates to after 2334 BC CMT (3885 BC ULT), indicating that while Assyriologists may not want to accept the fact that the Ubaid ruins are Sumerian, the Ubaidians did worship the same gods as the Sumerians and Akkadians.

The Egyptians were using papyrus from at least the 1st Dynasty, and as the two cultures were trading ideas about how to build massive stone platforms and then pyramids, it seems likely someone would have introduced papyrus to Sumer. The fact that we don't find papyrus in the ruins of Ubaid is not proof that they didn't use papyrus as Ubaid was built in marshland, while Egypt was built along a river, surrounded by what became desert after 6000 years ago.

Even in Egypt, we find virtually no surviving papyrus until the Middle Kingdom. We do find some, so we know they were using it, but we find very little. In Ubaid, the climate would have caused the papyrus to rot within centuries, and would naturally explain why they ultimately invented the clay tablet. In Egypt, when they wanted to create a document that would last a long time, they carved it into stone, however, the Sumerians had very little stone, and in fact, it was one of their main imports. Carving records into stone would have been far too expensive when they were surrounded by the exact same reeds the Egyptians used to make papyrus.

The development of Sumerian clay tablets has been traced back directly to Ubaid era clay tokens called bullae, which began to be used between 8,000 and 7,500 BC. These bullae represented grain and livestock which were often stored in communal facilities due to the limited amount of land available in the Ubaid cities. They also appear to have been used in trade, as a type of proto-money. The bullae remained virtually unchanged for over 4000 years, until approximately 4000 to 3500 BC, when they began to become more elaborate.

Bulla	Pictograph	Old Babylonian Cuneiform	Neo-Assyrian Cuneiform	Neo-Babylonian Cuneiform	Meaning
					Sheep
					Cattle
					Dog
					Metal
					Oil
					Garment
					Bracelet
					Perfume

During the Sumerian dynastic and later periods in Mesopotamia, bullae were accompanied by papyrus that explained their value, for example: 'this bulla is worth two cows at the livestock holding pen.' This made them more like a bankers' check than true money in the modern concept, however very much like early paper money that was once backed by gold. It is difficult to comprehend how the bullae could have ever been used without papyrus explaining what they were valued at, and is, therefore, a strong indicator that papyrus, and writing, were used in Mesopotamia since the introduction of the bulla circa 8000 to 7500 BC.

While Sumerian cuneiform is documented to have evolved out of Ubaid bullae, the two scripts are both used on the Daily Salary tablet AO 20052 at the Louvre, pictured below. As there is no reason for the two scripts to have been written at the same time, this indicates that the Sumerians were copying older Ubaid era tablets, much as later Mesopotamian civilizations would copy Sumerian texts.

The third period in the Mesopotamian timeline is the Akkadian era, which is also derived from the Sumerian King Lists and is a direct continuation from the Sumerian era. The Akkadian people are believed to have settled in the Sumerian civilization and eventually become dominant. King Sargon was the first Akkadian King, who overthrew the last Sumerian King and established the Akkadian Empire, eventually gaining control over all of the former Sumerian territories. This civilization generally continued the Sumerian civilization, however, the dominant language shifted to Akkadian, the ancestral language of Babylonian and Assyrian. The Akkadians continued to live in the Sumerian cities, and rebuild them, and therefore there are more Akkadian era relics than Sumerian or Ubaid.

Unlike the earlier Sumerians, the Akkadians were a Semitic people, whose language served as the basis of both the Old Babylonian and Old Assyrian languages.[23] Both Old Babylonian and Old Assyrian are very closely related to Akkadian, sometimes being classified as dialects of Akkadian, however, they are easily distinguishable from both each other and Akkadian. Both the Babylonians and Assyrians adopted Akkadian cuneiform for their written records, which for the Babylonians isn't a problem, as they conquered the Akkadians, however, it is a problem for the Assyrians. The Assyrians had records of their people's history long preceding the foundation of the Old Assyrian Empire, circa 1905 BC CMT (3278 BC ULT). This earlier period is known as the Early Assyrian Period, which either spans 2447 to 1906 BC CMT, or 3764 to 3278 BC ULT. As this period must have happened after the Akkadian Empire circa 2334 to 2154 BC CMT (3885 to 3700 BC ULT), it is generally ignored by Assyriologists as it begins over a century before the Akkadian Empire was founded in the CMT. In the ULT, the Early Assyrian Period began late in the Akkadian Empire, with the foundation of the Old Assyrian Empire happening near the end of the Neo-Sumerian Empire. Again this is a strong indicator that the conventional timelines are wrong as we either have to ignore the records of the Assyrians, or accept they were time-travelers to make their history fit into the CMT.

Babylonian Timeline

Babylonian Timelines

Period	CMT			ULT		
Old Babylonian Empire	1894 BC	to	1595 BC	3352 BC	to	3038 BC
Kassite Dynasty	1570 BC	to	1155 BC	3013 BC	to	1155 BC
Elamite Empire	1210 BC	to	1100 BC	1210 BC	to	1100 BC
Neo-Assyrian Empire	912 BC	to	612 BC	912 BC	to	612 BC
Neo-Babylonian Empire	612 BC	to	539 BC	612 BC	to	539 BC

The fourth period in the Mesopotamian timeline is the Late Era, which includes the Babylonian, Assyrian, and later civilizations. The Babylonian timeline is derived from the Babylonian King Lists and continues where the Sumerian King Lists end. The Babylonian civilization was largely a continuation of the Akkadian civilization, however, the capital city of Babylon was north of the marshlands. The fact that the Babylonian King Hammurabi was around at the same time as the Egyptian King Neferhotep I requires moving the entire Old Babylonian Empire to circa 3352 to 3038 BC ULT.

This does not affect the dating of the later periods, as there was a dark age after the Fall of Babylon at the end of the Old Babylonian Empire. The Hittite sacking of Babylon is considered one of the most important events in the Babylonian timeline and generally dated to somewhere between 1499 and 1736 BC depending on the version of the CMT used. If the ULT is used then the Fall of Babylon took place around 3038 BC, around 200 years after the collapse of the Egyptian Middle Kingdom. The ULT also sees the reign of the last Neo-Sumerian King, Damiq-ilishu, ending in 3227 BC, around the same time the Egyptian Middle Kingdom collapsed, shortly after the Great Shock of 3250 BC. This is the point in time that the world's climate changed significantly into a neo-glacial period that lasted until around 1500 BC.

There are a number of pieces of evidence supporting the existence of this Great Shock of 3250 BC. During this time the world's weather became stormier, and there was far more rain, which would have caused significant flooding along the Tigris and Euphrates, and significant flooding of the

Mesopotamian marshlands, as well as along other rivers and in other swamps throughout the world.[24] The GISP2 ice core samples from Greenland show there was a spike in atmospheric sulfate at 3250 BC, believed to have been from an increasing number of polynyas in the Arctic, caused by an expansion of oceanic surface ice.[25] The GRIP ice core sample from Greenland shows the 3250 BC point as being at a low point in atmospheric methane, followed by a rapid increase over the next 200 years, which is attributed to an abrupt increase in global wetlands.[26] Ice core samples from the Huascaran glacier in Peru, show an abrupt cooling at about 3250 BC.[27]

It is a historical fact that the Hittites sacked Babylon at the end of the reign of the Old Babylonian King Samsu-Ditana. Babylonia was left in a state of anarchy, and around 24 years later a people called the Kassites occupied Babylonia, and rebuilt the city, renaming it Karduniash. The Kassites ruled Babylonia for centuries, however, they left very little in the way of records until the 1300s BC. This time period is called the Babylonian Dark Age, or Mesopotamian Dark Age, as there are very few records of the time from Babylonia, Elam, Assyria, the Hittite Empire, and Canaan. This dark age either took place between 1524 and 1373 BC CMT, or 2965 and 1373 BC ULT. This means it either happened after the Second Egyptian Dark Age (Second Intermediate Period), which was between 1803 and 1549 BC CET, or it happened at the same time as the Second Egyptian Dark Age between 3246 and 1580 BC ULT.

If the Babylonian Dark Age happened after the Second Egyptian Dark Age, then there is no dark age, as the timeline of the Old Kingdom Assyrians can be continued in the New Kingdom Egyptians. Theoretically, there should be no inconsistencies if both conventional timelines are correct, however, there is the massive anachronism of the Hyksos, a Semitic and Hurrian people, that used Indo-Aryan words and technology, who invaded Egypt circa 1674 BC CET. According to the Egyptians the Hyksos invaded Egypt from the Middle East after conquering Canaan, yet according to the CMT, they were not there, or anywhere. Indo-Aryans didn't enter the Middle East until after the Sack of Babylon circa 1595 BC CMT. This is as clear as any evidence could be that the conventional timelines are wrong. In the ULT, Babylon was sacked in 3038 BC and the Hyksos occupied Egypt in 2533 BC, explaining why Indo-Aryan words were being used by a Semitic and Hurrian people.

Placing the Old Babylonian Empire in the ULT does not affect the later periods of the Mesopotamian timeline, however, it does affect the earlier Sumerian and Akkadian Periods. The *Sumerian King List* provides a continual list of king spanning thousands of years of history. If the Fall of Babylon was circa 3038 BC, then the life of Sargon of Akkad would date to circa 3885 to 3845 BC, and the life of Gilgamesh would date to between 7824 and 7698 BC, assuming all of the dynasties are in sequence other than the known dynastic overlaps. Assyriologists don't generally consider the dynasties to have actually been sequential, as they have been forced to compress all of Dynastic history into a period of only a few hundred years, in order to synchronize it with the CET.

Correlating the life of Hammurabi with the life of Neferhotep I according to the ULT is not problematic, however correlating the life of Zimri-Lim of Mari to circa 3230 BC, is a problem as Mari is generally regarded as being founded in 2900 BC. Unlike many other Sumerian cities, Mari did not start as some little village that grew into a larger city, it was founded as a colonial city during the Mesopotamian Early Dynastic period I. This however also resolves the issue, because if the Old Babylonian Empire was circa 3352 to 3038 BC, then the Mesopotamian Early Dynastic period I would have been thousands of years earlier, and according to the ULT interpretation of the *Sumerian King List*, existed by 4200 BC.

Assyrian Timeline

Assyrian Timelines

Period	CMT	ULT
Early Assyrian Period	2447 BC to 1906 BC	3764 BC to 3278 BC
Old Assyrian Empire	1905 BC to 1517 BC	3278 BC to 2965 BC
Mitanni Empire	1590 BC to 1460 BC	2967 BC to 1460 BC
Middle Assyrian Kingdom	1460 BC to 912 BC	1460 BC to 912 BC
Neo-Assyrian Empire	912 BC to 612 BC	912 BC to 612 BC

Synchronizing the timelines of the Middle East with the ULT also means synchronizing the timeline of the Assyrians. Like the Babylonian civilization in central Mesopotamia, the Assyrian civilization in northern Mesopotamia developed out of the Akkadian culture. The historic periods of the Assyrian civilization are divided into five eras, the Early Assyrian Period, the Old Kingdom, the Mitanni rule, the Middle Kingdom, and the Neo-Assyrian Empire. Linguistically the Assyrian language developed from the Akkadian language, meaning the Akkadian civilization should precede the Assyrian civilization, however in the CMT, the Early Assyrian Period actually preceded the Akkadian Empire. How the Assyrians adopted Akkadian cuneiform, instead of Sumerian cuneiform is not explained by Assyriologists. In the ULT the Assyrian Early Period starts near the end of the Akkadian Empire, which explains why the Assyrians adopted Akkadian cuneiform.

In the CMT, the founder of the Assyrian dynasty, Tudiya, existed roughly a century before Sargon, the founder of the Akkadian Empire, while in the ULT, Tudiya lived around a century after Sargon. As Tudiya could not have lived before Sargon, when the CMT was compressed to synchronize it with the CET, Tudiya and the entire Early Assyrian Period was discredited and demoted from history to mythology. The ancient Assyrians recorded the Early Assyrian Period as a record of the history of the 'kings who lived in tents,' meaning the Assyrians were still nomadic at the time and hadn't yet settled in the land later known as Assyria.

The Old Assyrian Kingdom timeline ran parallel to the Old Babylonian Empire and was for a while under the dominion of the Old Babylonian

Empire after Hammurabi ousted the Assyrian King Ishme-Dagan I, and forced his son King Mut-Ashkur to pay tribute. Assyria continued as an independent kingdom for some time after the destruction of Babylon, slowly or quickly losing territory to the rising Mitanni Empire, and then fell under the dominion of the Mitanni Empire entirely, which they didn't break lose of until the beginning of the Middle Kingdom era, sometime before the Egyptian New Kingdom destroyed the Mitanni army in the Battle of Megiddo. The Mitanni Empire rose during the Babylonian dark age, which in the ULT, corresponds with the Second Egyptian Dark Age in Egypt. The people of the Mitanni Empire were mostly Hurrian, with an Indo-Aryan nobility, and appear to be the source of the Hyksos that occupied Egypt during the Second Egyptian Dark Age, who were mostly Semitic, but with a Hurrian nobility, and who used Indo-Aryan words.

The Mitanni occupied the region that corresponds to modern Syria, creating the Mitanni Empire within a century of the Sack of Babylon, seizing territory from the Hittites to the north, and Assyrians to the east. In the CMT the empire was established by 1560 BC when they sacked the Assyrian capital of Ashur, while in the ULT the empire was established by 2967 BC when they occupied Yamhad. This was during the Babylonian dark age, so few records survive. It is known that the Mitanni Empire either very quickly or gradually conquered the Assyrian Empire, however, it had lost control of Assyria sometime before the Battle of Megiddo circa 1457 BC. While the surviving records seem to indicate that the wars between the Mitanni and Assyrians lasted for centuries before the fall of Ashur, the fact that the Assyrian timeline needs to synchronize with the CET forces Assyriologists to accept the premise that the Mitanni conquered, ruled and then lost Assyria between circa 1560 and 1457 BC CMT. In the ULT this is a long sequence of events that took place between 2967 and 1457 BC ULT, in fact, it is unclear when Assyria regained its independence from the Mitanni, and they could have been independent for centuries by the time of the Battle of Meggido. All that is known is that the Assyrians were independent at the time of the Battle of Megiddo, as they, along with the Babylonians and Hittites, sent tribute to King Thutmose III after he defeated the Mitanni army.

Synchronizing the Assyrian timeline with the ULT doesn't create any issues, as the Assyrian timeline has a dark age after the collapse of the Old Kingdom. The Assyrian Dark Age correlates with the Babylonian Dark Age, and the Second Egyptian Dark Age in the ULT. This dark age saw the rise of the Mitanni in Syria and the Hyksos in Egypt, two cultures that left very little in terms of written records. After the Egyptians had driven the Egyptianized-Hyksos 16th Dynasty out of Egypt, around 1731 BC ULT, they launched a series of invasions into Canaan, occupying most of the Mediterranean coast of modern Israel/Palestine, Lebanon, and Syria, culminating in the Battle of Megiddo in 1457 BC. The Battle of Megiddo was an insurrection against Egyptian rule led by the Kings of Kadesh and Megiddo, and backed by the Mitanni Empire. It ended with the Egyptian army destroying the Canaanite armies and the 330 princes and tribal leaders of the Mitanni. A few years later the Egyptians launched an invasion of the Mitanni Empire, and were able to enter the capital of Washukanni and capture King Barattarna without encountering a Mitanni Army. While they did not gain any territory from the Mitanni, they did show the weakness of the Mitanni, and by 1228 BC the Mitanni Empire effectively ceased to exist, becoming a vassal of the Assyrian Middle Kingdom.

Hittite Timeline

Hittite Timelines

Period	CMT			ULT		
Old Hittite Empire	1664 BC	to	1524 BC	3103 BC	to	2965 BC
Middle Hittite Kingdom	1524 BC	to	1400 BC	2965 BC	to	1450 BC
New Hittite Empire	1400 BC	to	1178 BC	1450 BC	to	1178 BC

Adjusting the dating of the Egyptian civilization and Old Babylonian Empire to correspond with the ULT, also means adjusting the Hittite Empire's dating. The Hittites sacked Babylon circa 3038 BC ULT and therefore the Hittite civilization needs to have existed by 3038 BC. Like the Egyptian civilization the Hittite civilization is divided into three kingdoms, the Old, Middle, and New Kingdoms. However, these kingdoms are not as ancient as the Egyptian kingdoms. The Hittite Old Kingdom is the Empire that destroyed the Old Babylonian Empire, which means that it had to be around circa 3038 BC.

There is only one known synchronism between the Hittite Old Kingdom and the Old Babylonian Empire, the sacking of Babylon. If this is set to circa 3038 BC, then the era of the Old Kingdom spans approximately 3103 to 2967 BC. The Hittites are believed to have begun migrating into Anatolia from the Balkans sometime between 100 and 200 years before the foundation of the Old Kingdom, placing the migration roughly around the time of the Great Shock of 3250 BC. The Hittite destruction of Babylon under King Mursili I was the Old Kingdom's furthest military reach, and after the lengthy campaign against Babylonia, the Hittite resources were strained, and the capital was left in a state of near-anarchy. King Mursili I was assassinated shortly after returning home, and the Hittite Kingdom fell into a state of chaos. The neighboring Hurrian culture emerged during the chaos to occupy the southern half of the Hittite Kingdom, from the Tigris River to the Mediterranean coast, forming the Mitanni Empire.

The Hittite Old Kingdom fought a series of wars against the Mitanni, however, the Old Kingdom was not able to regain its lost territory, and slowly withered. By the end of the Old Kingdom, circa 2967 BC ULT, the

Hittite civilization had been reduced to its core territory in central Anatolia, and virtually no records remain from the time. The Hittite Dark Age that followed is referred to as the Middle Kingdom era. Few records remain from the period, and although the names of some kings are known, it is unclear how long the Middle Kingdom era lasted. There are no synchronisms with either the Egyptian or Mesopotamian civilizations known from the Middle Kingdom. What is known is that there is a list of six kings believed to have ruled sometime during this era, however, even the capital of the kingdom during their rule is unclear, as the besieged Hittites repeatedly moved their capital.

The Hittite New Kingdom emerged by 1457 BC, as they paid tribute to the Egyptians after the Battle of Megiddo. The Hittite New Kingdom also called the New Hittite Empire, is well known from the Egyptian New Kingdom and Assyrian Middle Kingdom records. There is no conflict when the dating of the Hittite New Kingdom on the ULT, as both the Hittite and Egyptian New Kingdoms existed around the same time. This Hittite Empire became a dominant power in Anatolia and Syria during the era of the Egyptian New Kingdom and the Assyrian Middle Kingdom.

Kassite-Mitanni-Hyksos Timeline

Kassite-Mitanni-Hyksos Timelines

Civilization	Period	CMT	ULT
Babylonia	Kassite Dynasty	1570 BC to 1155 BC	3013 BC to 1155 BC
Mitanni	Mitanni Empire	1500 BC to 1300 BC	2967 BC to 1300 BC
Egypt	Canaanite 14th Dynasty	1705 BC to 1690 BC	2793 BC to 2533 BC
Egypt	Hyksos 15th Dynasty	1674 BC to 1535 BC	2533 BC to 2249 BC
Egypt	Egyptianized-Hyksos 16th Dynasty	1660 BC to 1600 BC	2249 BC to 1731 BC

Synchronizing the Hurrian civilization with the ULT is also required if the ULT is correct. The Hurrians were a people that lived in northern Syria and northern Mesopotamia, first attested during the Akkadian Empire. Sometime after the Hittite destruction of the Old Babylonian Empire, the Hurrians became united under an Indo-Aryan monarchy and forged the Mitanni Empire. This empire formed in the wake of the power vacuum created by the Hittite's conquest of the Kingdom of Yamhab in northern Syria, and the destruction of the Old Babylonian Empire in central Iraq, followed by the collapse of the power structure within the Hittite Empire. The rise of this empire was also possible as the Old Assyrian Empire was in decline at the time.

Very little is actually known about the Mitanni Empire, or the Hurrian peoples, as there are very few records from the time. The Hurrian people spoke a language related to the language of the Urartu people of the Old Armenian Highlands of eastern modern Turkey and may have been the indigenous people of northern Mesopotamia. The Hurrians were documented as living in northern Mesopotamia during the Akkadian and Old Babylonian Empires, however, did not constitute a separate civilization until the rise of the Mitanni Empire.

The fact that the civilization fell under the control of an Indo-Aryan nobility is strange regardless of when the civilization existed. The homeland of the Indo-Aryan culture is unknown but generally assumed to have been in Central Asia or the Eurasian Steppes. The Indo-Aryans did have quite a lot in common with the Hittites, who were also an Indo-European people, and shared several deities including Indra, Mitra, Nasatya, and Varuna.

During the declining years of the Hittite Old Kingdom, the Mitanni Empire occupied its southern territories, ranging from the Tigris River to the Mediterranean coast of Cilicia. This empire also occupied the western areas of the Assyrian Empire, which was also in decline at the time. In Canaan, the Mitanni occupied several kingdoms including Aziru and Amurru, and turned Alalakh and Kizzuwatna into vassal states. Eventually, the entire Assyrian Empire fell under the dominion of the Mitanni, although when this took place is unknown as both empires left virtually no records during this period. Like the other older civilizations, the Assyrian civilization had gone into rapid decline around the same time as the Hittites and Egyptians, however, had started recovering sometime before the Battle of Megiddo circa 1457 BC.

The Mitanni Empire left very little in terms of written records, however, it was around for either a very short time between 1590 and 1300 BC CMT, or a long time between sometime before 2967 and 1300 BC ULT. The Mitanni left no king lists, and their kings are only known from their interactions with neighboring civilizations. Several synchronizations can be made between the Mitanni kings and the kings of the Egyptian New Kingdom, Assyrian Middle Kingdom, and the Kassite Dynasty of Babylonia. Regardless of the timeline used the Mitanni Empire existed during a dark age.

The Babylonian Dark Age took place at approximately the same time as the Second Egyptian Dark Age, which was either between approximately 1524 and 1460 BC CMT, or 2965 and 1460 BC ULT in Mesopotamia, and between approximately 1803 and 1549 BC CET, or 3246 and 1580 BC ULT in Egypt. Using the ULT these dark ages overlapped, however, using the conventional timelines they don't overlap, which means there should not be a dark age.

The appearance of the Indo-Aryans in the Middle East at the time was not unique to the Mitanni Empire. After the Hittites laid waste to Babylon, Babylonia was occupied by a militant faction of people known as the Kassites, who appear to have had an Indo-Aryan nobility.[28] The Kassites themselves spoke a language which is only partially understood, as very little appears to have been written in it. The Kassite language has been identified by various linguists as either related to the Hurro-Urartian languages,[29] or the Caucasian languages.[30] These people are believed to have migrated into Babylonia from the Zagros Mountains of northern Iran, sometime after the Hittites destroyed Babylon.

The Kassite Dynasty was one of the longest in Babylonian history, although not popular with the general populace, who saw these Kassites as foreign occupiers. Like the Hyksos in Egypt, the Kassites tried to assimilate into the local culture and used Babylonian as the language of governance and business, however, they were also a brutal military dictatorship. The Kassites occupied Babylon around 1571 BC CMT or 3013 BC ULT, either way around 25 years after the Sack of Babylon.

The appearance of the Indo-Aryan led Kassites, could explain the rise of the Hurrians in northern Mesopotamia around the same time. The Hurrians were in northern Mesopotamia since at least the Akkadian era and could be the aboriginal population of northern Mesopotamia. If the Kassite language was related to the Hurrian and Urartu languages, as the dominant theory currently suggests, then the Kassites likely saw the Hurrians, who had been ruled by Akkadians, Babylonians, Assyrians, and Hittites for centuries, as long lost cousins. It is not unreasonable to see the rise of the Mitanni Empire as a Kassite backed plot, if for no other reason than to weaken the other powers in the region. It is well established that the two countries maintained strong relations throughout their existences.

It is unclear when the Hurrians began to rise against the Hittites and Assyrians, as this also happened in the dark age. It is nevertheless depicted in the CMT as happening almost instantaneously, as there isn't much time in the CMT, and the Mitanni had to build an empire that could sack Ashur by 1560 BC, and dominate the Hittites, conquer most of Canaan, then conquer Assyria itself, and then lose it all by 1460 BC. Fortunately, the ULT allows the Hurrians centuries to have built and then lost the Mitanni Empire.

The Hyksos, who invaded Egypt from Syria and Canaan, were a dominantly Semitic people, with a Hurrian nobility, that used Indo-Aryan names and loanwords, as one would expect the Mitanni to have developed into after a few centuries. According to the generally accepted CET, the Hyksos migrated into Egypt starting around 1674 BC, over a century before the Hittite sack of Babylon created the power vacuum that allowed the Kassites to invade Babylonia, and before the Mitanni Empire suddenly materialized from nowhere according to the CMT. In fact, if one accepts the CET, there is no explanation for a Semitic people with a Hurrian nobility using Indo-Aryan words and names originating anywhere in the Middle East, or anywhere else on Earth. Circa 1674 BC CMT there were the Old Babylonian, Old Hittite, and Old Assyrian Empires dominating the region, with no signs of Indo-Aryans anywhere nearby.

If the ULT is used, then the Egyptian Middle Kingdom collapsed into the Second Egyptian Dark Age starting around 3246 BC. The last of the Neo-Sumerian kings lost power in 3227 BC, likely due to the extensive flooding of the old Iraqi Marshlands caused by the Great Shock of 3250 BC. In the centuries that followed Babylon grew in power as the new focus of trade in Southern and Central Mesopotamia, and new powers rose in the formerly dry northern regions around of Ashur and Hattusa to the north. These northern regions thrived for a couple of centuries before ultimately drying back to their previous conditions as the global climate stabilized. As the crops failed in the north circa 3050 BC, the Hittites began expanding their first Empire, raiding first Yamhad in modern Syria, and then sacking Babylonia circa 3038 BC.

The ULT continues with a group of people known as Kassites migrating down from the Zagros mountains into Babylonia and establishing their rule over the region by 3013 BC. These people were ruled by an Indo-Aryan nobility and used both horses and wagons, a technology believed to have been invented by Indo-Aryans or their predecessors in the Eurasian Steppes or Eastern Europe, sometime before the Bronocice pot was made between 3635 and 3370 BC.[31] The earliest known surviving securely dated wheel is the Ljubljana Marshes Wheel, from Slovenia, which is carbon-dated to 3150 BC. In the ULT the Kassites introduce the chariot to Mesopotamia circa

3013 BC, and the Hyksos later introduce the chariot to Egypt circa 2533 BC.

In the conventional timelines, the Sumerians were using the horse-drawn chariot since at least 2600 BC, but it was not introduced to Egypt until the Hyksos Dynasty circa 1674 BC. This anachronism is not explained by Egyptologists, who simply accept that the Egyptians lagged almost a thousand years behind the Sumerians technologically by the Egyptian Middle Kingdom, even while they were trading extensively with the Sumerians. The idea that the Egyptians built the Grand Canal and terraced the Fayum depression by hand, instead of using horses and carts to carry away the debris is profoundly illogical, and it seems hopelessly implausible that the ancient Egyptians could have been that stupid.

It is even more absurd that the Sumerians were using horses and wagons during the Egyptian Old Kingdom, and instead of importing the technology, the ancient Egyptians chose to build the great pyramids with brute human strength. Using the conventional timelines the Egyptians and Sumerians exchanged ideas about how to build mastabas and pyramids, and taught each other the art of writing, and even exchanged ideas about mythical animals, but at no point did the Egyptians look at the horse, or even the wheel, and think, 'that might be useful.'

In the ULT the introduction of the wheel into Mesopotamia by the Kassites circa 3013 BC was at the beginning of the Babylonian Dark Age, and only two centuries into the more the 1600 year long Second Egyptian Dark Age. The Indo-Aryan Kassite nobility of Babylon extended their control into Syria, establishing the Mitanni Empire, by seizing control of the native Hurrian population, and using them to subjugate the Amorite population of Canaan. This new Mitanni Empire appears to have been more of a Steppes-style confederation than a Mesopotamian-style kingdom. As demonstrated at the Battle of Megiddo circa 1457 BC, and its aftermath. In the Battle of Megiddo, the Mitanni backed the kings of Kadesh and Megiddo in their attempt to resist Egyptian domination of Canaan. The Mitanni were described as the 330 princes and tribal leaders of the Mitanni, which were destroyed by the Egyptian forces. A few years later when the Egyptians launched an invasion of the Mitanni Empire, they were able to enter the capital of Washukanni and capture King Barattarna without meeting a Mitanni army. This strongly indicates that the Mitanni were not a unified kingdom with a standing army, but rather a confederation of tribes.

By 2793 BC ULT, a group of Canaanites, who had been living in Northern Egypt since the Middle Kingdom, seized power and established the 14th Dynasty. This Dynasty was in turn conquered by the Hyksos around 2533 BC ULT, who formed the 15th Dynasty. The modern name Hyksos is derived from the ancient Egyptian term 'heqa khasut,' which translates as 'rulers of foreign lands.' The term had been used since at least the Middle Kingdom for any foreign government, but this was the first time a foreign government was described as ruling Egypt. Egyptologists do not interpret the Hyksos as being a foreign government, as the Hyksos Dynasty occupied Egypt circa 1674 BC CET, while the Old Babylonian, Old Assyrian, and Old Hittite Empires were still around, and none of them bothered recording that they conquered Egypt, which one of them would have had to have done, as the Egyptians recorded the Hyksos conquering Canaan before entering Egypt.

Instead, Egyptologists cling to the idea proposed by the Jewish Historian Josephus circa 94 AD, that the Hyksos were a group of nomadic 'Shepherd Kings,' even though his etymology of Hyksos as 'Shepherd Kings' has, ironically, been thoroughly discredited by Egyptologists. The fact that the term Hyksos is derived from the ancient Egyptian term for 'foreign ruler' is not disputed by Egyptologists, yet clearly, there were no foreign powers that could have been ruling Egypt circa 1674 BC to 1535 BC CET. Conversely, there was a foreign power circa 2533 BC to 2249 BC ULT that not only could have, by should have conquered the Canaanite Dynasty of Egypt, the Mitanni Empire, who had conquered the Canaanites in Canaan.

The Hyksos formed the 15th Dynasty in Egypt, which in the CET overlaps with the 13th, 16th, Abydos, 17th, and 18th Dynasties in order to compress the timeline. This means that multiple Egyptian dynasties were concurrent in the CET, controlling different regions, and fighting various undocumented wars. In the ULT, these dynasties generally followed each other, except for the Abydos Dynasty which was not mentioned in Manetho's timeline. In the ULT, the Hyksos appear to have conquered the 14th Dynasty during a famine around 2533 BC. Seals from the 14th Dynasty have been found as far north as Tel Kabri, in modern-day Israel, and as far south as Dongola in modern-day Sudan,[32] indicating that the 14th Dynasty was still in control of the territory of the Middle Kingdom.

The Hyksos seized control of Egypt circa 2533 BC ULT, forming the 15th Dynasty, and in the process introduced the horse, the war-chariot, and compound bow to Egypt. This is itself an enigma, as in the CET the Hyksos invaded Egypt circa 1674 BC, introducing horses and war-chariots, almost a thousand years after they are known to have been in use in Sumer, as portrayed in the Standard of Ur from 2600 BC CMT. The Standard of Ur dates from the reign of King Ur-Pabilsag, who is not listed in the Sumerian King List, which would place his life sometime after the end of the Sumero-Akkadian Dynasty. He also is unknown from the later Old Babylonian, Old Assyrian, or Sealand King Lists, which would mean he must have existed somewhere during the Old Babylonian Dark Age between 3013 and 1373 BC ULT. This means that the Egyptians either lagged almost a thousand years behind the Sumerians technologically in the conventional timelines, or both cultures adopted the horse and chariot technology during the same dark age.

In the CET, the Hyksos 15th Dynasty was driven out of Egypt circa 1535 BC early in the 18th Dynasty, after the rise and fall of the 16th, Abydos, and 17th Dynasties. In order for these dynasties to all coexist, they have to have only ruled specific regions. In the ULT, the Hyksos 15th Dynasty was driven out by the 16th Dynasty circa 2249 BC, which was an Egyptianized-Hyksos Dynasty based in Thebes, Egypt. In both timelines, the Abydos Dynasty rose up as a nationalist faction that fought a 70-year long war against the 15th or 16th Dynasty. In the CET, the Abydos Dynasty formed the 17th Dynasty circa 1580 BC and was replaced by the 18th Dynasty of the New Kingdom in 1549 BC, who ultimately drove the Hyksos from Egypt circa 1535 BC. While in the ULT the Abydos Dynasty drove the 16th Dynasty from Egypt circa 1731 BC and then formed the 17th Dynasty which ruled until 1580

BC when the 18th Dynasty founded the New Kingdom. While we do have extensive records from the New Kingdom, there are no records of conflict with the Hyksos, the only existing record that Egyptologist use to date the war between the Hyksos and the 18th Dynasty is the military commentary on the back of the *Rhind Mathematical Papyrus*, consisting of brief diary entries, one of which reads:

> "*Regnal year 11, second month of shomu, Heliopolis was entered. First month of akhet, day 23, this southern prince broke into Tjaru.*"33

This diary entry does not state the name of either the ruling king or the rebel prince, and could just as easily be interpreted as the founder of the 18th Dynasty Prince Ahmose I's rebellion against his uncle King Kamose of the 17th Dynasty. In fact, it makes far more sense that the writer would refer to the enemy as a prince if he was the nephew of the king, than if he was ruling a rebel faction. The fact that Heliopolis was invaded should point it not being a reference to the war against the Hyksos, as the Hyksos were based in Avaris in the Nile Delta, not Heliopolis in modern Greater Cairo.

It should also be noted that the *Turin King List* from the 19th Dynasty, less than 300 years later, does not record the 15th Dynasty Hyksos and 18th Dynasty coexisting, but rather it records the same thing that Manetho translated into Greek a thousand years later. The fact that the New Kingdom era Egyptians believed the 14th, 15th, 16th, 17th, and 18th Dynasties were sequential, spanning over 1200 years of history is well documented, yet ignored by Egyptologists. Egyptologists also choose to ignore the fact that both the 13th Dynasty (1803 to 1649 BC CET) and 16th Dynasty (1660 to 1600 BC CET), ruled from Thebes in overlapping concurrent dynasties. Two competing governments sharing a capital city for eleven years is a pretty abstract notion.

In the CET, when the Hyksos were driven out of Egypt around 1535 BC, they seem to have simply disappeared. While the Old Babylonian Empire had already been occupied by the Kassites and very little is known of the time in Babylonia, the Old Assyrian and Old Hittite Empires were still around, and neither recorded the army of 480,000 Hyksos that Manetho mentioned leaving Egypt. In the ULT, the Hyksos Dynasty was driven out of Egypt circa 2249 BC, deep into the Babylonian Dark Age, centuries after the collapse of the Old Assyrian and Old Hittite Empires.

As the Hyksos appear to have been mainly Semitic people, with a Hurrian nobility, they likely reintegrated into the Mitanni and Kassite Dynasty Babylonians. The last king of the Hyksos Dynasty was recorded by the Turin King List as Khamudi. His name had also been found on scarab seals in Jericho,[34] and a seal believed to be from Byblos has been discovered with the name Khondy on it,[35] which is generally believed to refer to Khamudi, although some Egyptologists believe it was a different, previously unknown Egyptian king.

The first Kassite king we know anything of was Agum II, also called Agum Kakrime, who is believed to have been the 8th or 9th king of the Third Babylonian Dynasty, meaning that there was an entire dynasty between the Old Babylonian Kingdom and the known Kassite Dynasty that we have no records of. Unfortunately, the oldest records of Agum II are from the Neo-Assyrian era around 700 years later, and therefore we cannot even know if this is accurate information. There are eight kings listed before Agum II on ancient Mesopotamian king lists, however, nothing is known of them, other than that the first three ruled for a combined length of 70 years.

The first Kassite King that can be synchronized with the king lists of another culture is Burnaburiash I, who concluded a treaty with the Assyrian King Puzur-Ashur III, sometime around 1580 BC. Burnaburiash I was the 10th king listed in the Kassite dynasty, and if the first three king's reigns, ranging from 22 to 26 years, are of similar length to the first seven king's reigns, then the Kassite dynasty should have started approximately 225 years before the reign of Burnaburiash I, or approximately 1800 BC ULT. According to the ancient *Mesopotamian King List A*, the Kassites ruled Babylonia for 576 years and 9 months, over the course of 36 kings. As the last king of the Kassite Dynasty was Enlil-nadin-ahi, whose reign ended in about 1155 BC, this would indicate the Kassite Dynasty began in 1731 BC. This year is the same year that the Egyptianized-Hyksos 16th Dynasty was driven from Egypt in the ULT. As the monarchs of the Egyptianized-Hyksos Dynasty would have been used to living in opulence, the most likely place for them to have traveled to with their army of 480,000, was Babylonia, which would explain the foundation of a new dynasty at this point in time.

Unfortunately, the conventional Mesopotamian timeline does not allow this, as Babylon wasn't sacked until 1595 BC, meaning the Kassite dynasty must date to after that. As a result, Assyriologists ignore the early Kassite kings, and the CMT only allows 350 years for the Kassite dynasty. After the Egyptians drove the Hyksos from Egypt, they launched several campaigns deep into Canaan, crossing into Mitanni territory. The Egyptian King Thutmose III launched an invasion of the Mitanni Empire around 1457 BC, after defeating the combined forces of the cities of Megiddo and Kadesh and their allies, including the 330 Mitanni tribal leaders. The invasion of the Mitanni Empire was ultimately a failure, and Egypt acquired no territory from the Mitanni, however, the token Mitanni militia encountered was defeated.

The Assyrian homeland had already regained its independence from the Mitanni before the Battle of Megiddo in 1457 BC, and would go on to restore the lost Assyrian Empire in the following centuries. The capital city of the Mitanni, Washukanni, was sacked by the Hittites under Suppiluliuma I, sometime around 1320 BC, and they installed the vassal King Shattiwaza. Shortly thereafter the Mitanni fell under the domination of the resurgent Assyrian Empire. Washukanni was sacked again around 1250 BC, this time by the Assyrians after a failed attempt by the Mitanni to succeed from the Assyrian Empire. In Babylonia, the Kassite dynasty fought a series of losing wars against the Assyrian Middle Kingdom until they ultimately fell to the Elamites of southern Iran circa 1155 BC.

The fact that the Egyptians could launch a major offensive into Canaan in 1457 BC, invading the Mitanni Empire, yet finding no trace of the Hyksos, just 80 years after they were driven out of Egypt in 1535 BC CET, points to the CET being fundamentally wrong. If the Hyksos were driven out of Egypt in 2249 BC ULT, almost 800 years before the Battle of Meggido, it would explain why there was no trace of them in 1457 BC. Egyptologists also dispute the length of the last king of the Hyksos reign, providing estimates of 1 to 12 years, however, do agree that Khamudi was ultimately driven from Canaan.

For centuries historians have suggested that Khamudi may have been the legendary founder of the Greek city-state of Thebes: Cadmus (Κάδμος / Kadmos).[36] According to Herodotus, Cadmus lived sixteen hundred years before his time, which would mean he lived sometime before 2000 BC. The City of Thebes is believed to have been founded sometime during the Early Helladic III Period, between 2200 and 2000 BC. This generally corresponds to Khamudi leaving Egypt circa 2249 BC ULT, but cannot line up with Khamudi leaving Egypt circa 1535 BC CET. Cadmus was recorded by various ancient Greco-Roman sources as coming from Tyre,[37] Sidon,[38] or Egypt.[39] While the theory of Khamudi being Cadmus is far from generally accepted by Egyptologists, as Cadmus had to have founded Thebes in Greece long before Khamudi was driven from Egypt in the CET, this idea dates back to at least the time of ancient Rome, and is why Roman historian Diodorus Siculus recorded Cadmus originating in Egypt.

Dynastic Mesopotamia in the CMT

In the CMT, the Ubaid civilization existed from at least 8000 BC, based on the existence of bullae dating back to that period, which then evolved into Sumerian clay tablets, but somehow, the Sumerians knew nothing about them, and instead wrote elaborate nonsense about ancient Sumerian dynasties in the same cities and at the same time the Ubaidians were there. The Sumerian civilization then appeared fully formed building massive temple complexes identical to the Ubaidians, whom they didn't know anything about, around 2900 BC.

The Sumerian civilization was only around for a few hundred years, and then fell to the Akkadians around 2334 BC. The Akkadian civilization spanned Mesopotamia, and regional kingdoms rose to prominence in Assyria circa 1905 BC and Babylonia circa 1894 BC. The last of the Sumero-Akkadian dynasties fell to the Babylonians in 1788 BC, for no particular reason.

In approximately 1674 BC a group of Semites and Hurrians that appear to have been led by Mitanni, but weren't because there were no Mitanni yet, peacefully migrated into northern Egypt, and formed the Hyksos Dynasty. They appeared out of nowhere, which is convenient because when they were driven back out of Egypt around 1535 BC, they just vanished.

In 1595 BC, Babylon was destroyed by the Hittites, from Anatolia, and a couple of decades later the Kassites invaded and settled in Babylonia. They are believed to have been related to Hurrians, and had an Indo-European nobility, like the Mitanni. Immediately after the Hittites destroyed Babylon in 1595 BC, a group of Indo-Aryans seized control of the Hurrian population in modern Syria, and instantaneously formed the Mitanni Empire, driving back both the Hittite and Assyrian Empires. Around 1560 BC, during the reign of the Assyrian King Nur-ili, the Mitanni Empire sacked Ashur, capital of the Assyrian Empire, and shortly afterward the entire Assyrian Empire fell under the dominion of the Mitanni. This means that the Mitanni had less than 35 years to liberate the Hurrians from the Hittites and Assyrians, and conquer the Canaanites, before sacking Ashur.

Around 1457 BC the Egyptian King Thutmose III launched an invasion of the Mitanni empire in Syria, and met only token resistance from the local militia. By 1390 BC the Mitanni Empire was losing ground to the resurgent Hittite and Assyrian Empires, and circa 1340 BC the Hittites sacked the Mitanni capital Washukanni and installed a vassal king. In circa 1276 the Assyrians occupied Washukanni, and made the former Mitanni empire into part of their Middle Kingdom.

Dynastic Mesopotamia in the ULT

In the ULT, the Ubaid civilization was the Sumerian civilization, which existed from at least 8000 BC based on the existence of bullae dating back to that period, which then evolved into the Sumerian era clay tablets. The Sumerians did have records of that early time, which they recorded as the historic dynasties of Sumer.

The Sumerian civilization was around for thousands of years, before falling to the Akkadians around 3885 BC. The Akkadian civilization spanned Mesopotamia, and regional kingdoms rose to prominence in Assyria circa 3278 BC and Babylonia circa 3352 BC. The last of the Sumero-Akkadian dynasties fell to the Babylonians around 3227 BC, as a result of the Great Shock of 3250 BC when the southern marshlands of Mesopotamia would have been drowning under the extra rainwater.

In approximately 3038 BC, Babylon was destroyed by the Hittites, from Anatolia, and the region fell into chaos. This region was later colonized by a group of people called the Kassites, who were led by an Indo-Aryan nobility. These Indo-Aryans and Kassites backed an insurgent Hurrian uprising in Hittite and Assyrian lands, which then formed into the Mitanni Empire.

The Mitanni later conquered Egypt in circa 2533 BC forming the Hyksos 'foreign ruler' dynasty. The Hyksos rule was overthrown by an Egyptianized-Hyksos 16th Dynasty in 2249 BC which ruled from Thebes in southern Egypt. The Hyksos that were driven from Egypt around 2249 BC reintegrated with the Mitanni and Kassite population of Babylonia. The Egyptianized-Hyksos 16th Dynasty was later driven out of Egypt in 1731 BC and seized power in Babylonia forming the Third Babylonian Dynasty.

Around 1457 BC the Egyptian King Thutmose III launched an invasion of the Mitanni empire in Syria and met only token resistance from the local militia. By 1390 BC, the Mitanni Empire was losing ground to the resurgent Hittite and Assyrian Empires, and around 1340 BC the Hittites sacked the Mitanni capital Washukanni and installed a vassal king. In circa 1276 BC, the Assyrians occupied Washukanni, and made the former Mitanni empire into part of their Middle Kingdom. The Assyrians also conquered most of the Kassite ruled Babylonia, before it ultimately fell to the Elamites circa 1158 BC.

Section 3: Indo-European and Harappan Historic Era

Some of the oldest known texts have survived in South Asia, including the Vedas, Avesta, and Hindu Epics. Most of these texts are believed to have originated outside of South Asia, including the oldest Vedas, and the Avesta. The Avesta was used in Persia by Zoroastrians before they migrated into India after the Islamic conquest of Persia. Most of the Avestan texts no longer exist, as Alexander the Great destroyed both the Avestan Archives and the majority of Avestan scholars that could recite them after his conquest of the Persian Empire, however, Greek and Persian language texts do survive from before the time of Alexander that describe the ancient Archives. On the other hand, the Vedas have only been used in India throughout recorded history, and some do not believe they originate outside of Southern Asia. Nevertheless, a large amount of evidence has been amassed in the past century that show the ancient peoples of the Eurasian Steppes shared several elements with the society described in the Vedas, especially the oldest Vedas, and therefore the current view is that they were the people who composed these texts.

The question of which is older, the Vedas, or the Avesta has been debated by linguists and historians since the 1800s, with remarkably diverse views being proposed. The Vedas are generally dated by Indologists to no earlier than 1200 BC, the fabled 'beginning of the Iron-Age,' however, this view seems to be based on the European historians of the 1800s desire to have the Vedas be younger than the Torah, which was then believed to date to circa 1500 BC. Today the Torah is dated to between 800 and 500 by most historians, and clearly, the Vedas are older than that. In point of fact, the older Vedas must date back to the Bronze Age, meaning before 1200 BC, and as they appear to have arrived in India by the onset of the Indian Iron Age, the older Vedas must predate 2400 BC.

On the other hand, the life of Zoroaster, who composed the earliest sections of the Avesta, traditionally dated to between 6300 and 6200 BC but Greek and Persian scholars before the time of Alexander the Great. Modern historians don't generally accept this dating either, and often place his life circa 550 BC, around the same time as the earliest references to him living before 6200 BC. Some scholars have even proposed later dates, meaning he would have lived a century or two after the oldest references to him. Obviously, there are problems with some of the dates proposed, however, scholars have a wide variety of views on this issue.

The Vedas

The Vedas are the oldest known collection of literature in India, however, their origin is widely disputed. The term Vedas is often misused by laymen as a catch-all for any ancient or even recent Hindu text that claims to be divinely inspired, however, it is, in fact, a specific group of four texts: the Rig-veda, Sama-veda, Yajur-veda, and Atharva-veda.[40] These four specific texts have been accepted as 'the Vedas' for thousands of years, however, at one point there were only three.[41] This is established by the references found in the Rig-veda to the 'three Vedas' found in the Taittiriya Brahmana (verse 3.12.9.1) and the Aitareya Brahmana (verse 5.32-33). Likewise early Buddhist Nikaya texts also only reference the 'three Vedas,' specifically omitting the Atharva-veda.[42] Historians generally agree that the Atharva-veda wasn't considered a Veda until after 500 BC, meaning, well into the Buddhist age when the Vedic religion was in decline.

Understanding the origin of this collection of texts is critical to understanding the history of the ancient Indo-Aryan peoples, and by extension their Iranian and European relatives, unfortunately, the subject is complex. To simplify the explanation of these various texts, the below graph is added showing the various dialects of Sanskrit, and the Vedic texts composed in them in roughly chronological order. This work will also simply the naming of the various texts, referring to various Brahmanas Aranyakas, and Upanishads by the Veda they are associated with, instead of their specific names, as there would be dozens of more names on the chart below if each individual text was named.

Each of the four *Vedas* is divided into four sections, the: *Samhita, Brahmana, Aranyaka,* and *Upanishads,* which means that there are sixteen major divisions within the four *Vedas*.[43] Additionally, there are sections of text that have been added later and are treated as separate sections by scholars. While all of these sections were composed in the Sanskrit language, they were not composed in the same dialect, and therefore a rough chronological order can be worked out.

Rigvedic	Mantra Language	Samhita Prose	Brahmana Prose	Sutra Language
Rig-veda Samhita				
	Rig-veda Khilani			
			Rig-veda Brahmana	
			Rig-veda Aranyaka	
			Rig-veda Upanishads	
	Sama-veda Samhita			
			Sama-veda Brahmana	
				Sama-veda Aranyaka
				Sama-veda Upanishads
	Yajur-veda Samhita			
			Yajur-veda Brahmana	
				Yajur-veda Aranyaka
				Yajur-veda Upanishads
	Atharva-veda Samhita			
			Atharva-veda Brahmana	
				Atharva-veda Aranyaka
				Atharva-veda Upanishads

The *Samhita* sections are collections of hymns and form the core of the four *Vedas*. Generally, when someone refers to a 'Veda' they are specifically referring to the *Samhita* section of the *Veda*. The *Samhitas* are the oldest section of each *Veda*, however, they are not composed in the same dialect, but rather four dialects. The *Rig-veda Samhita* is composed in two similar dialects, generally called *Early-Rigvedic* and *Late-Rigvedic*, while the *Sama-veda Samhita* is composed in *Mantra Language*, and the other two *Samhitas* are composed in a combination of Mantra Language and Samhita Prose.

The *Rig-veda* is universally considered the oldest of the *Vedas* and has been throughout recorded history. The *Rig-veda Samhita* itself is a collection of 1028 hymns, comprised of 10,600 verses, and organized into 10 books called mandalas. Mandalas 2 through 9 are in the oldest form of Sanskrit known, *Early-Rigvedic*, while mandalas 1 and 10 are later additions in *Late-Rigvedic*. The differences between the two *Rigvedic* dialects are less noticeable that the later language shifts, however, have been noted for centuries. The *Rig-veda Samhita* also includes a section of hymns known as the *Khilani*[44] that is recorded in Mantra Language Sanskrit, like the *Sama-veda Samhita*, and parts of the *Yajur-veda* and *Atharva-veda Samhitas*. It is generally accepted that these four texts were composed in Mantra Language, were composed around the same time, after the earlier Rigvedic texts of the *Rig-veda Samhita*.

The fact that *Yajur-veda* and *Atharva-veda Samhitas* are composed in two distinct dialects of Sanskrit is accepted as an indicator that the texts were likely composed over a long period of time, and while the Mantra Language core did not change, the later additions were fluid, changing with the language. It is worth noting that while these are referred to as texts today, they are not believed to have been written at the time, but rather sung as hymns or recited as mantras. Rigvedic was a sung dialect, while Mantra Language was a spoken dialect intended for reciting mantras, which were generally spoken during prayer, and then later *Samhita Prose* was a more poetic dialect, for public recitals.

The second sections in the *Vedas* are called the *Brahmanas*, which are theological treatises on the hymns of the *Samhita* sections. These sections are composed in a dialect called Brahmana Prose, which dates to after the sections composed in Mantra Language and Samhita Prose. This dialect was also used to compose the third and fourth sections of the Rig-veda, the: *Aranyaka*, and *Upanishads*, which leads to the conclusion that these sections of the *Rig-veda* were composed around the same time as the *Brahmanas*.

The *Aranyakas* are the third section of the *Vedas*, which are esoteric, while the *Upanishads* are the deeply spiritual treaties. For the past couple of centuries, the *Upanishads* have gained a great deal of esteem within Hinduism, and are currently considered a core of Hindu spiritual traditions by many Hindus. The *Upanishads* of the three later *Vedas* are all composed in Sutra Language Sanskrit, while the *Aranyakas* are composed in a mixture of Brahmana Prose and Sutra Language Sanskrit, implying the *Aranyakas* may date back to the same period as the *Brahmanas*, however, were later edited in the Sutra Language era.

The Iron Ages

Iron Ages

Period	Meteoric (CET)	Meteoric (ULT)	Smelting (CET)	Smelting (ULT)	Common use
Hattic (Turkey)			2500 BC	4000 BC	550 BC
Aïr Mountains (Niger)			2500 BC		1500 BC
Telengana (Southern India)			2400 BC		600 BC
Haldummulla (Sri Lanka)			2400 BC		600 BC
Persia (Iran & Azerbaijan)		5000 BC	2000 BC		550 BC
Lejja (Nigeria)			2000 BC		200 AD
Egypt	4000 BC	5800 BC	1500 BC		550 BC
Malhar (Northern India)			1800 BC		300 BC
Yaz (Turkmenistan)			1500 BC		1300 BC
Sumer (Iraq)	4000 BC	5800 BC	1500 BC		550 BC
Akkad (Iraq)	2300 BC	3850 BC	1500 BC		550 BC
Assyria (Iraq-Syria)	1900 BC	3200 BC	1500 BC		550 BC
Nok (Nigeria)			1500 BC		200 AD
Termit (Niger)			1500 BC		200 AD
Balkans			1300 BC		550 BC
Greece			1000 BC		500 BC
Nubia (Sudan)			1000 BC		500 BC
Axum (Eritrea & Ethiopia)			1000 BC		500 BC
Jordan			930 BC		500 BC
China			900 BC		100 BC
Roman Empire			800 BC		100 AD

Unfortunately, knowing the order the Vedic texts were written in does not date the texts, and therefore various internal references are used to place the texts into specific cultures, which can then be used to date the texts themselves. These references are to specific metals and grains mentioned within the Vedas, specifically iron and rice. The earliest sections of the Rig-veda Samhita includes mention of metals (ayas) and therefore the entire collection must date to after the end of the stone age. The Rig-veda Samhita book 4 specifically refers to the gods smelting metal:

> "...the gods smelting like metal ore the human generations..."(Rig-veda 4.2.17)

The earliest mention of what is believed to be iron (krsna ayas / black metal) is found in the *Atharva-veda Samhita*[45] in the later Samhita Prose sections and the *Shatapatha Brahmana* in the *Yajur-veda*,[46] written in the Brahmana Prose. The mention of iron in this text is accepted as proof that the composition of this text took place after the onset of the Iron Age, however, the Iron Age began at different points in time across Eurasia. Meteoric iron had been used throughout the ancient world and was worth more than any other metal before the discovery of smelting. Iron artifacts have been found in the Iranian Plateau independently dated to 5000 BC,[47] as well as the pre-dynastic Badarian and Naqada cultures of Egypt and the Late Ubaid era of Iraq, both dated using the conventional dynastic timelines to circa 4000 BC CET/CMT[48] or 5800 BC using the Universal Long Timeline.

Several early iron-smelting sites have been found long preceding the general adoption of iron between 1200 and 550 BC, which is classically referred to as the Iron Age. The concept of the Iron Age dates back to the classic era Greeks, between 600 and 100 BC, who claimed the world had three historic eras, the stone age, the bronze age, and the iron age which they were in. The dating of the Iron Age is also based on their calculation, which held the Battle of Troy, circa 1200 BC, was at the end of the Bronze Age, and the conquest of the Iranian Plateau by the Persians took place after iron had become common.

Archaeological research in the 1800s brought this into doubt, as the Egyptians had some iron since the pre-dynastic era, and iron tools and weapons were found in small quantities throughout Egyptian history. The Egyptian word for iron was 'bi-a-n-pt' which translates as 'metal from the sky,' and is accepted as referring to any meteoric iron, however, the oldest known use of this word is from the 19th Dynasty, dated to between 1292 and 1189 BC CET (1322 to 1202 BC ULT). The word 'bi-a' was used since at least the Old Kingdom between 2686 and 2181 BC CET (4945 to 4003 BC ULT), where it appeared in the *Pyramid Texts*, however, it the word simply referred to any hard metal, and it appears that the Egyptians did not differentiate between hard metals at the time. Early Egyptologists concluded that all dynastic era iron was derived from meteors, and modern analysis generally agrees with this conclusion, as the surviving early Egyptian iron artifacts are high in nickel content, as iron-rich meteors generally are.

The development of iron smelting, which removes the impurities from the iron ore, was not significantly more advanced or complex than copper smelting, however, it does require a higher temperature. The melting point of copper is 1084° C (1984° F), while the melting point of iron is 1538°C

(2500° F). The melting of copper was itself preceded by the smelting of tin and lead which both have temperatures low enough to be melted over a campfire, however copper requires a higher temperature and is believed to have first been smelted in ovens or pottery kilns. Iron smelting was a slightly more advanced technology than copper and tin smelting, as it includes adding coke or charcoal as a reducing agent.

The earliest known civilization to engage in iron-smelting were the Hattians of Central Anatolia circa 2500 BC CMT[49] (4000 BC ULT), who treated iron as a precious metal, like gold and silver. The Hittites that settled in the Hattian lands by 1664 BC CMT (3103 BC ULT) continued to use iron as a precious metal. The next oldest known site of iron smelting is in the Aïr Mountains of Niger, where iron smelting took place between 2500 and 1500 BC. These dates are established by carbon-dating, and not dynastic chronologies, and are therefore the same regardless of the timeline used. It isn't known for sure which culture was living in the Aïr Mountains at the time, however, the Hausa people were living in the Aïr Mountains before the Tureg were driven south by the Arabs in the 8th-century AD, and therefore assumed to be the descendants of the iron-working culture from 2500 to 1500 BC. Whichever culture it was, it appears to have developed iron smelting independently of an earlier culture, and likely inspired the development of iron-working in the Lejja culture in Nigeria circa 2000 BC.

The oldest known iron smelting on the Eurasian continent other than the Hattians and Hittites, is from between 2400 and 1800 BC, at several sites across the Indian states of Telangana, Karnataka, Andhra Pradesh, and Uttar Pradesh. The earliest iron artifacts are found in the southern states,[50] while the oldest slag deposits that prove large-scale iron production are found in Uttar Pradesh on the Gangetic plains in the north of India, dating to 1800 BC.[51] As iron is missing from the *Rig-veda* and the *Sama-veda*, but found in the *Yajur-veda* and *Atharva-veda* the implication is that the latter two were written after the onset of the Iron Age, while the earlier two predate it.

Dating the Vedas

Sanskrit (Indo-Aryan) Timeline

Sanskrit Dialect	Culture (CIET)	Timeline (CIET)	Culture (ULT)	Timeline (ULT)
Rig-vedic	Early Vedic India	1800 BC ? to 1100 BC	Cucuteni-Trypillia and Sredny Stog	4800 BC to 3000 BC
Mantra Language			Maykop, Yamnaya, and Poltavka	3700 BC to 2100 BC
Samhita Prose	Late Vedic India	1100 BC to 600 BC	Oxus (BMAC) and Early Iron Age India	2400 BC to 1800 BC
Brahmana Prose			Early Vedic India	1800 BC to 1100 BC
Sutra Language			Late Vedic India	1100 BC to 600 BC
Classical Sanskrit	Classical India	600 BC to 1300 AD	Classical India	600 BC to 1300 AD

The oldest specific mention of iron in the Vedas is accepted as being in the Atharva-veda Samhita, in the later Samhita Prose sections, and the next oldest mention of iron was in the Yajur-veda Brahmana, in Brahmana Prose. This would place the introduction of iron to the Vedic people, around the time that the Sanskrit language developed the Brahmana Prose. The Atharva-veda Samhita is also generally considered to have been composed in a different land than the earlier three Vedas, as it has several inconsistencies with the earlier Vedas. It is believed by some Indologists that this was the first Vedic text composed in India as the Indo-Aryan peoples migrated into India.

This would date the Atharva-veda Samhita to sometime between 2400 and 1600 BC. This date is not generally accepted, as the early Indologists of the Colonial era believed that the Iron Age in India must have taken place centuries after the Iron Age in the Middle East, instead of a thousand years earlier. Conventional Indo-European dating for the Vedic Texts would place the entire collection between 1200 and 600 BC, which is now proven to be quite impossible. Some more recent estimates by Indologists have moved the estimated dating to 1800 to 600 BC, however, any attempts to place the dating to an earlier period is hampered by the fact that the Indo-Aryan Mitanni invaded the Middle East circa 1500 BC CMT, and therefore the closely related Sanskrit texts must date to the same period. However, in the Universal Long Timeline, the Mitanni invasion of the Middle East dates to circa 2967 BC ULT, which allows the Vedic texts to have predated the Indian Iron Age, which we now know dates back to 2400 BC.

If the Samhita Prose sections of the Artharva-veda Samhita were written in Northern India between 2400 and 1800 BC, then the Samhita Prose sections of the Yajur-veda Samhita must date to the same time period, however, as it does not mention iron, it must have been composed outside of India. Given many lines of evidence, it is accepted that the Indo-Aryans migrated into India from Central Asia, carrying their Vedic Texts. Several ancient Central Asian cultures have been proposed for the homeland of the Sanskrit speaking Indo-Aryans, including the Andronovo, Oxus, and Yaz cultures, as well as the ruins at Jeitun in Turkmenistan. Both the Andronovo and Yaz cultures are too late to be where the Yajur-veda Samhita was composed, and Jeitun was too early. The Oxus civilization, also called the Bactria-Margiana Archaeological Complex (BMAC), existed between 2400 and 1600 BC, at the same time as the development of iron smelting in India, and was, therefore, the most likely culture for the Samhita Prose Indo-Aryans to have started out, before migrating into India and coming into widespread contact with iron.

The Oxus civilization spanned the area of modern southern Turkmenistan, Uzbekistan, and Tajikistan, between 2400 and 1800 BC. Based on genetic analysis of the remains found in the civilization's cemeteries, several ethnic groups were living in the area, including Middle Easterners (J*, J1, J2), Indo-Europeans (R1b, R2), Caucasians (G, T), Dravidians (L), and East Africans (E1b1a, E1b1b). The various Y-chromosome R haplogroups are generally associated with the Indo-European peoples and are the most common haplogroups found in Europe as well as Iran, Afghanistan, Pakistan, and northern India. Middle Easterners constitute the largest number of remains analyzed from the Oxus civilization, however, as the latter Vedic religion taught cremation, it is unlikely that many remains would be left from Sanskrit speaking peoples from that time period.

As the Samhita Prose sections of the Vedic Texts were the latter sections of the Yajur-veda and Artharva-veda Samhitas, the earlier Mantra Language sections must have been composed before the Indo-Aryans settled in the Oxus civilizations. As the civilization of the Rigvedic and Mantra Language sections of the Vedas describe a culture very much like the Kurgan culture of the Eurasian Steppes, it is generally accepted that the steppes could be the origin of the Indo-Aryan peoples, or their cultural ancestors. These culture similarities include the use of horses and chariots, which are believed to originate on the steppes as the oldest remains of chariots have been found in the region. Additionally, horse burial sites have been found in the steppes that match the horse-sacrifice ceremonies found in the Rigveda Brahmana and Yajur-veda Samhita. These texts discussing horse burials are recorded in two dialects of Sanskrit, Samhita Prose and Brahmana Prose, which implies that the ancient Indo-Aryans were burying horses during the era they spoke these dialects, however, not during the earlier Rigvedic and Mantra Language eras, or later Sutra Language era.

Several closely related sites have been found across the steppes connected with the Kurgan cultures, including the Maykop, Yamnaya, Catacomb, and Poltavka cultures, spanning the era of 3700 and 2100 BC. The Maykop culture is often described as early Kurgan, although it was based farther south, in the Northern Caucasus region between 3700 and 3000 BC.[52] The Yamnaya culture is generally considered the height of the Kurgan culture, its name being the Russian term meaning 'related to yama' (Ямная). Yama (яма) is the Russian word 'pit,' which refers to the burial pits under the mounds which are commonly called kurgans. The word Yama / Jama means the same thing across the Slavic language family, appearing in all Slavic languages other than Polish. The Yamanaya Culture spanned the region of Ukraine, and southern and central Russia as far east as the Urals between 3300 and 2600 BC. Yama is also the name of the god of death and the underworld in the Rigveda, meaning that the word has been in use in the region for at least 5000 years.

The Yamnaya culture developed into the Catacomb culture in the west between 2900 and 2200 BC, and the Poltavka culture in the east between 2800 and 2100 BC. The Catacomb culture developed in Ukraine and southern Russia, while the Poltavka culture developed in the region between the Volga and the Urals. Genetic analysis of remains from these kurgan cultures show that almost all remains had the Y-DNA R haplogroups,[53] which are generally accepted as being Indo-European. Two Middle Eastern

(J*, J2a) males were also found in the region,[54] indicating long-distance trade with the Middle East existed by this time. One individual was also found belong to haplogroup I2a2a1b1b,[55] which is generally found today in Northern Europe and Britain, and associated with lighter features, which implies that Mantra Language speakers were also trading with Northern Europe. Based on the analysis of the DNA recovered, it appears these people were similar in appearance to modern Iranians, with generally dark hair and eyes, and tan-colored to light brown skin.[56]

The Kurgan cultures developed from the earlier Cucuteni-Trypillia, and Sredny Stog cultures of the Ukraine, Moldova, and Romania, between 4700 and 3500 BC. These cultures are widely accepted as the direct fore-bearers of the Maykop and Yamnaya cultures and have also been proposed as the potential homeland of the Indo-European people. Like the later kurgans, these cultures buried people in pits (яма / yama), however they did not pile mounds above the pits. They also are believed to have been the first people that had domesticated horses.[57]

Genetic analysis has proven a connection between the Cucuteni-Trypillia culture and the Yamnaya culture, with peoples from western Ukraine, Moldova, and Romania migrating east into the traditional homeland of the Yamnaya culture circa 3600 BC.[58] The various remains that have been found within the Cucuteni-Trypillia culture mostly belong to subclades of the Y-DNA R haplogroup, including R0, HV, and H. Individuals from the Middle Eastern J and T haplogroups have also been found, proving early contact between Eastern Europe and the Middle East by 6000 years ago. Given the common points between this culture and the culture of the Rig-veda Samhita, this is the most likely location of the composition of the Rig-veda. Mandala 1 of the Rig-veda mentioned chariots, which are proven to have been in use in Eastern Europe by 3500 BC.[59] Early wagons and chariots appeared near-simultaneously across Eastern Europe, Caucasia, and Mesopotamia at this time, however, are generally accepted to have originated in the Ukraine, where horses are believed to have first been domesticated by the Sredny Stog culture.[60]

The later appearance of horse sacrifices in the Mantra Language texts connect this dialect conclusively with the kurgan cultures circa 3700 to 2100 BC, meaning the earlier Rigvedic texts had to date to an earlier culture, which the Cucuteni-Trypillia and Sredny Stog culture appears to be. Given the genetic migration from the Cucuteni-Trypillia culture east through the Sredny Stog culture to the later Yamnaya culture, the indication is that the Early-Rigvedic texts were likely composed in the Cucuteni-Trypillia culture between 4800 and 3500 BC, while the Late-Rigvedic texts were likely composed in the Sredny Stog culture between 4500 and 3500 BC.

The Avesta

Avestan Timeline

Sanskrit Dialect	Culture (CIET)	Timeline (CIET)	Culture (ULT)	Timeline (ULT)
Old Avestan	Central Asia ?	Before 1800 BC?	Bug-Dniester	6500 BC to 5500 BC
Younger Avestan			Samara, Dnieper-Donets, and Khvalynsk	5500 BC to 3500 BC
Youngest Avestan			Afanasievo	3700 BC to 2500 BC
Rig-vedic	Early Vedic India	1800 BC ? to 1100 BC	Cucuteni-Trypillia and Sredny Stog	4800 BC to 3000 BC
Mantra Language			Maykop, Yamnaya, and Poltavka	3700 BC to 2100 BC

The Vedic texts are the oldest Indo-Aryan texts, however, they aren't the oldest Indo-European texts. The Old Avestan texts are generally considered the oldest Indo-European texts, however, this is an issue that has been widely debated for thousands of years. The Avesta is the holy book of the ancient Zoroastrian religion, which was once the dominant religion of the Persian Empire. Like the Vedic texts, it is generally accepted that the Avesta was not written down until late in its existence, and was recited by a priesthood until the Achaemenian dynasty of Persia ordered the creation of an archive of Avestan texts near Persepolis circa 600 BC. This took place after the Persians had conquered the Iranian Plateau, and had adopted the cuneiform script from the Mesopotamians.

According to Zoroastrian records from later periods, there were approximately 30,000 Avestan texts in the archive, spanning the history of the Avestan-speaking peoples. This archive was burnt by Alexander the Great when he conquered the Persian Empire. He is also reported to have executed the priests who could recite the texts from memory. The surviving text known as the Avesta was compiled from surviving copies of Avestan texts the following decades, as Alexander's heirs did not share his disdain for the Persians, however, the vast majority of the text were lost forever. The Avesta itself is composed in an ancient Indo-Iranian language which is only known from one source, the Avesta. Like the Vedic Texts, the Avesta is composed in more than one dialect, either two or three depending on interpretation. The two established dialects of Avestan are called Old Avestan, and Younger Avestan. Additionally, some texts appear to be composed in a poor quality dialect, which is often described as an attempt by a non-Avestan speaker to compose in Avestan. This third dialect, if it is treated as one, is considered the Youngest Avestan, and in any event, the texts composed in it are considered the last sections of the surviving Avesta to have been composed.

The two established dialects are believed to have been both separated in time and location. This is based on the fact that not only does the dialect change, but the geographic names mentioned also change. Additionally, the Youngest Avestan texts, regardless of whether it is a dialect or not, were written in another distinct location as the geographic names change again. Old Avestan is also called Gathic Avestan, as it is the dialect that the Gathas were composed in. The Gathas are a collection of hymns attributed to the ancient philosopher and poet Zoroaster which served as the core of the Zoroastrian religion. The life of Zoroaster, also called Zarathustra, has also been a matter of debate for thousands of years. The earliest records of the life of Zoroaster universally agreed that he lived between 6200 and 6300 BC. This view was endorsed by all pre-Alexandrian scholars, including Xanthus and Hermippus in the 5th-century BC;[61] and Hermodorus, Eudoxus of Cnidus and Aristotle in the 4th-century BC.[62] All of these early scholars lived before the Avestan archives were destroyed by Alexander, and therefore they must have been basing this obscure date in the extreme past on what was recorded there.

This view changed in the Christian era, as early Christian 'historians' rewrote the history books of the world to make sure everything fit into the timeline described in the Septuagint, in which the world had been created circa 5500 BC. In the 3rd-century AD, Diogenes Laërtius placed the life is Zoroaster at approximately 1000 BC,[63] and in the 4th-century Ammianus Marcellinus placed the life of Zoroaster around 550 BC. The later Islamic era Zoroastrian text called the Bundahishn appears to have used Ammianus Marcellinus as a source when it placed the life of Zoroaster circa 550 BC, a view which then became entrenched in Zoroastrianism.

Scholars in the past three centuries have repeated the views of all of the ancients, but generally date the life of Zoroaster sometime between 1700 and 500 BC. These dates are generally based on linguistic theories and are dated according to when the particular scholar believed the Avestan language developed in comparison to Sanskrit. Nevertheless, dating Zoroaster's life to circa 550 BC seems hopelessly illogical when the leading Greek scholars of the following century believed he had lived 5800 years earlier. Surely they would have known he had just recently lived and died.

The crux of the question of when Zoroaster lived, depended on two questions, when did Sanskrit develop, and when did Avestan develop in relation to Sanskrit. For those that believe that Sanskrit is older than Avestan, the life of Zoroaster could be any time before the Greeks mentioned his existence in the 5th-century. For those that believed that Avestan is older than Sanskrit, the life of Zoroaster must predate the composition of the Rig-veda. Unfortunately, the current school of Indology teaches that the Rig-veda was composed at the impossibly late date of circa 1500 to 1200 BC. This late date would allow Zoroaster to have lived as late at 1700 to 1500 BC. However, this late date is impossible based on the current knowledge of the earlier Iron Age in India.

The majority of linguists comparing Avestan to Sanskrit agree that the two languages were the most similar at the earliest phase, meaning that Early-Rigvedic was the closest Sanskrit dialect to Avestan. If the Avesta is divided by dialect, there are three sections, the Old and Younger Avestan sections, as well as the Vendidad, which is composed in the disputed Youngest Avestan dialect. A large body of commentary called the Zend is traditionally published with the Avesta written in Middle Persian, and dating to the late-Greek through early-Islamic eras, when Zoroastrianism was the dominant religion in Persia.

In addition to Zoroaster's hymns which are known as the Gathas, the Yasna Haptanghaiti is composed in the Old Avestan dialect. The Yasna Haptanghaiti is a collection of seven chapters of prose verses that were inserted into the Gathas by early followers of Zoroaster. Linguists agree that these texts must have been written by people living shortly after the time of Zoroaster, and speaking the same language, however, the Yasna Haptanghaiti does form a distinctive form of Old Avestan, similar to the difference between the two dialects of Rig-vedic.

The Younger Avestan sections of the Avesta comprise most of the text and are a distinctly different dialect from Old Avestan. This dialect is believed to have been spoken after Old Avestan was no longer being spoken, and is accepted as being spoken at a different geographic location based on the fact that the two texts do not contain the same geographic names. Some sections of these texts also seem to be pre-Zoroastrian, and my date back to an earlier Mithraic religion. Mithra was a major character in both the Rig-Veda and Avesta, and it is believed by some scholars that there were converts to Zoroastrianism during the Younger Avestan era from the Mithraic religion. As virtually nothing is known of what that religion was, other scholars dismiss the claim. There was a major Mithraic cult in the Roman Empire that did not seem to be directly related to either the Vedic religion or Zoroastrianism, and therefore it could have been a descendant of the ancient Mithraic religion, however, this too is considered impossible to prove by most scholars.

The third dialect is found in the Vendidad, a historical text and legal code, somewhat akin to the Jewish Torah. The name means 'the law against the devas,' as the Zoroastrians considered the Vedic devas (gods) to be devils. Like Jews, Christians, and Muslims, the Zoroastrians were monotheists, in their case worshiping a god called Ahura Mazda, roughly translating a 'Great Wisdom.' Unfortunately, as so little of the Avestan archives survived Alexander's conquest, we cannot be sure if the language of the Vendidad constitutes a third dialect that many texts were written in or a fake text written during the Greek era. It is clear that the text does not use the same geographic names as the earlier Old and Younger Avestan texts, and most of the place-names appear on the Persian Plateau or in Central Asia. It is possible that this was an attempt to reconstruct an older text from fragments, or an outright fraud, however, it has never been treated as anything other than original Avestan text by Zoroastrians. If it is an original Avestan text, the implication is that there was a third dialect of Avestan, Youngest Avestan, and that this dialect was somewhere between Younger Avestan and an archaic form of Median or Persian. Avestan is generally considered closer to Scythian, a language spoken in ancient Afghanistan, Central Asia, and Southern Russia, and therefore classified as an East Iranian language, however, if Youngest Avestan is treated as a distinct dialect, then the West Iranian languages become children of Avestan, making Avestan the parent language of both the Eastern and Western branches of Iranian.

Regardless of whether Youngest Avestan was a dialect or not, the Old and Younger Avestan dialects appear to be older than the Rigvedic dialect of Sanskrit. This view is held by most linguists, however, some historians argue the issue. Among Hindus, the idea that Zoroaster existed before the Vedas is considered heretical, as he rejected the gods (divas), and many are motivated to date the Avesta to a later date for religious reasons. Nevertheless, there are several reasons why linguists agree that Avestan must pre-date Sanskrit. One of these reasons is due to the number of non-Indo-European loan words in Sanskrit, and which languages they derive from. As Sanskrit evolved, its speakers encountered several peoples that spoke different languages, and they learned new words, and grammatical structures from these other people, however, Avestan is a very 'pure' language, containing no known words of Uralic, Dravidian, or Munda origin. Sanskrit has loan words from all these language groups, and they can be detected entering the Sanskrit language as the language evolved through the various forms used to compose the Vedas.

The earliest known dialects of Sanskrit, Rigvedic, already had words in it that linguists believe originated in the Uralic languages to the northeast of the Cucuteni-Trypillia and Sredny Stog cultures. Little is known of the ancient Uralic cultures, however, they do appear to have been using metals from an early era, and their word for 'slave' was 'orya' which many linguists believe is derived from the word Arya, the name the Indo-Iranians called themselves. This implies that the Kurgan people were either selling there people as slaves, or the Uralics were raiding the kurgan lands for slaves. The modern descendants of the Uralic peoples include the Finnish and Estonian peoples, along with several ethnic groups spread through northern Russia.

Linguists have been debating the relationship between the Uralic and Indo-European languages since the 1800s. The greater part of the Uralic languages' lexicon is shared by various Indo-European languages, however, it cannot be traced to a specific Indo-European group. Many of the borrowings can be traced to language groups found around the periphery of the Uralic lands including the Balto-Slavic, and Germanic language groups, however, some words are Indo-Iranian.[64] An example of the borrowing from Indo-Iranian languages would be the word 'sata' which means 'hundred' in Sanskrit and Avestan, as well in Uralic languages.[65] Specific borrowings from Sanskrit into Uralic languages have also been noted such as the Finnish word for hammer: 'vasara,' which is believed to be derived from the Sanskrit word 'vajra,' the name of Indra's hammer in the Rig-veda. The Sanskrit language also appears to have been modified by Uralic pronunciation, such as the shift from the Avestan *-tst- to the Sanskrit *-tt-. This Uralic inspired shift could only have happened in the northern steppes where the Sanskrit speaking Indo-Aryans would have encountered the Uralic speaking peoples of the Ural Mountains.

The Rigvedic dialect of Sanskrit was also missing the Dravidian loanwords that appeared in later Sanskrit dialects. The Dravidian languages are today indigenous to southern India, as well the highlands of Balochistan on the border of Pakistan and Iran, however, it is generally accepted by historians and Indologists that the ancient Indus Valley civilization was a Dravidian civilization. The era of the Indus Valley Civilization is also a matter of much debate, as its timeline was developed in the 1930s and correlated to the Conventional Mesopotamian Timeline, forcing the Bronze Age Indus Valley Civilization to be surrounded by the Iron Age Indian civilizations that are now known to have existed at the time. By comparing the Indus Valley Civilization to the timeline of Mesopotamia and Egypt on the Universal Long Timeline using Indus seals found in Mesopotamia, it is now clear that the Indus Valley civilization existed much earlier, reaching its mature phase between 5000 and 3500 BC, and finally fading away by 2600 BC, before the rise of the Iron Age civilizations of India.

The Indus Valley Civilization traded extensively with the Sumerians during the Kish and Nippur dynasties, as well as the later Elamites and Akkadians. Common iconography has been found among the Indus, Sumerian, and Egyptian civilizations dating to the earliest periods of these three cultures. During the height of the Indus Civilization, they appear to have dominated most of South Asia and developed extensive trading networks as far north as Shortugai on the Oxus River of Central Asia. Oxus River is the ancient name of the Amu Darya River, which flowed north from Afghanistan to the Aral Sea. In ancient times the Great Aral Sea was massive, filling the modern desert regions of the Kyzyl Kum depression, being at least half the size of the Caspian Sea before it started shrinking around 3250 BC. The Indus trading port on the Oxus would have provided easy access to the Aral Sea at the time, and the Mantra Language Yamnaya and Poltavka cultures to the north.

The dominant grain eaten by the Indus people was rice, which first appeared in the Vedas in the Mantra Language Yajur-veda Samhita which had to have been composed on the Steppes by the Yamnaya and Poltavka cultures between 3700 and 2100 BC. This appears to be one of the first loan-words into the Sanskrit language, although a few others also appeared in the Mantra Language dialect, which indicates that the Steppes peoples must have begun trading with the Indus civilization. By the era of the Samhita Prose sections of the Vedas, Dravidian words begin to appear, although are few, however by the Brahmana Prose sections, they become more common. The later Sutra Language sections have so many Dravidian words, that it is generally agreed that the Sanskrit speaking peoples must have been permanently settled among Dravidian speaking peoples by the time these sections were composed.

Nevertheless, there appear to be no Dravidian or Uralic elements within the Avestan language, nor any reference to rice in the Avesta, supporting the conclusion that the Avestan language pre-dates the later Sanskrit language. The one argument often given for the late dating of the Avesta is that it does reference iron, called 'aysan,' however, this word is derived from the Avestan words meaning sky and stone, meaning the Avestan-speakers were referring to meteoric iron, and not smelted iron like the later Rigvedic 'krsna ayas.' It is also unclear if the Avestan-speakers were actually referring to iron, or if the word simply meant 'metal.' The lack of any Uralic or Dravidian elements within the debated Youngest Avestan dialect in the Vendidad supports the early composition of the texts, and by extension, the concept that it predated the later west and east Iranian dialects, nevertheless, as only one text survives in this language, linguists are unwilling to ascribe an entire culture to it, and generally settle on the idea that it was a later dialect or pseudo-dialect spoken by an impostor or in a remote culture that had become disconnected from the general advancement of the Indo-Iranian dialects.

As the Young Avestan dialect has to predate Rigvedic Sanskrit, regardless of the situation with Youngest Avestan, it must point to an even earlier civilization on the steppes, which is known from the archaeological record as a group of closely related cultures: the Samara, Dnieper-Donets, and Khvalynsk Cultures. Remains from these cultures belong to the same Y-DNA R haplogroup as the later Cucuteni-Trypillia and Sredny Stog cultures, proving the later kurgan cultures descended from these earlier cultures. The Samara culture was located on the Volga River near the city of Samara beginning around 5500 BC. The Samara culture developed into the Dnieper-Donets culture north of the Black Sea by 5000 BC, and the Khvalynsk culture in the Volga region by 4900 BC. The Khvalynsk culture of the Volga region continued until 3500 BC, while in Ukraine the Dnieper-Donets culture developed into the Early Rigvedic Cucuteni-Trypillia and Sredny Stog cultures between 4700 and 4200 BC.

These cultures used to bury their dead with the head of a horse, goat, or sheep, although it is unknown if the horses were domesticated or being hunted, however, it is generally accepted they were being eaten. Several mass graves have been found which are interpreted as sites of human sacrifice, however, they could also be interpreted as burial sites of the remains from plagues or raids. Metals appear to have used as a sign of wealth, in these cultures, with tools and weapons still being made of flint. The metals used in this culture were imported from the more technologically advanced cultures of the Ural and Caucasian mountains, or melted from meteors, explaining the use of the word 'aysan' meaning 'sky stone.'

In addition to the western Cucuteni-Trypillia and Sredny Stog cultures, the Younger Avestan cultures also gave rise to the Afanasievo culture to the east. The Afanasievo culture occupied southern Siberia, eastern Kazakhstan, and western Mongolia between 3300 and 2500 BC, and were both culturally and genetically descended from the Dnieper-Donets and Khvalynsk cultures. Like the earlier cultures, the Afanasievo continued to use flint tools, and the only known metals found in their graves were jewelry imported from other lands. Their existence runs parallel to the early bronze age Rigvedic culture in the western Steppes, and therefore they could not be trading greatly with the early Sanskrit speakers, as they did not import metalworking processes from them. Depending on one's view of the Youngest Avestan language debate, this culture could either be seen as the Youngest Avestan speaking people or Proto-Scythians. In either event, the Scythians would later rise in the region, speaking a language that linguists agree is the most like Avestan of the languages still spoken in the classic era of Greco-Roman civilization.

Linguists also agree that the Old Avestan speakers lived earlier than the Younger Avestan speakers, and in a different region. The precursor to the Samara and Dnieper-Donets cultures is generally regarded as being Bug-Dniester culture, in the chernozem region of Moldova and Ukraine between 6500 and 5500 BC. The people of the Bug-Dniester culture are believed to have settled in the region from the Volga region, after crossing Siberia from the Lake Baikal region. The idea that these people originated originally in the Lake Baikal region of Siberia is based on the pottery style that originated there spreading across the Steppes to the chernozem region. This concept is supported by genetic research into remains discovered in the Baikal region that show the population there around 24,000 years ago belonged to the Y-DNA R* haplogroup, the ancestral group of most Europeans and South Asians. Additional studies have found the R haplogroup subclades in the remains at Afontova Gora, in southwest Siberia circa 18,000 years ago, and the subsequently in then later in the remains of the various steppes cultures before they spread out throughout Eurasia. The Bug-Dniester culture is the earliest culture associated with the Indo-European peoples that are believed to have been a farming society, cultivating einkorn, emmer, and spelt, as well as raising cattle.[66]

As the Bug-Dniester culture appears to be the latest culture that the Old Avestan speaking people could have resided in and that they would have been there between 6500 and 5500 BC, the life of Zoroaster may well have been between 6300 and 6200 BC as the ancient scholars claimed. The society of Zoroaster was clearly described as being very primitive, and his teaching appears to have had little impact on the overall culture. Both the Younger Avestan sections of the Avesta and the Vendidad describe the followers of Zoroaster surrounded by heathens, implying the religion did not become widespread until the Achaemenian dynasty when it became the state religion of the Persian Empire. The majority of the Avestan speaking peoples appear to have been following the Vedic religion, and before that pre-Vedic cults. The name of the Zoroastrian God confirms this, as Ahura Mazda, includes the word Ahura, the Avestan version of Asura, the ancient gods of the early-Vedic era. Indra, Rudra, Varuna, and several ancient Vedic gods were called Asuras in the Rig-veda, however, this term fell out of use, and today they are considered divas (gods) by Hindus, while Asuras are seen as ancient demons or evil gods.

The Old Avestan Bug-Dniester culture appears to have been extremely successful, and the Y-DNA R haplogroup subclades spread from there back across the steppes and into Asia, creating several new cultures as it went. The oldest known remains belonging to the R* haplogroup are approximately 24,000 years old and were found in the Baikal region of Siberia. Based on the rest of the genome it is known that the boy had tan-colored skin, brown eyes, black hair, and Mongolian-type physiology. All early remains containing R haplogroup subclades have similar features until approximately 14,700 years ago when blond hair and lighter eye shades begin to appear in the genome of the remains.[67] These lighter tones were most likely a result of interbreeding with Uralic peoples encountered as the R haplogroup peoples moved west from Siberia, and may have also been present in the indigenous population in Eastern Europe when they arrived. The Avestan language most-likely developed within the Bug-Dniester region, as there would have already been several Indo-European languages in the region when the R haplogroup people settled in the area. The almost artificial seeming specific and precise rules of Old Avestan point to a language adopted by an immigrant population that adapted the linguistic rules they already knew and applied them to a new language.

The Greco-Aryans

Greco-Aryan Timeline

Language Group	Culture (CIET)	Timeline (CIET)	Culture (ULT)	Timeline (ULT)
Greco-Aryan	Eastern Europe?	Before 1800 BC?	Iron Gates Mesolithic	11,000 BC to 3500 BC
Greco-Armenian	Eastern Europe?	Before 1800 BC?	Starčevo-Kőrös-Criş	6200 BC to 5300 BC
Paleo-Balkan	Balkan Peninsula	Before 1800 BC?	Turdaş-Vinča	5700 BC to 4500 BC
Proto-Greek	Balkan Peninsula	Before 3200 BC	Gumelniţa-Karanovo	4700 BC to 3950 BC
Helladic Greek	Greece	3200 BC to 1060 BC	Greece	3200 BC to 1060 BC
Mycenaean Greek	Greece	1600 BC to 1100 BC	Greece	1600 BC to 1100 BC

Old Avestan was not the earliest Indo-European language and must have been in the general vicinity of several other Indo-European languages, all spoken by non-Y-DNA R haplogroup people. The exact evolution of the various Indo-European language groups is a matter of great debate among linguists, however, most agree that there was a Proto-Indo-Iranian or Greco-Aryan or Indo-Slavic language that would have preceded Old Avestan. This language group would have been the mother language of the various Indo-Aryan, Iranian, Armenian, Greek, and Albanian languages. This Greco-Aryan language could not have been spoken by a steppes culture as they would have carried the Y-DNA R haplogroup at an earlier point if they were from the steppes.

Archaeological evidence shows a great deal contact between the Bug-Dniester culture and the cultures of the Danube River and the Carpathian Mountains, especially the Starčevo-Kőrös-Criş culture between 6200 and 5300 BC. This culture was not an R haplogroup people, instead of being composed of H and G Y-DNA haplogroups. These haplogroups are commonly found today in the Dravidians of southern India, and peoples of the Caucasus Mountains and northwest Iran. These haplogroups are believed to have been common in the indigenous peoples of southern Europe before the R haplogroup became dominant. The ancestral culture of the Starčevo-Kőrös-Criş culture is believed to be the Iron Gates Mesolithic culture which was based in the Danube region since 11,000 BC.

Given the long contact between these cultures and the Bug-Dniester culture, these cultures must have been Indo-European speaking, and the earlier Iron Gates culture must have been the source of the Greco-Aryan language which the haplogroup R peoples adopted. The Iron Gates Mesolithic culture existed in the region of Iron Gates where the Danube River crosses from Serbia into Romania. It includes the ruins of Lepenski Vir, nicknamed 'the first city in Europe.'[68] Lepenski Vir was a stone-age town with at least ten satellite villages that existed between 6300 and 6000 BC. While Lepenski Vir may have been the peak of the culture, similar artifacts in the region go back to at least 11,000 BC, indicating an extremely long period of habitation. While it is the most likely location of the Greco-Aryan speaking people, it would have been quite different from the later steppes cultures, as it was a river-based culture instead of a culture that traveled by horseback. The Danube River would have given them access not only to the chernozem region where the Bug-Dniester culture was located, but also deep into the European continent, as today it passes through, or serves as a border to Germany, Austria, Slovakia, Hungary, Croatia, Serbia, Bulgaria, Romania, and Ukraine, before finding its way to the Black Sea.

If the Greco-Aryan language was the language of the Iron Gates culture, then the origin of the Indo-European languages would date back to the Magdalenian cultures of Europe, between 17,000 and 12,000 years ago. These cultures roamed across the European continent hunting the game that spread into the region as the glaciers retreated. Their ancestors are believed to have mainly been from the Caucasus and Anatolia. A significant number of stone tools and weapons have been found across Europe that bear a striking resemblance and the production of tools is believed to have been fairly standardized, implying a common culture. This culture seems to have formed into a northern culture focused on the then massive Lake Ancylus that filled the Baltic Sea, and a southern culture that existed in the Balkans along the Danube River. The northern culture was likely the origin of the other surviving branch of the Indo-European languages, the West-European languages.

The Starčevo-Kőrös-Criş culture emerged from the Iron Gates culture along the Danube and a tributary river called the Kőrös Hungarian and Criş in Romanian, roughly contemporaneously with the Old-Avestan culture in the Bug-Dniester region. This culture covered a sizable area in the Balkan peninsula, including regions of the modern states of Serbia, Montenegro,

Bosnia-Herzegovina, Bulgaria, Croatia, Hungary, Macedonia, and Romania. Like the earlier Iron Gates culture, it appears to have been a principally river-going stone-aged culture and based on similarities between the Indo-Iranian languages and the Greco-Armenian languages the Starčevo-Kőrös-Criş culture likely spoke the Greco-Armenian language. The Greco-Armenian language is a theoretical language that the Greek, Armenian, and Albanian languages descend from. This theoretical language is not universally accepted, however, these three language groups do have significant similarities indicating a common region of origin with significant prolonged contact and borrowing between the languages, and therefore even if the Greco-Armenian language did not exist, the Starčevo-Kőrös-Criş culture is the most likely region where these languages originate.

This same region was later home to the Turdaş-Vinča culture between 5700 and 4500 BC, which seems to have developed directly from the earlier Greco-Armenian culture in the area. Based on the linguistic analysis the Armenian branch of this language group must have split off by then, and it is possible that they were either living in the steppes among the Sanskrit speakers or had already migrated to the northern Caucasus region. The Turdaş-Vinča culture was in both the right time and place to be the locus of the Paleo-Balkan culture, which was the ancestral mother culture of the Greek and Albanian language groups. Paleo-Balkan is also a disputed proto-language, however, it is generally more accepted than Greco-Armenian, as there are a large number of similarities between Greek and Albanian that are difficult to explain from cultural borrowing.

The Turdaş-Vinča culture is generally considered one of the earliest cultures to use a form of writing by advocates of the conventional timelines, as this culture is dated based on scientific evidence to between 5700 and 4500 BC when the conventional timelines claim Egypt and Sumer did not even exist. When viewed on the Universal Long Timeline, all three cultures, along with the Indus Civilization in South Asia developed writing systems around the same time as the Turdaş-Vinča culture in the Balkans. The Danube script itself is highly debated as only short phrases have been found using the script, generally scratched into small coin-like tokens. These tokens are not dissimilar to the tokens used in the Ubaid and Uruk periods of Mesopotamian Archaeology, which are dated to between 6500 and 3100 BC CMT (8331 to 4931 BC ULT). In the case of the Mesopotamians, the symbols of the tokens are later found in the early pictographic script of the Jemdet Nasr and Early Dynastic eras between 3100 and 2334 BC CMT (4931 to 3555 BC ULT), which proves the symbols were used for writing.

Unfortunately, there are no longer known works from the Balkans that prove this text was used for writing more than names or simple terms like cow or fish. Of the 5421 artifacts found inscribed with this script, only 1178 have more than one symbol.69 Almost all of these symbols, that aren't on the tokens are carved into pottery, implying they may have been names of the artisans that created the work. If this is the case, it implies either a literate society in which everyone could read the symbols or, a non-literate society in which the symbols were merely a primitive trade-mark system. The symbols themselves are abstract, unlike the pictographic symbols used in early Sumer, the hieroglyphs of Egypt, and the Indus Valley Script. This implies a script that had been in use for a long enough time that the symbols had evolved from their original form which was likely pictures of animals and objects. The development of more iconic scripts from simple pictures is well established in Egypt, Mesopotamia, South Asia, China, and Mexico, where indigenous scripts all evolved from pictures, and therefore, it seems highly probable that this script was a later development of a script recorded on a medium that is now lost to time, such as parchment or vellum. An alternate interpretation for these tokens with unique symbols of them is that they were being used as seals, which would imply a form of parchment that could be rolled and sealed with wax, like in Mesopotamia and the Indus Valley Civilization.

Like the Sanskrit speakers on the steppes at the time, the Paleo-Balkans seem to have only used metal for jewelry and continued to use flint tools, although, unlike the Sanskrit speakers, they were working copper mines to produce the jewelry themselves. This culture gave rise to several smaller cultures in the western Balkans, as well as the Gumelnița-Karanovo culture spanning much of modern Bulgaria and Romania between 4700 and 3950

BC. Like the earlier Paleo-Balkan culture in the Turdaș-Vinča region, the Gumelnița-Karanovo culture continued to use the Danube script, which by the end of their civilization was in use for at least a thousand years.

Like the smaller west Balkans cultures, the Gumelnița-Karanovo culture seems to have collapsed by 4000 BC, although no signs of conquest and resettlement have been found. At this point, the Kurgan culture was thriving on the steppes, and the Sanskrit speakers likely introduced the horse to the Balkans at this time, which would have allowed the people to spread out farther from the rivers, likely fragmenting the culture that had been living along the rivers of Bulgaria and Romania into several closely related tribes over the next millennium. Given the location of the Gumelnița-Karanovo culture, it seems highly probable that this was the Proto-Greek culture, which is generally accepted as having been somewhere in the Balkans at the time.

Farther south in Greece, another culture had been developing since 7510 BC referred to as the Sesklo or Neolithic Greece culture. This culture is generally accepted as having not been a Greek culture, however, some Greek nationalists would like to draft it into the Greek pre-history. The main reason why historians have traditionally claimed the Greeks migrated south into Greece from the Balkans, is because the earliest Greeks recorded this as their ancient homeland. This migration into Greece took place sometime before the battle of Troy, as the Greeks had settled in Greece and built cities by that time.

The Sesklo culture itself was related to the cultures farther north in the Balkans at an early point, and similarities have been found between pre-Sesklo artifacts and Iron Gates artifacts. This implies an early off-shoot culture that traveled south, likely by boat, and settled in Greece by 7510 BC. This culture seems to have developed generally isolated from the cultures of the Balkans, however, would have been impacted by the spread of horses after 4000 BC. The Selko culture disappeared around 3200 BC, implying the people had left Greece for some reason. This time period is shortly after the Great Shock of 3250 BC, a time period when the world's climate changed significantly into a neo-glacial period that lasted until around 1500 BC.

There are several pieces of evidence supporting the existence of this Great Shock of 3250 BC. During this time the world's weather became stormier, and there was far more rain, which would have caused significant storms in the Aegean Sea, and significant flooding along rivers and swamps throughout the world.[70] The GISP2 ice core samples from Greenland show there was a spike in atmospheric sulfate at 3250 BC, believed to have been from an increasing number of polynyas in the Arctic, caused by an expansion of oceanic surface ice.[71] The GRIP ice core sample from Greenland shows the 3250 BC point as being at a low point in atmospheric methane, followed by a rapid increase over the next 200 years, which is attributed to an abrupt increase in global wetlands.[72] Additionally, the ice core samples from the Huascaran glacier in Peru, show an abrupt cooling at about 3250 BC.[73]

The disappearance of the Sesklo culture from Greece mirrors the appearance of the Hittite culture in Anatolia, and given the stormy weather at the time, it is probable that the Sesklo culture transitioned from being a primarily maritime culture to a horseback culture around this time. The fragmented and mountainous nature of Greece would have been far less appealing than the open spaces of Anatolia, although the reason for their movement was more likely to find food, as they would have been depending on the sea as a source of food until that time. Akkadian records from the time mention the Hittites progressively conquering the Hattian culture over the next century, and ultimately established their Old Kingdom circa 3103 BC ULT (1664 BC CMT).

This would naturally lead to the conclusion that the Sesklo culture was a proto-Hittite culture. The Hittites are well established as one of the early off-shoots of the Indo-European culture, however, their language is so different from the other Indo-European languages that they must have developed in isolation for several millennia before invading Anatolia. This is a significant problem for the supporters of the conventional timelines, as there is no time for Hittite to develop. The conventional timeline of Indo-European linguistics is itself a matter of great debate, with different researchers placing the origin of the Indo-European culture anywhere between 5500 and 1800 BC. Most linguists point to the earlier periods, as Indo-European languages have gone through several shifts throughout their existence. Tracing the changes in Indo-Iranian languages, which is possible thanks to the existence of the Avesta and Vedas, we see no less than eight distinct linguistic eras before the emergence of Classical Sanskrit and Old Persian circa 600 BC. Before this, there had to have been several linguistic eras, which had to at least include a Greco-Aryan (or Indo-Slavic) and Indo-European era, although most linguists would place more eras between the emergence of Old Avestan and Rigvedic Sanskrit from the Proto-Indo-European language.

To resolve this lack of time in the conventional timelines, some linguists have proposed an Indo-Anatolian language that preceded the Indo-European languages, as this would have allowed enough time for the Hittite language to deviate so far from the other Indo-European languages. However, when viewing the development of these cultures and languages on the Universal Line Timeline, it becomes clear that Hittite could have developed long after the Proto-Indo-European, in relative isolation from the other Indo-Europeans to the north. Little can be known for certain of the original Hittite homeland, other than the likelihood that it was a mountainous land, as their name for themselves was the Nesi, which is believed to be derived from the word 'mountain.'

After the Hittites left Greece, the Greeks began settling the region. The earliest artifacts attributed to the Greeks, date to around 3200 BC and are referred to Helladic, or 'Early Greek.' These artifacts begin to appear at the same time the Sesklo people disappear, however, there are no signs of massacres, and it appears the Greeks simply expanded down into the vacated lands. Not all the Sesklo likely left Greece, however, those that stayed behind were assimilated into Greek culture by the Mycenaean era, between 1600 and 1100 BC. The Proto-Greeks in the Balkans were likely dislodged by flooding rivers during the Great Shock of 3250 BC, which would have led to migrations into a mountainous territory, however, this was also a period of rapid cooling, which would have driven the Proto-Greeks south. In any event, according to their records, not all Greek tribes moved south at that time, as the Dorians were later recorded as having migrated into Greece after the collapse at the end of the Mycenaean era, circa 1100 BC.

The Mycenaean Greeks were the first Greeks that are known to have used a written script, the Linear-B script, that they appear to have adopted from the Minoans. Linear-A is the still undeciphered Minoan version of the script, which was used alongside Minoan Hieroglyphs. The earliest surviving Linear-B inscriptions are dated to circa 1450 BC and provide the earliest glimpse into the Greek minds of the time. At that time the Greeks were worshiping some of the same gods as their classical era descendants, including Poseidon, Dionysus, Persephone, and Hades. Some of these names have also been found in Linear-A, however, while the sounds of the symbols are believed to be the same as the sounds used by the Greeks, the language itself is undeciphered.

The West-Europeans

West-European Timeline

Language Group	Culture (CIET)	Timeline (CIET)	Culture (ULT)	Timeline (ULT)
Proto-West-European			Ahrensburg	12,900 BC to 11,700 BC
West-European			Swiderian	11,000 BC to 8200 BC
Late-West-European			Maglemosian	9000 BC to 6000 BC
Italo-Celtic	Baden and/or Beaker Culture	4300 BC to 1800 BC	Baden and Bell Beaker	4300 BC to 1800 BC
Proto-Germanic	Nordic Bronze Age	1700 BC to 500 BC	Funnelbeaker, Globular Amphora, and Corded Ware	3200 BC to 1060 BC
Celtic	Atlantic Bronze Age	1700 BC to 700 BC	Atlantic Bronze Age	1700 BC to 700 BC
Proto-Nordic	Viking Era	800 AD to 1100 AD	Nordic Bronze Age	1700 BC to 500 BC

As the last possible culture that could have been the Old Avestan culture appears to have been the Bug-Dniester Culture of 6500 to 5500 BC, making their Greco-Aryan ancestral culture likely the Iron Gates culture in the Danube between 11,000 and 6000 BC, the other surviving branch of the Indo-European languages, the West-European languages, had to be around at the same time. The West-European languages include the Germanic, Italic, and Celtic languages, which all share certain common elements. The existence of a proto-Italo-Celtic language has long been accepted by some linguists, while others argue that the Celtic languages are an offshoot of Proto-Italic, or that the Italic languages are an offshoot of Proto-Celtic. This debate seems to be somewhat arbitrary, and no-doubt influenced by nationalism to an extent. In any event, there was a common Italo-Celtic language at one point, regardless of how it is classified.

The inclusion of Germanic with Italo-Celtic is more contentious, as the Germanic languages also share a great deal with the Balto-Slavic languages, however, the Germanic and Balto-Slavic similarities can be attributed to later contact during the formative period of the Balto-Slavic languages, which is generally dated to around the time of the Greco-Roman cultures of the classic era. The similarities between Germanic and Italo-Celtic cannot be dismissed as late developments as all of these language groups long precede the classical era. 11,000 years ago, there was another significant stone-aged culture in Europe besides the Iron Gates Culture, the Swiderian culture of modern Poland, and Lithuania. The Swiderians were also a river-going people, who used the rivers emptying into the Baltic sea as highways across Eastern Europe the same way the Vikings would thousands of years later.

This culture had similar technology to the Iron Gate culture on the Danube but appears to have been less artistic, and most likely had a harder time surviving in the climate of Eastern Europe than the Greco-Aryans had on the Danube. This culture was descended from the Ahrensburg culture, who inhabited northern Germany through southern England between 12,900 and 11,700 BC, and was in turn a descendant of the Magdalenian cultures that migrated into Europe between 17,000 and 12,000 years ago. The Ahrensburg culture appears to have moved east into the more sheltered region of the Baltic from the more exposed region of the North Sea, although the exact reason is unknown, it was likely due to climatic shifts. The Baltic was at the time an ice lake formed from melting glaciers which persisted until approximately 8300 BC when it was exposed to the sea and became a brackish sea archeoclimatologists call the Yoldia Sea.[74]

This transition from ice lake to brackish sea circa 8300 BC seems to have led to the end of the Swiderian culture, as within a century the culture disappears from the archaeological record. An offshoot culture called the Maglemosian culture formed around the coasts of Baltic ice lake beginning around 9000 BC, which seems to have thrived as the Baltic ice lake warms and became the brackish Yoldia Sea, and they continue along the shores of the Yoldia until approximately 6000 BC. During this time the Yoldia Sea became isolated from the North sea again, forming a massive freshwater lake called Ancylus Lake by archeoclimatologists. This transition does not seem to have affected the Maglemosian culture in the region, however, the subsequent draining of the Ancylus when the lake reconnected to the North Sea seems to have destroyed the civilization. Ancylus Lake was significantly higher than the sea-level of the ocean, covering large low-lying sections of modern Sweden, Finland, and Estonia, which rapidly drained around 6000 BC when the lake reconnected to the North Sea, and the Maglemosian culture disappeared at the same time.

Assuming this was the original West-European speaking homeland, then the Funnelbeaker culture of Poland, Denmark, Northern Germany, and Southern Sweden between 4300 and 2800 BC would no doubt be a northern descendant of West-Europeans, and likely the Proto-Germanic culture. The Baden culture to the south, in the lands of Hungary, Czechia, Austria, and Slovakia between 3600 and 2800 BC is occasionally proposed as the original homeland of the Italo-Celts by proponents of that proto-language, and therefore could easily be a southern branch of West-European peoples that migrated back into the Danube area.

In the north, the Funnelbeaker culture developed into the Globular Amphora culture between 3400 and 2800 BC, and then the Corded Ware culture between 2900 and 2350 BC. This last culture encompassed all of the lands east of the Rhine that the Romans traditionally attributed to the Germans, but also expanded northeast through Poland and the Baltic into Finland and north-western Russia. Likely, some of this culture was not Proto-Germanic, however, it is plausible that Proto-Germanic was used as a common language of trade and politics across the region, which would explain the Germanic words in Uralic languages, as well as the common elements of between Germanic and Balto-Slavic languages, assuming the Balto-Slavs were a northern offshoot of the Greco-Aryans or Sanskrit speakers that fell under the Germanic sphere at that time.

To the south and west, the Baden culture seems to have evolved into, or been drawn into the Bell Beaker Culture, which is often associated with the spread of the Celtic or Italo-Celtic culture. The Bell Beaker Culture spread from the northern Danube out across Western Europe between 4300 and 1800 BC, and at its peak encompassed most of France, Spain, Portugal, and Britain, as well as parts of Italy. In the west, this culture was later replaced by the Atlantic Bronze Age between 1300 and 700 BC, which may have been spread by the Proto-Celtic language. Proto-Celtic is generally accepted as having been a creole of various old languages in western Europe that was used as a trade language. It is likely the Celts never spoke a common language, but a spectrum of similar languages influenced by Proto-Italo-Celtic.

The Balto-Slavs

Balto-Slavic Timeline

Language Group	Culture (CIET)	Timeline (CIET)	Culture (ULT)	Timeline (ULT)
Greco-Aryan	Eastern Europe?	Before 1800 BC?	Iron Gates Mesolithic	11,000 BC to 3500 BC
Rig-vedic	Early Vedic India	1800 BC ? to 1100 BC	Cucuteni-Trypillia and Sredny Stog	4800 BC to 3000 BC
Mantra Language			Maykop, Yamnaya, and Poltavka	3700 BC to 2100 BC
Proto-Germanic	Nordic Bronze Age	1700 BC to 500 BC	Funnelbeaker, Globular Amphora, and Corded Ware	3200 BC to 1060 BC
Proto-Balto-Slavic	Eastern Europe	Before 1500 BC ?	Trzciniec-Komariv	1900 BC to 1200 BC
Balto-Slavic	Eastern Europe	Before 1500 BC ?	Lusatian	1300 BC to 500 BC
Proto-Slavic	Eastern Europe	500 AD to 900 AD	Pomeranian	650 BC to 150 BC
West-Slavic	Eastern Europe	700 AD to 1400 AD	Oksywie-Wielbark	200 BC to 400 AD
East-Slavic	Eastern Europe	800 AD to 1200 AD	Przeworsk	300 BC to 500 AD

The development of the Balto-Slavic language group in north-central Europe is another highly debated issue. Some linguists believed the language group did not even exist, instead claiming the two language groups merely co-existed in the same region. In either case, the Baltic and Slavic languages share a great deal, and both appear to be an offshoot of either Sanskrit or Greco-Aryan, and then influenced by Proto-Germanic.

If the Balto-Slavic language did exist, it creates another problem for the Conventional Indo-European Timeline, as linguists have stated it could not have existed more recently that around 3000 to 3500 years ago, meaning that it existed at the same time as Sanskrit, which is should be a descended of. This issue is sidestepped if one dismissed the Balto-Slavic language and simply claims that they are very similar languages, that developed in the same region, from the same proto-language, say Greco-Aryan, and were then influenced by the same foreign languages, such as Proto-Germanic, however, one then needs to explain the large number of identical words and concepts shared in the Balto-Slavic languages and Sanskrit, yet not shared by Avestan.

The division of the Slavic languages into the Eastern, Southern, and Western Slavic language groups is another debated issue, as the Conventional Indo-European Timeline requires all of this to have happened in the Middle Ages. This means that in the Conventional Indo-European Timeline there were no Poles or Czechs or Bulgarians, or Serbo-Croats until after the year 500 AD, and no Russians or Ukrainians until around the year 900 AD.

This determination is based on the fact that the Slavs were mostly illiterate until 900 AD, and the writing that does remain from the time period is all in Old Slavonic, the script developed in Bulgaria and Serbia at that time. Old Slavonic was used by Slavic peoples, throughout Greek-influenced lands, while the Roman-influenced Germanic and Celtic lands adopted the Latin alphabet.

This concept that the Slavs did not begin to separate into differentiated language groups until after the year 500 AD is required in the Conventional Indo-European Timeline as there is no time for them to have separated earlier. Unfortunately, it contradicts all logic. For a non-literate people to maintain a common-dialect they would all need to live in a common area, which in the Conventional Indo-European Timeline is modern Poland. After 500 AD, they began to rapidly breed and cover Eastern Europe, expanding south to Bulgaria and Serbia almost instantly, where they came into contact with the Greeks and developed the Old Slavonic alphabet, but did not bother teaching it to the relatives back in Poland, who they broke off all contact with. Then the Old Slavonic-using Bulgarians expanded up into modern Ukraine, Russia, and Belarus, becoming the dominant population before the Viking expanded into the region starting around 800 AD. Somehow, the Slavs also picked up a large number of Sanskrit terms and concepts in the Conventional Indo-European Timeline, before they began to separate into different groups. This means that one must accept the idea that a group of Vedic Indians circa 1800 to 1100 BC CIET settled in Poland, and taught the Vedic religion to early Slavs and neighboring, but unrelated, Balts. They apparently had no contact either with the other Sanskrit-speaking peoples of India, but then did have contact with the Scythians living in Russia and Ukraine, as the later developments within Sanskrit did not affect the Slavic and Baltic languages, while the Scythian language did. Scythian was a language related to Avestan and more distantly, Persian, which left a clear imprint on the East Slavic languages, somehow, even though in the Conventional Indo-European Timeline the Scythians had been driven from Europe a thousand years before the Slavic languages began to separate.

On the other hand, in the Universal Long Timeline all of the layers of cultural influence make perfect sense and correspond to archaeological evidence. The Proto-Balto-Slavic language would have developed in Belarus and neighboring regions within what archaeologists have labeled the Trzciniec-Komariv culture, between 1900 and 1200 BC. This language group would have been based on Mantra Sanskrit, which was previously spoken in the area by the Kurgan peoples, who themselves had begun migrating south to the Great Aral Sea. By the time that Balto-Slavic formed, the region was under the cultural domination of the Proto-Germanic Corded Ware culture, although the Germanic influence would have been limited so far to the east. The Balto-Slavic culture would have reached a peak, and likely started to separate into Baltic and Slavic groups under the Lusatian culture of Poland and Ukraine, circa 1300 to 500 BC. The following Pomeranian culture of the same region would have been the Proto-Slavic culture, between 650 and 150 BC. Around 300 BC a group of Slavs moved into the Scythian lands to the east as they headed south, where the remnants of their culture left the imprint on the Eastern Slavic dialect that formed in that region. This Eastern Slavic culture was the Przeworsk culture of the western Steppes, which lasted until around 500 AD, while the Slavs that stayed in the west formed the Oksywie-Wielbark culture between 200 BC and 400 AD. These two Eastern and Western Slavic cultures would have both been impacted by the environmental shift around 400 AD, and migrants would have flowed south into East Roman lands, where the South Slavic culture formed and the Old Slavonic alphabet was invented.

The Hattians and Hittites

Anatolian Archaeological Timeline

Dynastic Periods	CMT	ULT
Hattian Culture	Pre-2500 BC to 1664 BC	Pre-4000 BC to 3103 BC
Old Hittite Empire	1664 BC to 1524 BC	3103 BC to 2965 BC
Middle Hittite Kingdom	1524 BC to 1400 BC	2965 BC to 1450 BC
Mitanni Empire	1500 BC to 1300 BC	2967 BC to 1300 BC
New Hittite Empire	1400 BC to 1178 BC	1450 BC to 1178 BC
Middle Assyrian Kingdom	1178 BC to 912 BC	1178 BC to 912 BC
Neo-Assyrian Empire	912 BC to 612 BC	912 BC to 612 BC
Regional Sites	Carbon-dated Timelines	
Natufian	13,050 BC to	7505 BC
Qaramel	13,000 BC to	6783 BC
Tell Abu Hureyra	13,000 BC to	5000 BC
Göbekli Tepe	9130 BC to	7370 BC
Nevalı Çori	8400 BC to	8100 BC
Çayönü	8630 BC to	6800 BC
Aşıklı Höyük	8200 BC to	7400 BC
Hassuna	7750 BC to	6780 BC
Çatalhöyük	7500 BC to	5700 BC
Tell Sabi Abyad	7500 BC to	5500 BC
Jarmo	7500 BC to	5000 BC
Bouqras	7400 BC to	6200 BC
Hacilar	7040 BC to	5000 BC

The Hattians are a little understood culture that existed in Anatolia before the Hittites moved into the region. Little of their culture survived the later expansion of the Hittites, who according to Akkadian records from the time slowly conquered the Hattians between approximately 3200 and 3103 BC ULT (1750 to 1664 BC CMT). As far as we can tell from the archaeological record, the Hattians were not a literate people, however, the Akkadians that were trading with them did record some of their names. These names have been interpreted by some as being Caucasian, distantly related to the modern Georgian and Abkhazian languages. This conclusion is far from accepted, however, there are no other competing theories, other than that the culture may not have survived to the present.

The Hattians are also often connected to the Hurrians that lived in northern Syria before the Mitanni and Assyrians conquering the area. This cultural affinity is generally accepted, however, the evidence is also limited as the Hurrian language was not recorded, other than in names recorded by the

Akkadians, Hittites, Mitanni, Hyksos, and Assyrians. The Hattian culture was nevertheless a highly advanced culture, being the first known culture in the region, or anywhere, that was engaging in iron-smelting, by as early as 4000 BC ULT (2500 BC CMT/CIET). This iron was used for jewelry, but not tools, which mirrors its use in many other ancient cultures. The pre-dynastic and dynastic Egyptians used iron for jewelry since at least 5800 BC ULT (4000 BC CET), and in the Uruk period of Iraqi history since approximately the same time. Further north in the Samara culture on the Steppes of Eurasia, metal was only used as jewelry between 5500 and 3500 BC (as established by carbon dating).

The Hattian culture is also often connected to the ancient ruins in the region of southeast Turkey and northern Syria, and northern Iraq, such as Mureybet, Tell Abu Hureyra, Göbekli Tepe, Çayönü, Çatalhöyük, Hacilar, and Tell Sabi Abyad. Unfortunately, in the conventional timelines there is a significant gap between the ends of these civilizations, the last of which ended circa 5000 BC, and the earliest the Hattian culture can be firmly dated to, circa 2500 BC, or approximately 150 years before Sargon the Great of Akkad, circa 2334 BC CMT. This was not the foundation point of the Hattian civilization, but the earliest the civilization can be proven to be smelting iron, indicating that they were likely around for several centuries by 2500 BC, perhaps even a millennium, however, this is still a gap of 2500 years since the end of the last earlier civilizations. Using the Universal Long Timeline the Hattians began smelting iron circa 4000 BC ULT, which is a significantly shorter period of time than the 2500 year gap, but still not clear evidence that the cultures were connected.

These earliest archaeological sites do however support the Universal Long Timelines in proving that there were cities around when the Sumerians claimed there were, pre-dating the 1st Uruk Dynasty which began in Sumerian records circa 9868 BC. The Natufian Culture of the Levant, as well as the Tell Qaramel and Tell Abu Hureyra ruins all date back to before 9868 BC, and other ruins in the region might as well, as very little archaeology has been done in the region due to ongoing ethnic violence and the rise and fall of the Islamic State.

The most famous site in the region is arguably Göbekli Tepe near the Syrian border of Turkey. The site was originally surveyed by a joint team from the Istanbul University and the University of Chicago in 1963, who, after doing virtually no work on the site, decided it was a Byzantine ruin from around a 1000 years ago, which is how it was listed until 1994 when Klaus Schmidt of the German Archaeological Institute decided to take a second look. He had been excavating nearby Nevalı Çori, and was expecting to find other sites in the region that dated back to circa 8000 BC, and what he found when he excavated Göbekli Tepe quickly overturned the earlier assumption that it was a Byzantine gave yard. The upper layer which was first uncovered where scientifically dated to between 7560 and 7370 BC, and the earlier layers that have subsequently been uncovered have pushed the date back to 9130 to 8800 BC, however, these are just the three top levels. Some sites in the region have been shown to have dozens of distinct layers, and therefore very little is actually known about this culture. Additionally, ground-penetrating radar has shown that the site covers a large region around the hill that is the focus of the current work, and less than 5% of the site has been excavated. The other sites in the region have had even less work done on them, nevertheless, these archaeological sites prove there was a civilization in the Northern Mesopotamia region by 10,000 BC, making the claims of the Sumerians at least plausible.

If there was a civilization spread across the Northern Mesopotamian region, it seems impossible that it did not trade along the Tigris and Euphrates, and therefore the question demands an answer: Where are the ruins of whoever the North Mesopotamians were trading with, if as Assyriologists insist, there was nothing in southern Iraq until circa 6500 BC. Are we to believe these people that did not have horses or the wheel, also did not know how to built boats, or even rafts? It is a scientific fact that people in the region have been using boats for at least 130,000 years, as that is when Crete was colonized,[75] yet, these advanced cultures 10,000 years ago had somehow forgotten that wood floats? Clearly, they were using the Tigris and Euphrates for trade as several sites are at the old courses of these rivers, and so, there must have been someone in southern Iraq at the time, as the Sumerians recorded.

The Kassites, Mitanni and Hyksos

Regardless of when the Sumerian civilization started, it was eventually subsumed into the Akkadian culture. The first Akkadian king, Sargon the Great, conquered the Sumerians circa 3885 BC ULT (2334 BC CMT), and although there was brief Neo-Sumerian era circa 3568 to 3462 BC (2112 to 2004 BC), the Sumerian civilization died out, replaced by the various Semitic cultures that settled in Mesopotamia. These Semitic cultures built the Old Kingdoms of Babylonian and Assyrian empires between by 2965 BC ULT (1517 BC CMT). To the north, the Hittites had conquered the Hattians and built their own empire by that time, however, then something happened, and these civilizations collapsed. The era that followed was a dark age in the Mesopotamian history of unknown length.

During this era when very little was recorded the Kassites conquered Babylon, and the Mitanni conquered the Assyrian Empire and most of the Hittite Empire. Both of these peoples are a general mystery, as they seem to have been illiterate when they invaded Mesopotamia and used the Babylonian and Assyrian languages for trade and diplomacy. The one known exception was when dealing with the Hittites, where they used the Hittite language. The Babylonians and Assyrians did leave some literature during this time, and it is clear from the names of these people, their gods, and the loan words that entered into the Semitic languages at the time, that these people were Indo-Aryans.

It has been argued that the gods of the Indo-Aryans were likely the same as the Avestan-speaking peoples, and therefore, these could have been any Indo-Iranian peoples, however, there are many names and terms, mainly to due with horses and chariots that are specifically Indo-Aryan, and not Iranian, and therefore most linguists have agreed that these were Indo-Aryans. This raises several problems for the conventional timelines, as the closes Sanskrit dialect appears to be Rigvedic or Mantra Language, which would mean that these Indo-Aryans would have to date to early in the period that the Vedic texts were being written in. This was explained by dating the Vedic texts to after 1800 BC CIET, however, with ironworking taking place in India by 2400 BC this dating is impossible, and therefore one has to assume a large group of Indo-Aryans somehow became cut-off from the rest for 1500 years as the Sanskrit language evolved, and then launched a massive invasion of Mesopotamia.

The fact that the Semitic peoples of Mesopotamia adopted Indo-Aryan terminology for horses and chariots is even more perplexing as they have already had the technology for almost a thousand years, as proven by the Standard of Ur, which showed horses and war-chariots in use in Sumer as early as 2600 BC, while in the convention timelines the Mitanni didn't conquer their empire until circa 1500 BC CMT, and Kassites didn't arrive in Babylon until 1570 BC CMT. One is left with the idea that for over 1000 years the Mesopotamians were using horses, wagons, and chariots but without ever naming them. The vision of these highly literate cultures simply pointing and grunting at horses and literally anything with a wheel for over a thousand years is apparently what Assyriologists want us to believe.

The situation is even more confusing when one adds the view of Egyptologists to the mix, as in the conventional Egyptian timeline has the Hyksos invading Egypt from the north Mesopotamian region circa 1674 BC, using horses and war-chariots, apparently, something the Egyptians had never encountered before, even though they were trading with the Sumerians since pre-dynastic times, and the Sumerians and later Mesopotamians had had horses and wagons for almost a thousand years by the time the Hyksos invaded. In fact, Egyptologists expect people to believe that the ancient Egyptians copied the concept of the ziggurat from the Egyptians, which is what the earliest pyramid: Djoser's Pyramid is, according to Egyptologists, yet, did not think to import horses, wagons, or even the wheel. For comparison, the Standard of Ur, which shows both the horse and the war-wagon is dated to circa 2600 BC by Assyriologists, while the entire Old Kingdom of Egypt, when all the largest pyramids were built, is dated to between 2685 and 2161 BC by Egyptologists. Compounding this bizarre timeline, the entire Middle Kingdom is dated to between 2061 and 1803 BC by Egyptologists, which is when the greatest work of environmental engineering ever done, was apparently done without and beasts of burden or even the wheel. This was the creation of the vast lake-land and terraced hills of the Fayum, in the desert east of Cairo. The Fayum is still part of the agricultural heartland of Egypt, however, at its height during the Middle Kingdom the lake in the center, today called Lake Qarun, was 63 meters higher than it is today, and covered an area over ten times as large. This was accomplished by digging a canal to the Nile that allowed the annual floods to fill the area each year, all, without either using horses or wagons, both of which had been used by the Mesopotamians for 600 years.

This would be like Australia choosing to build a large sea in the interior of the outback, but choosing to do it using only technology that was widely available in the 1400s. One is left with the impression that the Egyptians must have been both the most brilliant engineers in all of history to do what they did and the most idiotic to do it that way. Of course, this is only a valid perspective if the conventional Egyptian timeline is correct, which it clearly is not, as the Hyksos invading from Northern Mesopotamia circa 1674 BC, is impossible. The Hyksos were a Semitic people, with a Hurrian nobility, and some Indo-Aryan loanwords, and there was no culture like this in Mesopotamia, or anywhere else, until a couple of hundred years later. If the Hyksos traveled through Mesopotamia circa 1674 BC CMT, they did it at the height of the Old Babylonian, Old Assyrian, and Old Hittite Empires, and yet, no one noticed? Not only did no one in Mesopotamia notice them entering Egypt, but when the Egyptians finally drove them out in 1535 BC CET, no one in Mesopotamia noticed that either, even though the Old Assyrian and Old Hittite Empires were around at the time. In the conventional Mesopotamian timeline, the Babylonians had been conquered by the Kassites circa 1570 BC, however, they didn't notice this band of warriors passing through their territory either, and to put it in perspective, it is recorded that there were 480,000 Hyksos that were driven out of Egypt circa 1535 BC CET, not counting slaves. You'd think someone would notice an army of a half-million passing through their territory.

The simple truth is that the conventional timelines of Egypt and Sumer simply do not correlate. There was a culture in Mesopotamia exactly like the Hyksos, the later Mitanni, but they didn't exist until late into the Mitanni era, when the local Hurrian culture had eclipsed the Indo-Aryan culture that conquered the empire, and that would have after 1500 BC CMT.

Naturally, none of these issues exist in the Universal Long Timeline, as the Kassites occupied Babylon circa 3013 BC ULT, introducing the horse, chariot, and terminology long before the Standard of Ur was created circa 2400 BC by one of the later Sea Dynasty kings. This is five hundred years after the chariot was apparently invented on the steppes by the earlier Kurgan/Indo-Aryans peoples. Some of these Indo-Aryans went on to conquer a large region of northern Mesopotamia over the next few decades, apparently, by freeing the Babylonian's Hurrian slaves, who then led insurrections in the Assyrian and Hittite Empires which the Indo-Aryans capitalized on, establish the Mitanni empire, or more properly confederation by 2967 BC ULT. Hundreds of years later, the Hyksos invaded Egypt in 2533 BC ULT, from the Mitanni confederation, and when they were ultimately driven from Egypt in 1731 BC ULT, they returned to the Mitanni confederation, which then fought a series of wars against their neighbors before being completely conquered in 1460 BC.

In the ULT, the Egyptians didn't choose to build the pyramids, and dig the great canal, and terrace a region the size of Wales the hardest way imaginable because they, one would assume, had nothing better to do. They simply didn't have access to more advanced technology. In the ULT, the Kassites did not introduce wagon and chariot technology to the Mesopotamians until circa 3013 BC, while the Egyptian Middle Kingdom had collapsed circa 3249 BC.

The Harappans

Perhaps no archaeological ruins have been as hotly disputed as the Indus Valley Civilization, also called the Harappan Civilization after the initial ruin excavated: Harappa. The ruins of this civilization were discovered in the 1920s and dated according to where they fit into the conventional Egyptian and Mesopotamian timelines, as there was no better method at the time. Subsequent attempts to carbon date the artifacts from the ruins have given such a wide and conflicting number of results that the data is essentially useless. It is clear that the Harappans were trading with the Sumerians from an early date, as Harappans artifacts have been found in Iraq dating to the 2nd Kish Dynasty, between 7025 and 4998 BC ULT (2700 to 2600 BC CMT). These artifacts were used to date the early Harappan Phase, Harappan 1, to circa 3300 to 2800 BC, and subsequently, the entire Indus Valley Civilization to between 3300 and 1300 BC, finishing up just before the beginning of the iron age circa 1200 BC, as there are no iron artifacts found in the ruins of this civilization. Of course, this is now an impossible range of dates for this civilization, as by 2400 there was ironworking in other parts of India, and by 1800 iron smelting in Uttar Pradesh state, which is within the region of this civilization, and by 1500 BC iron smelting had spread from India to Yaz in modern Turkmenistan, meaning it had to have traveled through the Indus civilization if it was still there. Yet, there is no iron found in this civilization's ruins, and therefore, it was not there at the time.

Using the Unified Long Timeline, the Harappan artifacts found in the 2nd King Dynasty from the Harappan 1 phase can be dated to roughly sometime between 7025 and 4998 BC ULT. Additional Harappan artifacts from the Harappan 3B phase have been found at Nippur corresponding to the life of Sargon the Great, which would be circa 3885 BC allowing for that phase to be roughly dated. The most recent Harappan artifacts found in Sumer date to the Isin Dynasty, circa 3462 to 3227 BC ULT, which are from the Harappan 3C phase. Harappan 3C was the last phase of the mature period of the Indus Civilization, which either went into sudden decline circa 1900 BC on the conventional Harappan timeline due to climatic changes that were entirely unique to Pakistan and India, or, went into sudden decline circa 3246 BC ULT as part of the global weather changes of 3250 BC, known as the Great Shock of 3250 BC. This was a period known from several sites and ice-cores from around the world, as a time period when the world's climate changed significantly into a neo-glacial period that lasted until around 1500 BC. In the ULT it is linked with the collapse of the Egyptian Middle Kingdom, the Isin Dynasty in Iraq, the end of the Protopalatial period of Minoan civilization, and several migrations of various cultures in the Eurasian Steppes and Central Asia.

Indologists have estimated that there were approximately 600 years from the end of the Mature period until the ultimate demise of the Indus Civilization, which, if applied to the ULT would place the end of this civilization circa 2846 BC, centuries before the time that ironworking appeared in southern India. It also requires the Indus civilization to have existed by the 2nd King Dynasty, ending circa 4998 BC ULT, something that is inconsistent with Indologists' initial assumptions about when the culture formed. These early Indologist's assumptions were not simply based on correlations with the Sumerian and Akkadian civilizations, and the assumptions about the iron age starting in the Middle East somewhere, but also based on two centuries of research into the Vedas and more than a century of research into the Avesta. By the time that the ruins of the Indus Civilization were discovered both European and Indian scholars studying the ancient literature, had concluded that the origin of the Indo-Iranian peoples must be somewhere northwest of India, in Central Asia or Europe, and some went so far as to suggest the Indo-Iranians had originated in a sunken continent at the north pole. This idea, generally considered absurd today, was based on the fact that in the Avesta the 'High Watchpost' is built at a point around which the stars revolve. This was assumed to be the north pole, around which the stars at least appear to circle in the northern hemisphere. Additional texts were found that mentioned a day and a night lasting an entire year, which only happens in the polar regions, and resulted in the idea by 1900, that the Indo-Iranians had originated in the far north somewhere before migrating south into India.

This idea was by no means original, the Zoroastrians had migrated to India after Iran had become predominantly Islamic, and a thousand years before the Scythians had migrated to India from the Eurasian Steppes as the Goturks expanded into the region. The idea that the Vedic Aryans had done the same at some point was a natural conclusion, however, some strongly disagree with this conclusion, claiming that all Indo-European peoples originate in India, not further north. This idea seems to have developed as an anti-Imperial view, even though there were Indian Nationalist that were involved with the scholarship that developed the theory that the Indo-Aryans migrated into India. At the time, in the late 1800s, no known ruins were supporting this thesis, however, they were found throughout the 1900s, spread across the Eurasian Steppes.

In the view of the Out-of-India proponents, the ruins of the Indus Civilization are the ruins of the bronze age Vedic Civilization of the Rig-veda. This theory has yet to explain the lack of horses, chariots, yama graves, horse burials, and many other aspects of the Rig-veda that are lacking from the Indus ruins. The primary reason that so many Hindus believe that the Indus Valley Civilization is the ruins of the ancient Vedic Civilization, is because the Indus Civilization is remarkably similar to the civilization described in the Mahabharata, Ramayana, and other great ancient Indian epics. The assumption among many Hindus is that this is the same civilization that wrote the Vedas, however, the Vedas and epics have virtually nothing in common.

The earliest Vedic texts have different heroes, gods, technology, and geography from the epics. Indologists theorize that the epics may have been translated from, or inspired by, older Dravidian language texts or stories dating from the Harappan civilization. Iravatham Mahadevan, the epigraphist who successfully deciphered the Tamil-Brahmi inscriptions, and who is world-renowned for his expertise on the epigraphy of the Indus Valley Civilization once described the situation as:

> "It is not a migrant civilization, it is not that a handful of settlers came and settled on the sea coast. This is a large, native, indigenous civilization. It is surprising that people hardly realize

the extent of the Harappan civilization. It was more than a million square kilometers in area, much larger than modern Pakistan, much larger than all the other ancient civilizations, excepting China of course, put together. The Sumerian, the Akkadian, the Egyptian, Hittite and so on. Over such a large and fairly populous area, judging from the number of villages and cities. Several estimates of the population of Harappa and Mohenjo-daro have been made and they seem to have been very large cities by ancient standards. This only goes to confirm our supposition that you must look for a local language as a candidate for the Harappan script...

...the scale and the magnitude of the Harappan civilization speaks against its total extinction. As all scholars who have studied the problem agree, the incoming Aryans were relatively a very small minority and they were able to dominate only culturally and ultimately, in the assimilated Indo-Aryan or north Indian people, the indigenous racial element must have slowly surfaced. That is why we have no such thing as early Aryan pottery, because the pottery continued to be made by the local people. As someone has said jokingly, archaeology knows of no Aryans, only linguistics knows of Aryans. This is true. The answer to this is that the incoming Aryans were small in number. In this respect there was no cultural discontinuity. The real discontinuity was in language, principally, and in religion and ritual in the earliest levels, but in later levels, modern Hinduism as we know it is a composite of both pre-Aryan, native, animistic and tribal religions and the incoming Aryan religion. Perhaps when the Indus script is deciphered, I would not be surprised to find that the greater part of modern Hinduism has a Harappan lineage."[76]

Traditional Hindu gods found in the epics began to appear in the Vedas in the Brahmana Prose sections, which in the ULT would have been written in Iron Age India between 1800 and 1100 BC, meaning they would have been living among the Dravidian speaking ancient Hindus of the Harappan civilization by this point. For example, the Shatapatha Brahmana in the Yajur-veda contains the earliest mention of Garuda in the Vedas, in the Brahmana Prose. The Mahabharata, which is believed to have been written between the 7th century BC and 4th century AD, claims that Garuda is also Garutman, who was in the Rigveda, and therefore Hindus generally accept that Garuda was in the Rigveda. Likewise, other epic gods, heroes, and geographic locations have been spliced into the early Vedic Texts by simply stating that the names in the Vedic Texts are another set of names for the same gods, heroes, and geographic locations found in the epics. This is naturally, an undisprovable hypothesis if any name simply means whatever you want it to, then any text could have been written anytime, and be about anyone. By this logic, the Torah could have been written by ... Confucius? Why not?

The fact is, the ancient Indian epics are clearly based in India, but the Vedas were not. The Vedas were written by people who used the horse, while the epics were written by people who lived along rivers, and traveled by boat. Horses and iron, and even airplanes have been added to the epics, but there is no reason to believe they were not added at a later date, as the oldest known versions are believed to have been first written in Classical Sanskrit, long after the Indo-Aryans would have settled in northern India, and brought their horses with them. The airplanes are s curious addition to the epics, but not a recent addition, although the translation of the word 'vimana' as 'airplane' was developed after the invention of the airplane in the 1900s. Older English to Sanskrit dictionaries translated 'vimana' as 'flying car,' 'flying carriage,' or 'flying machine,' and some scholars postulated that these were references to a carriage mounted on the backs of elephants, although there is no evidence of this in the texts themselves. As some vimanas were said to travel to other planets, or be the size of cities, the elephant carriage hypothesis is generally considered as a plausible inspiration for the idea, but in most surviving texts, historians generally view vimanas as purely literary devices intended to show the power of the over of the vimana.

Horses and chariots far more common in the epics than elephants, however, the technology found in the epics, other than the flying machines, reflects the technology of Iron Age India, when they were likely first written, at least in the Sanskrit language. These epics are generally considered by Hindus to be accurate descriptions of ancient events, and Indologists generally are willing to accept the idea that the stories are set in the ancient Indus Valley Civilization, even if the stories are themselves later fiction. In most respects, the culture and geography described in the ancient epics match what Indologists think the Indus Civilization was like. Major characters are often described as having dark skin, which Dravidian people have, and many names are believed to be Dravidian loan-words.

Hanuman, the monkey-god: The orientalist F. E. Pargiter theorized that Hanuman the monkey-demigod from the epics was a proto-Dravidian deity, and the name 'Hanuman' was a Sanskritization of the Old Tamil words Aan-mandhi meaning 'male monkey.' The Hindu scholar Ray Govindchandra influenced by Pargiter's opinion suggested in 1976 that the early Indo-Aryans may have invented a Sanskrit etymology for the deity's name after they accepted Hanuman in their pantheon.[77] Garuda, the name of the eagle-god does not appear to be a Sanskrit word and is not found in the Vedas until the Shatapatha Brahmana in the Yajurveda, written in Brahmana Prose after the Indo-Aryans would have migrated into India. In the earlier sections of the Vedas, a similar creature called Śyena is found, which is the Sanskrit word for eagle. The name Garuda is believed to be based on the old Dravidian word *karug-u* meaning 'eagle,'[78] and therefore many Hindus view this as the same character. Even if it is, the shift in the name shows that the Indo-Aryans had come under a strong enough Dravidian influence that they were changing the names of their own gods to fit into the new culture they were surrounded by.

The changing of one's god's name is no small affair but does happen. Most Christians living in the Middle East call their god Allah, which in Arabic translates as 'the God.' While this is a perfectly valid translation of any monotheistic god, it is an Islamic title, and therefore something the Middle Eastern Christians adopted from the Muslims, and something not noted in the Middle East until almost a thousand years after the time of Mohamed. A similar transition has taken place in Southeast Asia, were in nations that have become mainly Islamic, older Hindu literature has been Islamized, for example, Allah has replaced Brahma in local versions of the Ramayana.[79] This transition only took a few hundred years, however, it also included the adoption of a new religion, which the Vedic people do not appear to have done.

Unlike the Vedas, there is no surviving literary evidence for the epics before Classical Sanskrit, although there is a general acceptance that at least the core of the story must be much older. This is a strong indicator that the epics were translated at that point into Sanskrit, which is why Old Dravidian names and places in the Indus Civilization are described. The setting of the Mahabharata is northern India and Pakistan, approximately 3200 to 3100 BC. This fact has never been in doubt, even before archaeologists actually found ruins in the region that date to that time. Before that, it was simply considered, by non-Hindus, a fictional tale designed to present the central thesis of the Bhagavad Gita, which is the philosophical view of Krishna that takes up a quarter of the text. Since the discovery of ruins in the region the Mahabharata was set in and dating to the time period, the fictional assumption is now questioned by many, although like many early assumptions by Indologists, Assyriologists, and Egyptologists, it is still generally accepted as some sort of divine inspiration by the followers of those cult-like disciplines.

In the Mahabharata, Krishna and his brothers the Yadavas were driven from their home town of Mathura when the city was attacked, and occupy the ancient island fortress formerly called Kushasthali, which they rebuilt[80] and renamed Dwarka.[81] This fortress served as their base and home through the ensuing war, and after their ally, King Arjuna had won, there were a few decades of peace. However, a fight broke out between the Yadava brothers, which resulted in them all dead, and when Arjuna hear this, he ordered Dwarka to be abandoned, following which it sank into the sea. The island didn't simply become abandoned and eventually sink into the sea, the event leading up to it was described quite traumatically:

> "Winds, dry and strong, and showing gravels, blew from every side. Birds began to wheel, making circles from right to left. The great rivers ran in opposite directions. The horizon on every side seemed to be always covered with fog. Meteors, showering (blazing) coals, fell on the Earth from the sky. The Sun's disc, O king, seemed to be always covered with dust. At its rise, the great luminary of day was shorn of splendour and seemed to be crossed by headless trunks (of human beings). Fierce circles of light were seen every day around both the Sun and the Moon. These circles showed three hues. These edges seemed to be black and rough ans ashy-red in colour. These and many other omens, foreshadowing fear and danger, were seen, O king, and filled the hearts of men with anxiety."[82]

The traditional dating of Krishna's life is between 3228 and 3102 BC. Completely coincidentally, 3,103 BC is the year the Hittite Empire was founded in the ULT, and given that the Hittites conquered the much older and more technologically advanced Hattians, something significant must have happened to cause them to suddenly become aggressive. As the Middle Egyptian Kingdom had collapsed by 3100 BC ULT, we only have fragmented record from the time, however, there is one text that is sometimes dated to the 13th dynasty, the inscriptions in the tomb of Ankhtifi in Mo'alla. This text is generally dated to the end of the 8th Dynasty and may date to that period, however, there is no evidence to support it either way, and internal evidence can also be used to date it to the 13th Dynasty.

> "...I fed Hefat (the town of Mo'alla), Hormer, and [gap in text] in the time when the sky was storms and the land was in the sandstorms of starvation on this sandbank of the Hell (tzw – the Underworld where Apophis, the great serpent, that tried to eat the Sun)."

Little is known from Ankhtifi's life, other than that when he was young, Abydos was still the residence of the Overseer of Upper Egypt, and by the end of his life there was no longer an Overseer of Upper Egypt, and Ankhtifi was the nomarch (count) of Hierakonpolis and Edfu, two of Egypt's southernmost nomes (counties). Whenever Ankhtifi lived, it appears to be at the collapse of a kingdom, which would either mean either the 7th/8th dynasty or 13th dynasty, however, Abydos was not abandoned in the 7th/8th dynasty, yet was abandoned during the 13th dynasty, so why do Egyptologists date it to the 8th dynasty. Simply put, Egyptologists have compressed the 1666 years of the Second Egyptian Dark Age (Second Intermediate Period) into 254 years, forcing multiple dynasties to coexist, creating a complicated mess of competing dynasties that even sometimes used the same capital city at the same time. As a result, there just isn't any time for Ankhtifi's life, and the storms and sandstorms and famine that led to the collapse of Abydos, so Ankhtifi's life is moved to the First Egyptian Dark Age, even though Abydos survived that dark age.

If in fact, Ankhtifi's life was at the beginning of the 13th Dynasty, then he would have lived between approximately 3246 and 3200 BC ULT, at the same time as the traditional dating of Krishna's life. The specific date of the birth of Krishna was calculated by the Indian mathematician and astronomer Aryabhatta in the early 6th century AD, based on the astronomical references found in the Mahabharata, and while the date of his death is also attributed to Aryabhatta it is unclear where it came from, as the Mahabharata only mentioned the alignment of the planets when Krishna was born, not when he died. As Krishna lived so long ago, and the earliest written copy of his life was written in Classical Sanskrit, one must allow for errors in transmission. It was translated, at least once before being written in Sanskrit, and no doubt copied hundreds of times before that in the original language if it was written before that. If it wasn't written before that, then it must have been recited, meaning hundreds of people would have had to learn the story and repeat it verbatim for thousands of years.

Likewise, the records of the ancient Egyptians cannot be accepted as exactly correct down to the year or even decade either due to the gaps that exist in the dark ages, and therefore, these two events could be the same event. If so, then the time of Krishna would be circa 3246 BC in the Universal Long Timeline.

Above and below, are two pictures of the ruins in Harappa, the above photograph shows a close-up of the foreground area of the photograph below.

According to all ancient sources, the author of the Mahabharata was the scribe Vyasa Dwaipayana, who lived sometime between 5000 and 4000 years ago and was said to have been born on an island in the Yamuna River, which is a major tributary of the Ganges in northern India. This places him in the Harappan 1 Phase of the Indus Valley Civilization according to the Conventional Harappan Timeline, and the Harappan 5 Phase in the ULT, so either way Vyasa lived in the Indus Valley Civilization, which included the western Ganges region where the Yamuna River is located, assuming he is not fictional, as most Indologists seem willing to accept.

The island of Dwarka where Krishna and his brothers lived was located off the coast of western India, near the modern city of Dwarka, and does exist as a sunken island with a stone fortress on it, and it is not the only ruin located off the coast of northwest India. In the Gulf of Khambhat, another ruin was discovered in 2001, which has been studied in more detail. This ruin is the remains of a stone metropolis 9 kilometers long, which ran along an ancient shoreline that is now around 40 meters below the waterline, and debris found within it has been carbon-dated to between 7545 and 7490 BC.[83] It seems improbable that this metropolis is unrelated to the ruins of the Indus Valley Civilization or the earlier Mehrgarh Civilization, however, in the Conventional Harappan Timeline there is a gap of 4200 years between this metropolis and the Indus Valley Civilization, and 500 years before the Mehrgarh Civilization's early phase.

Conversely, in the Unified Long Timeline, this coastal metropolis still existed during about 2700 years before the Harappan 1 Phase, however, at the same time as Mehrgarh Civilization's early phase. Several specific artifacts can be used to correlate the Harappan civilization with the Unified Long Timeline, including the Harappan artifacts recovered from Susa, Nippur, and Kish in Sumeria, and the assumed time-period life of Krishna. Only one artifact can be dated to a specific historical person, an artifact from the Harappan 3C phase found in Nippur believed to date to the time of Sargon the Great, king of Akkad, who seized control of Mesopotamia circa 3885 BC ULT. An artifact from the Harappan 3C phase was found in Susa, which would have to date to before the end of the Isin dynasty circa 3227 BC ULT.

The earliest Harappan artifact found in Iraq was found in the ruins of Kish, which in the ULT existed from 7025 BC onward, and therefore this artifact could date to anytime before Sargon the Great. Below are two photos of the ruins in the Gulf of Khambhat, which show their similarity to the ruins of Harappa, Mehrgarh, and Bhirrana.

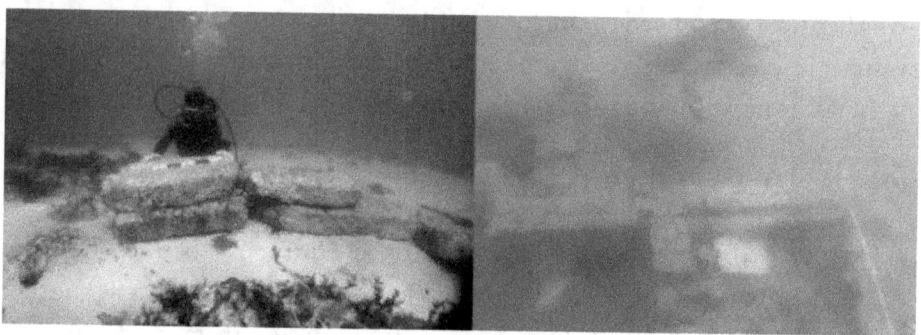

Using the general outline of the Indus Valley Civilization that has been worked out by Indologists, and assuming the life of Krishna was circa 3246 BC ULT, correlating with both the collapse of the Egyptian Middle Kingdom and the end of the Harappan Mature Phase, then the general framework places the Indus Valley Civilization as between 6546 and 2846 BC ULT. Using this timeline, the artifacts found in Mesopotamia do correlate with the Harappan phases they are believed to date to. There can be little doubt that future excavations in India will support the Universal Long Timeline, and hopefully find enough of the Indus Valley Script that we can confirm the stories found in the Classic Sanskrit epics do date to those civilizations.

An additional factor worth considering from a historical perspective, but considered sacrilegious by many Hindus, is the date of life of Rama. Rama was the hero of the Ramayana, which exists in over a dozen significant variations across South and Southeast Asia. While the story, which includes everything from mermaids to space stations in some version, might be largely fictional, it is clearly an ancient story. The hero-king Rama is generally believed to be the king of India that the ancient Greeks and Romans reported as King Dionysus. As early as 1784, Sir William Jones pointed out the clear correlations between the Indian King the Greeks called Dionysus and Rama, consider the following two quotes from his essay 'On the Gods of Greece, Italy, and India.'

> "Meros is said by the Greeks to have been a mountain of India, on which their Dionysus was born, and that Meru is also a mountain near the city of Naishada, or Nysa, called by the Grecian geographers Dionysopolis, and universally celebrated in the Sanskrit poems."

> "...deems Rama to be the same as the Grecian Dionysos, who is said to have conquered India with an army of satyrs, commanded by Pan; and Rama was also a mighty conqueror, and had an army of large monkeys or satyrs, commanded by Maruty, son of Pavan. Rama is also found, in other points, to resemble the Indian Bacchus."

Above is a photograph of the 'Pre-Harappan' ruins at Mehrgarh, and on the next page are the ruins of Bhirrana, which show the multiple layers of construction from different eras. The 'Maruty, son of Pavan' was Hanuman, using an older translation of the name. The idea that Rama was considered important in the time of the Greco-Roman civilization is not in doubt, as the Ramayana dates back to at least this time, however, what is relevant is what the Greek and Roman historians recorded about the date of his life. All Greco-Roman records of Rama, or the Indian Dionysus, or the India Bacchus, depending on the language of the author, place Rama's life at approximately 6,451 years before the time of Alexander the Great, and that there were 154 kings ruling between them. This would be approximately 6600 BC, before the Indus Valley Civilization existed, yet during the Mehrgarh Civilization. This is not what Hindus generally believe, as the current Hindu calculation for his life places it over 2 million years ago. While the Greco-Roman historians like Pliny[84] and Arrian[85] were clearly quoting an Indian source that had access to a significant King list, that source no longer exists. Naturally, just because people believed something 2000 years ago, does not mean it is accurate, however, the fact that there are ruins from the region, dating to the time of these 154 kings does at least make their existence plausible, as someone built those cities.

Brahmi and Kharosthi

Many Vedic gods found their way into the Classic Sanskrit epics, but generally as vague heavenly beings that were only peripherally involved in the stories being told, such as the Vedic Aruna, the personification of the sun-rise from the Vedic Texts, that incarnated as Aruni, a woman who gave birth to two monkey-men in the epics. Not only is are these two unrelated stories, but if there wasn't a similarity of the name no one would ever connect them. Comparing the red-glow of sun-rise to a woman who gives birth to monkey-men, is like comparing the Moon to ... a woman who gives birth to monkey-men.

While the Vedic gods were added to the much later epics does not seem difficult to understand, the fact that they were added so 'inconsistently' as Indologists call it, draws into question just how many people were still even aware of who they were by the Classical Sanskrit era, as most seem to simply be the reuse of the older names, completely unconnected to what the Vedic god actually was. On the other hand, the appearance of the epic gods and heroes in the Vedas allows confirmation that the latter sections of the Vedas were written within the Dravidian speaking culture then dominant in northern India.

The name Rama appears in the Atharva-Veda, however, wasn't a name but a descriptive term, meaning 'dark-colored' or 'black.'[86] There is a mention of 'Devaki's son Krishna' in the Chandogya Upanishad of the Sama Veda, however, this is written in Sutra Language, which would place its origin in India between 1100 and 600 BC. It is generally assumed that this was a reference to the Krishna from the Mahabharata, although the reference is vague. Both Garuda and Vishnu are mentioned in the Rig-veda, but again in the Brahmana Prose sections, like Garuda, which dates to between 1800 and 1100 BC ULT. Vishnu, today one of Hinduism's supreme deities, was not a major god in either the epics or the Vedas, however, based on when he entered into the Rigveda, must have been a Harappan god, although, he appears to be somewhat like the Vedic gods in the epics, and may represent another ancient tradition within South Asia that was also being grandfathered into the epics. Brahma was not mentioned in the Vedic texts until the Maitrayaniya Upanishad of the Yajur-veda, which was composed in Sutra Language, and would, therefore, date to between 1100 and 600 BC ULT. The word shiva exists in the Vedas, but as an epithet meaning 'auspicious,' often linked with the Vedic gods Rudra, or Indra, or Angi. As a result, some Hindus believe that Shiva is Rudra, while others believe he was Indra, and others believe he was Angi. As it is logical to assume the Vedic texts did shape the evolution of Hinduism after they became part of Hinduism, the modern Shiva likely drew from all of them, however, a god named Shiva was not mentioned in the Vedic Texts.

Clearly, a great deal of what is today Hinduism is drawn from the Vedic Texts, such as the Rigvedic concept of Atman, however, the earliest Vedic Text were not created in the same region or culture as the ancient Sanskrit epics. The epics as they exist today, are generally dated by scholars and linguists to the Classic phase of the Sanskrit language before various regional languages rose in India to supplant Sanskrit. Classical Sanskrit was based on the Aṣṭādhyāyī treatise of the ancient Indian grammarian Pāṇini. It is unclear exactly when Pāṇini lived, however, his life is generally dated to between the 7th and 4th-century BC. The various dating methods used for his life are tragically pointless, for example, at one point he mentioned writing in the Aṣṭādhyāyī, which has led many scholars to assume he lived after the Greek conquered Pakistan and introduced the Greek alphabet, meaning he would have to have been alive as late as approximately 320 BC. This is a preposterously-ignorant argument for an academic to make, as the Greeks simply conquered the Persian Empire, which was literate, and had previously annexed parts of Pakistan by 540 BC. Moreover, the ancient Indus Valley Civilization had a form of writing which Indologists acknowledge was in use since at least 3000 BC, yet, the Greeks introduced writing to India after 320 BC?

Little is truly known about the life and death of Pāṇini. It is believed he was born in northern Pakistan to a woman named Dākṣī, and was killed by a lion, much later, in between he reinvented the Sanskrit language. Pāṇini's

Aṣṭādhyāyī was the most advanced grammatical standard ever produced in the ancient world and made use of a technical metalanguage consisting of syntax, morphology, and lexicon. There was nothing like it ever produced for the Persian, Greek, or Latin languages. Grammarian did not come close to reproducing work like it until the 1700s, and even then it is arguable. As it sits, the dating of Pāṇini's life is largely based around the question of when Classical Sanskrit emerged, and Surta Language Sanskrit stopped being used. It was believed universally in ancient times that he lived before Siddhartha Gautama, the Buddha. However, which the entire evolution of the Sanskrit language forced to date to after the Mediterranean Iron Age, circa 1200 BC, this became impossible, and each new generation finds a way to shift him a century of so forward in time, in a few decades he'll probably be that guy that Gandhi knew, after all, if he wasn't talking about Indian writing, or Persian writing, why assume he was talking about Greek writing? English, obviously he was talking about English! Hey, Gandhi knew English... Seriously, the methods used to date his life are that haphazard.

The other piece of internal evidence that was originally used to date Pāṇini's life to after Siddhartha's, before linguists caught on the to maybe 'writing' meant 'Greek' idea, was that in the Aṣṭādhyāyī he mentioned 'kumāraśramaṇa' which as the Buddhist version of nuns, so clearly this was after the life of Siddhartha. But Siddhartha did not invent nuns or even Buddhism! Siddhartha was a Buddha, which means 'teacher,' but not the first in any school of Buddhism, in fact, some schools claim the first Buddha lived over 50,000 years ago! Additionally, the Jain religion, which existed long before Siddharta's life also has nuns, called kumāraśramaṇa, meaning this argument that Buddha invented nuns was as feeble-minded as the 'topsy-turvy' Greek idea. However, none of these preposterous ideas would have even been proposed if scholars weren't forced to date all of Sanskrit's evolution, which linguistically should have taken thousands of years, to just a few hundred.

The issue of 'writing' is even more complicated by the question of not just which script was he talking about, but, did he know how to write himself? Which is a bit like asking did Einstein actually know how to do mathematics, or did he just see some people doing it, and say 'Huh, math? Anyway, did you know E=MC2?' Pāṇini's Aṣṭādhyāyī is undeniably the greatest known grammatical treatise of the ancient world, and yet it is debated whether be bothered to write it down, or just mentioned his musing to some people he knew. Seriously? Yes! It is hotly debated, because, you know... Greek anyone?

The core issue is the fact that virtually no writing exists from ancient India. This does not mean that ancient Indians were not writing, just that if they were, the texts have not survived to the present. There are clay tablets and some engraved stones in the ruins of the Indus Valley Civilization, and there are some later engravings on rocks, but there are no surviving paper, papyrus, parchment, vellum, or palm-leaf texts surviving to the time of Pāṇini. In South Asia, the most common writing medium has been palm-leafs, but due to the humidity across the subcontinent the leaves generally deteriorate within a decade, and therefore someone needs to be constantly making copies in order for the texts to not be lost. Any interruption of the copiest's work would lead to the rapid disappearance of the text. So, wars, storms, and everything in between have ravaged almost all ancient Indian literature, and even major works like the Vedas and epics have regional differences as portions have been lost in some areas.

The question of what script was Pāṇini talking about is central to the question of when Pāṇini lived, and if one is forced to accept that all of Sanskrit's dialects evolved and supplanted the former dialects within a few centuries, with the conventional Indo-European timeline demands, mainly due to the Mitanni presence in Mesopotamia circa 1500 BC CMT, then one needs Classical Sanskrit to be as recent as possible in order to leave as much time as possible for the old Sanskrit dialects to have formed and been abandoned. However, the conventional timelines contain far too many inconsistencies to be taken seriously and in the ULT there is more than enough time for Pāṇini to have lived before Siddhartha.

The life of Siddhārtha Gautama is universally date to sometime between 563 and 400 BC, although the specific years are debated. This means that Classical Sanskrit was in use for approximately 1000 years when it was finally replaced by the emergence of regional dialects. This timeline of Sanskrit in

India, parallels the thousand years of Latin in Western Europe before it was replaced by regional dialects, and the thousand years of Classical Arabic before it was replaced by regional dialects. There is no thousand-year rule about the regionalization of languages, however, the parallels are notable. Clearly, in Europe, the regionalization of the Romance languages was influenced by the collapse of the Roman Empire, and invasions of Germanic tribes, as the collapse of the Caliphate and the invasions of Mongols and Turks no doubt impacted the regionalization of Arabic. In India, the cause of the regionalization is less clear, however, is generally tied to the collapse of the Gupta Dynasty, and invasions of the Huns from Central Asia.

However, unlike what happened in Europe with the fracturing of Latin into the Romance languages, which nevertheless continued to use the Latin alphabet, in India, the Sanskrit derived Indo-Aryan language each developed a unique script. This points to the Indians being in at least one way, very different from the Europeans of the time, as the Indians obviously had a relatively high literacy rate. In Western Europe, as Christianity took over, literacy rates fell. This was because of several specific causes, such as mass deaths from diseases that were rampant at the time, but also as Christians actively burned libraries, something the Indians apparently did not do, at least on the same scale. The maintenance of the Latin alphabet was due to the fact that there was very little literacy in any West European language, and so West Europeans that wanted to read and write, did so in Latin. In India, the rapid regionalization of the Brahmi script into local scripts was possible because texts needed to be copied constantly, and so each new development of the script would be standard across all texts in that language within a decade or so.

The script being used in India the Classical era of Greco-Roman civilization was the Brahmi script, which looks vaguely like Greek, which is where the idea that the Indians learned to write from the Greeks came from, however, the ancient Greeks themselves never reported this, it is a theory proposed in the 1700s. The majority of Brahmi script carvings that have been found are from Northern India and are written in Sanskrit, however, this is not the only Indian language written in Brahmi, there are also Brahmi carvings in Tamil and Ceylonese in Southern India and Sri Lanka, which date back to the same period. Since the 1970s the idea that the Brahmi script even originated in Northern India has come under attack by Tamils and Sri Lankans, although that had always been the assumption. The oldest Sanskrit Brahmi carvings that can be firmly dated in Northern India date to around 250 BC, while in Southern India Tamil Brahmi inscriptions have been both radiometrically and carbon-dated to dated between 520 and 490 BC, and in Sri Lanka the Ceylonese Brahmi inscriptions are dated to around the same time.

Naturally, this does not prove that the script was invented in Southern India and adopted by the northerners, however, that is one possibility. The more relevant fact is that three versions of Brahmi were already different at the earliest point we have found examples of them. Both the Tamil and Ceylonese variants had symbols for sounds made in Dravidian languages that are not present in Indo-Aryan languages, although the language being written in the Ceylonese Brahmi script was Indo-Aryan, obviously with a large number of Dravidian loanwords. Wherever this script originated, it had already been adopted and adapted by two, possibly three, cultures circa 500 BC, and therefore must have been in use in at least one of these cultures for a significant period of time. Somewhere, a culture had developed this script, and become so influential that their neighbors or trading partners started using the script, and by 500 BC it may have already been spread across the Indian subcontinent and was clearly widespread in the south.

The Brahmi script was a fairly complex script in comparison to the Phoenician, Aramaic, Greek, and Latin scripts used to the west, and bore no resemblance to the older Egyptian, Cuneiform, or Chinese scripts. Brahmi is an abugida in which each letter represents a consonant, while vowels are written with an obligatory diacritic. The following is a chart of the symbols used in around 250 BC when the Greeks first translated it. Each of the 34 consonants could have one of 8 diacritics, meaning there was a total of 272 symbols. This is a notable difference from the 24 letters of the Greek alphabet, 21 letters of the archaic Latin alphabet, 22 letters of the Phoenician abjad, and 22 letters of the Aramaic abjad.

	-a	-ā	-i	-ī	-u	-ū	-e	-o
k-	+	₣	ƒ	₣	ŧ	ŧ	₮	₮
kh-	ꓩ	T	T	T	ꓩ	ꓩ	ꓞ	ꓞ
g-	ʌ	ʀ	ʀ	ʀ	ʌ	ʌ	ʌ	ʌ
gh-	ʮ	ʮ	ʮ	ʮ	ʮ	ʮ	ʮ	ʮ
ṅ-	⸦	E	⸦	⸦	⸦	⸦	⸦	⸦
c-	ɗ	ɗ	ɗ	ɗ	ɗ	ɗ	ɗ	ɗ
ch-	ɸ	ɸ	ɸ	ɸ	ɸ	ɸ	ɸ	ɸ
j-	ɛ	ɛ	ɛ	ɛ	ɛ	ɛ	ɛ	ɛ
jh-	ʮ	ʮ	ʮ	ʮ	ʮ	ʮ	ʮ	ʮ
ñ-	ħ	ħ	ħ	ħ	ħ	ħ	ħ	ħ
ṭ-	⸦	ɛ	⸦	⸦	⸦	⸦	⸦	⸦
ṭh-	O	O	O	O	Q	Q	O	O
ḍ-	ɾ	ɾ	ɾ	ɾ	ɾ	ɾ	ɾ	ɾ
ḍh-	ƍ	ƍ	ƍ	ƍ	ƍ	ƍ	ƍ	ƍ
ṇ-	I	I	I	I	I	I	I	I
t-	λ	λ	λ	λ	λ	λ	λ	λ
th-	⊙	⊙	⊙	⊙	⊙	⊙	⊙	⊙
d-	⟩	⟩	⟩	⟩	⟩	⟩	⟩	⟩
dh-	D	D	D	D	D	D	D	D
n-	⊥	⊥	⊥	⊥	⊥	⊥	⊥	⊥
p-	ʟ	ʟ	ʟ	ʟ	ʟ	ʟ	ʟ	ʟ
ph-	b	b	b	b	b	b	b	b
b-	□	□	□	□	□	□	□	□
bh-	⊓	⊓	⊓	⊓	⊓	⊓	⊓	⊓
m-	⋈	⋈	⋈	⋈	⋈	⋈	⋈	⋈
y-	⊥	⊥	⊥	⊥	⊥	⊥	⊥	⊥
r-	l	ɾ	ɾ	ɾ	ʟ	ʟ	ꓶ	T
l-	ꓩ	J	J	J	J	J	J	J
v-	ɓ	ɓ	ɓ	ɓ	ɓ	ɓ	ɓ	ɓ
ś-	ʌ	ʌ	ʌ	ʌ	ʌ	ʌ	ʌ	ʌ
ṣ-	t	ɛ	ɛ	ɛ	ʟ	ʟ	ʟ	ɛ
s-	ᴧ	ᴧ	ᴧ	ᴧ	ᴧ	ᴧ	ᴧ	ᴧ
h-	ʟ	ʟ	ʟ	ʟ	ʟ	ʟ	ʟ	ʟ
ḷ-	ꓩ	ꓩ	ꓩ	ꓩ	ꓩ	ꓩ	ꓩ	ꓩ

The difference between Brahmi and the western scripts is so significant it is difficult to believe that anyone could think Brahmi is based on the western alphabets, regardless of whether there are some physical similarities in the shapes of some Brahmi symbols and Greek letters. In the end, there are only so many shapes that one can quickly draw, and most alphabets have some similar symbols in them. As complex as the 272 symbols may seem, the system is remarkably simple once learned, and provides exacting and very specific sounds, unlike Latin, which requires accents and additional symbols to represent most languages, or, clairvoyance in the case of English, which is impossible to sound out without first learning the language. Which sound does the letter J correspond to in English, or G, C, S, V, W, D, T, Y, X, A, O, E, I, Y, U, or R? It depends on the local dialect, and the actual sounds may be reversed in one country versus another, such as V and W in Indian versus American English, the completely different pronunciation of R in British versus Canadian English. In Brahmi this was not possible, however, that is also why so many scripts developed from it as the languages fragmented.

The various Mediterranean scripts that were used in the iron age are all believed to be derived from the Phoenician script, as the Phoenicians colonized the Mediterranean during the iron age, and traded with everyone. The Greek, Latin, Aramaic, Tifinagh, Etruscan, and other Mediterranean scripts are all believed to be based on Phoenician and generally work the same way, either as an abjad or an alphabet, and either way with only 22 to 26 letters, nothing complex like Brahmi. The origin of the Phoenician script is itself unknown, however, it has variously been traced to ancient Egyptian Hieroglyphs or Hieratic, Minoan Linear-A, or the Proto-Sinaitic script, which itself is virtually unknown. The wide-scale adoption and adaption of the Phoenician script throughout the Mediterranean, even replacing older scripts like Linear-B and Cuneiform is believed to have happened because it was simple, which contradicts the idea that Brahmi developed from it, or its child scripts Aramaic and Greek.

Like the western scripts, Brahmi is a system of abstract symbols, and there is no surviving pictographic phase. In all known regions where writing was developed, it was preceded by a pictographic system. In Egyptian, Hierarchic developed from Hieroglyphs, and then later developed into the more abstract Demotic. In Iraq, Cuneiform developed from a pictographic script which was itself preceded by small clay tokens in the image of birds, fish, and cow's heads. Chinese Characters developed from an earlier system of pictograms which have been found on ancient Chinese oracle bones. Minoan Hieroglyphs were in use before the development of the Linear-A script. There is debate about where the shift first took place, and which ancient script influenced which, but the pattern of development was identical, and even if the Sumerian, Egyptian, and Minoan systems of writing were all influencing each other, Chinese is believed to have developed in isolation, much like Mayan in the Americas.

A similar development process can be seen in the Mayan script, which developed from pictures into a collection of glyphs, which while still resembling pictures and sometimes used to mean the picture drawn, also meant specific sounds in the Mayan language, allowing for the pronunciation of abstract concepts which cannot be drawn. This jump from drawing a fish or a cow-head, to having sounds that represent abstract concepts is what separates a series of pictures from a written script. Many concepts cannot be drawn, like blue, or cold, or 'this is how you bake bread.' Pictures and tokens can still be useful, if a token of a cows head can be exchanged for a cow, then it is essentially money but does not allow the expression of stories that can be read thousands of years later. Human remains date back hundreds of thousands of years, but if our ancestors were telling epic tales back then, those stories are lost forever, but, some of what the Sumerians and Egyptians recorded still survives, due to the leap from pictures to symbols.

On the other hand, Brahmi simply appears, fully formed in its earliest known varieties, indicating that the majority of its developmental history must be missing. It is clear that it was not being carved into the sides of massive stone blocks like in Egypt, or pressed and baked into clay tablets like in Mesopotamia, and therefore one is left with the notion that the script was mainly used for writing on palm leaves, or some other medium that has been lost to time. Of course if one assumes that someone was writing something, one is still left with the question of what? Brahmi was not a simple writing system designed for scratch names and lists of items like the Phoenician script. Brahmi was clearly designed artificially or developed over a long period, to exactly replicate the entire range of sounds that were possible, with 272 just for the Sanskrit language. This means that the entire range of human thoughts and ideas could have been written in the language. In Phoenician and other abjads there are a large number of sounds that are implied, which is fine if you know the language, but leads to several debates among linguists today as we cannot be sure what many of the words mean.

Abjads do not include letters for the vowels, and therefore even well known ancient texts written in abjads can be confusing. For example, the Jewish Torah, which is one of the most well studied ancient texts, yet the meaning of approximately a quarter of the words is unclear. There are accepted assumptions about what they mean, and a great deal of debate within Rabbinical literature going back over a thousand years. Christian translators usually fall back to the ancient Greek translation done at the Library of Alexandria when they aren't she what a word means, however even the ancient Greeks didn't always know what the words meant. A simple example of this is found near the beginning of the Torah, in Genesis 1:21: תנין גדול. What do these two words mean? The ancient Greeks translated them as 'great whales,' as they did not know what the Torah said. This translation was subsequently placed into the King James translation, as the language professors at Oxford did not know what the words meant. Depending on the translation גדול can mean great, large, number, intense, loud, older, important, god, or haughty, while תנין can mean dragon, dinosaur, sea monster, river monster, serpent, or snake, but not a whale. So what do these two words mean: the great dragon, large dinosaur, number of sea monsters, intense river monster, loud serpent, older snake, important dragon, dinosaur god, haughty sea monster, or some other thing entirely? None of this vagary was possible using the Brahmi script.

To farther complicate the issue for scripts in Northern India, there was another script used to write Sanskrit, and it was at least partly based on Aramaic. This other Sanskrit script is called Kharosthi and was in use in Pakistan alongside Brahmi when the Greeks conquered the region, and continued in use until the 3rd century AD, dying out a couple of centuries before Brahmi in South Asia, however, continued in use in Central Asia until the 7th-century. Like Brahmi, Kharosthi was an abugida, however, it was influenced by Aramaic according to virtually every scholar that has studied it. Kharosthi also does not distinguish between long and short vowels, meaning that it is a simplified abugida in comparison to Brahmi, and was likely created to make a 'modern-looking' script, that looked more like Aramaic, the official script of the Persian Empire after Darius' reforms around 500 BC. Naturally, this raises the question of why two different, and radically different scripts were both developed from Aramaic in Pakistan under Persian rule. Logically, one of them wasn't, and since we have discovered Brahmi carvings predating Darius, we can now state categorically that Brahmi predated Kharosthi, likely by many centuries, as it would have taken time to develop.

Unlike Brahmi, Kharosthi does not appear to have been used extensively in the south, where the Tamils continued to use Tamil Brahmi script until the 5th century AD, which has been found scattered throughout the regions they traded with, ranging from Egypt to Thailand. It is equally possible that the Brahmi script developed in southern India or Sri Lanka, and was later adopted by the Northern Indians, or, that it was already in use in Northern India long before the Persians occupied Pakistan. Unfortunately, this debate is largely dominated by national and ethic arguments, as there is no clear evidence supporting either option at this time. Regardless, it is a complex system and must have been in development long before the 'final' versions of it that appear at the beginning of recorded history across South Asia. Someone must have been writing something phonetically complex in order to need a script like this.

Few documents are complex enough to need so many specific sounds, however, the Vedas are one such collection of documents. The various forms of Sanskrit that evolved over the millennia are only known today because they were written down in the classic era in Brahmi and Kharosthi, two scripts capable of showing the differences in pronunciation that different texts were compiled in. If they were written using the Greek or Latin alphabets all of this complexity would have been lost, and we would assume they were written shortly before the time of Siddhartha. This issue of the limits of scripts to record the progress of dialects makes most proto-historic era text impossible to date. Consider for example Sanchuniathon of Beirut, who was, according to his ancient Greek biographers a Phoenician scholar that lived sometime before the Battle of Troy, circa 1200 BC. He apparently wrote a history of the Phoenicians, and a history of the Jews, neither of which survive to the present. His works were translated into Greek by Philo of Byblos in the 1st century AD, whose works also do not survive. What does survive are a few quotes of Philo's translation in Eusebius' Praeparatio Evangelica, written circa 313 AD. Assuming Sanchuniathon actually lived and wrote the works attributed to him, and Philo translated his works accurately, and Eusebius quoted them accurately, how, after at least one translation, assuming one were able to read Praeparatio Evangelica in Greek, and with most of Sanchuniathon's texts missing, could one know when he lived, based on his dialect?

Furthermore, there is no reason to believe either Philo or Eusebius were treating Sanchuniathon fairly, as both were quoting him to push their own religious agendas. Compounding this is the fact that Sanchuniathon claimed his information on earliest history was translated into Phoenician from the pillars in the Temple of Amun, which would themselves date back to at least the 11th Dynasty of Egypt, circa 3502 to 3459 BC ULT (2061 to 1991 BC CET) during the Middle Kingdom, and therefore there was at least one more layer of translation that has been lost before one even read Sanchuniathon's original work. In the early Christian era after Eusebius, Sanchuniathon was often dismissed as a fool of even a hoax by Philo, and as a result, Philo's works weren't copied, and once the papyrus they were written on had deteriorated, they were lost. One of the primary points Christians used to discredit him was that his early era of the gods was so similar to Hesiod's, which they assumed he was plagiarizing, and Hesiod had lived around 700 BC, so how could Sanchuniathon have plagiarized him over 500 years earlier. In all fairness, the same could be said of the original Greek translation of the Torah, which has most of the same gods in it as Hesiod, so: did Moses plagiarize Hesiod too? or was it the Rabbis at the Library of Alexandria? or did Hesiod maybe not invent the story but simply tell one version of a very old tale?

Interest in Sanchuniathon resurfaced during the enlightenment, however, with no evidence supporting his existence he was more of a historical question mark. Archaeology of the 1900s seems to have vindicated him though, as excavations in Ugarit (near modern Latakia in Syria) have confirmed the Phoenicians or their ancestors had worshiped the same collection of gods that Sanchuniathon described since at least 1800 BC, and trading with Egypt since at least the Middle Kingdom when Amun was the dominant god. While this is not itself evidence for the existence of Sanchuniathon, it is evidence that some intermediary had existed between the ancient Phoenicians and Philo, and therefore Sanchuniathon's existence is considered likely by most historians.

Two ancient civilizations left us enough translatable texts, over a long enough period of time to observe multiple dialect shifts, similar to that which is observed in Sanskrit and Avestan: Egypt, and Mesopotamia. In Egypt, the Old, Middle, and New Kingdoms each had a distinct dialect of Egyptian, although it is harder to detect than with the Indo-Iranian languages as Hieroglyphs and Hieratic do not convey the exact sounds of the language like the abugidas of Southern Asia. In Mesopotamia, a string of Semitic languages and dialects existed: Akkadian, Old Babylonian, and Neo-Babylonian in the south, and Akkadian, Old Assyrian, and Neo-Assyrian in the north. Both Old Babylonian and Old Assyrian were regional dialects of Akkadian, but emerged as separate languages circa 3350 BC ULT (1800 BC CMT).

Using the better understood Egyptian timeline as a metric, consider that there was 1443 (ULT) or 625 (CET) years between the emergence of the Old and Middle Kingdoms, and then 1922 (ULT) or 512 (CET) years between the emergence of the Middle and New Kingdoms. Therefore, there were either 3365 or 1137 years, depending on the timeline used for the transition from Old through Middle to Late Egyptian. That was simply two dialects, and even the most conservative timeline Egyptologists can imagine gives over 1100 years, and according to the ancient Egyptians was over 3300 years. Sanskrit went through five or six of these shifts, depending on one's interpretation of the two Rigvedic dialects, before the shift to Classical Sanskrit, with should have happened by 500 BC at the latest. This means that the time when the Old-Rigvedic texts were composed should have been 2 to 3 time the lengths of the dialects shifts in Egypt, in other words somewhere between the very broad range of 10,600 and 2800 BC, but certainly not after 1500 BC when the Mitanni were invading the Middle East according to the conventional Mesopotamian timeline. Adding the Avestan dialects to the timeline as precursors to Sanskrit as most linguists agree on, would add another two or three dialects to the timeline since the life of Zoroaster, placing him anywhere between 14,000 and 3900 BC, but certainly not 50 years before Aristotle, who himself reported Zoroaster having lived between 7200 and 7300 BC. Does anyone actually believe the 'father of logic' was that stupid?

Clearly, evolutionary-linguistics is not an exact science, as demonstrated by the preceding wide range of possible points in time, nevertheless, the minimum plausible dates, using the already impossibly short conventional timelines already show that Sanskrit and Avestan must be much older than many historians are willing to consider. These purely linguistic estimates show that if anything the framework of Indo-Iranian cultures proposed in this work may be too conservative, and much older cultures were the sources of these texts, however, if there were older cultures using horses, we have yet to find their remains, moreover, the estimated time period of the use of Old-Avestan at approximately the same time that the ancients reported that Zoroaster lived seems to confirm this framework as at least more historically valid than the existing system being taught.

Nevertheless, Brahmi appears fully formed in the oldest rock-carvings it is found in, and while it must have had a developmental phase, this phase is entirely missing from the ruins we have found to date. Logically, either Brahmi is derived from another, older script, or it evolved completely independently, in which case we would expect to find a pictographic ancestor script as we have found in other regions where scripts evolved independently. This missing pictographic script could be missing because it was only ever used to write on something that deteriorates quickly, like palm leaves, however, it could also be missing from the records because it has simply been ignored.

As the Greek and Roman historians recorded, the Indians had a list of 154 kings preceding Alexander going back to the time of Rama, circa 6600 BC, it is logical to assume this would have been written down, and one of the earliest documents to have been written down. If it was a king list of north Indian kings from 6600 BC onward, then in either the CHT or ULT, it would date back to the Mehrgarh civilization and likely would have been written in the Indus script, also called Harappan script, which has been proven to actually predate the Indus Valley Civilization in the CHT, dating back to the Mature Mehrgarh Phase. The script appears late in the mature Mehrgarh phase, circa 3500 BC CHT, meaning in either timeline it was over 1500 years after the recorded life of Rama. Of course, the oldest surviving examples cannot be assumed to be the very first attempts to write something down, in fact, only a small sample of Indus Script can be assumed to have survived to the present. Nevertheless, the remnants of the Indus script that survive to the present only become common in the Mature Harappan phase between 4150 and 3450 BC ULT (2600 and 1900 BC CHT). The Indus script disappeared abruptly at the end of the mature phase of the Indus civilization, circa 3446 BC ULT (1900 BC CHT).

The sudden disappearance of the script is strange as the civilization itself did not suddenly disappear, the implication is that they had switched to writing on a new medium such as palm leaves or copper plates. There is of course the evidence found within the Harappan ruins themselves that the Harappans were using a medium like papyrus or parchment to write on, the seals. Seals are used to seal documents with wax, these documents have always been scrolls, in every known civilization that used seals, and therefore it is a natural conclusion that the Harappans were using some kind of papyrus-like medium.

A few pieces of pottery do survive from later periods that have similar symbols of them and have been dated to as late as 1528 BC using thermoluminescence dating,[87] which implies the script was still in use 2000 years after the end of the mature phase, and around 1000 years before the appearance of Brahmi script. Another late inscription of the Indus script was found in southern India dating to the early 2nd-millennium BC,[88] indicating that the script was used in at least two regions were the Brahmi script would later emerge.

The earliest Brahmi scripts that survive to the present are rock carvings and graffiti, neither of which is a true measure of a society. In later periods it is known that the Indians were writing on palm leaves, which deteriorate quickly but are cheap and plentiful, making them an excellent medium for most documents. Documents that were intended to survive for a long time were engraved in copper, unfortunately, these plates would have been melted down by anyone that stole them, and so would disappear quickly after the collapse of any kingdom. If either medium was in use from the Harappan Late Phase, then it would have allowed the Indus script to evolved into the Brahmi script without leaving a trace. In either event, the Brahmi script was in use across the Indian subcontinent by 500 BC, and therefore was likely the script the ancient king list was recorded on when the Greeks arrived. If the ancient king lists or any other ancient documents from between 3500 and 500 BC were engraved on copper plates, they have likely deteriorated by now if they weren't melted at some point, however, it is still possible that some may be found. At this time the oldest known surviving copper plate inscriptions found in India date back to the 3rd-century BC.

Dating the Harappans

Unlike in Egypt and Iraq, there has been a great deal of interest in dating the Indus Valley Civilization using scientific methods, unfortunately, the results have been so contradictory that it leaves one scratching their head. The initial timeline developed by Indologists in the 1920s was based largely on the assumption that the timeline used in Assyriology was correct, which itself was based on the timeline of Egyptian civilization popularized by James Henry Breasted around the turn of the century. Breasted had become the first American citizen to earn a degree in Egyptology, at the University of Berlin, and then wrote a series of books that tried to integrate the history of the world into the biblical timeline, specifically the Biblical timeline of the Methodist college he had started his academic career in. By the 1920s he was the head of the Oriental Institute in Chicago, which he had founded and was funded by the Rockefellers. He used the institute's wealth and influence to provided funding to Egyptologists, Assyriologists, and Indologists that supported his biblical-based timeline for world history.

Modern Egyptologist likes to ignore the fact that he was a biblical fundamentalist. His compressed timeline was developed by Christians and thoroughly debunked by Egyptologists in the 1800s, and yet by the 1920s was considered the standard timeline, even though the surviving earlier generation of Egyptologists, like Petrie, dismissed it as impossible. After that generation of Egyptologists died out the current Biblical chronology of the Conventional Egyptian Timeline became the only timeline even taught in universities, even though it is neither what the ancient Egyptians recorded, nor even possible. In the 1920s Breasted traveled extensively visiting India, Mesopotamia (British Iraq), Syria, Palestine, and Egypt, to garner supporters for his timeline.

The Indologists in the 1920s through 1950s that worked out the timeline of the Indus Valley Civilization were dependent on the Assyriologist that were significantly funded by Breasted and therefore worked out a timeline for the entire civilization that spanned 3300 to 1300 BC. This timeline placed the birth of the Indus Valley Civilization in the same year that Breasted's own theories placed the birth of Egypt: 3300 BC. This civilization was immediately assumed by many Hindus to be the ruins of the ancient civilization of the epics, however, that would mean they should span the time of over 2 million years ago until at least 3100 BC, the time of Krishna. Below is a picture of Breasted (pictured left), with his team sailing from Bombay (modern Mumbai) in India to Basra in Iraq, in 1920.

The very small time period that the ruins are attributed never seemed right to Hindus who assumed the Indologists were allowing a western bias to shape their theories, which, of course, is correct whether the theories are correct or not, as the chronology they worked out was dependent on the timeline of Mesopotamia, who the Harappans were trading with. This has resulted in many Indians and Pakistanis wanting scientific dating as opposed to the 'hearsay' approach that the early Indologist were forced to use. In the 1960s samples were taken from the ruins at Harappa and tested using radiocarbon dating techniques that were new at the time, and apparently confirmed the approximate dates of the Conventional Harappan Timeline, however, these samples were taken from the exposed upper levels of the ruins, and to date, no excavations of the lower levels have been possible as they are built below the waterline. This is a significant issue. Indologists claim that the civilization failed because the climate changed and the water table dropped, yet, the

Indus is higher today than when Harappa was initially built, and therefore the foundation must go back to before the Indus river rose to its current level.

Between 1986 and 1996 a large number of carbon-dating tests were carried out from sites across the region which are described in western papers as confirming the CHT, however, they are still only taken from the upper exposed levels of the sites, as the water level is too high to excavate to the lower levels. Clearly, the water levels were even higher at the peak of the civilizations, as, like in Sumer, the cities were built up well above the surrounding land which must have been at least seasonally flooded. Most of the major sites in the Sind region are 12 meters (36 feet) above the surrounding land, implying that this civilization experienced significant flooding for a long period of time. Based on the fact that we have still never been able to excavate the lower levels of these cities, it seems irrational to attempt to date them at all, and the Harappan Phases of the CHT are most-likely just the tail end of this civilization, which based on the rising water levels, likely dates back well over 10,000 years.

The carbon dating that supposedly supported the CHT, did include a large number of earlier dates, so many in fact, that the CHT became untenable and was quietly changed by Indologists to 5000 BC to 1300 BC. Western history books still use the early Indologist's assumptions about the Indus Valley Civilization starting no earlier than Breasted's version of the Egyptian Civilization: 3300 BC, however Indologists no longer use these dates. Currently, the mainstream of Indology places the 'Early Food Producing Era' of the Harappan Civilization at between 6500 and 5000 BC, with the Early Harappan Phase then running to 2600 BC when the early Indologists found correlations with the Assyriologist's timeline. This chronology doesn't make a great deal of sense, as many of the earliest sites appear no less advanced than the sites of the Mature Phase, but the Mature Phase can't be moved as it is tied to the Conventional Mesopotamian Timeline.

An example of the problem in Indology is Mehrgarh, a ruin in Pakistan that was not discovered until 1974, and therefore the early Indologists did not clairvoyantly decree a date for it. Mehrgarh was a city that existed for a long time, and ran the full development process of the Indus and other civilizations, through early, mature, and late phases, which spanned approximately 5500 years. In many respects the Mehrgarh civilization was exactly the same as the rest of the Indus Valley Civilization, even sharing identical dentistry techniques, however, the carbon dating of Mehrgarh places almost its entire history before the early Indologists claimed that the Early Harappan Phase began. The Mature Mehrgarh Phase ends at approximately 3300 BC, and the Late Mehrgarh Phase ends at approximately 2600 BC, which coincidentally, is approximately the timeline the ULT requires for the Indus Valley Civilization to have existed. It seems bizarre that anyone could believe that this completely unique civilization developed all alone and went through the entire life-cycle of the Indus Valley Civilization, but then died and the Indus Valley Civilization started from scratch and redeveloped everything identically to the Mehrgarh Civilization. Two different civilizations, where the latter inherited some of the technology of the former perhaps, but this is not the case.

The Early Harappans did not have the technology of the Late Mehrgarhans, they had the technology of the Early Mehrgarhans, who had not existed for thousands of years, and then reinvented everything exactly the same. The idea is so preposterous that Indologist adjusted the timespan of the Indus Valley Civilization, taking it back from 3300 BC to 5000 BC to allow for this earlier Mehrgarhan technology to enter into the Early Harappan Phase, however, the two timelines still don't overlap, and now the Early Harappans are some-how getting Early Mehrgarhan technology from the Mature Mehrgarhans. While this is better, it is still not correct, it would be like a modern country only exporting 500 to 2000-year-old technology. The Mehrgarhans were no longer using those techniques, so how were they exporting them? Some of the technology can be dismissed as parallel thinking, the climate and resources are the same regardless of when they lived, but some of the technologies are specific, like the techniques used to make fake eye-balls or to drill holes in teeth, and these cannot be dismissed as simply parallel development. These cultures were clearly around at the same time.

Other ruins have been found more recently that show this was part of a wide-scale civilization across the region, such the excavations at Bhirrana,89 Haryana, where ruins were excavated between 2006 and 2009 that have been carbon-dated to between 7380 and 6201 BC.90 These ruins also show what is considered 'advanced pottery' like the pottery of the Mature Indus and Mature Mehrgarh Phases, yet, again, cannot be Harappan as it is too early according to the CHT, yet, it is completely in sync with the ULT.

The Minoans

In the Mediterranean, another early culture had developed writing that also has not been deciphered yet, the Minoans as they are called today. The Minoan civilization died out before the rise of the Classical Greek civilization and was rediscovered around 1900 by a British archaeologist named Arthur Evans. He noted several parallels between Minoan and Egyptian civilization, and worked out a rough timeline of the Minoans based on the known history of Egypt, dividing the civilization into Pre-Palatial, Proto-Palatial, Neo-Palatial, and Post-Palatian periods, which roughly corresponded to the Old Kingdom, Middle Kingdom, New Kingdom, and Late Period of Egyptian history. His original work used the dates of Egyptian civilization that was universally accepted a the time, before the rise of Breasted's para-biblical timeline, and so early works listed the Minoan Civilization as beginning during the time of the Old Kingdom, around 4600 BC, as there were some huge cut-stone blocks used for building in Crete that looked like the style of cut-stone masonry of the Old Kingdom. This dating was adjusted to Breasted's para-biblical timeline once it became dominant in the mid-1900s, and so now most books incorrectly state that Evans used dates that support Breasted's timeline.

For cultures that are known to have been trading, there is surprisingly little evidence of contact until the Egyptian Middle Kingdom. The earliest Minoan artifacts have been found in northern Egypt from the reign of Amenemhat II of the 12th Dynasty, circa 3459 to 3246 BC ULT (1991 to 1803 BC CET). These artifacts are believed to date to the early Proto-Palatial period of Evan's timeline, around the same time that the Minoans began using the Linear A script. The Minoan hieroglyphs were in use earlier, by at least the late Pre-Palatial period. Neither script appears to be a direct import from either Egyptian hieroglyphs or hieratic, however, it is generally assumed both scripts were influenced by the Egyptian scripts.

There are earlier signs of contact between the Minoans and the Egyptians, such as seals found in Crete that look similar to the seals used in Egypt in the 1st Egyptian Dark Age (1st Intermediate Period), however, virtually nothing survives from that time period, and so it is the most poorly understood period of Dynastic history. Nevertheless, the seals are considered to prove contact between the Minoans and Egyptians between 4003 to 3502 BC ULT (2900 to 2300 BC CET), in the middle of the Pre-Palatial Period of Cretan history. Earlier contact is assumed during the Old Kingdom, as the oldest stone blocks in Crete resemble the oldest stone blocks in Egypt, however, this is not considered conclusive proof of contact.

Later contact between the Minoans and other cultures are documented, such as the Minoan style frescoes discovered in ancient Canaanite ruins at Tel Kabri in Israel in 2015. The ruins of Tel Kabri where the frescoes have been found dated to the Middle Bronze era, dated anywhere between 2100 and 1550 BC, however, the site itself dates back as early as 6400 BC. The style of the frescoes matches the style of the late Neo-Palatial Period, and therefore is approximately the same time period in either timeline. The dating of this entire period is hampered by the dispute between researchers in Crete and Egypt over the dating of the eruption of the Thera volcano on the island of Santorini in the Aegean sea.

The dating for the eruption of Thera has been debated for most of the last century, with a variety of views entering into the debate. The dating of the eruption is central to the dating of the late Minoan civilization, as it makes the beginning of the decline of the civilization. The volcanic eruption covered most of Crete in several meters of ash, and ash fall from Thera is recorded as far as northern Egypt. This ash is problematic as the Egyptologists decided it was circa 1500 BC, based on which dynasty the ash fell during, however, no one else seems to understand that Egyptologists know everything, and Aegean Prehistorians argued it was at least a century earlier, based on the pottery being used at the time when the eruption buried entire towns. This debate between Egyptologists and Aegean Prehistorians continued until the 1970s when early carbon-dated samples from the region confirmed the Egyptologists' view. Aegen Prehistorians rejected the carbon-dated data, insisting that it must be from circa 1650 BC, not circa 1500 BC, and in the 1990s new calibrated carbon-dating methods were used which confirmed the Aegen Prehistorians' view, which lead to the

Egyptologists' rejecting the new carbon-dated data. As it stands, the best current data shows that plants buried in the ash from the eruption took place between 1627 and 1600 BC. However, this is still debated by the Egyptologists, because, if the eruption took place over a century earlier than the Conventional Egyptian Timeline states, then there is at least one century missing from the history of Egypt, and they simply don't want to re-examine the timeline again. Last time the Rockerfellers paid to have the history of Egypt changed, whose going to pay for it now?

In any event, the timeline of Crete is not significantly effected whether it is viewed on the Conventional Aegean Timeline or the Universal Long Timeline. In either timeline, most of the early Minoan history remains unknown. The Minoans appear to have been in contact with the Egyptians by the Old Kingdom, but this cannot be proven conclusively by the evidence so far found. They were using similar seals during the 1st Egyptian Dark Age, which would mean they were most likely trading by 3500 BC ULT (2300 CAT). Cretan hieroglyphs are found in the strata after 3363 BC ULT (1900 BC CAT) indicating a significant Egyptian influence by this time, and Minoan artifacts are found in Egypt confirming the trade between the cultures. This was during the Egyptian Middle Kingdom when the Egyptians dug the great canal that flooded the Fayum Depression west of modern Cairo.

This period of trade between the Egyptians and Minoans seems to have continued throughout the later periods of Minoan history, as well as trade with the Canaanite cultures in the modern states of Lebanon, Israel, and Syria. The Minoan civilization seems to have been rocked by several massive earthquakes during its existence, which was followed by massive rebuilding eras. These rebuilding eras and the changing pottery styles have led to a more developed timeline of Minoan history that divides the civilization's existence into around a dozen eras. The original era model had nine eras: Early Minoan 1, 2, and 3; Middle Minoan, 1, 2, and 3; and Late Minoan 1, 2, and 3, however, further divisions have taken place as more findings have been discovered, and now Middle Minoan 1 has an A and B era, as do others.

By the end of the Middle Minoan 2B era, Cretan hieroglyphs disappear, however, Linear A was still in use. Neither script has been deciphered, however, it is believed that they were both used for the Minoans language, like the Egyptians parallel use of hieroglyphs and hieratic. In Egypt, hieroglyphs seem to have mainly been used for religious purposes, along with anything to do with the monarchy, which was itself seen as a religious institution, while hieratic was used for more mundane things like shipping inventories, so, perhaps the situation is the same in Crete. Some proper names have been deciphered in Linear A, by comparing to Linear B, which was used to write Greek, and so we know that had some of the same gods, or at least used their names.

After the eruption of Thera, the Minoans rebuilt again, although their civilization could never recover its glory as their cities seem to have been attacked consistently after Thera, with most showing signs of being repeatedly burnt down between whenever Thera erupted, and the ultimate disappearance of the Minoans circa 1425 BC. If the Egyptologists are right, then the Minoans rebuilt from Thera and had their cities burnt down, and then rebuilt the cities again, and then had then burnt down again, in just 75 years. Naturally, Aegean Prehistorians disagree, as using the carbon-dated timeline the Minoans had around 200 years to go through this final phase of their existence, as they were slowly conquered by the Greeks. By 1425 BC Linear-A disappeared and was replaced by Linear-B, which has been deciphered as early Greek, so there is no doubt that the Minoans were conquered by the Greeks, who were themselves less knowledgeable and adopted the Minoan script, as well as some of their gods.

Section 4: Pre-Dynastic Egypt

Before the dynastic period, Manetho and other ancient sources stated there was a series of older civilizations in the Nile. Little has been found from the period, however, some findings do support his claims. While much of the Pre-Dynastic era may be fiction, it would be irresponsible to propose returning to Manetho's timeline without looking at what the Egyptians believed came before.

Pre-Dynastic Egyptian Timeline

Period	Manetho			Turin		
Reign of the Gods				53,155 BC	to	29,955 BC
Kings from Horus to Bydis	30,435 BC	to	16,535 BC	29,955 BC	to	16,535 BC
Demigods	16,535 BC	to	15,280 BC			
1817 Year Long Rule of Kings	15,280 BC	to	13,463 BC			
30 Kings of Memphis	13,463 BC	to	11,673 BC			
10 Kings of Thinis	11,673 BC	to	11,323 BC			
Spirits of the Dead and Demigods	11,323 BC	to	5510 BC			
Dynastic Egyptian Timelines	5510 BC	to	30 BC	5510 BC	to	30 BC

Zep Tepi

One might read the history of Christian scholars re-writing Egyptian history, and wonder why? What difference does it make when the Ancient Egyptians thought their civilization was founded to a Christian? If someone believes the world was created in 4004 BC, what difference does it make if ancient Egyptians thought their civilization was founded in 5510 BC? After all, they weren't Christian. The reason early Christians were so insistent on re-dating the ancient Egyptian timeline, was because it was tied directly to the Egyptian concept of Zep Tepi, or the First Time.

The First Time was what came before the unification of Egypt at the beginning of the 1st Dynasty. Zep Tepi was a time when Gods and Spirits ruled Egypt, and this brought it into direct conflict with early Christianity, and the idea that there was only one God. This obsession with 'proving Christianity' continued to be mainstream thought well into the 1900s, although it is now generally not a concern to academics, other than to the 'agnostic' David Rohl.

Nevertheless, modern Egyptologists continue to ignore Zep Tepi, as their Christian precursors did, using the same reasoning: those gods and spirits didn't exist, so why bother studying them? It seems strange that people who have dedicated their lives to studying ancient Egypt would simply not bother studying parts of Egyptian history based on their personal assumptions that these parts of history didn't happen, yet that is the state of current Egyptology. Whatever the ancient Egyptians were trying to remember and record in their history, is apparently not important to modern Egyptologists, which is why the CET can be not only the dominant timeline but only timeline studied by Egyptologists, when it directly contradicts the records of the ancient Egyptians.

This arrogance regarding recent assumptions is ubiquitous in modern history, where it is considered appropriate to dismiss all ancient records predating 3000 to 4000 BC. Most historians go so far as to claim these ancient records do not exist at all, yet they clearly do. Whether they are accurate or nonsensical, the ancient Mesopotamians had records going back to over 200,000 years ago. The Avesta, the religious holy book of the Zoroastrian faith, includes a reference to the Arctic before the last glacial period began circa 130,000 years ago and a description of the onset of the glaciers that destroyed that world. The oldest sections of the Rig-Veda, a Hindu holy book, are believed to date to around the same age as the Avesta, as the two languages used are virtually identical. Other Hindu holy books contain histories apparently that go back millions of years. And in Egypt, there was Zep Tepi, the First Time.

The records of Zep Tepi are even more fragmentary than the records of the Old Kingdom, however, should be considered, when considering the roots of Egyptian history. That the ancient Egyptians believed that their civilization was originally founded by, and ruled by gods cannot be disputed, as these gods show up in ancient Egyptian king lists, such as the Turin King List from circa 1250 BC. The Turin King List is a list of kings that lived in ancient Egypt up until the New Kingdom when it was compiled. It was written on a piece of papyrus, which was miraculously preserved in the Egyptian desert for thousands of years, and then quickly deteriorated once taken to the humid climate of Italy. The part of the papyrus that was damaged the worst was the beginning of the king list which dealt with the Zep Tepi.

All that remains of that section is a few scattered fragments and the summation at the bottom of the section. This summation is generally restored as:

Reign of Spirits and Followers of Horus 13,420 years,

their lifetime until the Followers of Horus, 23,200 years.[91]

This reference to the Reign of Spirits and Followers of Horus seems to be a reference to what Manetho recorded in the Aegyptiaca regarding the Zep

Tepi. In Aegyptiaca, Manetho recorded that before the unification of Egypt in 5510 BC, Egypt was ruled by a series of gods, followed by a series of human, spirit, and demigod rulers. The sequence as recorded as Eusebius follows along with his first draft of the short-timeline:

"THE AEGYPTIACA OF MANETHO: MANETHO'S HISTORY OF EGYPT

Excerpted from the Eusebius' Chronica

BOOK I.

Reign of Spirits and Followers of Horus

Dynasties of Gods, Demigods, and Spirits of the Dead.

From the Egyptian History of Manetho, who composed his account in three books. These deal with the Gods, the Demigods, the Spirits of the Dead, and the mortal kings who ruled Egypt down to Darius, king of the Persians.

1. The first man [or god] in Egypt is Hephaestus [Ptah], who is also renowned among the Egyptians as the discoverer of fire. His son, Helios [Ra], was succeeded by Sosis [Shu]: then follow, in turn, Cronos [Geb], Osiris, Typhon [Set], brother of Osiris, and lastly Orus [Horus], son of Osiris and Isis, These were the first to hold sway in Egypt. Thereafter, the kingship passed from one to another in unbroken succession down to Bydis through 13,900 years. The year I take, however, to be a lunar one, consisting, that is, of 30 days : what we now call a month the Egyptians used formerly to style a year.

2. After the Gods, Demigods reigned for 1255 years, and again another line of kings held sway for 1817 years: then came thirty more kings of Memphis, reigning for 1790 years; and then again ten kings of This [Thinis], reigning for 350 years.

3. There followed the rule of Spirits of the Dead and Demigods, for 5813 years.

4. The total [of the last five groups] amounts to 11,000 years, these however being lunar periods, or months. But, in truth, the whole rule of which the Egyptians tell — the rule of Gods, Demigods, and Spirits of the Dead — is reckoned to have comprised in all 24,900 lunar years, which make 2206 solar years.

5. Now, if you care to compare these figures with Hebrew timeline, you will find that they are in perfect harmony. Egypt is called Mestraim by the Hebrews; and Mestraim lived not long after the Flood. For after the Flood, Cham (or Ham), son of Noah, begat Aegyptus or Mestraim, who was the first to set out to establish himself in Egypt, at the time when the tribes began to disperse this way and that. Now the whole time from Adam to the Flood was, according to the Hebrews, 2242 years.

6. But, since the Egyptians claim by a sort of prerogative of antiquity that they have, before the Flood, a line of Gods, Demigods, and Spirits of the Dead, who reigned for more than 20,000 years, it clearly follows that these years should be reckoned as the same number of months as the years recorded by the Hebrews: that is, that all the months contained in the Hebrew record of years, should be reckoned as so many lunar years of the Egyptian calculation, in accordance with the total length of time reckoned from the creation of man in the beginning down to Mestraim. Mestraim was indeed the founder of the Egyptian race; and from him the first Egyptian dynasty must be held to spring.

7. But if the number of years is still in excess, it must be supposed that perhaps several Egyptian kings ruled at one and the same time; for they say that the rulers were kings of This, of Memphis, of Sals, of Ethiopia, and of other places at the same time. It seems, moreover, that different kings held sway in different regions, and that each dynasty was confined to its own nome : thus it was not a succession of kings occupying the throne one after the other, but several kings reigning at the same time in different regions. Hence arose the great total number of years. But let us leave this question and take up in detail the timeline of Egyptian history."

Modern Egyptologists entirely reject the idea that the Egyptians didn't know the difference between months and years, however, his multiple concurrent dynasties hypothesis managed to return to mainstream Egyptology after being thoroughly debunked in the 1800s. Regardless of Eusebius' intent, he did leave us one of the few large excerpts of Manetho. His interpretation of Manetho attempts to compress Manetho's timeline to 24,900 years, then further compresses it to 2206 years to make it fit into the 'Hebrew timeline,' that the Christians were trying to convert everyone to in the first few centuries of the Christian Era. However Manetho didn't state that the History of Egypt was 24,900 years long, he stated there were 24,925 years between the rule of Horus and the beginning of the 1st Dynasty, circa 5510 BC. This breaks down as:

- Unspecified length of time when the gods ruled,
- 13,900-year-long chain of kings from Horus to Bydis,
- 1255-year-long rule of demigods,
- 1817-year-long rule of kings,
- 1790-year-long rule of 30 kings of Memphis,
- 350-year-long rule of 10 kings of Thinis (This),
- 5813-year-long rule of the Spirits of the Dead and Demigods,
- 5510 BC beginning of the 1st Dynasty.

The last of the gods to rule was Horus according to Manetho, followed by the 13,900-year-long rule of the kings ending with Bydis, which seems to be a near-parallel with the 13,420-year-long rule of the 'Spirits and Followers of Horus' recorded in the Turin King List. This would mean that the rule of the gods would be 23,200 years long, as recorded in the Turin King List, placing the beginning of the rule of Ptah the first god at approximately 53,155 to 53,635 BC. Manetho was clearly using a different source than the Turin papyrus, however, the difference of 480 years, or 3.5%, is quite insignificant considering the tremendous time-span being described.

According to Manetho the 13,900-year-long period of rule by kings ending with Bydis, was followed by the rule of demigods for 1255 years, then another line of kings for 1817 years, followed by thirty more kings based in Memphis who reigned for 1790 years, and then again ten kings based in This, who reigned for 350 years. This was then followed by the rule of spirits of the dead and demigods for 5813 years, followed by the unification of Egypt, in 5510 BC.

These additional 'dynasties' between the 'Spirits and Followers of Horus' and the Old Kingdom are missing from the Turin King List, however, given the condition of the papyrus, it is not surprising. Adding all these gods, demigods, and 'archaic dynasties' together pushes back the foundation of Egypt to 53,635 BC. This is a completely different concept than Egypt being founded either circa 5510 or 3100 BC. If there is any truth in this claim of extreme antiquity to Egypt, it changes not only our concept of Egyptian history but our understanding of civilization itself.

How would anyone prove that Egypt is older than... Egypt? One could look into the archaeological record for any evidence of older structures, however, all known ancient structures in Egypt have already been attributed to the dynastic period even when there are no records of them being built. While there are those who believe the sphinx, megalithic temples, and even the great pyramids date back to pre-dynastic times, using them as evidence is problematic, as they are already generally accepted as being dynastic in origin. Perhaps it would be best to start with the dates recorded by Manetho and see if anything was happening in Egypt at the time.

Rule of Spirits of the Dead and Demigods

The era that directly preceded the 1st Dynasty in Aegyptiaca was the so-called 'rule of spirits of the dead and demigods' which lasted for 5813 years. 5813 years before 5510 BC was approximately 13,323 years ago. Archaeological evidence has been found of several cultures in the Nile during the time period, the Isnan, Sebilian, and Qadan cultures, all of which lived in southern Egypt at the time. The Isnan and Sebilian cultures were essentially destroyed by the so-called 'Wild-Nile' period, while the Qadan was severely damaged, and ultimately faded away a few centuries later.

The Wild-Nile was a period late in the Late Paleolithic when the glaciers of the Ethiopian highlands were melting, which resulted in significantly higher annual floods than later periods in Egyptian history. This was particularly bad circa 13,500 years ago, when there were also heavy rains in Central Africa, which caused Lake Victoria to overflow, sending massive amounts of water up the White Nile. These annual floods were averaging between 5 and 10 meters higher than during dynastic times and deposited a great deal of sediment along the shores of the Nile. Many Sebilian settlements are buried in over 25 meters of flood deposits. This period of extreme and erratic annual floods began around 13,500 years ago, and continued, decreasing in magnitude, until shortly before the beginning of the dynastic era.

The time has been described as the most important catastrophic event in the Late Pleistocene history of the Nile,[92] and caused the Nile to be virtually abandoned for thousands of years until shortly before the beginning of the 1st Dynasty. This actually does sound like something that could be described poetically as the 'rule of spirits of the dead and demigods,' if one accepts that the Egyptians of the time didn't know why the Nile goddess was behaving so chaotically and blamed it on demigods.

The 10 Kings of Thinis

Prior to the 'rule of the spirits of the dead,' was the rule of 'ten kings of This,' who reigned for 350 years. The city of This, also called Tjenu or Thinis, is a pre-dynastic city that is believed to exist in the region of Abydos by Egyptologists, however, has never been found. It is almost certainly the 7300-year-old village found in the vicinity of Abydos in 2016, but Egyptologists need it to date to around 5100 years ago for their timeline to work, so they'll have to keep looking for it.

It is mentioned in many early texts, and according to Manetho was the home-town of King Menes who founded the 1st Dynasty in 5510 BC. It is believed to have been in the vicinity of ancient Abydos, modern Girga. If the records of there being a dynasty based in Thinis between 13,673 and 13,323 years ago are correct, then there should be some archaeological evidence, and there is.

While it cannot be definitively proven yet that the Qadan Culture had anything to do with the city later called Thinis, it was in the general vicinity of where Thinis is believed to have later been. Without having officially discovered the ruins of Thinis, it is impossible to conduct excavations which could determine its age, therefore we cannot know if Thinis was rebuilt on the ruins of an older city, however, it is clear that there was a culture between 14,000 and 13,500 years ago in the vicinity of where Thinis would eventually stand, the Qadan culture. It is difficult to imagine how Manetho could have known this, nevertheless, the archaeology does support at least the possibility that there was an archaic dynasty in the region of Thinis, between 14,000 and 13,500 years ago.

Naturally given its age, and the massive flooding that followed its demise, very little remains from the Qadan culture. The Qadan culture seems to have been a hunter-gatherer society that largely survived on the wild grains that grew in the Nile valley, and hunted and fished along the shores of the Nile. Based on remains exhumed from cemeteries, the Qadan people used projectile weapons, including spears, slings, and bows and arrows.[93] This culture seems to have been very warlike, as most of the exhumed remains show signs of damage inflicted by weapons. It is unclear who they were fighting.

The culture itself is believed to have started around 15,000 years ago in northern Sudan, and then slowly spread north up the Nile. The region around Thinis was likely as far north as the culture spread and would have only been present in the region for a few centuries before the Wild-Nile period started, which would have effectively ended the settlement near Abydos. Once the Wild-Nile period began the battered Qadan culture shrank back to its cultural hearth in southernmost Egypt, where it slowly weathered until disappearing sometime around 12,000 years ago.

The 30 Kings of Memphis

According to Manetho, before the rule of the 10 Kings of Thinis, there was a dynasty of 30 kings based in Memphis who ruled for 1790 years. The location of the dynastic city of Memphis is known, it's near the modern town of Mit Rahina, 20 km south of Giza. The city of Memphis was the capital of the Egyptian Old Kingdom, said to have been founded by King Menes after he unified Egypt circa 5510 BC ULT (or 3100 BC CET). It was a major city throughout most of Egyptian history and is the root of where the name 'Egypt' is derived. While the city of Memphis founded by Menes could be at the location of the earlier city of Memphis, it is not necessarily the case.

The name Memphis is derived from the ancient Egyptian words 'Hut-ka-Ptah,' meaning 'Enclosure of the ka of Ptah.' The term 'ka of Ptah' translates as essentially the 'spirit of Ptah,' or more literally 'craftsmen,' as Ptah was the patron deity of craftsmen. Therefore the name of the city could be read as the 'enclosure,' or 'fortress' of the craftsmen. This basic term is found in several ancient cultures across the region, such as the ancient Sumerian Bad-tibira, which also meant 'fortress' of the smiths or craftsmen. Like the Egyptian city of Memphis, Bad-tibira was both a historic city in Iraq and an ancient quasi-mythical city from a time period thousands of years before the foundation of Sumer. This concept of the 'city of the smiths,' whatever it might have originally meant, is so ingrained in the ancient Middle Eastern culture that it even found its way into the Tanakh (Biblical Old Testament). In the earliest part of the Bible, the first city was built by Cain, the first metalsmith.

Naturally, it is possible that King Menes built his capital where he thought the ancient city of Memphis was, however, there is no reason to assume that he did. If one does assume that Menes' Memphis was in the vicinity of the ancient Memphis, then one faces the fact that Menes' Memphis was in the area that is today covered by modern Greater Cairo. Finding the original Memphis under all that might not be possible.

BROKEN TIMELINES - BOOKS 1-3: EGYPT, MESOPOTAMIA, THE INDO-EUROPEANS AND HARAPPANS

According to Manetho, this dynasty should have existed between 15,463 and 13,673 years ago, presumably in the Greater Cairo area. While there were several different cultures known to have been in southern Egypt during the period in question, in northern Egypt, there is virtually nothing known. The reason for this is that the average depth of the Nile is significantly higher today than it was 15,000 years ago. Currently, the average depth of the Nile north of Cairo is less than 1 meter higher than the Mediterranean Sea, however, 15,000 years ago the Mediterranean was over 100 meters lower than it is today. Between 14,700 and 13,500 years ago the global ocean level is believed to have increased around 25 meters due to the melting of glaciers. Therefore if there was any culture along the Nile in northern Egypt between 15,463 and 13,673 years ago, it would have been drowned as the ocean levels rose and caused the Nile depth to rise. Unless this very early Memphite dynasty built something inland, away from the Nile, whatever they built could now be 70 to 100 meters below the ground-level of Cairo.

For thousands of years, there have been rumors of an underground city in the region of Memphis that dates back to 15,000 years ago, however, there have been no recent archaeological digs that support this. One site does look promising, the rumored underground labyrinth reported by the ancient Greek historian Herodotus circa 450 BC in the Fayum depression, near Lake Moeris. Herodotus recorded the labyrinth in *The Histories, Book 2: Euterpe*, 148-149:

> "148. Moreover they resolved to join all together and leave a memorial of themselves; and having so resolved they caused to be made a labyrinth, situated a little above the lake of Moiris and nearly opposite to that which is called the City of Crocodiles. This I saw myself, and I found it greater than words can say. For if one should put together and reckon up all the buildings and all the great works produced by the Hellenes, they would prove to be inferior in labour and expense to this labyrinth, though it is true that both the temple at Ephesos and that at Samos are works worthy of note. The pyramids also were greater than words can say, and each one of them is equal to many works of the Hellenes, great as they may be;

but the labyrinth surpasses even the pyramids. It has twelve courts covered in, with gates facing one another, six upon the North side and six upon the South, joining on one to another, and the same wall surrounds them all outside; and there are in it two kinds of chambers, the one kind below the ground and the other above upon these, three thousand in number, of each kind fifteen hundred. The upper set of chambers we ourselves saw, going through them, and we tell of them having looked upon them with our own eyes; but the chambers under ground we heard about only; for the Egyptians who had charge of them were not willing on any account to show them, saying that here were the sepulchres of the kings who had first built this labyrinth and of the sacred crocodiles. Accordingly we speak of the chambers below by what we received from hearsay, while those above we saw ourselves and found them to be works of more than human greatness. For the passages through the chambers, and the goings this way and that way through the courts, which were admirably adorned, afforded endless matter for marvel, as we went through from a court to the chambers beyond it, and from the chambers to colonnades, and from the colonnades to other rooms, and then from the chambers again to other courts. Over the whole of these is a roof made of stone like the walls; and the walls are covered with figures carved upon them, each court being surrounded with pillars of white stone fitted together most perfectly; and at the end of the labyrinth, by the corner of it, there is a pyramid of forty fathoms, upon which large figures are carved, and to this there is a way made under ground.

149. Such is this labyrinth; but a cause for marvel even greater than this is afforded by the lake, which is called the lake of Moiris, along the side of which this labyrinth is built. The measure of its circuit is three thousand six hundred furlongs (being sixty schoines), and this is the same number of furlongs as the extent of Egypt itself along the sea. The lake lies extended lengthwise from North to South, and in depth where it is deepest it is fifty fathoms. That this lake is artificial and formed by digging is self-evident, for about in the middle of the lake stand two pyramids, each rising above the water to a height of fifty fathoms, the part which is built below the water being of just the same height; and upon each is placed a colossal statue of stone sitting upon a chair. Thus the pyramids are a hundred fathoms high; and these hundred fathoms are equal to a furlong of six hundred feet, the fathom being measured as six feet or four cubits, the feet being four palms each, and the cubits six. The water in the lake does not come from the place where it is, for the country there is very deficient in water, but it has been brought thither from the Nile by a canal: and for six months the water flows into the lake, and for six months out into the Nile again; and whenever it flows out, then for the six months it brings into the royal treasury a talent of silver a day from the fish which are caught, and twenty pounds when the water comes in."

Herodotus' description of the Fayum depression being artificial is partially correct because although it is a natural depression, it was artificially terraced by the Middle Kingdom, creating what almost all ancient authors described to be an artificial lake region. The Roman-era historian Strabo was one of the few classical historians who claimed it was a natural formation. The Labyrinth he described was dismantled in the Greco-Roman era, so the stone could be used to build new buildings in Alexandria and Memphis. The site of the labyrinth was discovered by W. M. Flinders Petrie in 1889, who described it in *Ten Years Digging in Egypt*, pages 91-92:

"Though the pyramid was the main object at Hawara, it was but a lesser part of my work there. On the south of the pyramid lay a wide mass of chips and fragments of building, which had long generally been identified with the celebrated labyrinth. Doubts, however, existed, mainly owing to Lepsius having considered the brick buildings on the site to have been part of the labyrinth.

When I began to excavate the result was soon plain, that the brick chambers were built on the top of the ruins of a great stone structure; and hence they were only the houses of a village, as they had at first appeared to me to be. But beneath them, and far away over a vast area, the layers of stone chips were found; and so great was the mass that it was difficult to persuade visitors that the stratum was artificial, and not a natural formation. Beneath all these fragments was a uniform smooth bed of beton or plaster, on which the pavement of the building had been laid: while on the south side, where the canal had cut across the site, it could be seen how the chip stratum, about six feet thick, suddenly ceased, at what had been the limits of the building.

No trace of architectural arrangement could be found, to help in identifying this great structure with the labyrinth: but the mere extent of it proved that it was far larger than any temple known in Egypt. All the temples of Karnak, of Luxor, and a few on the western side of Thebes, might be placed together within the vast space of these buildings at Hawara. We know from Pliny and others, how for centuries the labyrinth had been a great quarry for the whole district; and its destruction occupied such a body of masons, that a small town existed there. All this information, and the recorded position of it, agrees so closely with what we can trace, that no doubt can now remain regarding the position of one of the wonders of Egypt."

In 2008 a group of Belgian and Egyptian researchers using ground-penetrating radar discovered that this massive stone platform that Petrie's team discovered does, in fact, have a lower level that appears to contain hundreds of large regularly spaced rooms, approximately 8 to 12 meters below the surface. So far they have not found the entrance to the lower level, which is fortunately well hidden. The team published their results in Egypt's *National Research Institute of Astronomy and Geophysics* (NRIAG), however, shortly afterward the Secretary-General of the Supreme Council of Antiquities in Egypt put a stop to all communications regarding the labyrinth, apparently due to Egyptian National Security sanctions.

The strange underground labyrinth exists on both sides of the modern Bahr Wahbi canal, encompassing the entire Hawara region south of the Hawara pyramid, which Herodotus referred to as one of the labyrinth's corners. Unfortunately, the water level has increased significantly since the labyrinth must have been built, as today the mean water level in the Fayum is only 4 meters below ground level in the Hawara region, meaning the entire subterranean labyrinth must be submerged, as it lays 8 to 12 meters below ground level.

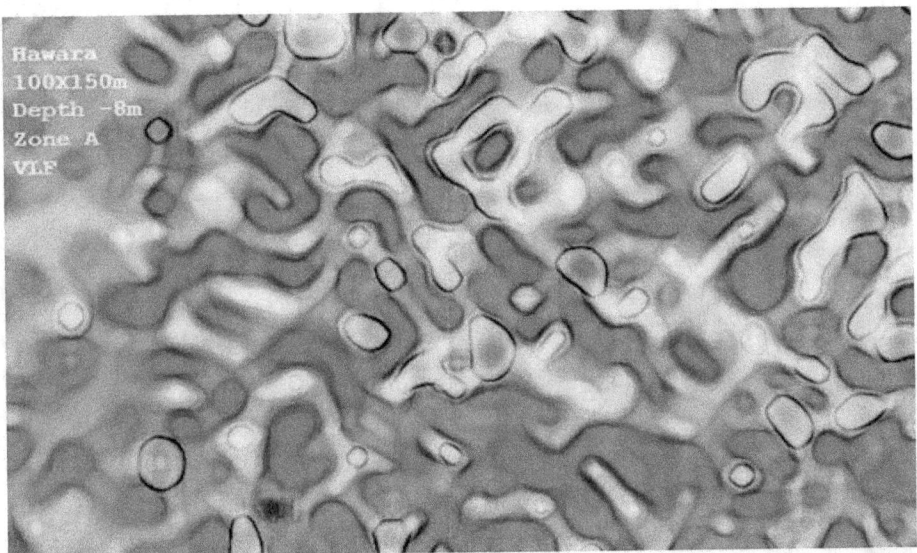

The average water level in the Fayum is significant when considering when this labyrinth was built, as it has to predate the modern high level of water in the Fayum, and naturally had to predate the time of Herodotus. Nevertheless, in the time of Herodotus, the water level was even higher than today, statues that he claimed were out in the lake were discovered in the 1800s miles from the shore of the lake, which had shrunk significantly during the intervening 2300 years. This means the priests at the labyrinth that refused to give Herodotus access to the lower level, couldn't have given him access even if they'd wanted to, as the area would have been filled with water even back then.

This means that we need to look back in time to see when the Fayum had significantly less water than it does now, in order to determine when the underground labyrinth was built. The area was extensively altered during the Middle Kingdom when the Pyramid of Hawara was built. The terraces surrounding the lake were built, and the canal linking the Fayum to the Nile was dug, allowing the Nile floods to fill Lake Qarun in Fayum each year. This massive project to rebuild the Fayum to the productivity level of the Old Kingdom era seems to have been the primary focus of the Middle Kingdom. The Pyramid of Hawara is recorded as being built by Amenemhat III, during the 12th Dynasty, who is also recorded to have dug the Grand Canal connecting the Fayum to the Nile.

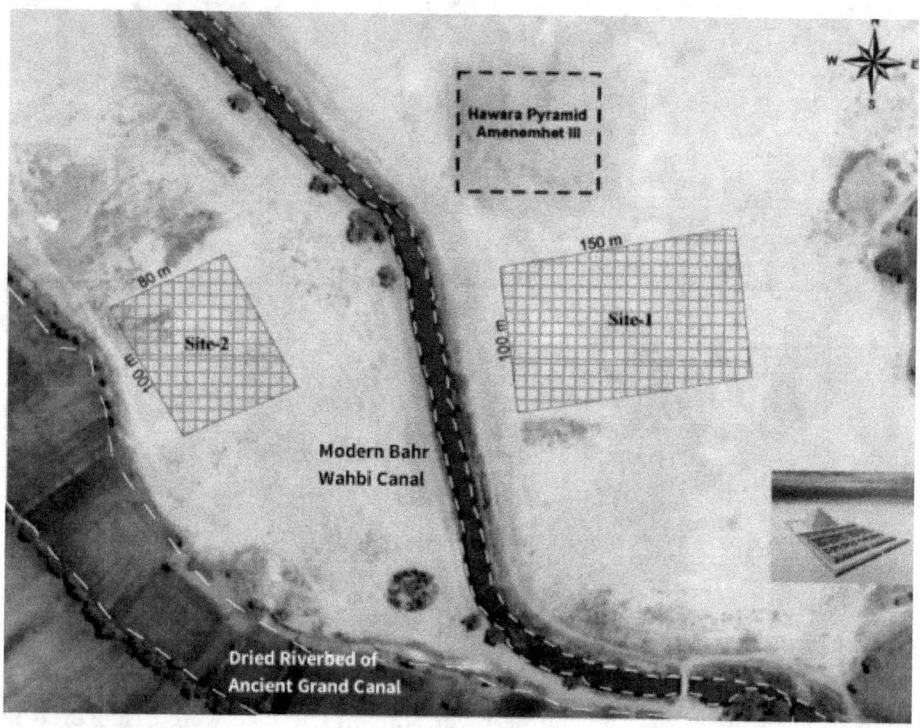

Clearly, the subterranean labyrinth could not have been built after the Fayum was flooded, and therefore it had to have been built sometime before Amenemhat III's reign. Creating the Grand Canal was, in fact, more of a dredging operation, clearing debris from the Bahr Yussef channel that had connected the Nile and Fayum during the African Humid period, prior to 6000 years ago. During this earlier period, the Fayum was flooded annually by the Nile floods, and the lake in the Fayum was significantly deeper than either today or during Herodotus' time.

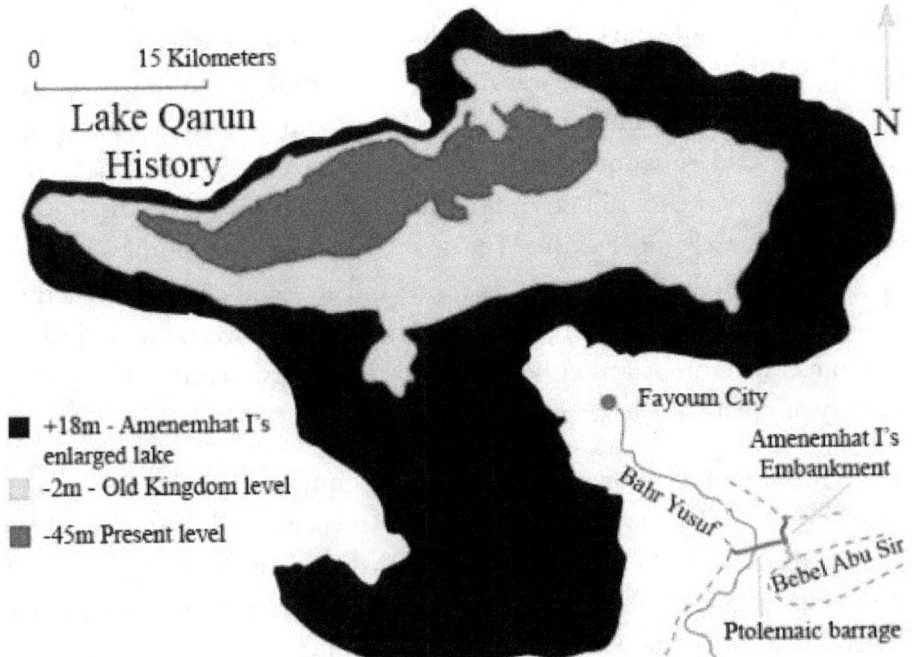

This means that the subterranean labyrinth was either built after the water levels dropped, sometime between 6000 years ago and the 12th Dynasty, or significantly earlier. Therefore knowing when the Old and Middle Kingdoms were, is extremely important when considering this ancient labyrinth's construction. Theoretically, if the Old Kingdom existed between 2686 and 2181 BC as the CET states, then the Bahr Yussef channel should have been dried out, and the water level in the Fayum should have been very low, leaving a dried out region. However, this is not what Old Kingdom sources record. The Fayum region was known to during the Old Kingdom as Ta-She meaning the 'Land of the Lakes.' It was a lush land where the Kings from Memphis went hunting. It was in fact far more humid than during the later Middle Kingdom, indicating that either the Bahr Yussef was open, or there was rain in the region or both. In fact, Egyptologists believe that the water level in the Fayum was over 40 meters higher in the Old Kingdom than it is today. This is further evidence for the ULT being correct.

Nevertheless, whether the Old Kingdom was between 2686 and 2181 BC CET or 4945 and 4003 BC ULT, the Fayum was flooded and fertile, meaning that the water level was high. The labyrinth could not have been built during the First Intermediate Period, as it is described as being larger than all the Old Kingdom and Middle Kingdom temples combined. This means that it was either build during the first few centuries of the Middle Kingdom, or much, much earlier. The first 150 years of the Middle Kingdom was focused on the war of reunification, and it seems unlikely that they would have built a massive labyrinth near the border between the competing kingdoms, therefore it was either built during the first century of the 12th Dynasty or much, much earlier.

Between the reunification of Egypt at the beginning of the 12th Dynasty circa 3459 BC ULT (1991 BC CET), and Amenemhat III becoming King in 3328 BC ULT (1860 BC CET) were the reigns of five kings. Each of these kings engaged in major pyramid building works, however, only one is associated with the Fayum before Amenemhat III. Amenemhet III's grandfather Senusret II built the Pyramid at El-Lahun in the Fayum, however, unlike most other pyramids at the time, this one wasn't built with bricks, but with packed mud. Clearly, the Fayum wasn't dried out before the reopening of the Bahr Yussef channel, as no one would carry mud into the desert to build a pyramid, when there were rocks nearby that could be quarried. The mud must have been locally sourced, which means the Fayum wasn't dry, and Amenemhet III's projects in the Fayum and Bahr Yussef were intended to increase the local food production, not create a lake land from a desert.

This means that there is no point in dynastic Egyptian history when the subterranean labyrinth could have been constructed, meaning we have to look back to a much earlier point. Regardless of when the Old and Middle Kingdoms were, the Fayum was too wet for the subterranean labyrinth to have been built then, therefore, we have look to the paleoclimatological record to see when the water level in the Fayum was low enough for the labyrinth to have been built. We know it could not have been during the African Humid Period which spanned approximately 14,600 to 6,000 years ago, as there was both high water flow down the Nile that would have flooded the Fayum each year, and heavy rainfall, which would have also flooded the Fayum. This means that the labyrinth could have only been built before the onset of the African Humid Period, before 14,600 years ago, which is consistent with Manetho's 30 Kings of Memphis. The paleoclimatological record also shows that prior to the onset of the African Humid Period, Egypt was very dry, and the water level would have been significantly lower than in later periods.

Clearly, any civilization capable of building a labyrinth that was larger than all the temples and palaces of the dynastic Egyptian kingdoms combined had to be a significant civilization. Perhaps if Egyptologists ever acquire the technology to examine the region of Cairo 70-100 meters below the current ground level, an ancient city of Memphis from circa 15,000 years ago will be found, however, it is equally possible that the labyrinth in the Fayum is the ancient city of Memphis.

The limited information gathered of the Labyrinth from ground-penetrating radar does not look like the majority of Egyptian architecture, however, it does resemble a couple of strange structures. The apparent use of large solid blocks of stone weighing tonnes as square columns does match the architecture in the Osireion and the Red Granite Temple of Giza. The Osireion is a strange subterranean temple next to the Temple of Seti I, in Abydos. The upper level of the Osireion was excavated in 1925, and is no longer subterranean, however, it was when Strabo visited it sometime before he described it in Geographica first published in 7 BC:

> *"Above this city [Ptolemaïs] lies Abydus, where is the Memnonium, a royal building, which is a remarkable structure built of solid stone, and of the same workmanship as that which I ascribed to the Labyrinth, though not multiplex; and also a fountain which lies at a great depth, so that one descends to it down vaulted galleries made of monoliths of surprising size and workmanship."*[94]

The Memnonium Strabo mentioned is the Temple of Seti I, his other name was Menmaatre, which was then used to reference his temple. The fountain Strabo mentions is the Osireion which he went on to claim was built by Amenemhet III since it was so much like the Labyrinth in the Fayum. Modern Egyptologists generally assume it was built at the same time as the Temple of Seti I from the New Kingdom, who ruled circa 1294 to 1279 BC. The Osireion is today partially below the water table, as it was during the life of Strabo 2000 years ago, and as it was during the life of Seti I 3250 years ago. Historically the water table was higher during Strabo's time than it is today and even higher during the time of Seti I. How exactly the ancient Egyptians built a subterranean structure underwater, and why it was built in a very different style than almost every other structure in Egypt, is generally ignored by Egyptologists.

The image on the previous page demonstrates the massive solid granite stones used in the construction of the Osireion. The obvious differences between the construction techniques of the Osireion and the Temple of Seti I have been noted since early Egyptologists began studying the Osireion. In

1914 Swiss Egyptologist Henri Édouard Naville published a paper in The Journal of Egyptian Archaeology, in which he described the uncovering of the Osireion, and gave his opinion on the structure:

"When we reached the end of the passage, on both sides we found wide openings which evidently were chambers, and in front a huge monolithic lintel 15 feet long. It looked at first like an entrance to another passage, but we soon perceived that it was merely an opening in a stone wall about 12 feet thick, built of enormous blocks of sandstone and red quartzite. This wall separates the two rooms we had first reached from other rooms in the direction of the temple. We could clear only the southern room. The west wall leans against a mound of marl and is thinner. The southern one has outside a kind of rough casing in limestone and I believe it was not subterranean at that place. The erection was roofed over with large stones which have been used since as building material. Over the roof was probably sand, so that the whole construction looked like a huge mastaba.

The wall on the east side of the chamber is built of enormous stones very well joined. It reminds one of the masonry of the time of the pyramids, of the so-called Temple of the Sphinx. It seems probable that it is much older than the temple of Seti. It may have been part of the first sanctuary, for there was certainly one at an early date, at least of the time of the 12th dynasty. Otherwise one would not understand why there was such a large cemetery of that epoch, and of the following dynasty, such as is found in the hill called Kom-es-sultân, where Mariette made such productive excavations. Beyond this wall, going towards the temple, we could trace two more rooms, so that what we are now excavating is not a mere passage, it is a series of rooms, the last of which is probably under the temple of Seti.

This is one of the questions raised by this unique construction. Are we here in the oldest sanctuary of Osiris? For we cannot suppose that there was none at the time when the kings of the first dynasties built their funereal monuments at Umm el Ga'ab. There must have been a settlement of some importance in a place which already, at that early time, had a sacred character. This character would naturally be derived from the existence of a sanctuary, from its being the abode of a most venerated divinity.

Abydos has always been the city of Osiris, as Heliopolis was the city of Tum. When did Abydos begin to be the residence of the god? When was the first place of worship erected there, and when did Osiris take that name instead of Apuatu? I am going to risk an opinion which, I confess, is at present only a conjecture. The name of Osiris means "he who makes a seat or an abode," and Apuatu, as we have seen, is "the opener of ways," the guide whom the conquerors follow. Did the change of name not take place when an abode, a sanctuary, was first built at Abydos, and he ceased to be the wandering god, the standard of a tribe of migrating conquerors? If this hypothesis were confirmed, it would explain also why Abydos was the first capital of the early kings, and the starting point of Menes."[95]

Prior to the upper level of the Osireion being excavated, most of it was filled with debris, as the roof stones had been quarried since the time of Strabo, and sand and rocks had filled the interior. Based on ancient descriptions it seems to have still been fully covered in the Greco-Roman era. This naturally brings up the question of what it was covered with. Naville postulated that it was originally built above ground level, and covered in sand, making it look like a giant mastaba. Mastabas were large flat-topped tombs built during the Old Kingdom that are believed to have evolved into pyramids during the 4th Dynasty, meaning Naville was proposing the Osireion dated to the earliest era in Egyptian dynastic history.

The Osireion was clearly known of when the Temple of Seti I was built, as they built around it and possibly on top of it, however, it was a known holy site for thousands of years before the time of Seti I. The 13th Dynasty King Neferhotep I, circa 3237 BC ULT (1786 BC CET) during the Middle Kingdom era, erected a boundary stele at Abydos which it stated that none should set foot there. The region around the Osireion was also used extensively as a burial ground in the Old Kingdom, and back into pre-dynastic times. Clearly, the site was holy before Seti I built his New Kingdom Temple circa 1280 BC. The above image is the site of the upper level of the Osireion being excavated in 1914.

If one accepts the premise that the Osireion predates the building of the Temple of Seti I, then it was likely uncovered while the temple was being built. The land where the temple was built is an ancient floodplain, that was flattened out by digging out a level area for the temple to sit on. The floodplain was deposited by the Nile during the Wild-Nile period, meaning that the Osireion would need to date back to before 13,500 years ago when the massive Nile floods began. The previous photograph shows the Osireion and the floodplain layers behind it, which clearly would have covered the building if it was there before the flooding started. On the next page is a diagram showing the work of Petrie and Murry in 1903, who discovered and excavated the entrance, and the subsequent work done in 1912 through 1914 by the Egypt Exploration Fund.

Currently, only the upper level of the Osireion is excavated, as the lower levels are below the water level. Based on historical accounts and historic water levels of the nearby Nile, it is clear that this was the only level known to ancient visitors to the Osireion. Due to the water level, no attempts have been made to excavate down into lower levels, and the Osireion was assumed to be just what we now know is only the top level. The currently excavated top level is 13 meters below the surrounding ground level, and the channel in the middle of the Osireion was initially cleared another 4.3 meters in 1925, however, this was not the bottom of the Osireion, simply the level that could be cleared to with 1920's technology.

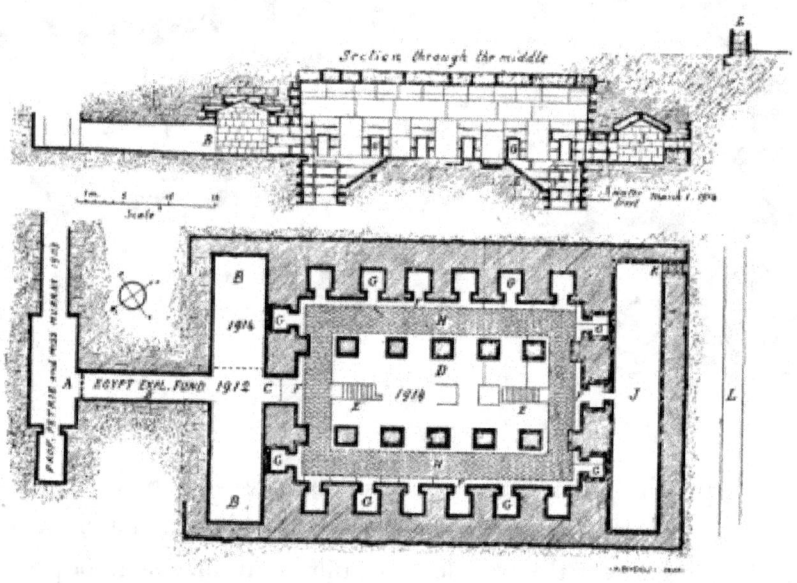

In 2008 a paper was published that reported the soil in the channel had been successfully penetrated to 10.4 meters using a metal rod, and seismic data indicated that the wall of the channel may extend to 15 meters below the current water level.[96] As the current water level fluctuates around 13 meters below ground level, and the Osireion's marble walls descent an estimated 15 meters below that, it means the Osireion's base must be at least 28 meters (90 feet) below the current ground level.

While this area has not been excavated, Sebilian settlements south of Abydos have been excavated from under 25 meters of sediment dating the Wild-Nile phase, so the Osireion could have been buried around the same time, between 13,000 and 7500 years ago. If this structure was still above the surface of the then ground-level during the 10 Kings of Thinis era, between 11,673 and 11,323 BC, it could be why there was a dynasty based out of the Abydos region. In fact, there could be numerous structures buried in the region that just aren't tall enough for us to have stumbled across, from both the 10 Kings of Thinis, and earlier periods.

The fact that Naville stated the masonry looks older than the Temple of Seti I, and that is looked like the 'so-called Temple of the Sphinx' brings us back to the megalithic temples of the Giza Plateau. These two temples are today called the Sphinx Temple and the Valley Temple of Khafre. The Sphinx Temple is built directly in front of the Sphinx, east of the Sphinx between the Sphinx and the old Nile harbor. The Causeway of Khafre runs from the Pyramid of Khafre to the Sphinx Temple complex, where the harbor for the Khafre Causeway was located.

Naville's statement that the masonry of the Osireion looks like the 'so-called Temple of the Sphinx,' refers to the lower level of the Khafre's Valley Temple, which had not been distinguished from the adjacent Sphinx Temple during Naville's day. The two temples are immediately next to each other, however very little of the Sphinx Temple survives to the present, while a significant amount of the Khafre Valley Temple survives. The valley temple was built using two very different types of stone, and two very different construction techniques. The lower level was built using red granite, while the upper level was built using limestone, quarried on the Giza Plateau. The Sphinx Temple was built using limestone cut from the Sphinx enclosure. In both temples the surviving limestone blocks are heavily eroded after so many centuries, however, the granite blocks are still in remarkably good shape.

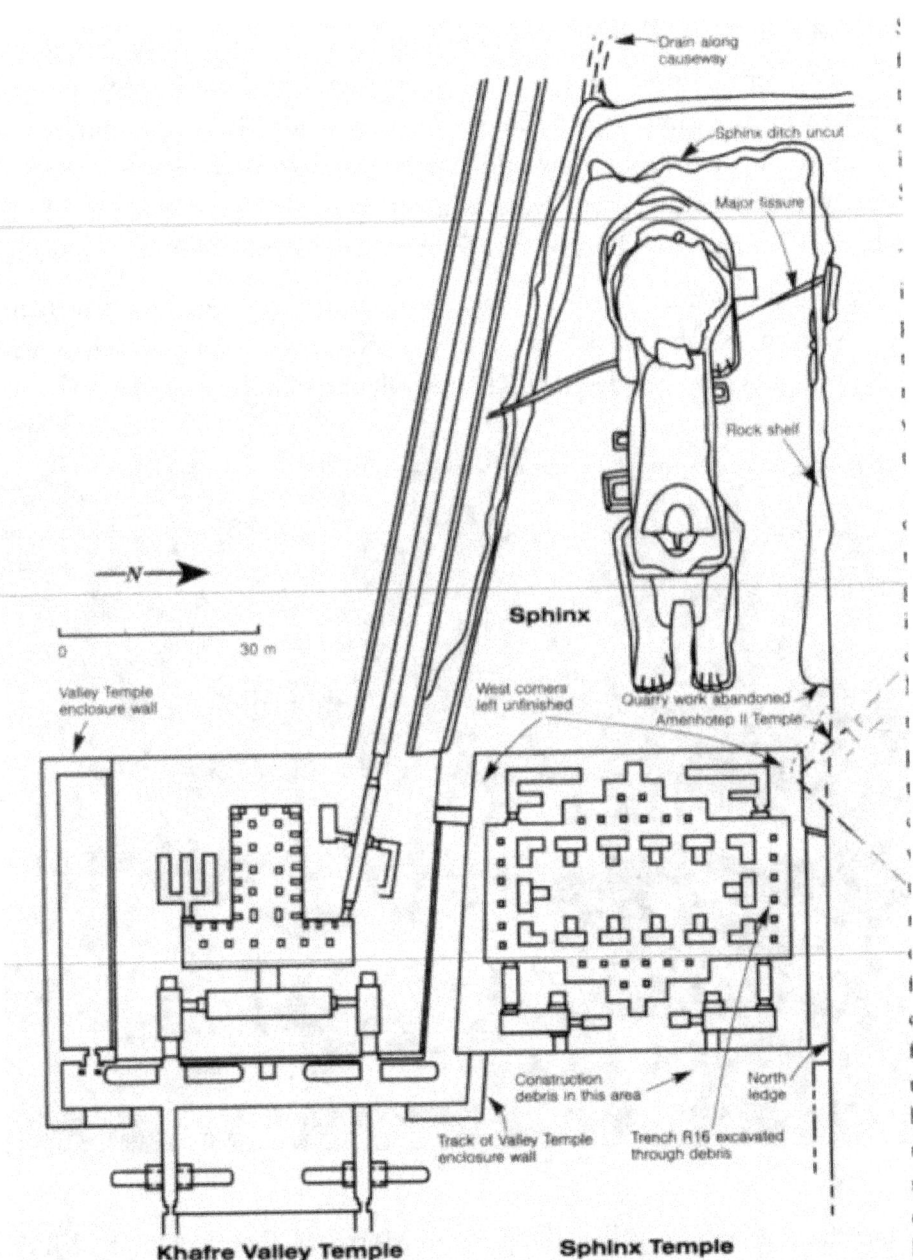

The reason for the lower level of the Khafre Valley Temple being built of a different stone is unknown, however, the remnants of the limestone Sphinx Temple directly to the north show a great deal of similarity of design, indicating whichever temple was built later seems to have been an expansion of the earlier temple. The style of the upper level of the valley temple does seem to be the same as the Khafre Mortuary Temple at the foot of the Pyramid of Khafre, strongly indicating that the two temples and the causeway connecting them were built at the same time, presumably by Khafre. The name of Khafre was found in the debris at both the valley temple and mortuary temple,[97] and the pyramid's ancient Egyptian name was Wer(en)-Khafre, which translates as 'Khafre is Great,' which is why Egyptologists have decided that Khafre built the complex.

The Khafre Pyramid, Valley Temple, and Mortuary Temple, like the Khufu and Temple complexes, were built from limestone excavated from the Giza Plateau, red granite from the Aswan quarries, and white limestone from the Tura quarries. While the red granite of the lower level of the valley temple is believed to have come from Aswan and therefore indicates it was built at the same time as the rest of the Khafre structures, the architecture is dramatically different, which has caused some Egyptologists to doubt if it is from the same period, or an earlier phase of construction that was adopted by Khafre. The view of early Egyptologists of the Khafre Valley Temple was summed up by Auguste Mariette in 1890:

"About six hundred yards to the S.E. of the Great Pyramid is the Sphinx. The Sphinx is a natural rock, to which has been given, more or less accurately, the external appearance of that mystic animal. The head alone has been sculptured. The body is formed of the rock itself, supplemented, where defective, by a somewhat clumsy masonry of limestone. The total height of the monument is 19 metres, 80 centimetres, equal to 65 English feet. The ear measures 6 feet 5 inches; the nose 5 feet 10 inches; and the mouth 7 feet 8 inches. The face, in its widest part, across the cheek, is 4 metres 15 centimetres, that is 13 feet 7 inches. Its origin is still a matter of doubt. At one time it was supposed to be a monument of the reign of Thothmes IV (XVIIIth dynasty). But we know now, thanks to a stone in the 'Boolak Museum, that the Sphinx was already in existence when Cheops [Khufu] (who preceded Chephren [Khafre]) gave orders for the repairs which this stone commemorates. It must also be remembered that the Sphinx is the colossal image of an Egyptian god called Harmaehis.

Near the Sphinx is a singular construction which, even to a greater degree than the Sphinx itself, is an enigma to Egyptologists. It is certain that this construction is as ancient as the Pyramids. But is it a temple, or is it a tomb? Its external appearance, it must be confessed, is rather that of a tomb. From a distance it must have presented the appearance of a mastabah, scarcely exceeding in size those which are actually found, for example, at Abousir and Sakkdrah. In one of the chambers of the interior there are six compartments, place done above the other, which certainly seem to have been constructed, like those of the third Pyramid and of the Mastabat-el-Faraoun, for the reception of mummies. Moreover, the place does not differ essentially from that of certain other tombs which are found in the vicinity. It may therefore be fairly argued that the monument in question was a tomb, without violating any rules of criticism; can the contrary opinion, which calls it a temple, be equally well supported? It is true, the Ancient Empire having left us no other temple with which to compare this one, it is not unnatural to suppose that at this remote period Egyptian temples might have been constructed on the extraordinary plan of the one we are now considering. Nor is it unnatural either to assume that, since the Sphinx is a god, the adjoining monument may be the temple of that god. But are these arguments sufficient? And, after all, to put the case plainly, is the monument an annex of the Sphinx, or is not rather the Sphinx an annex of the monument? Does not the whole of this represent a very ancient tomb, adorned, for the sake of greater dignity, with a colossal statue of a god? The question is pending."

By the 1930s Egyptologists had generally agreed that the complex must have been built by Khafre, and so the pyramid, mortuary temple, causeway, and valley temple were all grouped together as 4th Dynasty buildings. The valley temple was connected to the mortuary temple at the foot of the pyramid via the causeway, and all of the buildings were built of locally sourced limestone, red granite from the Aswan quarries, and/or white limestone from the Tura quarries. The fact that the lower level of the valley temple was designed as a tomb and built in a different style of masonry was simply written off as an odd thing that once happened in Egypt. However, the question of the Sphinx Temple remained.

Only the lower level of the Sphinx Temple remains, and while the design is similar to the lower level of the valley temple, it is not made from red granite, but limestone quarried from the Sphinx enclosure. The Sphinx Temple shows no signs that it ever had stones quarried from Aswan, or Tura, or even the Giza Plateau other than the Sphinx enclosure. Comparative analysis of the surviving stones of the temple has even determined approximately where they were quarried from in the enclosure. This means that the Sphinx and Sphinx Temple, which were clearly made at the same time, could have been produced by a local Giza culture, potentially long before the 4th Dynasty.

When Mariette asked the question of whether the Sphinx was an annex of the Khafre Valley Temple, or the Khafre Valley Temple was an annex of the Sphinx, it was because they appear to have been built at different points. The earliest Egyptologists to uncover the Sphinx believed it was built by the New Kingdom King Thutmose IV, circa 1400 BC who erected the Dream Stele between the paws of the Sphinx. This idea was overturned when the Inventory Stele was found in 1857 which stated that King Khufu of the 4th Dynasty had found the Sphinx buried in sand and restored it. The specific language of the Dream Stele was later determined to be Late-Egyptian and not Old-Egyptian and therefore the story can only be dated back to the New Kingdom or later, and is generally dated to the 26th Dynasty. It is possible that the story is a Late-Egyptian translation of an older story that may have originally been written in Old or Middle-Egyptian, and if nothing else proves that the ancient Egyptians of the Late Period believed the Sphinx predated the pyramids of Khufu and Khafre. Unfortunately, without any documentation of who built the Sphinx prior to Thutmose IV's claims of uncovering it during the New Kingdom, Egyptologists have been left with no recourse but to including it in with the Khafre structures, which clearly are designed to fit together. The situation was described by Hassan in 1949:

> *"Taking all things into consideration, it seems that we must give the credit of erecting this, the world's most wonderful statue, to Khafre, but always with this reservation: that there is not one single contemporary inscription which connects the Sphinx with Khafre; so, sound as it may appear, we must treat the evidence as circumstantial, until such time as a lucky turn of the spade of the excavator will reveal to the world a definite reference to the erection of the Sphinx."*[98]

That 'lucky turn of the spade' may have already happened. In 1980 Egyptian Egyptologist Zahi Hawass drilled a series of holes to determine the level of the water table, approximately 68 meters east of the Sphinx. After passing through 16 meters of soft debris the drill hit red granite, which is not indigenous to the Giza region, and had to have been imported from Aswan. The area drilled is covered in flood debris that settled over the region since the granite blocks were placed there, however, is significantly lower than the harbor used by the Old Kingdom, and certainly hasn't been exposed since the Old Kingdom. This would imply that someone was building the Giza region significantly earlier than the Old Kingdom, as the water level was high at the time and had been throughout the African Humid Period preceding it. This means that whatever this red granite building is, it dates back to at least 15,000 years ago, and it raises the possibility that the lower level of Khafre's Valley Temple may date back to that time as well.

If the red granite lower level of the Khafre Valley Temple does date back to 15,000 years ago, the Sphinx and Sphinx Temple could have been built as an annex to the Red Granite Temple at a later time, when the Giza culture no longer had access to the Aswan quarries. If this is the case then the Sphinx building culture would have had to have been sometime after the era of the 30 Kings of Memphis, and before the Old Kingdom. This reopens the possibility that Khufu did uncover the Sphinx and restore it as described in the Inventory Stele.

If the Red Granite Temple and buried red granite buildings of Giza, Osireion or Abydos, and underground Labyrinth of the Fayum date to circa 15,000 years ago then this would have been a significant Nile civilization, equivalent in some respects to the later Egyptian Kingdoms. Strabo's account of the upper level of the Labyrinth looking like the Osireion is interesting, as there are no records of the Labyrinth being built. It is assumed to have been built by Amenemhat III, who dug the Grand Canal and built the Pyramid at Hawara, next to the Labyrinth. Amenemhat III was initially building another pyramid, the so-called Black Pyramid at Dahshur, but abandoned that pyramid in order to build the pyramid next to the Labyrinth.

The course of the Grand Canal runs to the west of the area where the underground Labyrinth has been found, however as we do not know exactly how big the structure is, the canal may have broken through the roof of the underground Labyrinth while being dug. It is logical to assume the longer path of the Grand Canal, in comparison to the modern Bahr Wahbi Canal, was due to an obstruction that no longer exists, which raises the possibility that the upper level of the Labyrinth was already there, presumably covered in sediment from the Wild-Nile phase, and was discovered by the 12th Dynasty while digging the Grand Canal. This would explain why the ancient historians described it as greater than all the temples of Egypt combined, and why it was reported as looking like the Osireion.

Unfortunately, until the Egyptian government opens the lower level of the Labyrinth for exploration, we may never know what exactly it was, however once opened it should provide samples of ancient debris that could be used to date the Labyrinth allowing us to know for sure when it was built. The simple fact is that while the 30 Kings of Memphis era is the most recent time these archaic structures could have been built, based on the fact that the water level has been too high ever since it isn't the earliest time they could have been built. All of these structures could have been built at earlier dates, and may not even date to the same ancient culture. Until we have access to the Labyrinth we simply cannot know if these sites are actually related or simply built in similar styles.

1817-Year-Line of Kings

Before the 30 kings of Memphis, Manetho listed the rule of another group of kings for 1817 years. Very little is known about this period that apparently existed between approximately 17,280 to 15,463 years ago. This was deep into the glacial drought when Egypt was extremely dry. The period around 17,000 years ago Lake Tana in the Ethiopian highlands dried out, which was the source for 80% of the Nile's water during the later dynastic period. This led to the Nile's water level falling to one of its all-time lowest points. Lake Tana did not recover until sometime after 15,100 years ago.

The other primary source of water for the Nile has traditionally been the White Nile, which flows from Lake Victoria in central Africa. The White Nile is currently the source for around 20% of the Nile's water, however, during the time when Lake Tana was dried out, it would have been the source for most of the Nile's water. However, Lake Victoria was very low at this time as well, ultimately drying out entirely by 15,000 years ago, meaning that the Nile itself, had almost dried out by the end of this very ancient dynasty. It is theorized that the Nile was a seasonal river during this period, flowing only part of the year, and possibly dammed by sand dunes in multiple places where lakes would have formed behind the dams.[99] There is very little that has been discovered dating from this period. Some stone tools have been found along the higher banks of the Nile, however, the majority of artifacts from this period would likely be buried under the Nile's riverbed, as people would have clustered around the water, not at the top of the surrounding cliffs.

Reign of the Demigods

Before the dynasty of kings that lasted for 1817 years, Manetho listed the rule of the demigods for 1255 years. Whatever this era was about, it apparently existed between approximately 18,535 to 17,280 years ago. This was deep into the glacial drought when Egypt was extremely dry, however, before Lake Tana or Lake Victoria dried out. Ice core samples from Antarctica show that between approximately 17,700 and 17,500 years ago, the atmosphere contained a very unusual chemical anomaly of high concentrations of halogens, including chlorine, bromine, and iodine. These halogens were similar to the CFCs emitted by modern civilization in the past century and also created holes in the ozone layer. The cause of this sudden spike in halogens is theorized to have been a 192-year-long volcanic venting from Mount Takahe in Antarctica. Whatever the demigods were or represented, any remains from the time period along the northern Nile would likely be around 110 meters below the current ground level in the Nile delta. Given the ozone depletion at the time, the reference to demigods could have simply been a memory of people that were deformed by malignant melanoma.

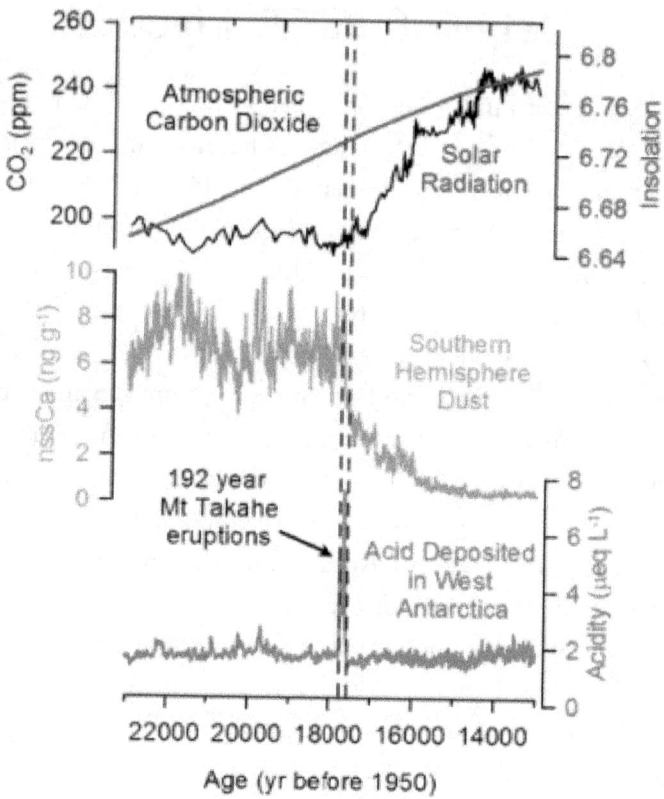

Spirits and Followers of Horus

Prior to the Rule of the Demigods, Manetho claimed there was a 13,900-year-long period where kings ruled, ending with the rule of King Bydis. This corresponds to the 'Spirits and Followers of Horus' listed in the Turin King List, who ruled for 13,420 years. This would have been between approximately 31,955 or 32,435 and 18,535 years ago. This time period generally corresponds to the Last Glacial Maximum (LGM) when the glaciers were at their greatest extent, and the global ocean level was at its lowest point. The LGM is generally considered to have existed between 31,000 and 16,000 years ago[100] with its peak circa 26,500 years ago. At the time the world was very dry, and human settlements are believed to have been clustered along the coastlines and riverbanks. Given the fact that the Nile would have been significantly lower, probably over 100 meters lower than today, finding any evidence of a culture at the time would be difficult.

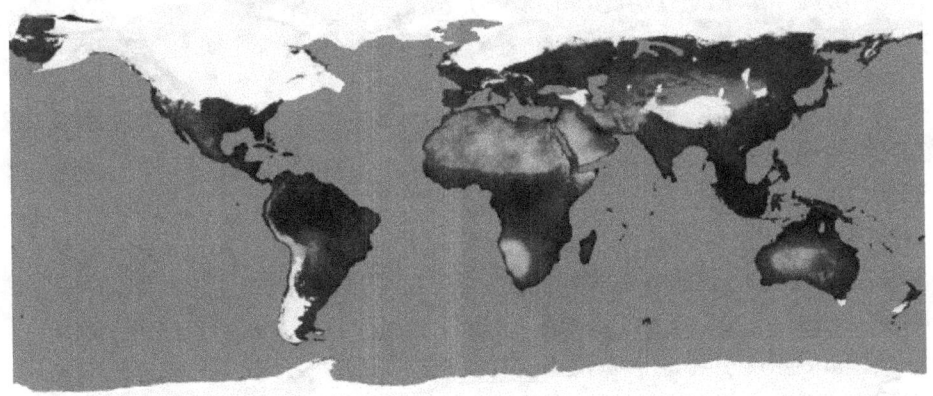

Reign of the Gods

Before the reigns of Spirits and Followers of Horus, the Palermo King List stated that there was a time period 23,200 years long that was referred to simply as the Reigns before the Spirits and Followers of Horus. This time period would range from circa 55,155 to 31,955, or 55,635 to 32,435 years ago, depending on whether using the Turin or Manetho King Lists. Manetho broke this period down into the rule of a series of gods, however, did not specify how long each one reigned. The fragments of the Turin King List from that period show the Egyptians of the New Kingdom did believe what Manetho had written over a thousand years later.

One of the few portions of the first two columns of the Turin King List that is still legible is translated as:

The Dual King Djehuty (Thoth), life, prosperity, and health 7726 years.

While Thoth wasn't listed in Manetho's list of gods that ruled, the names of other gods that ruled have been reconstructed from the fragments, including Geb (Column 1.14), Osiris (Column 1.15), Set (Column 1.16), and Horus (Column 1.17). Thoth is mentioned in Column 1.18, followed by Ma'at in Column 1.19, and then Horus again in Column 1.20. The discrepancy between Manetho's list and the Turin List is connected to a religious text that Manetho did not use: the Book of the Dead, or as the ancient Egyptians called it: Book of Coming Forth by Day.

In the Book of the Dead, Osiris was murdered by Set who became king of Egypt, and raised Osiris' son Horus as his own son, after marrying Osiris widow Isis. Horus ultimately challenged Set in front of a court of gods over-which Thoth presided. The gods decided to uphold Ma'at, which translates as balance, or in context, the law, and restored Horus. This story is believed by Egyptologists to have been created during the Second

Intermediate Period when an ethnic Egyptian dynasty was trying to drive out the Asiatic Hyksos dynasty. The story metaphorically illustrated the war in Egypt, where Osiris represented the earlier great Egyptian kingdom that was murdered by the Hyksos, whose patron god was Set. The ethnic Egyptian dynasty was represented by Horus who would eventually be restored to the throne of Egypt by the gods when the rule of law returned to Egypt.

The Turin King List was made during the reign of Ramses II in the New Kingdom when the Book of the Dead was the dominant religious text. Thoth, Ma'at, and the second Horus, being added to the list makes political and religious sense as it confirms the authenticity of the Book of the Dead. The fact that Manetho didn't include these extra gods likely means that he was using an older source than the Turin King List. As Manetho was a Gnostic and not a follower of any of the ancient Egyptian religions it is unlikely he would see any value in using King Lists that included extra gods that were likely added for political reasons, if he had access to older lists that did not.

Only some of the gods on Manetho's list can be found among the fragments of the Turin papyrus, however, there is clearly several names missing from column one before Geb, and therefore it is plausible that the names Manetho listed were once on the Turin King List. Manetho listed Hephaestus (Ptah), Helios (Ra), Sosis (Shu), Cronos (Geb), Osiris, Typhon (Set), and Orus (Horus) as ruling before the Spirits and Followers of Horus. If the correlation between the 13,900-year-long reign of the kings between Horus and Bydis listed by Manetho, and the 13,420-year-long reign of the 'Spirits and Followers of Horus' is accepted, then the rule of the gods was the 23,200-year-long period before the 'Spirits and Followers of Horus.'

The sequence of gods listed in Manetho's list is clearly drawn from the New Kingdom creation epic of Ptah. In the New Kingdom Ptah became one of the dominant gods, who after building the world passed control of it to the Sun god Ra. After that, the rule of the world passed through the hands of a sequence of gods: Shu, Geb, Osiris, Set, Horus, Thoth, Ma'at, and finally Har. As both Thoth and Ma'at are also listed on the Turin King List, it seems likely that they were added to the king lists of the New Kingdom for religious reasons.

In the Old Kingdom, there was a precursor to the creation epic of Ptah, in the creation epic of Atum. In the creation epic of Atum the rule of the world passed from Atum directly to Shu, and from him onto Geb, Osirus, Set, Horus. Whatever this sequence of gods may represent will likely never be known, and may in fact simply represent a creation myth woven into the ancient Egyptian history.

It appears as if there were once alternate predynastic histories in Egypt, however, we only know about them today because of references to them found in some of the ancient surviving texts. Around 450 BC, Herodotus recorded the history of the Egyptians from the beginning of their civilization, down to the last king before the Assyrians conquered Egypt, a king he called the 'priest of Hephaestus.' After recording the Egyptian dynastic history Herodotus mentioned what came before. Herodotus, Book II, chapters 142 to 144 recounts the following:

> *"142. Thus far went the record given me by the Egyptians and their priests; and they showed me that the time from the first king to that priest of Hephaestus, who was the last, covered three hundred and forty-one generations of men, and that in this time such also had been the number of their kings, and of their high priests. Now three hundred generations make up ten thousand years, three generations being equal to a century. And over and above the three hundred the remaining forty-one cover thirteen hundred and forty years. Thus the whole sum is eleven thousand three hundred and forty years; in all which time (they said) they had had no king who was a god in human form, nor had there been any such thing either before or after those years among the rest of the kings of Egypt. Four times in this period (so they told me) the sun rose contrary to his wont; twice he rose where he now sets, and twice he set where now he rises; yet Egypt at these times underwent no change, neither in the produce of the river and the land, nor in the matter of sickness and death.*

143. Hecataeus the historian was once at Thebes, where he made for himself a genealogy which connected him by lineage with a god in the sixteenth generation. But the priests did for him what they did for me (who had not traced my own lineage). They brought me into the great inner court of the temple and showed me there wooden figures which they counted up to the number they had already given, for every high priest sets there in his lifetime a statue of himself; counting and pointing to these, the priests showed me that each inherited from his father; they went through the whole tale of figures, back to the earliest from that of him who had lateliest died. Thus when Hecataeus had traced his descent and claimed that his sixteenth forefather was a god, the priests too traced a line of descent according to the method of their counting; for they would not be persuaded by him that a man could be descended from a god; they traced descent through the whole line of three hundred and forty-five figures, not connecting it with any ancestral god or hero, but declaring each figure to be a "Piromis" the son of a "Piromis," that is, in the Greek language, one who is in all respects a good man.

144. Thus they showed that all whose statues stood there had been good men, but wholly unlike gods. Before these men, they said, the rulers of Egypt were gods, but none had been contemporary with the human priests. Of these gods one or other had in succession been supreme; the last of them to rule the country was Osiris' son Horus, called by the Greeks Apollo; he deposed Typhon, and was the last divine king of Egypt. In Osiris is in the Greek language, Dionysus."

The list of gods that are mentioned at the end, Osiris, Horus, and Typhon (Set), are clearly part of the list of gods that reigned in the timeline of Manetho and the Turin Papyrus. According to Herodotus, these gods were not contemporary with human priests, who had recorded the existence of 345 generations of humans during the span of Egyptian history. The Hecataeus mentioned by Herodotus was no doubt the historian and geographer Hecataeus of Miletus, who wrote *Periodos ges* circa 500 BC. These ancient generations apparently added up to 11,340 years, which if then added to the 2500 years since then would place the beginning of these generations circa 13,840 years ago, during the time of the 10 Kings of Thinis, before the Rule of Spirits of the Dead and Demigods. While there is no known evidence of a priestly cast existing through the Wild-Nile Period, it is nevertheless plausible that a cast of priests could have survived in the regions near the Nile during the African Humid Period.

There is evidence of astronomers living in the Sahara during the Wild-Nile Period, at Nabta Playa in southwest Egypt. Nabta Playa is the site of an ancient wetland that existed until the 5.9 Kiloyear Event, where numerous archaeological sites have been discovered dating back to the African Humid Period. Currently, the oldest known human artifacts found at Nabta Playa date to between 10,000 and 8,000 BC.[101]

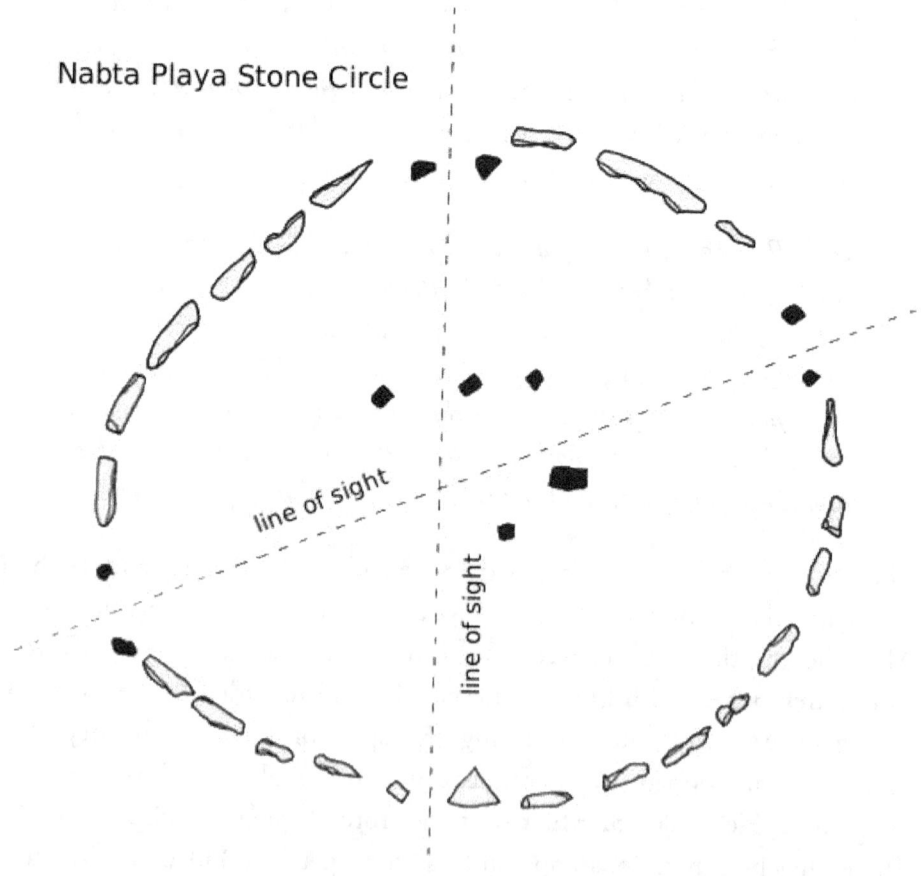

At Nabta Playa are a number of stone circles and aligned standing stones that appear to be ancient star calendars. The most famous is a group of small standing stones that appear to be a star calendar, like a small scale stone henge. These star calendars have been a source of much debate among scholars, with different scholars correlating the calendars with different stars at different points in time. The growing consensus is that the star calendars align with Sirius and Orion circa 6000-6500 BC.

In 2005 astrophysicists Thomas Brophy and Paul Rosen showed that the standing stone orientations and star positions were pointing towards Sirius circa 6088 BC. At the time Sirius had a declination of -36.51 degrees for a rising azimuth, which is where on the C-line average points. The C-line is a line of standing stones within the calendar that has been central to much debate. Near the calendar circle, there is a group of aligned large megalithic stones, the southern line of which aligns to the same stars as the smaller calendar, however, at approximately 6270 BC. Both of these star calendars could also be aligned with Orion, however, in the much larger window of 6400 to 4900 BC. Carbon dated remains of a campfire near the group of megaliths confirm this general timeline, of circa 6000 BC.[102]

It should be noted that while this is the growing consensus, it is not the only proposed dates for the site. Brophy has also pointed out in his book 'The Origin Map' that the alignments at Nabta Playa are also consistent with the alignment of the Milky Way, and Orion, between 17,500 and 16,500 years ago. Orion is the only modern constellation known to have been viewed as an asterism by the ancient Egyptians as early as the Old Kingdom. During the Old Kingdom, circa 4945 to 4003 BC ULT (or 2686 to 2181 BC CET), Orion was known as Sah, 'the father of the gods.' His wife was Sopdet, the star we call Sirius, and their child was the falcon god Sopdu, the planet Venus. These gods were syncretized with Osiris, Isis, and Horus during the First Egyptian Dark Age, which again points to how long that dark age lasted. However, in the Old Kingdom, this triad clearly represented a calendar.

Venus and Earth have orbits around the Sun that causes Venus to realign with the stars exactly the same every 8 Earth years. This means that the ancients could reset their calendars every 8 years, which happens to be 13 Venus orbits around the Sun, and thereby keep their calendars in sync with the seasons. This Earth/Venus orbital co-synchronicity was known to the ancient Mesopotamians and Mesoamericans who both used it to reset their calendars every 8 years. Sirius was also known in Egypt as the star which predicted the annual flooding of the Nile, and as such was used to predict the seasons. Once a year, for approximately five days, Sirius would rise right before dawn, which is referred to as the Heliacal Rising of Venus. This happened right before the annual flooding of the Nile, which was caused by the beginning of the wet season in Ethiopia, where most of the Nile water started out.

Herodotus also claimed that the Egyptian priests who had recorded the 345 generations of humans had also claimed the during the entire length of Egyptian history, including the reign of the gods, "Four times in this period (so they told me) the sun rose contrary to his wont; twice he rose where he now sets, and twice he set where now he rises." This is a clear reference to the passage of long spans of time. In Herodotus' time, the Sun was rising in Cancer during the Heliacal Rising of Sirius, approximately July 14-19. The Sun setting Cancer during days of the Heliacal Rising of Sirius would have been 12,960 years earlier. This is due to what astronomers call the precession of the equinoxes.

The precession of the equinoxes is an observable shifting of the constellations over a span of around 25,920 years, during which time the constellations appear to slowly rotate around the earth. Astronomers call it the precession of the equinoxes because Eurasian cultures were more concerned with predicting the course of winter than the heat of summer, however, the ancient Egyptians were more concerned with the summer heat, and the inevitable flooding of the Nile. If it is accurate that "twice he [the Sun] rose where he now sets, and twice he set where now he rises," then that would refer to a span of time about 51,840 years long, starting approximately 2,450 years ago, when Herodotus wrote it down. In other words, the reign of the gods began approximately 54,290 years ago according to the priests Herodotus spoke with, and around 55,155 to 55,635 years ago according to Manetho and the Turin Papyrus. Whatever this time was supposed to represent, it clearly meant something to the ancient Egyptians.

Section 5: Pre-Dynastic Mesopotamia

Pre-Dynastic Mesoptoamian Timeline

Civilization	Dynasty	ULT		
Eridug	Alulim	266,379 BC	to	237,579 BC
Eridug	Alalngar	237,579 BC	to	201,579 BC
Bad-tibira	En-men-lu-ana	201,579 BC	to	158,379 BC
Bad-tibira	En-men-gal-ana	158,379 BC	to	129,579 BC
Bad-tibira	Dumuzid	129,579 BC	to	93,579 BC
Larag	En-sipad-zid-ana	93,579 BC	to	64,779 BC
Zimbir	En-men-dur-ana	64,779 BC	to	43,779 BC
Shuruppag	Ubara-Tutu	43,779 BC	to	25,179 BC
Kish	1st Kish	25,179 BC	to	7698 BC
Dynastic Era		9868 BC	to	3227 BC

Like the Egyptians, the Sumerians recorded a long pre-dynastic history. The Sumerians recorded a series of king lists for different cities, which they claimed ruled Mesopotamia in sequence, with the kingship being taken from city to city. Modern Assyriologists generally disregard the idea that the kingship passed from city to city in a long line of dynasties, as this would push the foundation of Sumer back to approximately 23,645 BC, after the Flood of Ziusudra. Adding the dynasties listed before the flood, human history would have begun approximately 264,845 BC.

This is a tremendous period of time and is generally disregarded by both Assyriologists and historians as being nothing more than myths. However, humans were around at the time, and the brief records of the time-periods in question do correlate with significant events in human prehistory as determined by research into geology, paleoclimatology, and archaeogenetics.

Kish Civilization

1st Kish Dynastic Timeline

King	ULT		
Jushur	25,179 BC	to	23,979 BC
Kullassina-bel	23,979 BC	to	23,019 BC
Nangishlishma	23,019 BC	to	22,349 BC
En-tarah-ana	22,349 BC	to	21,929 BC
Babum	21,929 BC	to	21,629 BC
Puannum	21,629 BC	to	20,789 BC
Kalibum	20,789 BC	to	19,829 BC
Kalumum	19,829 BC	to	18,989 BC
Zuqaqip	18,989 BC	to	18,089 BC
Atab	18,089 BC	to	17,489 BC
Mashda	17,489 BC	to	16,649 BC
Arwium	16,649 BC	to	15,929 BC
Etana	15,929 BC	to	14,429 BC
Balih	14,429 BC	to	14,029 BC
En-me-nuna	14,029 BC	to	13,369 BC
Melem-Kish	13,369 BC	to	12,469 BC
Barsal-nuna	12,469 BC	to	11,269 BC
Zamug	11,269 BC	to	11,129 BC
Tizqar	11,129 BC	to	10,824 BC
Ilku	10,824 BC	to	9,924 BC
Ilta-sadum	9,924 BC	to	8,724 BC
En-me-barage-si	8,724 BC	to	7,824 BC
Aga	7,924 BC	to	7,698 BC

The earliest kings whose names we have found on ancient artifacts, are Enmebaragesi and Aga, the last two kings of the 1st Kish Dynasty. According to the Epic of Gilgamesh King Enmebaragesi conquered Elam, in southern Iran, and then turned his eye towards Uruk. King Dumuzid, the fisherman, of Uruk ultimately conquered Kish, and then apparently forced the former King Enmebaragesi to live as a woman. As transgender men and women are documented as part of the Sumerian culture, it is unclear if this indicates that Enmebaragesi was a female living as a male while he was king, or if Dumuzid, the fisherman, was a sadist who forced the conquered male king to live as a woman.

Assyriologists generally accept that Enmebaragesi and Aga existed, along with Dumuzid and Gilgamesh, however, don't accept the earlier kings in the 1st Kish Dynasty. One of the issues of dating the 1st Kish Dynasty is that it is unclear if the different Kish Dynasties were located in the same City of Kish, or even in a city at all during the early era. The ruins of the City of Kish are believed to have been near Tell al-Uhaymir, close to the city of Babylon.

The unclear nature of the 1st Kish Dynasty has led to the proposal by the Assyriologist Ignace Gelb, that early Kish may have been a culture, and not a city. In Gelb's proposal, Kish was the original Semitic culture that the Akkadians and Amorites descended from. There is some evidence supporting this theory in the Sumerian King List itself, as many of the kings of the 1st Kish Dynasty do have Semitic names. Unfortunately, this cannot be seen as conclusive evidence for a Semitic dynasty as some of the names are Sumerian, and the oldest copies of the Sumerian King List date to the Akkadian era, and therefore the Semitic names could simply be translations of the original Sumerian names. There is some evidence that the Akkadians did translate parts of the king list into Akkadian, as the second name on the list, Kullassina-bel, translates as 'All of them (were) lord' in Akkadian. This is generally read as a sign that the period was either without government or was some kind of republic. The period of Kullassina-bel was recorded as being 960 years long.

If one accepts the premise of the ULT, that the Ubaid civilization was the Sumerian dynastic period, from the 1st Uruk Dynasty through the end of the 3rd Uruk Dynasty, when Sargon of Akkad seized control of Mesopotamia, circa 3885 BC ULT, then the Kish civilization would have happened between 25,179 and 7698 BC. This Kish civilization started in the aftermath of a great flood that was the precursor for the later story of Noah's flood from Jewish folklore, which then found its way into the Christian and Islamic religions.

It is a very strange time period for the ancient Sumerians to have stated there was a major flood, as it is at the approximate date that the ice-sheets reached their greatest extent during the last glacial maximum, which is estimated at 26,500 years ago. The lowest level that the ocean level reached during the last glacial maximum is estimated at 135 meters below the current sea level, sometime between 29,000 and 21,000 years ago.[103] After the ice-sheets reached their peak, the ice-sheets began melting, and global coastlines began drowning as the ocean levels began to rise. The Sumerian King List places this date as about 25,179 BC.

After the flood of Ziusudra, the first king on the Sumerian King List was Jushur who rained for 1200 years. As the following 'king' was Kullassina-bel, whose name means 'All of them (were) lord,' which clearly isn't the name of a king, but rather the description of the time. This implies that Jushur and the rest of the long-lived 'kings' were in fact periods of time, or possibly dynasties or even civilizations. There is very little information that remains from the Kish civilization, the first 12 'kings' are completely unknown other than their mention in the Sumerian King List.

The 13th king, Etana, is known from later Babylonian and Assyrian stories about him. He was known as 'the shepherd, who ascended to heaven and consolidated all the foreign countries.' In the story of Etana, he became involved in a struggle between an anthropomorphize serpent, and an anthropomorphize eagle. The serpent-man mutilated a cow, and when the eagle-man came to investigate the carcass the serpent-man caught the eagle-man and locked him in a pit. Etana found the pit and freed the eagle-man, after which the eagle-man flew Etana up to heaven, where Etana found the cure for impotence. While this story is quite strange, it does seem to be a precursor to the war between the man-bird angels and serpent-devil of the Judaeo-Christian religions. This time period of King Etana, between 15,941 and 14,441 BC ULT, is also interesting as it is roughly the same period as Manetho's 30 Kings of Memphis.

No other information about the Kish Dynasty survives until Enmebaragesi who was captured by Dumuzid the Fisherman circa 7836 BC ULT. Aga continued to rule Kish for some time after Enmebaragesi's capture, however, according to the king list, the kingship was transferred to Uruk, meaning Aga would have simply been a local governor. If the Kish culture was a

Semitic culture, the transfer of the kingship to Uruk was the beginning of the Sumerian period.

Antediluvian Shuruppak

Before the beginning of the Kish civilization, the *Sumerian King List* claims that there was the Flood of Ziusudra. While this flood served as a forerunner for the Flood of Noah, it was not depicted as being a worldwide phenomenon the way the later Jewish story was. The early Jews most likely knew of the many flood stories from across their world and interpreted them as one world-wide flood. The coastal regions of the world have been flooding since the height of the glacial maximum during the last glacial period, sometime between 29,000 and 21,000 years ago.

The melting of the ice-sheets has not been consistent and has occasionally reversed, as the ice-sheets temporarily increased in mass during brief reversals. Nevertheless, the global ocean levels have been generally rising since the Last Glacial Maximum. This sea-level increase has generally been slow, however, has included rapid sea-level change periods, when large amounts of ice suddenly melted. Ice-core samples from Antarctica and Greenland, along with studies of a variety of submerged land features, have shown there has been a series of rapid ocean rise periods, called meltwater pulses. These meltwater pulses are known as MWP-1A0 around 19,000 years ago, MWP-1A between 14,700 to 13,500 years ago,[104] MWP-1B between 11,500 to 11,200 years ago,[105] and MWP-1C between 8200 and 7600 years ago.[106]

These meltwater pulses are no doubt the cause of many of the world's flood myths, and if the Sumerian King List is to be believed, the first one was circa 25,179 BC. There are several versions of Ziusudra's flood from throughout the history and cultures of Mesopotamia where he had several names. Ziusudra and Zin-Suddu were the names used by the Sumerians, Utnapishtim was his Akkadian name, and Atrahasis was later used by the Babylonians. None of these appear to be real names, Ziusudra translates as 'life of long days,' Utnapishtim translates as 'he who saw life,' and Atrahasis translates as 'exceedingly wise.' While it's possible that someone would name their child 'exceedingly wise,' the other names are clearly not proper names, and as the 'exceedingly wise' Atrahasis was the most recent name used by Mesopotamians, circa 1894 to 1595 BC CMT (3352 to 3038 BC ULT), it is clear that we don't know what his name actually was.

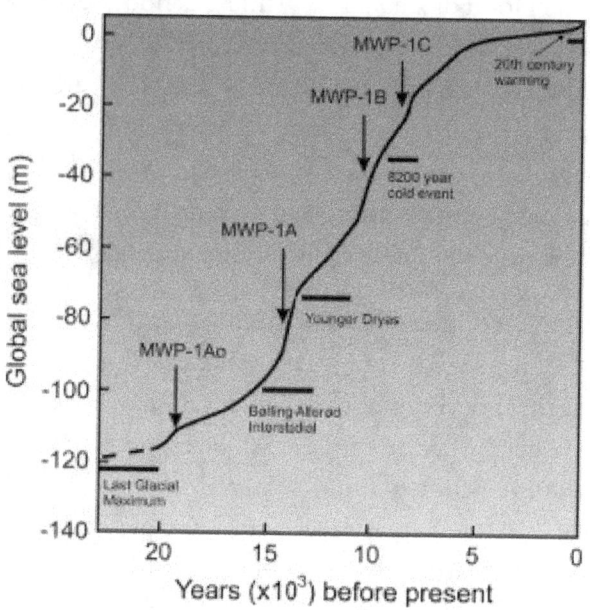

Ziusudra, Utnapishtim, and Atrahasis

The stories of Ziusudra, Utnapishtim, and Atrahasis, are all essentially the same, although embedded in larger narratives of their respective cultures. The *Epic of Atrahasis* from circa 3352 to 3038 BC ULT (1894 to 1595 BC CMT), was the most comprehensive. It began with the gods dividing control of the world between them, Anu getting control of the sky, Ellil getting control of the land, and Ea getting control of the water. This story is mirrored in many ancient mythologies, such as the Hurrian Anu-Kumarbi-Teshub triad, the Canaanite Hadad-Mot-Yamm triad, the Greek Zeus-Hades-Poseidon triad, the Latin Jupiter-Orcus-Neptune triad. As all of these cultures rose to prominence after the time of the Old Babylonian Empire, the stories could have been copied from the Babylonians.

The *Epic of Atrahasis* continued with Ellil assigning a group of lesser gods to work as farmers and engineers, however, after working for some time they rebelled and refused to continue working for Ellil. Ea suggested that the gods create a new race to work as farmers and engineers, and so humans were made. Unfortunately, the humans bred rapidly, and the land became so overpopulated that Ellil decided to limit the human population by releasing plagues and famines every 1200 years, however, that was not enough to stop the human population growth, so Ellil decided to flood the land to wipe out humanity. Ea warned Atrahasis of the coming flood, and so Atrahasis pulled down his house and built a boat large enough for his family and friends to survive. The river where Atrahasis lived then flooded, and Atrahasis and his family and friends survived. Like the earlier Sumerian and Akkadian versions of Atrahasis, he was identified as being the King of Shuruppak before the flood.

The earlier Akkadian version of the story is found embedded in the *Epic of Gilgamesh*. King Gilgamesh, bereaved by the death of his best friend Enkidu, set off to find the ancient survivor of the flood Utnapishtim. It is explained within the epic that Utnapishtim was awarded immortality after the flood, which is why he was still around thousands of years later. The flood is also described, generally similar to the later Epic of Atrahasis. In the Utnapishtim version, Ea appeared to Utnapishtim in a dream and told him to build a cube-shaped ship, 200 feet long, wide, and high. Inside this wooden building were seven stories, each divided into nine sections, where Utnapishtim's family, friends, workers, and some domesticated animals lived during the flood. In this version of the flood, the ship floated to the hills of northern Iraq, where Utnapishtim and his crew disembarked.

The earliest version of the story we have is found on a broken clay tablet recovered from the ruins of Nippur called the *Eridu Genesis*. In this version, the gods An, Enlil, Enki, and Ninhursanga created humans and made parts of the world safe to live in. Then the gods descended to Earth, and the first cities were built: Eridu, Bad-tibira, Larak, Zimbir, and Shuruppak. Later the gods decided to not save humanity from a coming flood, both the cause of the flood and the reason the gods would not help humanity are unknown due to damage to the tablet. Where the tablet's damage ends, Ziusudra is in a huge boat with his friends and family, and some livestock. After the flood An and Enlil award Ziusudra with immortality for saving mankind.

There is one significant difference between the story of Ziusudra and his Akkadian and Babylonian decedents. In Ziusudra's story, the city he was not named Shuruppak, Shuruppak was the king. The *Eridu Genesis* tablet was found in the ruins of Nippur and dated to approximately 1600 BC CMT (2977 BC ULT). The dating itself is based on the debris the damaged tablet was found in, and it clearly dates to a much earlier time. 1600 BC CMT was the end of the Old Babylonian Empire, and the city of Nippur was neglected by the Old Babylonian Empire, as the religious focus of the empire had been turned to Babylon, and the supreme god of the Babylonians was Marduk, not Nippur's patron god Enlil. This broken tablet was clearly being thrown away in 1600 BC CMT, which is fortunate for us, as it is the only known copy of the *Eridu Genesis* to survive to the present.

As the text is written in Sumerian it is logical to assume it was written sometime during the Sumerian era. According to the ancient Sumerian *Tummal Chronicle*, the first king to build up the Temple of Enlil at Nippur was Enmebaragesi. Alabaster vase fragments bearing his name have been found at the ruins of Nippur, lending credence to this claim that he was involved in building the temple. Many other kings built up the Temple of Enlil over the rise and fall of dynasties, including Aga of Kish, Gilgamesh of Uruk, and Mesannepada of Ur.

The *Eridu Genesis* tablet was written in Sumerian cuneiform, and so the tablet must date to the Sumerian era, however, if the Sumerians were writing their pictographic script on papyrus before they started using clay tablets, then the story could be from any point in Sumerian history. This means that the *Eridu Genesis* could date from thousands of years before the dynastic city of Shuruppak was even founded.

Dynastic Shuruppak

The ruins of the dynastic city called Shuruppak are near modern Tel Fara, in southern Iraq. The city is believed to have been founded around 3100 BC CMT (or 4600 ULT), after a major river flood. Below the city's ruins are a layer of alluvium that has not been excavated, so, if the city was built on an older city that was flooded, we do not know. During its height, the dynastic city of Shuruppak was a major trading center, with more grain solos than any other known Sumerian city.

Assyriologists generally consider the story of antediluvian Shuruppak's flooding to relate to the layer of alluvium found under the city, meaning that the story of Ziusudra/Utnapishtim/Atrahasis' life can be dated to approximately 3100 BC CMT. While this is a convenient way to avoid having to deal with the idea that the flood happened at the height of the Last Glacial Maximum, it does seem to ignore the story of antediluvian Shuruppak being flooded, as the ruins of dynastic Shuruppak are built on top of the alluvium, not covered in it.

If the story of antediluvian Shuruppak's flooding is correct, then it is unlikely it will ever be found. If it was built near a coastal area, then it is under over 100 meters of water now, and if on a river mouth near a coast, probably under more than 25 meters of sediment. If it was along an inland river, it would be closer to the surface, but still buried for 25,000 years. Unless the ancient builders were building with materials that could have survived the elements for that long, there should be nothing left of it.

In the *Sumerian King List*, the city of Shuruppak was the fifth city built before the flood. This happened 18,600 years before Ziusudra's flood, approximately 45,800 years ago, after the city of Zimbir fell. The name Shuruppak means 'the healing place,' implying that the fall of Zimbir was traumatic, unfortunately, no information about this event survives. In the *Sumerian King List*, Ubara-Tutu is listed as the only king, having a reign of 18,600 years, however in the ancient Sumerian text *The Instructions of Shuruppak*, Shuruppak is listed as being Ubara-Tutu's heir, and Ziusudra is listed as being Shuruppak's heir, so Ubara-Tutu could not have been the only king. It seems likely given the names recorded in the following 1st Dynasty of Kish, that the Sumerians knew very little of the early times, and that no doubt included the antediluvian dynasties.

Shuruppaki Genetics

This time period is also interesting from a genetic perspective. Human mitochondrial DNA haplogroup-K is believed to have developed from haplogroup-U between 30,000 and 22,000 years ago, as the ocean levels were approaching their lowest level. This implies that during this time there was a significant population of mtDNA-HG-U people that settled somewhere, and some developed into mtDNA-HG-K people. This culture clearly had a large enough population that they could leave a significant genetic contribution to modern humanity. Haplogroup-K is found in approximately 10% of the native European population[107] and 6% of the Middle Eastern and North African population, with some groups having higher percentages, such as the Ashkenazi Jews at 32%,[108] Kurds at 17%,[109] French, Norwegians, and Bulgarians at 13.3%,[110] and Gurage of Ethiopia at 10%.[111]

Haplogroup-U did not disappear and continues to exist alongside haplogroup-K in Europe, the Middle East, and North Africa. The fact that haplogroup-U is also common in South Asia, while haplogroup-K is rare there, indicates that the culture that developed haplogroup-K was likely somewhere in the Middle East, North Africa, or Europe. This development of haplogroup-K from haplogroup-U circa 30,000 and 22,000 years ago is undeniably at the same time as the Glacial Maximum of the last glacial period, circa 29,000 to 21,000 years ago. Given the global atmospheric dryness of the period, wherever this culture was, it was likely near a large body of water. This points to a coastal location on either the Arabian sea or Mediterranean coasts, approximately 130 meters below the modern sea level. Given the fact the haplogroup-K is common in Europe and North Africa, but rare in South Asia, the Mediterranean seems more likely than the Arabian Sea.

If one were considering the Mediterranean Sea, the Nile river also seems an obvious option. This time period is when the ancient Egyptians claimed there was an uninterrupted line of kings, from the time of Horus to King Bydis. This time period is the first one the Egyptians described as ruled by human kings and apparently existed between 30,435 and 16,535 years ago. As Bydis is believed to simply be the ancient Egyptian word for 'king,'[112] this clearly is only a very dimly-remembered time by dynastic Egypt, however, it was recorded as being in Egypt. As the Nile was even then the only major river emptying into the Eastern Mediterranean, it does seem likely that a culture would have settled in the ancient Nile delta. Unfortunately, that would leave the ruins of Shuruppak under 130 meters of water and alluvium that have accumulated in the past 25,000 years.

Antediluvian Zimbir

According to the Sumerian King List before the time of Shuruppak, the kingship was in Zimbir for 21,000 years. Meaning that Zimbir would have been founded approximately 64,800 years ago, after the city of Larak fell. Zimbir is the direct translation of the ancient Sumerian name, generally used by historians when dealing with the antediluvian city, however, Assyriologists prefer the Akkadian name Sippar when referring to the dynastic city. There were at least two cities called Sippar in dynastic Sumer: Sippar-Amnanum and Sippar-Yahrurum. Unfortunately, early archaeologists in the 1800s did not keep good records of where they excavated artifacts from and simply labeled items as coming from Sippar. This has resulted in some confusion over which Sippar ancient tablets came from, Sippar-Yahrurum or Sippar-Amnanum.[113] Sippar-Yahrurum was the larger of the two, said to have been founded by Ziusudra after the flood to serve as a library. The classical Babylonian historian Berossus claimed Ziusudra buried the records of the world from before the flood at Sippur-Amnanum.[114] Clearly, this Sippur was not the Zimbir that would have been destroyed around 45,800 years ago.

The ruins of Sippar-Yahrurum are found at Tel Abu Habbah near Yusufiyah, in central Iraq. Sippar-Yahrurum is known to have been occupied since at least the Early Uruk period, which would fall between 9900 and 7500 BC ULT (4000 to 3100 BC CMT). In either timeline the city of Sippar-Yahrurum predates the flooding of dynastic Shuruppak, meaning that this city could not have been founded after the flooding of dynastic Shuruppak by Ziusudra. This supports the idea that dynastic Shuruppak was not the city that was flooded during Ziusudra's life.

The name Zimbir is believed to be the source of the Sumerian word 'sipru' which means writing.[115] The implication is that the Sumerians either invented or originally taught writing in the city of Sippar-Yahrurum. The city of Sippar is one of the known sources for ancient waxed wooden writing boards, that were used as early as the Late Uruk period, circa 5231 to 4931

BC ULT, (3400 to 3100 BC CMT). These writing boards were used for a wide range of purposes, from training scribes in cuneiform, to administering the city. It appears that they may have been the major form of record-keeping during later periods of Sumerian history,[116] unfortunately, few have survived from the Sumerian era.

The name Zimbir itself is believed to translate as 'bird city' in Sumerian,[117] which when combined with the root of the word for writing, forces us to consider the possibility that carrier pigeons could have originated at Zimbir. It is known that the Mesopotamians were using carrier birds of some kind by the time of Sargon circa 3885 to 3845 BC ULT (2334 to 2299 BC CMT), called the 'iṣ-ṣur-tú.'[118] Carrier pigeons were used for carrying messages between cities and even countries in ancient times. They were still in use by western militaries through World War 2 and reported to be in use by the Islamic State as recently as 2016. It is believed that the ancient Egyptians were using carrier pigeons by the end of the 1st Dynasty circa 5510 to 5247 BC ULT (3100 to 2890 BC CET).[119]

Axis-Mundi

According to the Sumerian King Lists, the king of Zimbir was Enmendurana. His name is generally translated as 'chief of the powers of Duranki.' Duranki translates as approximately 'the meeting-place of heaven and earth.'[119] This means that Enmendurana's name translates as approximately 'chief of the powers of the meeting-place of heaven and earth.' However, the Sumerian word 'en' was also used in archaic Sumerian to mean 'time' or 'era.' Meaning that Enmendurana can also be translated as 'time of the meeting-place of heaven and earth.' Whatever this is supposed to mean, it is clearly a description of a time period, and not a proper name, much like the later names of kings during the 1st Kish Dynasty.

This concept of the meeting-place of Heaven and Earth is known throughout many ancient cultures, generally referred to as the axis-mundi by academics. Many ancient cultures claimed that specific mountains were the axis-mundi, such as the Canaanites, who claimed Mount Hermon was the axis-mundi. In the ancient Jewish *Book of the Watchers*, the Watchers first descended to Earth on Mount Hermon, which is possibly descended from an earlier Canaanite story.[120] In the Jewish religion, Mount Zion is the axis-mundi, the hill that Jerusalem is built on. In Christianity the axis-mundi is not currently on Earth, it is God's City, which will eventually land on Mount Zion becoming the New Jerusalem.[121] The ancient Armenians believed that the gods had once lived on Mount Ararat, much as the ancient Greeks believed the gods lived on Mount Olympus. In traditional Chinese beliefs, the Kunlun Mountains were the axis-mundi, where the peach-tree of immortality could be found.[122]

In Hindu, Jain, and Buddhist beliefs the name of the mountain is Meru. Meru is a mythical mountain, which has been identified with several actual mountains, including the Pamir Mountains of Kashmir,[123] Mount Kailash in Tibet,[124] and Mount Sumeru in Java.[125] The fact that Mount Meru has been identified as several modern mountains clearly points to the fact that the original location is lost. In the ancient Zoroastrian holy book the Avesta, the axis-mundi was the Hara Berezaiti, which translates as High Watchpost. This mountain was surrounded by the steppes of the Aryan ancestral homeland, Airyanem Vaejah. The Airyanem Vaejah is described as being in the Arctic, before the beginning of the last glacial period, which if interpreted literally would be the Byrranga Mountains on the Taymyr Peninsula in Siberia. This name 'High Watchpost' has an odd similarity to the early-Jewish story of the Watchers descending on Mount Hermon, indicating that the Persian-era Jews may have been partially inspired by the Avestan story, merging it with the ancient Canaanite story, as they appear to have merged several flood narratives.

There is an old Akkadian story of Enmendurana, where he is called Emmeduranki, that seems like a half-way point between the ancient Sumerian story of Enmendurana, and the Jewish story of Enoch and the Watchers. In the story, Emmeduranki was taken to heaven by the gods Utu and Adad, where he was taught the secrets of heaven and earth,[126] *much as Enoch was in the Book of the Watchers.*[127] Additionally, both Enoch and Enmendurana are the seventh antediluvian monarchs/patriarchs in their respective cultures.[128]

The Akkadians had their own version of the axis-mundi, Mount Mashu, which Gilgamesh had to pass through to get to the Garden-of-the-Gods on his way to meet Utnapishtim. Mount Mashu's location is also unknown, it was described as being a long way to the east of Uruk. These axis-mundi mountains are found in diverse cultures throughout the world, and in countries without mountains, people for some reason built them and then treated them as the axis-mundi. This was the case for the Giza pyramids in Egypt, the E-anna Ziggurat in Uruk, and the pyramids of Teotihuacán in Mexico. This concept of axis-mundi is clearly very old, with many specific points across Eurasia and North Africa being identified as being the axis-mundi, along with some in the Americas. This means that the idea must date back to a very early point in human pre-history before humanity settled in the Americas. The settlement of the Americas is a topic that causes a great deal of debate, however, remains of a settlement at Monte Verde in Chile have been carbon-dated to 33,000 years ago,[129] meaning that the concept of the axis-mundi is likely older than that.

The axis-mundi was not always a mountain, it was also commonly depicted as a tree in Eurasian cultures, such as the German Yggdrasil, Baltic Austras koks, Hungarian Égig érő fa, Turkic Ağaç Ana, Mongolian Modun, and Chinese Jianmu. The Ashvattha from the Vedic texts of ancient India is interpreted by many as an axis-mundi.[130] World-trees are a common element of Native American beliefs, found depicted in Aztec, Izapan, Mayan, Mixtec, and Olmec architecture. In the ancient Mayan *Book of Chilam Balam*, the world-tree was called the Yax imix che.[131] The fact that world-tree axis mundi is generally found in the cultures of the Eurasian Plains or those that had long contact with them, as well as the native American cultures points to the origin of the world-tree axis-mundi as a story these cultures once shared, presumably before they migrated away from a common area. These tree axis-mundis also have counterparts in many of the mountain axis-mundis. In ancient Chinese folk religion, the Peach Tree of Immortality was located in the Kunlun Mountains. In the Sumerian religion on top of Mount Kur, was the Garden-of-the-Gods, where the Good Tree was located. This has been interpreted as a forerunner of the Jewish Tree of Knowledge in the Garden of Eden, which has also been interpreted as an axis-mundi.

Laschamp Event

Whatever the original axis-mundi event, the Sumerian King List places it between 64,779 and 43,779 years ago, which is odd timing if purely fictitious, as many Assyriologists would claim. The end of this time period correlates with the beginning of the Laschamp event, which was a short reversal of the Earth's magnetic field. The Laschamp event is estimated to have taken place between 43,400 to 39,400 years ago. During this time, magnetic north became astronomical south, and magnetic south became astronomical north. If anyone was watching the skies and looking at a compass the world would have seemed upside down. The reversed magnetic field lasted for about 440 years, with a 250-year transition to and from the upside-down world. The reversed field was 75% weaker than the normal field strength of the Earth's magnetic field. The increased amount of radiation reaching the surface of the Earth caused increased production of beryllium 10 and higher levels of carbon 14.[132] This event was first recognized in the late 1960s, as a geomagnetic reversal in the Laschamp lava flows of Clermont-Ferrand, France,[133] since then the magnetic excursion has been found in geological records from many parts of the world.

The cause of the Laschamp event is unknown. The fact that it happened at the time when the Sumerians claim Zimbir fell, could be incidental, however, it is difficult to explain why they would name the king as Enmendurana, the 'time of the axis-mundi,' and claim he was taught the secrets of heaven by Utu, the sun,[134] and Adad, the storm god,[135] implying a stormy time when there was a problem with the sun. If Zimbir did in fact use carrier pigeons, the reversed magnetic field would have also wreaked havoc with the bird's navigation, and likely caused the failure of the civilization's communication network.

The end of this era, when Zimbir fell, is not just the time of the Laschamp Event, it is also the time of very cold periods that seem to match the beginning and end of the Laschamp Event. These very cold and very dry periods happened between approximately 44,300 to 43,300 years ago, and

40,800 to 40,000 years ago.[136] They have been detected in both ice-core samples from Greenland, and the study of carbon isotopes from caves in Europe. During this time in Eastern Europe, the average temperature is believed to have dropped to subzero year-round, and permafrost spread down from the Scandinavian glaciers. This period of increased European permafrost is believed to have contributed to the downfall of the European neanderthals.[137] The combination of the sudden onset of this cold period, combined with the magnetic reversal and weakened geomagnetic field of the Laschamp event, would have been traumatic to any culture at the time. The fact that modern-humans began to migrate into neanderthal territory at this time, both in Europe and Siberia, does indicate that something major had changed within modern-human culture.

Zimbari Genetics

The time period when Zimbir fell is also notable in terms of human archaeogenetics. Human mitochondrial DNA haplogroup-U is believed to have developed from haplogroup-R between 49,800 and 43,200 years ago.[138] This haplogroup is widespread, and found in the indigenous populations of Europe, the Middle East, South Asia, North Africa, and the Horn of Africa. It diverged into nine subclades as the populations separated from their common source, which seems to be Zimbir. The oldest known sample of haplogroup-U mtDNA was recovered from a Siberian skeleton dated to circa 45,000 years ago.[139] Archaeogenetic studies have found haplogroup-U mtDNA in the remains of dynastic Egyptians, the remains of the indigenous Guanche people of the Canary Islands,[140] and the remains of ancient Europeans. Today this haplogroup is found in between 8% and 15% of Indians,[141] and 11% of the native population of Europe.[142] The highest percentage are found in the Berbers at 29% and the Copts at 27.6%. Given that these are the two known descendants of the native North African populations, it is plausible that Zimbir could have been in North Africa.

In order for this haplogroup to have developed, there would have needed to be a significant number of mtDNA-HG-R people, within which the mtDNA-HG-U group developed between 49,800 and 43,200 years ago. This new Zimbiri population would later found the Shuruppaki population, perhaps in the ancient Nile delta. The location of Zimbir itself was logically somewhere in the region where haplogroup-U is found today, Europe, the Middle East, North Africa, or South Asia, although Europe should be excluded as a potential location, as it was inhabited by Neanderthals at the time, and modern humans only began entering the region between 45,000 and 43,000 years ago, around the time Zimbir fell. The source of haplogroup-U is generally assumed to be somewhere in the Middle East, Anatolia, or the Caucasus Mountains.

Antediluvian Larak

In the *Sumerian King List*, before the kingship was in Zimbir, it was in the city of Larak, which fell approximately 64,800 years ago, after being around for 28,800 years, meaning it was founded circa 93,600 years ago. So far, no ruins have been found in Iraq associated with a dynastic city called Larak, however, it is believed they may lie somewhere near the ruins if Isin. Almost nothing is known about Larak. The King of Larak was said to be En-Sipadzidana of which there are no surviving stories. The name En-Sipadzidana translates approximately as 'time of the shepherd for the faithful of heaven,' which doesn't really enlighten us as to what Larak was, other than that they were apparently shepherding.

Sheep are believed to have been domesticated in the Middle East, approximately 13,000 years ago,[143] however, the wild mouflon species which sheep were domesticated from, have been around for approximately four million years,[144] and therefore sheep could have been domesticated earlier than 13,000 years ago. In fact, some studies have suggested that sheep may have been domesticated up to three times from three different wild mouflon species. Of course, the term shepherd could have been used metaphorically, as it is being used within the concept 'shepherd for the faithful of heaven,' which sounds like something a Christian minister might describe himself as being.

The world was different between 94,000 and 65,000 years ago, and modern-humans weren't the only people on it. The Neanderthals and Denisovans of Eurasia were the other humans on the planet at the time. Modern-humans are believed to have initially left Africa sometime between 110,000 and 95,000 years ago,[145] and by 100,000 years ago humans and Neanderthals had begun interbreeding.[146] While modern-human remains are found in the Middle East earlier than 80,000 years ago, after 80,000 years ago they were replaced by Neanderthals. It is believed that modern-humans left the region because the world was cooling, which allowed the neanderthals to migrate down into the area from Eastern Europe or Central

Asia. Somewhere in Eurasia, a group of modern-humans with some Neanderthal DNA did survive,[147] presumably in South Asia.[148] Between 55,000 and 45,000 years ago these modern-humans returned to the Middle East, as the neanderthals withdrew to Europe and Siberia.

If Larak existed between 94,000 to 65,000 years ago, and if its inhabitants were modern-humans, then it could not have existed in the Middle East. Based on the archaeogenetic evidence most likely regions for this culture would have been South Asia,[149] or Southeast Asia.[150] This early shepherding civilization of Larak would have suffered a near extinction-level set-back when the Toba Volcano exploded in Indonesia around 75,000 years ago. This volcanic super-eruption is estimated to have ejected so much ash and poisonous gasses into the atmosphere that it is believed to have caused a volcanic winter that would have lasted for up to ten years.[151] In India, the ash-fall left a layer 15 cm thick.[152] Until recent genetic research confirmed that the early Eurasian population had survived, it was believed that they had been wiped out by the Toba super-eruption.

Laraki Genetics

As is the case for the later Zimbir and Shuruppak civilizations, archaeogenetics has identified a mitochondrial DNA haplogroup that is believed to have arisen during this time, haplogroup-R. This haplogroup is the direct ancestor of haplogroup-U, which arose during the late Zimbir period, which was the direct ancestor of haplogroup-K, which arose during the late Shuruppak period. There were other mitochondrial subclades around, R gave rise to B, F, R0, and pre-JT, other than U, however, these groups arose at different times. The *Sumerian King List* points to specific periods in time when apparently significant civilizations existed, and these points in time follow a specific human lineage, back through K to U to R.

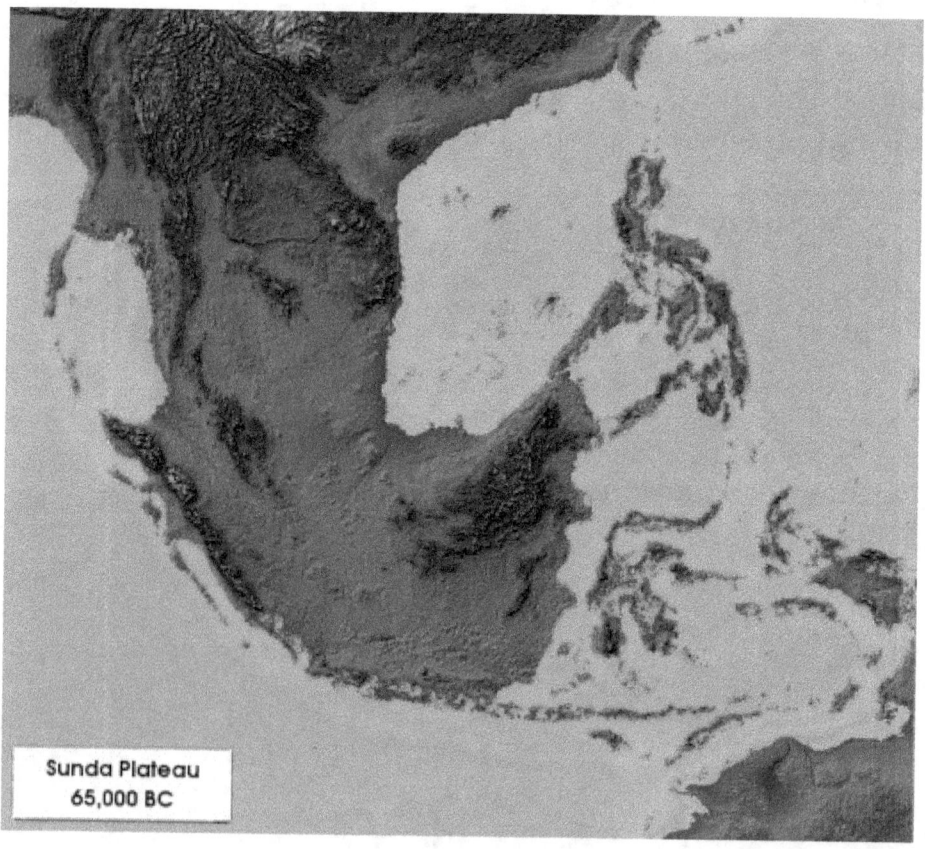

Haplogroup-R is believed to have arisen around 66,000 years ago,[153] in either South Asia[149] or Southeast Asia.[150] Haplogroup-R gave rise to several haplogroups: B, F, R0, pre-JT, and of course U, meaning that haplogroup-R and its descendants are spread over a vast swath of the world. Haplogroup-R and its descendants a found among the native populations of the Americas, Australia, Central Asia, Europe, the Horn of Africa, North Africa, the Pacific Islands, Papua, South Asia, and Southeast Asia. In fact, the only region where haplogroup-R and its descendants are rare is Sub-Saharan Africa. This has led to the logical conclusion that it originates in Asia.

These early Laraki people colonized South Asia, the Southeast Asian Sunda Plateau, and the continent of Sahul (Australia and Papua) by 65,000 years ago.[154] Along the way, they encountered the Denisovans, who they interbred with. They could not have reached Sahul without boats of some kind, meaning that the Larak culture had to have been sea-faring. Given the high percentage of Denisovan DNA found in Papuans and Melanesians, it has been proposed that the Denisovans had also crossed to Sahul, where the primary interbreeding took place.[155] This would mean that the Denisovans were also seafaring, however, it is also possible that the two groups crossed to Sahul together after making contact on the Sunda Plateau. Based on the subclades that developed within the R haplogroup, it is possible to trace the migrations of peoples out of Larak.

Haplogroup-R0a is mostly found in the Middle East, North Africa, the Horn of Africa, and Central Asia. The highest percentage is found on the island of Socotra in the Arabian Sea, at 40%.[111] This suggests that this haplogroup may have originated in the now-submerged continental shelf of Arabia or East Africa.

Haplogroup-HV and its subclades are mainly found in Europe, the Middle East, Central Asia, South Asia, and North Africa. It is believed to have originated around 24,000 years ago in Anatolia or Caucasia.[156] The H subclade is the most common in Europe and is believed to have developed around 20,000 years ago in Southwest Asia.[157] The V subclade is found at low frequencies throughout Europe, its highest percentage is found among the Sami people of Northern Europe, at 40%.[158]

Haplogroup-R1 and its descendants are mainly found in the Caucasian Mountains, with traces found in the Slavic populations to the north,[156] and the Brahmins of Uttar Pradesh[159] in India. This haplogroup is sometimes used as evidence that the Indo-Aryans originated on the Pontic Steppes north of Caucasia. R1's subclades R1a and R1b are also found in a high percentage in the indigenous population of the North American great lakes regions, and smaller percentages in Siberia and among the Fulani tribes of West Africa, although the cause for this wide distribution remains controversial.

Haplogroup-R2 is mainly found in Balochistan,[160] Pakistan, with smaller percentages across Rajasthan and Uttar Pradesh in India, and Iran, Turkey, and Georgia. If Balochistan was the location of the founder population, they may have been related to the Harappans or Elamites.

Haplogroup-J is mainly found in the Middle East, with the highest percentage found in Saudi Arabia at 21%.[161] Approximately 10% of Europeans, 8% of Caucasians, and 6% of North Africans carry mitochondrial DNA from this haplogroup. It is also believed to date from around 45,000 years ago, like U, and is almost nonexistent in East Asia, indicating the strong possibility that both originated in Zimbir.

Haplogroup-T is mainly found in the region around the Caspian Sea, in the Caucasus Mountains, Northern Iran, and Turkmenistan.[160] It is found in almost 10% of the European populations, with smaller percentages across the Middle East, Central Asia, South Asia, North Africa, and the Horn of Africa. It is believed to have developed in Anatolia sometime around 25,000 years ago.

Haplogroup-R3 is a rare haplogroup found in Armenia.

BROKEN TIMELINES - BOOKS 1-3: EGYPT, MESOPOTAMIA, THE INDO-EUROPEANS AND HARAPPANS

Haplogroup-R5 is widely spread across South Asia but is focused in Madhya Pradesh, India, at 17%,[148] indicating a possible location for the founder population.

Haplogroup-R6 is a rare haplogroup found in South Asia, mainly in the Tamil and Kashmiri populations.[148]

Haplogroup-R7 is primarily found in eastern India, among Austroasiatic and Dravidian speaking populations.[162] Among the Austronesian speaking people of India, this haplogroup represents 10% of the population.

Haplogroup-R8 is mainly found in eastern India, mainly in Orissa, in Andhra Pradesh. It is also found in Gujarat. In Orissa, it represents 12% of the population and is focused in the Austroasiatic speaking population.[163] Orissa may have been the location of the founder population.

Haplogroup-R9 (R9b, R9c) is mainly found in Southeast Asia, throughout Indonesia, Malaysia, and Vietnam. The Batak people of the Philippines may have the highest percentage of R9 mitochondrial DNA at 58%.[164]

Haplogroup-F is a major subclade of R9 spread across East and Southeast Asia. It is found in the populations of China, Indonesia, Thailand, and Vietnam. The highest percentages are found in remote regions around the periphery of East Asia, with 50% reported in the Nicobar Islands,[148] and 44% in the Shor people of Siberia.[165] This haplogroup is believed to have developed circa 43,400 years ago, somewhere in Asia.[153] As this haplogroup is not found in Native American populations, it likely developed in Southeast Asia. The collapse of this civilization may have been caused by the same climatic events that caused the collapse of Zimbir.

Haplogroup-R11 is found in Cambodia, China, Japan, Laos, Thailand, and Vietnam, as well as Rajasthan, India. The largest concentrations seem to be in Yunnan, China, at 12.5%.[166]

Haplogroup-B is a common haplogroup among East Asian, Southeast Asian, Siberian, Oceanic, and Native American populations. This haplogroup is believed to have developed sometime around 50,000 years ago, somewhere in Asia. The greatest variety of this haplogroup is found in China, indicating that it underwent its earliest diversification in China.[167] The subclade B4b is one of the five haplogroups found in the Native American population.

Haplogroup-R24 is a rare haplogroup found in the Philippines.[168]

Haplogroup-R12 is a rare haplogroup found in Australian Aboriginal peoples.[169] This haplogroup is closely related to the R21 haplogroup of Southeast Asia.

Haplogroup-R21 is found in the Negrito population of Southeast Asia, including the Jahai of Malaysia at 63%,[170] Senoi in Malaysia at 37%, and the Maniq people of Thailand. This haplogroup is closely related to the R12 haplogroup of Australia.

Haplogroup-R14 is found in Papua, Timor, and Lembata in Indonesia.[171]

Haplogroup-R22 is mainly found in Indonesia, with smaller percentages in Thailand, Vietnam, and Cambodia.[172] Within Indonesia, it is found on Bali at 7.3%, and Borneo at 1.9%, as well as on Java, Lombok, Sulawesi, Sumatra, Sumba, and Timor in lower percentages.[173]

Haplogroup-R23 is a rare haplogroup found in Bali and Sumba in Indonesia.[173]

Haplogroup-R30 is mainly found in South Asia, although also found in Japan.[174] Within India, it is found in Andhra Pradesh, the Punjab, and Uttar Pradesh. It is also found in Nepal and Sri Lanka.[162]

Haplogroup-R31 is a rare haplogroup found in Andhra Pradesh, Rajasthan, and Uttar Pradesh, in India.

Haplogroup-P is widespread throughout Papua,[175] Australia,[176] Melanesia, and Polynesia.[177] Smaller percentages are also found in the Philippines and eastern Indonesia. This group is considered to have formed in Sahul, sometime around 50,000 years ago.

Haplogroup-U is widespread throughout Western Eurasia and North Africa, from South Asia to the Atlantic Ocean. The highest percentages for this haplogroup are found in the Berber and Copts of North Africa, indicating a potential location for the founding group.

Based on the multitude of haplogroups originating from R, it is clear that the founder group for R could have been anywhere in a large swath of Eurasia and North Africa. Europe and Siberia would have to be excluded as Neanderthals were dominant in those regions, and Sahul does not appear to have been colonized until this period, however, it is possible that it was colonized by the Larak civilization. After the fall of Larak, the Laraki people seem to have been migrating in several directions. Those that migrated into Sahul seem to have developed the haplogroup-P mutation by 50,000 years ago. Around the same time, the Larakis that migrated north into China seem to have developed the haplogroup-B mutation, that would later become dominant in East Asia, and contribute to the Native American population.

The Larakis that migrated to the west resettled the Middle East after 55,000 years ago[178] began interbreeding with Neanderthals again,[179] and ultimately developed the U and J mutations by 45,000 years ago, which the *Sumerian King List* suggests was in the Zimbir civilization. Around the same time, another mutation developed in the Laraki that had remained in Southeast Asia, the haplogroup-F mutation. Many additional mutations are listed above, however insufficient research has been published to date to have any clear ideas of when or where these mutations took place.

Meanwhile, the Neanderthals and Denisovans appear to have begun interbreeding around 90,000 years ago, creating an Altai population of Neanderthals with some Denisovan DNA, that modern-humans would later encounter.[180] A modern-human population began interbreeding with the

Altai population around 60,000 years ago,[181] creating one of the ancestral populations for the East Asian and later native American populations.[182] The genetic evidence suggests that Larak was in Southeast Asia, most likely in a region of the Sunda Plateau that is now submerged. Given that the continent of Sahul was colonized during this time, it does seem that there was some level of civilization, as boats would have been required. This does not suggest a particularly advanced civilization but does suggest that they knew how to build houses, and likely had other stone-age technologies, if not something more advanced.

Antediluvian Bad-tibira

The Sumerian King List recorded that before Larak, the kingship was in Bad-tibira for the lives of three kings: Enmenluna, Enmengalana, and Dumuzid the Shepherd. As the first two names are translatable as descriptions of eras, it is clear that these were not the names of kings, but rather dynasties or civilizations. These dynasties were listed as spanning the time period of approximately 201,600 to 93,600 years ago. This covers a long span of human pre-history. The first two dynasties of Enmenluna and Enmengalana covered the time-span of 201,600 to 129,600 years ago, which mostly fell within the Penultimate Glacial Period of circa 196,000 to 130,000 years ago.[183] The following dynasty of Dumuzid the Shepherd covered the period of 129,600 to 93,600 years ago, which coincided with the Eemian Interglacial Period of circa 130,000 to 115,000 years ago,[184] and the onset of the Last Glacial Period, which started around 115,000 years ago.

Bad-tibira was also the name of a major Sumerian city in the dynastic period, located at the modern site of Tell al-Madineh, in southern Iraq. Bad-tibira translates as 'fortress of the smiths,'[185] or 'wall of the copper-workers,'[186] which is remarkably similar to the root of the name of the Egyptian city of Memphis. The name Memphis is derived from the ancient Egyptian words 'Hut-ka-Ptah,' meaning 'Enclosure of the ka of Ptah.' The term 'ka of Ptah' translates as essentially the 'spirit of Ptah,' or more literally 'craftsmen,' as Ptah was the patron deity of craftsmen. Therefore the name of the city could be read as 'enclosure of the craftsmen,' or 'fortress of the craftsmen.' Like Bad-tibira, Memphis also had a mythical pre-dynastic forebearer with the same name. Archaeological research in dynastic Bad-tibira has been hampered by the fact that the city was destroyed sometime in the Neo-Sumerian era, circa 3575 to 3467 BC ULT (2119 to 2011 BC CMT). The destruction was so devastating that the bricks that remain from before the destruction are vitrified,[187] meaning the fire that destroyed the city was hot enough to melt bricks and wide-spread enough to melt a city. Little else survives from before the city was burnt. After the destruction of the city,

King Lippit-Eshtar of Isin rebuilt the Temple of Righteousness in Bad-tibira around 3360 BC ULT (1920 BC CMT),[188] and Governor Sin-Iddinam of Larsa rebuilt the walls of the city around 3270 BC ULT (1830 BC CMT) during the war against the Old Babylonian Empire.

Antediluvian Bad-tibira's kings were listed as Enmenluana, Enmengalana, and Dumuzid the Shepherd. Assyriologists have not agreed on the translation of the names Enmenluana and Enmengalana, mainly as there is justifiably very little interest in arguing the correct translation of a 'mythical' person's name. However, the Sumerians did try to preserve some information, and translating what these names mean is intrinsic to understanding what they left us. The two names are composed of the cuneiform logograms EN, MEN, LU, GAL, and ANA.

EN: can be translated as: dignitary, lord, high priest, ancestor, rule, noble, or time

MEN: is translated as: crown. It is a metaphor implying the EN, meaning ruler.

LU: can be translated as: many, man, men, people, or sheep

GAL: is translated as: great, or big

AN: is translated as: heaven, An (god of heaven), or grain

A: when placed at the end of a word is a nominative.

This means that Enmenluana can be translated as 'the time of the crown of many heavens' although it could also be translated other ways, none of which make any more sense. Enmengalana can be translated as 'the time of the crown of the great heaven.' Neither of which shed much light on the time period, however, this time-span ends with the end of the Penultimate Glacial Period around 130,000 years ago. There are no known surviving stories about either of these kings, however, there is an extensive story about Dumuzid the Shepherd.

Dumuzid the Shepherd

King Dumuzid the Shepherd ruled approximately 129,600 to 93,600 years ago. This means his rule would have begun at the beginning of the Eemian Interglacial Period around 130,000 years ago.[184] During the Eemian Interglacial Period the world warmed as it has in the past 10,000 years, and the glaciers that had been covering the northern continents melted. The Eemian was ultimately warmer than our current world, and the Arctic Ocean became ice-free in the summers, however, Antarctica and Greenland remained glaciated. Wild hippopotamuses, which are currently confined to the African continent, ranged as far north as modern Germany and England.[189] Today the hippopotamus has been hunted to the point that they only survive in remote river regions of Africa, however, a few thousand years ago they ranged throughout almost all of Sub-Saharan Africa, and up to the Mediterranean along the Nile River, and into Canaan.[190]

Dumuzid the Shepherd was a major Sumerian hero and is found in several Sumerian era stories. He was so important that there was a month, in midsummer, named after him. As the Sumerian calendar is believed to predate the life of the later King Dumuzid the Fisher of Uruk, it is clear that they are different people. The original Dumuzid was the inspiration for the later Babylonian and Assyrian god Tammuz, which was also the name of the sixth month on their calendars,[191] which continues to be used in the Hebrew calendar.

In Greece, he was known as Adonis,[192] and the festival for him, in midsummer, was called the Adonia.[193] The name Adonis is believed to originate in Canaan, in the Canaanite word 'adon,' which translates as 'lord.' This belief in Adonis continued to be practiced in Canaan well into the Greek age, as documented by Lucian in his work: *On the Syrian Goddess*, in the second century AD. Adon continues to be used in the Hebrew language, meaning 'lord,' and when pluralized into 'Adonai' somehow means God. Adonis appears to have been adopted by the Greeks during the Greek dark age through contact with the Canaanites/Phoenicians. There is an older version of him that was apparently inherited from the Mycenaeans, who may have adopted him from the Minoans:[194] Dionysus.

There are also several similarities between the Sumerian myths surrounding Dumuzid and some of the earliest stories in the Tanakh, meaning that the Babylonian era Jews must have had access to these ancient stories. Additional correlations between the stories and festivals of Adonis and the Etruscan Atunis, the Phrygian Attis, and the Egyptian Osiris are well documented.[195] An additional very strong correlation is found between Dumuzid and the ancient Aryan Yima/Yama king/god, even though there is no clear connection between the ancient Sumerians and the ancient Indo-Iranians, meaning that the story of Dumuzid the Shepherd, is very, very old.

The Shepherd and the Smith

Dumuzid the Shepherd is known from various Sumerian epics, four of them form an epic saga: *Inanna Prefers the Farmer*, *Inanna's Descent into the Underworld*, *The Dream of Dumuzid*, and *The Return of Dumuzid*. Other Dumuzid stories tell alternate versions of the same basic story, with generally minor but sometimes major differences, these stories include *Inanna and Bilulu*, *Dumuzid and Geshtinanna*, *The Most Bitter Cry*, and *In the Desert by the Early Grass*.

The main epic serial of Dumuzid begins with *Inanna Prefers the Farmer*, which could be read as either a literal story of a woman choosing one husband over another, or, a metaphorical story explaining why shepherding flocks is better for the earth than engineering canals to water farms. *Inanna Prefers the Farmer* is also known as *Dumuzid and Enkimdu*, depending on who is translating it. The story begins with Utu, the Sun, convincing Inanna that she must get married. She courts both Dumuzid the shepherd, and Enkimdu the farmer, and decides to marry Enkimdu, but Utu and Dumuzid gradually persuade her that Dumuzid is the better choice, and ultimately she changes her mind and decides to marry Dumuzid the shepherd.

This story of the Farmer and the Shepherd is the basis of the story in the Judaeo-Christian book of *Genesis* about Cain and Abel.[196] In *Genesis* chapter 4, the brothers Cain and Abel each decided to make a sacrifice to the god Yahweh, Cain from the crops he'd grown, and Abel from one of the sheep he was shepherding. Yahweh for some reason refused Cain's vegetables which caused Cain to become so angry that he killed Abel, which then confused Yahweh because he couldn't find Abel. However, Cain felt guilty, and so to make sure no one killed Cain, Yahweh 'marked' him. It is unclear what this is a reference to, however, several ancient authors claimed it was a disease that caused 'groaning and tremors,' which was the translation used in the original version of the Christian *Old Testament*.[197] This may have been a reference to the diseases that many metal-smiths had in ancient times, which was caused by arsenic poisoning. Many ancient gods associated with metal-smithing were described as having limps or other health problems.[198]

Cain ran away from Eden, where Yahweh was living, to the land of Nod, and built a city called Enoch, the first city in the Judaeo-Christian timeline. While it is possible the later Jewish story only drew the most basic premise for the Cain and Abel story from *Dumuzid and Enkimdu*, it is also possible that the Babylonian Jews drew on sources we no longer have.

The Mountain in the Steppes

In order to understand these stories, it is imperative to understand the language being used, and what the various names mean. Dumuzid is derived from the Sumerian words DU MU meaning 'son of,' and ZI meaning 'life,' making Dumuzid's name mean 'Son of Life.' In the early dynastic period, Dumuzid was also called Ishtaran in the cities of Nippur and Der. Ishtaran's consort was called Sharrat-Deri meaning 'the Queen of Der.' The name Ishtaran may be a remnant of the older Kish civilization's name for Dumuzid, as it sounds like Ishtar, which the Sumerians called Inanna. Ishtar is generally considered to be a Semitic name, as there are a variety of Semitic variations including the Aramaic Attar, South Arabian Athtar, Amharic Astar, Moabite Ashtar, and Ugaritic At'tar. Some of these variations of Attar were male, while others were female, which is consistent with other Semitic gods which changed gender depending on whether the local clan was patriarchal or matriarchal.

Inanna's name is believed to mean 'Lady of Heaven,'[199] however, the Sumerian cuneiform logograms do not translate as that,[200] and she is therefore interpreted by Assyriologists as a goddess that was adopted into the Sumerian religion from another culture. According to the Sumerian epic sagas *Lugal Banda and the Mountain Cave* and *Lugal Banda and the Anzu Bird*, the goddess Inanna moved to Uruk during the life of Lugal Banda of

Uruk, sometime around 9124 BC ULT. Prior to relocating to Uruk, Inanna was in the land of Aratta, somewhere northeast of Uruk, past the Zagros Mountains. Aratta was also mentioned in the *Baudhayana Sutra*, an ancient Sanskrit text, most likely compiled between 800 and 600 BC,[201] although Aratta's location was not given. In both cases, lapis lazuli was mentioned in connection with Aratta, which suggests Aratta was in the Badakhshan region of modern Afghanistan and Tajikistan, as most of the lapis lazuli mined in the ancient world was mined in Badakhshan.[202] While this story of Lugal Banda is generally considered a myth, as no definitive proof has been found of Aratta's existence, it would explain why Inanna has a non-Sumerian name.

Dumuzid's sister was recorded as being Geshtinanna, and his mother's name was recorded as Sirtur, although the name of his father has not survived. Geshtinanna's name translates as approximately 'wine/vine of the heavens.'[203] In the later Akkadian and the Assyrian and Babylonian religions, she became the goddess Belet-Seri, which translates as 'Lady of the Steppes.' Belet-Seri was also called the 'scribe of the Earth,' and after marrying the god Amurru became known as the 'queen of the deserts.' Above are a couple of photographs showing the Gate of Ishtar as it was in the 1920s, and a Mushhushshu on a modern reconstruction of the Gate of Ishtar.

The cuneiform logogram for the Akkadian word 'seri,' was the Sumerian logogram EDIN, which was the Sumerian word for 'steppe.' The Sumerian Garden-of-the-Gods is theorized to be the basis of the later Jewish Garden of Eden,[204] where the name Eden was based on the Sumerian logogram EDIN. In several Sumerian stories such as *Debate Between Sheep and Grain*, *Enki and Ninhursag*, and *Song of the Hoe* the Garden-of-the-Gods is described as being on a mountain, surrounded by a steppe explaining how the word 'edin' would have been associated with the story.

Geshtinanna's Akkadian name Belet-Seri, records she began as King Dumuzid's sister, as the 'Lady of Edin,' then she married Amurru, and became the Queen of the Desert. Amurru, called Martu in Sumerian, was a Semitic god and was the primary god of the Amorites. Like Dumuzid, he was also called 'the shepherd,' which implies he was also a leader. He was also called 'belu shadi' meaning 'lord of the mountain,' which is the origin of the later Jewish phrase 'El Shaddai,' meaning 'god of the mountain.'[205] Amurru was also called several variations of 'belu shadi,' including 'dur-hur-sag-ga sikil-a-ke' meaning 'he who dwells on the pure mountain' and 'kur-za-gan ti-[la],' which means 'who inhabits the shining mountain.' The implication is that Geshtinanna married Martu, while they lived on the mountain in the steppes, and Martu ruled after Dumuzid died, but the steppes became a desert.

Geshtinanna was also said to be married to Nin-Gishzida,[206] a strange character similar to Ishtaran's companion Nirah. Nin-Gishzada is a title that translates as 'Lady of the Good Tree,' in Sumerian, however, was depicted as male. Many Sumerian female deities appear to have been emasculated as the Akkadians subsumed the Sumerian civilization. Nin-Gishzada and Nirah were both depicted in Sumerian art as a snake, or as an anthropomorphize snake. The modern caduceus symbols, used to represent both medicine and commerce are derived, via the Greeks, from an ancient Sumerian emblem in which the two serpents are entwined around the Good Tree, accompanied by the two Guardian dragons, pictured above on the Libation vase of Gudea.

Below are a rubbing of a pictorial brick from the Eastern Han Dynasty, in China circa 25 to 220 AD, and a photograph close-up of Fuxi and Nuwa. The pictorial brick also includes several other features of ancient Chinese religion, including the Peach Tree of Immortality, and the Great Bear, who is similar to Jambavan from the Indian epics.

The Guardian dragons, which the Sumerians called Mushhus, and were later called Mushhushshu by the Akkadians, Babylonians, and Assyrians, were the

Guardians of the Good Tree. The Gate of Ishtar was one of the gates to Babylon built in 575 BC. This is a clear forerunner of the Tree of Knowledge in the Jewish Garden of Eden. Like in the Sumerian story, the Jewish story has a snake associated with the sacred tree, which, like Nin-Gishzada, could speak. The Guardians also showed up in the Jewish story, as the two cherubs at the entrance to Eden, who were posted there to keep out humanity after Eve was convinced by the serpent to eat the sacred fruit, and then gave some to Adam.[207] In the *Book of Ezekiel* the cherubs are described as being winged creatures combining human, lion, bull, and eagle features,[208] much like the Assyrian and Babylonian era depictions of Mushhushshu.

The second serpent in the original caduceus was Amashilama, Nin-Gishzada's sister. Similar iconography of a pair of snake-people at the dawn of history is depicted in several ancient cultures, including Fuxi and Nuwa from China, and Osiris and Isis from Egypt. Isis doesn't appear to have been depicted as a serpent until the New Kingdom, when she merged with the Egyptian Old Kingdom god Renenutet, becoming known as Isis-Renenutet. Above is an excerpt from the New Kingdom book *Amduat* (left) which depicts both Isis and Nephtys as serpents, along with a Greco-Roman era Egyptian carving (right) of Isis-Renenutet, Serapis, and the baby Horus. Renenutet was a similar, yet reptilian, mother-goddess that dates back to pre-Dynastic times in Egypt.

Osiris was replaced by Serapis as Isis consort during the Greek era, who was a merged god, combining Osiris and the Old Babylonian god Ea, previously known as Enki by the Sumerians. Ea was known as Shar Apsi in Neo-Babylonian, meaning 'King of the Apsu.' The reason the Greeks believed Osiris and Enki were originally the same god is unclear, however, they did have ancient Egyptian and Babylonian texts that we no longer have access to. Below are two photos showing statues of Renenutet (left) and a similar Ubaid era reptilian mother-goddess (right) from Mesopotamia, dating to between 8331 and 5831 BC ULT (6500 to 4000 BC CMT).

These snake twins also seem to be the root of the story found in the Mahabharata of the two giant poisonous serpents in Indra's heaven that were stationed as Guardians of the amrita, the elixir of immortality. This is reminiscent of the Jewish version of the story, where the cherubs were placed at the entrance to Eden to stop humanity from eating from a second sacred tree: the Tree of Life, which would make humans immortal if they ate from it. While snake-people and dragons guarding a tree growing immortality-fruit makes the story of Dumuzid seem like fiction, it is nevertheless, even if it is fiction, certainly an ancient story embedded in many ancient cultures, and continues to influence the modern Abrahamic religions.

Jewish Antediluvian Bloodlines

In the Jewish story of Cain and Abel, the two brothers fought for the approval of Yahweh, and Cain ultimately killed Abel. Cain is written in Hebrew as קין and is translated in the King James Bible as either Cain or Kenite depending on the translator's choice. The Kenites were a tribe that lived in southern Canaan during the time of Abraham and Moses, whose name translates as Smiths, and are reported to have been copper-smiths.[209] They are believed to be the descendants of Cain in some interpretations of Jewish timelines.[210] While Cain is generally assumed to be the son of Adam, many ancient Jewish scholars[211] such as Philo and Pirke De-Rabbi Eliezer[212] believed he was the son of the serpent from the garden of Eden, called Samael, whose name means 'Venom of God.'

In the book of *Genesis*, Cain named the city Enoch after his son, who apparently isn't the Enoch that later encountered the Watchers, but a different Enoch. The book of *Genesis* describes two genealogies descending from Adam and Eve, the genealogy of Seth, and the genealogy of Cain. These two bloodlines both have people named Enoch and Lamech, and most of the names are similar in both genealogies. Theologians have suggested that the two bloodlines represent two competing pre-Judaic bloodlines, the Sethite and Cainite bloodlines. It is believed by many that the Sethite bloodline is inspired by the Sumerian Antediluvian Dynasties.[213]

Cainite bloodline:

- Adam
- Cain
- Enoch
- Irad
- Mehujael
- Methusael
- Lamech

- Naamah

Sethite bloodline:

- Adam
- Seth
- Enosh
- Cainan
- Mahalaleel
- Jared
- Enoch
- Methuselah
- Lamech
- Noah

Sumerian Antediluvian dynasties:

- Alulim
- Alalgar
- Enmenluanna
- Enmengalanna
- Dumuzid
- Ensipaziana
- Enmendurana
- Ubara-Tutu

If the Sethite bloodline was inspired by the Sumerian King List, then it is logical to assume that the very similar Cainite bloodline must have been inspired by the Sumerian King List as well. In fact given the similarities in the names, the two must have had a common ancestral bloodline. This has been reconstructed as the combined bloodline:

- Adam
- Seth-Cain/Cainan
- Enosh-Mehujael/Mahalaleel

- Irad/Jared
- Enoch
- Methusael/Methuselah
- Lamech
- Naamah/Noah

In this combined bloodline, Seth and Cain are still the sons of Adam, and Cainan is an alternate name for Cain. Enosh would be the cousin of Mehujael, who is also Mahalaleel. Irad and Jared are the same person, and father on Enoch, whose son is Methusael or Methuselah, who is the father of Lamech, who is the father of Naamah or Noah. Naturally, this cannot be proven as thousands of years have passed since the two bloodlines were recombined into *Genesis*, however, it does show that the story of these patriarchs was very old by the time the early Jews were compiling *Genesis*.

The story of Cain and Abel does include some other details which could descend from an older account of *Dumuzid and Enkimdu*. In the Jewish story, Abel was the shepherd who died, like Dumuzid the Shepherd. After that Cain went east to the land of Nod and built the city of Enoch. While Cain's name indicates he was a smith, as one would expect if he came from Bad-tibira, the book of *Genesis* claims the city he founded was the City of Enoch. If one accepts the correlation between King Enmendurana and the idea both Enochs were divergent stories of the same Enoch, then the city Cain founded was Zimbir, which would later rise to prominence between 65,000 and 43,000 years ago.

This city of Enoch was built in the land of Nod, 'on the east of Eden' according to Genesis 4:16. Based on the correlation of Eden and 'edin,' the Sumerian word for steppe, the land of Nod would have been somewhere on the same steppe as the mountain where the Garden-of-the-Gods was. Nod translates as approximately Wanderers, implying that whoever was living there were nomadic, explaining why Cain had to build his own city. Naturally, there are the internal contradictions within the Genesis narrative, in which there are three people in the world, Adam, Eve, and Cain, and Cain goes off on his own and has a child, then builds a city for that child. Clearly whoever wrote this, and whoever edited it, and whoever compiled it into what is today the book of *Genesis*, knew there had to be other people around.

Recent Out of Africa Theory?

If one accepts the Recent Out-of-Africa theory for modern-human origin in Africa, then the lifespan of Dumuzid was during the first phase of modern-human migrations out of Africa into the Middle East and South Asia. The current version of the Recent Out of Africa theory proposes that modern-humans first migrated into southern Eurasia between 110,000 and 95,000 years ago, and by 100,000 years ago modern-humans and Neanderthals had begun interbreeding.[214] Meanwhile Dumuzid's lifespan was listed as approximately 129,600 to 93,600 years ago. Given that Cain was leaving Eden traveling east, the original Garden-of-the-Gods must have been in North Africa somewhere. As Zimbir was required to still exist in 65,000 and 44,000 years ago, the City of Enoch would have to have been in South Asia. This would then suggest that Cain settling in Nod, and being 'marked' as different from other people, was the first wave of modern-humans settling in southern Eurasia and creating light-skinned children with the native Neanderthals. The light-skin genes in modern Eurasian and Native American populations are believed to be inherited from Neanderthal ancestors.[215]

This is of course, only valid if the current version of the Recent Out-of-Africa theory is correct. Modern-human remains have been found in Eurasia long predating the current version of the Recent Out of Africa theory, indicating that modern-humans either ventured out of Africa earlier than previously thought, or that they originated elsewhere. The immediate ancestor of the modern humans was thought to be homo-heidelbergensis until genetic analysis of the Sima de los Huesos fossils showed homo-heidelbergensis to be primitive Neanderthals, and pushed back the splitting of the modern-human and heidelbergensis-neanderthal bloodlines to roughly 600,000 to 800,000 years ago.[216] This raises the question of who our primary ancestors were if they weren't homo-heidelbergensis. The ancestor species of homo-heidelbergensis is currently believed to be homo-erectus, which could be the last common ancestor the modern-human bloodline had with the Neanderthal and Denisovan bloodlines.

Homo-erectus ranged over most of the African and Eurasian landmass, however, they were replaced across that entire range by homo-heidelbergensis by 500,000 years ago. One of the last homo-erectus enclaves is believed to be in Java, Indonesia from around 143,000 years ago.[217] Another later enclave was found in Bilzingsleben, Germany from around 370,000 years ago.[218] Somewhere, modern-humans are assumed to have evolved from homo-erectus or an intermediate species, and by 200,000 years ago seem to have spanned a vast region of Africa and Eurasia.

Modern-human teeth discovered in the Qesem Cave, in Israel, have been dated to between 400,000 and 200,000 years old, and appear to be physiologically similar to the remains found in the Qafzah and Es Skhul Caves, in Israel, dated to between 120,000 and 80,000 years ago.[219] In Morocco, the remains recovered from the Jereb Irhoud Cave have been dated to between 350,000 and 280,000 years ago.[220] In Dali County, Shaanxi, China, the so-called Dali-Man remains have been recovered, which have not been dated themselves, however, ox teeth recovered with the Dali-Man remains have been dated via uranium-series dating to 260,000 years ago.[221] The fact that the Dali-Man remains were recovered with ox remains indicates that humans could have had domesticated cattle a quarter million years earlier than generally assumed. Dali-Man has been described as being either early homo-sapiens or late homo-erectus, indicating a potential transitional species in Eastern Asia.

Between 200,000 and 100,000 years ago a large number of modern-human sites appear across Eurasia and Africa, calling into question why anyone would support the recent Out of Africa theory. By 177,000 years ago modern-humans were living in Israel,[222] the UAE by 127,000 years ago,[223] China by 120,000 years ago,[224] and Oman by 106,000 years ago.[225] The reason that the recent Out of Africa theory has support is due to the limited genetic diversity found among non-Africans compared to the genetic diversity found on the African continent. Genetic studies from the early 2000s showed higher levels of genetic diversity within Africa than in the rest of the world,[226] however larger studies conducted since then have shown that the Eurasian and Oceanic populations were driven by natural selection to selectively breed out certain traits,[227] and the greater diversity within Africa was caused by Eurasians migrating into Africa.[227]

At least one human species was apparently living in North America by 130,000 years ago.[228] Given that other animals were able to cross between Siberia and Alaska, it seems illogical that archaic humans couldn't have. The dominant genes in the Native American population are modern-human, like the rest of the planet's population, however, there are traces of both Neanderthal and Denisovan DNA found in the Americas. The Neanderthal DNA is easy to explain, as all native Americans have some Neanderthal DNA inherited from their Eurasian ancestors.

The Denisovan DNA is more difficult to explain, as it is found in the northern Andes, in South America. If the Denisovan alleles were carried into the Americas by migrants from Eurasia traveling with the other migrants, the Denisovan DNA would be spread through the entire native American population, and not contained in a region of South America. Either a group of modern-humans with a higher percentage of Denisovan DNA migrated into the Americas before the rest of the ancestors of the Native Americans, or the Denisovans migrated into the Americas, and didn't settle or survive in North America. As the Denisovan DNA in the Asia-Pacific region is focused on the equator, it is possible that the Denisovans didn't like the cold, meaning the extreme cold of the glacial periods, that covered most of North America in ice-sheets miles high, could have driven the Denisovans south. The time period of the ancient human presence in North America does happen to correlate with the beginning of the Eemian Interglacial Period around 130,000 years ago, and coincidentally perhaps, the beginning of Dumuzid's reign on the Sumerian King List.

The Underworld in the Mountain

Regardless of where modern-humans originated, they were widespread by 200,000 years ago, and while the Sumerian Edin could be interpreted as North Africa, various Eurasian stories point to the Eurasian steppes. Wherever Dumuzid's Bad-tibira was, his story wasn't about his city, but rather, his death. His story continues in the epic poem *Inanna's Descent into the Underworld*, in which Inanna visited her sister Eresh-Kigal in the Underworld, to attend the funeral of Eresh-Kigal's husband Gugalanna. Eresh-Kigal's name translates as 'Queen of the Great Earth,' and she lived in a place called Ganzir in the Kur, with her husband Gugalanna, before his death. Below is a photograph of the Queen of Night Relief dating to the Old Babylonian Empire, circa 3352 to 3038 BC ULT (1894 to 1595 BC CMT), believed to either depict Eresh-Kigal or Ishtar (Inanna) standing on lions.

Kur was the Sumerian word meaning 'mountain,' although in the later Sumerian period her abode became known as Irkalla. The Akkadians later called it Ersetu, their word for the ground, or used the various Sumerian euphemisms as names. Irkalla meant 'bringer of precious wealth,' which seems to be the same meaning as the Greco-Roman Plouton/Pluto whose name meant 'wealth,' and referred to the mineral wealth that miners pulled from the Earth.[230] The Sumerians also used several euphemisms for Kur in later Sumerian stories, which translate as 'House of Dumuzi,' 'Mountain of No Return,' 'Darkness', or simply 'Great Earth.' Below is an Assyrian stela depicting Ishtar (Inanna) riding a lion.

In the Sumerian era, Ganzir was described as a dark, dreary cavern located deep below the ground,[231] where inhabitants were believed to continue 'a shadowy version of life on earth.'[232] This underworld was no fiery abode, like the Greek Underworld. It was dark, boring, and the food was described as dry as dust with bread as hard as clay. It also didn't matter what someone had done before going to the Underworld, the conditions were the same for everyone. Below is an Assyrian stela depicting Ishtar (Inanna) riding a lion.

Eresh-Kigal's husband was Gugalanna during the Sumerian era, but was replaced by Nergal during the later Akkadian, Babylonian, and Assyrian eras. Gugalanna's name is also a title, which translates as 'canal-inspector of heaven,' an odd title for someone in the Underworld. The name Ganzir is also odd, it is made up of the logograms GAN and ZIR, which translates as approximately 'foundation water-pump,' which when combined with Gugalanna's title makes this Underworld sound more like a subterranean water pumping station. Nergal was described during the Akkadian and Old Babylonian eras as the god of drought, indicating he may be the same character as the failed 'canal-inspector' Gugalanna. From there he evolved through the Neo-Babylonian era into a god of plague and pestilence, and took over the rule of the Underworld from his wife.[233]

The Dumuzid Saga

In the epic *Inanna's Descent into the Underworld*, Inanna decides to visit Ganzir, which seems like an odd thing to do, if the Underworld referred to the state of being dead. As the law stated that no one could leave Ganzir other than messengers from Ganzir, she ordered her minister Nin-Shubur to intercede with the gods Anu, Enki, Enlil, and Nanna if she wasn't back within three days.[234] Nin-Shubur translates as 'Lady of the East,' and as minister of Inanna she could apparently speak directly with the gods, implying this civilization was a pantheocracy, like the later Sumerian civilization. Early Assyriologists assumed she was male, because women weren't allowed in government when 'modern' Assyriologists first discovered references to her, and the Akkadian version of her was a male: Papsukkal the messenger of the gods.[235] However this concept was proven in error, and she is now considered female again.[236]

Inanna dressed up in her most elaborate attire in order to impress everyone in Ganzir, and headed down to the gates of Ganzir, but when she got there she was stripped of her fancy clothes and her lapis lazuli measuring rod, which appears to be an archaic precursor to the royal scepter.[237] Apparently her fancy clothes and measuring rod weren't permitted in Ganzir, where everyone was dressed in filthy rags, and so she had to proceed into Ganzir naked. When she reached her sister's palace she was apparently quite angry about it and tried to oust Eresh-Kigal, ordering her to relinquish her throne. Unfortunately for her the seven judges of Ganzir, turned against her and ended up hanging her naked body from a hook, leaving Eresh-Kigal on the throne.[238]

After three days minister Nin-Shubur went to the temples of An, Enki, Enlil, and Nanna, begging them to free Inanna from the Underworld. An, Enlil, and Nanna all refuse to intercede as Inanna knew the law before heading down to Ganzir, but the compassionate Enki decided to help. Enki sent two androgynous beings down into Ganzir to heal Eresh-Kigal, and ask her for Inanna's body. These two androgynous beings were named Galatura and Kurjara, and while they are described as androids made from the dirt under Enki's fingernails in the oldest surviving version of *Inanna Descends to the Underworld*, the name Galatura betrays a plausible earlier version of the story. The logograms GA-LA, and TU-RA translate as 'Priest of the Sick.'

During the Sumerian era, the priests at the Temple of Inanna at Uruk were called galas. This priesthood was composed of both cis-gender women and transgender women, or in older translations transvestites.[239] Transgender priests were common in ancient Sumerian temples[240] and continued to be common in the Middle East until the Roman period. During the Roman Republican era, the Cult of Cybele was adopted into the Roman pantheon, in 204 BC.[241] The priests of Cybele were called gallus, and they were described as eunuchs that dressed as women,[242] which in modern terminology would be trans-gender women. These gallus worshiped Cybele and her mate Attis, which was the Phrygian version of Adonis,[243] himself a later version of Dumuzid the Shepherd. This means that the belief in Dumuzid and Inanna was not just widespread, but lasted a long time. Above is a photograph of a Sumerian statue of gala priests.

When Enki sent the two priests to Eresh-Kigal, she was described as being very sick, in agony like a woman giving birth. They were advised to offer to help her if she agreed to give them Inanna's body. Enki provided Kurjara with the food-of-live, and Galatura with the water-of-life. Then he instructed them to sprinkle the food-of-life and water-of-life over Inanna's body to bring her back to life.

This odd instruction from Enki served as the basis of the later Akkadian, Babylonian, and Assyrian Tammuz festivals, as well as the identical Adonia in Greece. In these midsummer festivals women would sprinkle seeds and water them, which would cause them to sprout, but then die as it was too late in the season for them to grow. Similar festivals were practiced by the Etruscan for Atunis and the Egyptians for Osiris. Why so many ancient cultures wasted seeds like this in midsummer is unknown, but it was practiced over a large territory for thousands of years. It is also reminiscent of the Christian Eucharist, in which eating a cracker, representing human flesh, and drinking some wine, representing human blood, grants immortality... after you die.

While this story is central to the ancient returning from death rituals of many religions, it could also be interpreted slightly differently. While the oldest surviving version does portray Inanna as dying after the judges yelled at her, hanging a dead body on a hook does seem like beating a dead horse. Why torture a corpse? If she wasn't actually dead, giving her food and water after removing her from the hook does seem like the logical thing to do.

When the judges saw her heading back up to the surface, they stated that as no one was allowed to leave Ganzir, she would have to have someone take her place. They sent a number of 'galla' with her to make sure she sent someone back to Ganzir to take her place. The word 'galla' is often translated as 'demon' by Assyriologists, especially in relation to Ganzir, and that does seem to be how the Akkadians and later Mesopotamian civilizations interpreted the term. Nevertheless, the term is composed of the Sumerian logograms

BROKEN TIMELINES - BOOKS 1-3: EGYPT, MESOPOTAMIA, THE INDO-EUROPEANS AND HARAPPANS

GAL and LA, meaning 'great man,' and was the Sumerian term for their concept of a policeman, deputy, or bailiff.[244] Translating the term as bailiff does make more sense, as these 'galla' were sent by a group of judges, to make sure someone that was essentially on probation carried through on her agreement to send someone down into the Ganzir to take her place. Nevertheless, this term did evolve into the Akkadian 'galla,' meaning demon in the contemporary Judaeo-Christian-Islamic and Buddhist concept of the term.

Outside the gates of Ganzir, Inanna and the bailiffs found the minister Nin-Shubur waiting for her to return. The bailiffs wanted to take Nin-Shubur back to Ganzir as her substitute, but Inanna refused to let them, stating Nin-Shubur was too loyal. Next, they found Shara, Inanna's brother, who the bailiffs wanted to take. Inanna objected stating he was her 'singer, manicurist, and hairdresser,' who was still mourning, and so Inanna wouldn't let the bailiffs take Shara. Then they found Inanna's other brother Lulal, who was still mourning, so Inanna wouldn't let them take him either.

Then they found Dumuzid sitting on the throne, apparently not grieving the loss of Inanna, and in a fit of rage, she told the bailiffs to take Dumuzid to Ganzir. In some of the later versions they found Dumuzid being entertained by a slave-girl, however, this seems to be a late addition to the story.

The story continued in the Sumerian poem *The Dream of Dumuzid*, in which Dumuzid told his sister Geshtinanna a dream he'd had.[245] In the dream Dumuzid escaped the bailiffs who were trying to take him to Ganzir, and they began searching Bad-tibira for him. They interrogated his sister Geshtinanna, but she would not tell them where he was hiding. Then they interrogated one of his friends who gave up Dumuzid's hiding place. The bailiffs captured him and dragged him to Ganzir.[246] This poem may also be a later addition to the saga, however, is generally included as it fits between *Inanna's Descent into the Underworld* and *The Return of Dumuzid*.

The Return of Dumuzid picks up where *The Dream of Dumuzid* ends: Dumuzid had been taken to Ganzir, and Geshtinanna was bereaved.

Geshtinanna and Dumuzid's mother Sirtur were lamenting the loss of Dumuzid, when Inanna joined them, regretting her rashness in letting the bailiffs take Dumuzid. They decided to visit Dumuzid in Ganzir, and while there Inanna arranged for Geshtinanna and Dumuzid to each spend only half the year in Ganzir, and be free the rest of the year.[247]

Ishtar and Tammuz, and Zababa

The Akkadian and Babylonian version of Inanna and Dumuzid was Ishtar and Tammuz. This version drew the most directly and demonstrably from the Sumerian version, as the Akkadians literally lived in Sumerian cities, and they adopted Sumerian gods and heroes into their pantheon, either adding them as new gods or syncretizing them with existing Semitic gods. As the Babylonians and Assyrians were the cultural descendants of the Akkadians they inherited these gods, yet expanded and changed the pantheons over time.

The largest difference between the Sumerian and Akkadian-Babylonian narratives of Ishtar versus Inanna revolves around Eresh-Kigal's husband. In the Sumerian era Eresh-Kigal's husband was Gugalanna, who was sometimes represented as being alive, and subservient to his wife, but by the time of *Inanna Descends to the Underworld* was dead, and was the reason Inanna was entering Ganzir, to attend his funeral. In the Akkadian and Babylonian era, Eresh-Kigal's husband Nergal was alive and they rule the Underworld together.[248] The Babylonian story *Nergal and Eresh-Kigal* tells the story of how these gods met and ended up married. This story dates back to at least 1350 BC, as a copy of it was recovered from Tel El-Amarna in Egypt, typically dated to this period.

In *Nergal and Eresh-Kigal* the gods in the Heights were planning a feast, and as Eresh-Kigal was unable to leave the Underworld, they sent a messenger down to ask if she wanted to send someone to represent her at the feast. She decided to send her Minister Namtar, who then ascended the long staircase to the Heights to attend the feast. When Namtar arrived at the feast all the gods rose to show respect for the minister of Eresh-Kigal, all the gods except the brash young Nergal.

Nergal was summoned to the Underworld to answer for insulting the minister of Eresh-Kigal, and before he descended to the Underworld Ea, the Akkadian version of Enki, advised him to not eat the food of the Underworld, not to accept any gifts Eresh-Kigal might offer, and to not have sex with her. He didn't listen, and the two ended up making love for six days. On the sixth day, Nergal decided to return to the Heights, and sneaked off while Eresh-Kigal was still asleep, ascending the long staircase to the Heights without anyone seeing him.

When Eresh-Kigal woke up and found him missing, she went into a psychotic rant, and sent Minister Namtar up to the Heights to bring Nergal back down to the Underworld as she 'did not have enough delight with him before he left!' Namtar ascended the long staircase back up to the Heights, but could not find Nergal, and returned to the Underworld. This happened a few times before he finally found Nergal, and brought him back down to the Underworld for Eresh-Kigal to 'get more delight with.' In a later Babylonian version, Nergal returned on his own, and 'seized her by the hairdo, and pulled her from the throne,' following which he 'took some delight' from her. These two versions have been noted by Assyriologists as being part of a pattern of marginalization and privatization of goddesses[249] during the Akkadian, Babylonian, and Assyrian eras. After the two were reunited they made love for seven days, and Anu ordered his minister Kakka to go to Mount Nugi, and descend into Irkalla and tell Eresh-Kigal and Nergal that they were married.

Most of this story is odd, the idea that someone might be offer food, gifts, or sex, as a punishment for insulting the Queen of the Underworld, is odd. The fact that Nergal ran away and hid, suggests that this story parallels the Rape of Persephone from Greek mythology, but with the genders reversed. Nergal was even described as cringing while he was hiding from Minister Namtar, implying he was for some reason afraid of Eresh-Kigal. This story is completely incongruous with the general marginalization and pacification of female deities in the Akkadian and Babylonian eras and suggests that it dates to an earlier period. During her rant after finding out that Nergal had escaped the Underworld, Eresh-Kigal referred to herself as the Great Judge of the Underworld, which implies that she was the leader of the seven judges that had stopped Inanna from taking over Ganzir in *Inanna Descends into the Underworld*.

The fact that the ministers and Nergal could simply walk up and down a staircase to travel between the Underworld and the Heights, portrays these as actual places, not the state of Death and Life, as Akkadian and Babylonian beliefs generally depicted Irkalla, the land of the dead. This matches the geography of the Dumuzid saga, where one could walk down from the Garden-of-the-Gods on top of a mountain, to Ganzir in a cave in the mountain. This geography is confirmed by Anu when he sends his minister Kakka to Mount Nugi, with orders to descend into the mountain to Irkalla to find Eresh-Kigal and Nergal. Mount Nugi is composed of the Sumerian logograms KUR, NU, and GI, which translate as 'Mountain of no return.' Which does match the Sumerian term 'land of no return,' the euphemism for Ganzir in the Dumuzid saga.

In the Sumerian era, Dumuzid wasn't the only husband of Inanna. According to the ancient records in the city of Kish, Zababa was married to Inanna from the earliest dynastic period. As Zababa was identified as Inanna's husband in the 1st Kish Dynasty, he may be a Kish Civilization precursor to Dumuzid, although Dumuzid was not depicted as a war god or even a warrior. Zababa was a war-god, whose iconography included lions, implying the Guardians from the Garden-of-the-Gods, however, he was not depicted as a cherub or lion-man hybrid, he was depicted as a man with a lion or panther. If Zababa was a Guardian, then the Kishite story might have conflated the goddesses Inanna and Geshtinanna, as Geshtinanna married Amurru after Dumuzid's death, who seems to have been a Guardian.

In the Akkadian era, *Myth of Adapa and the South Wind*, Dumuzid and Gishzida were the two Guardians of the Gates of heaven. The *Myth of Adapa*, was originally recovered from a dig in Tel el-Amarna in Egypt, and typically dated to the archives of King Akhenaten, from circa 1350 BC. Additional copies have been recovered from the Library of Ashurbanipal of Assyria, from circa 650 BC, indicating that this tale was popular over a wide area, and for a very long time.

The story is about a priest of Ea (the Akkadian Enki), who was fishing in the Persian Gulf when a strong wind capsized his boat, and in a fit of rage, he cursed the South Wind to not blow for a week. Anu, the Akkadian version of An, called Adapa to heaven to account for his action, and Ea instructed him to gain the sympathy of Tammuz, the Akkadian Dumuzid, and Gishzida, the Akkadian Nin-Gishzida, the two guardians of the gates of heaven. Ea also told Adapa not to eat any of the food in heaven, because it was poisonous. When he got to the gates of heaven, the guardians offered him the food-of-life, and the water-of-life, which he refused, and when Anu later asked why he refused them, he stated that it was because Ea advised him to. This caused the gods to laugh, as Adapa had unknowingly refused immortality. Anu then cursed humanity with diseases because of Adapa's stopping the south wind from blowing. While the story is entertaining, it appears to be an Akkadian or Old Babylonian fiction, unrelated to the other myths of Dumuzid, and can clearly not be the inspiration for the Adonis, Attis, or Atunis cults across the Mediterranean.

Dumuzid is also mentioned in the Akkadian era *Epic of Gilgamesh* when Ishtar attempted to seduce Gilgamesh, and he rebuffed her advances by reminding her of how she treated Dumuzid. This version does match the Dumuzid saga, however, dates to much later and does not add any new information to the story. Many Akkadian and Babylonian stories were written that either added to the Dumuzid saga, or changed the connotations of the saga. In *The Most Bitter Cry*, the Underworld was described as a place where everything both 'exists' and 'does not exist,' implying an insubstantial existence.[168] Likewise in the Akkadian epic *In the Desert by the Early Grass* Dumuzid became a disembodied spirit in the Underworld and traveled around encountering other disembodied spirits.

These Akkadian era stories changed the narrative from something that could be interpreted in the mundane world, to something that was clearly supernatural. The bailiffs became demons. The judges became devils. Ganzir, which was originally described as a subterranean prison or gulag became the Netherworld, and the Queen of Kigal, became the Queen of the Dead. Likewise, the Garden-of-the-Gods became Heaven, another Netherworld, but with better food.

Adonis, Attis, Atunis, Tithonus, and Osiris

The story of Dumuzid being trapped in the underworld with Eresh-Kigal for half the year, and free to be with Inanna for half the year is clearly the basis of the Greek myth of Aphrodite and Adonis.[251] In the Greek myth Adonis ended up spending a third of the year in the Greek Underworld with Persephone, the Queen of the Underworld, and two-thirds of the year with Aphrodite. The earliest mention of Adonis that has survived is from the Greek poetess Sappho circa 600 BC, however, most of the surviving narrative of the story was added later by Greek and Roman writers. Below is a depiction of Aphrodite and Adonis painted on a vase from circa 410 BC.

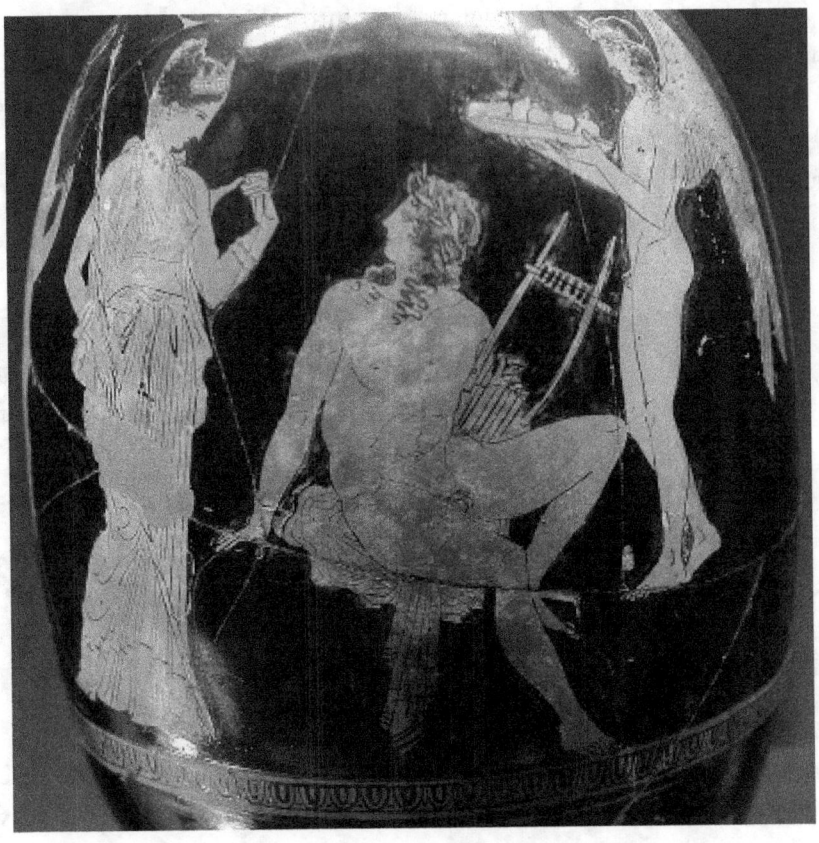

Various other cultures across the region had similar goddess-god duos with similar life-and-death annual cycles, including the Phrygian Cybele and

Attis, whose cult can be traced back firmly to between 500 to 600 BC, thanks to a Phrygian rock-cut shrine dedicated to the 'Mother of the Mountain.'[252] In the Phrygian version of the story, Cybele was originally Agdistis and took the name Cybele after her male genitals were removed. A statue of a seated woman accompanied by lions has been recovered at Çatalhöyük, Turkey, and dates from 6000 BC, calling into question when the Cult of Cybele began, as it is exactly how she was represented in the classical era.[253]

If one accepts that this is an 8000-year-old representation of Cybele, and thereby Inanna, one either has to accept the ULT of Mesopotamian history, in which Sumer was Ubaid, and existed since by at least 8000 BC, or that the Sumerians adopted a Phrygian deity into their pantheon, and put her right up at the top, with An, Enki, and Enlil, around 3000 BC in the CMT. Below are photos of three statues, a Roman-era statue of Cybele (left) from 100 to 200 AD, the Çatalhöyük Statuette (center) from circa 6000 BC, and an ancient statue of Cybele riding a lion (right) recovered from Roman-era ruins, but believed to predate Rome.

Significant similarities were noted between Dumuzid and Osiris in the early 1900s by anthropologist James Frazer. Both Dumuzid and Osiris were considered gods of the dead,[173] and were connected with grain,[255] and festival involving planting grains at the wrong time of the year, and were killed tragically, but then brought back to life by their wives, Inanna and Isis.[256] In both versions of the story, there is a special kind of food and water, in Sumer the food-of-life and water-of-life, in Egypt the food-of-the-gods and the water-of-the-gods.[257] Both Osiris and Dumuzid were also described as 'permanently youthful.'[258]

Below are photographs of an ancient Egyptian painting of Osiris' mummy sprouting grains, and a 'grain mummy.' Grain mummies were dried mud and seed statues, used in ancient Egypt to plant grain, likely to keep the Nile floods from washing the grain away. In mid-summer, grain mummies shaped like Osiris were used in a ceremony in which they were watered, sprouted, but then died as they weren't planted. This ceremony could have simply originated as a way to use up extra grain mummies or could be related to the similar festivals in Eurasia.

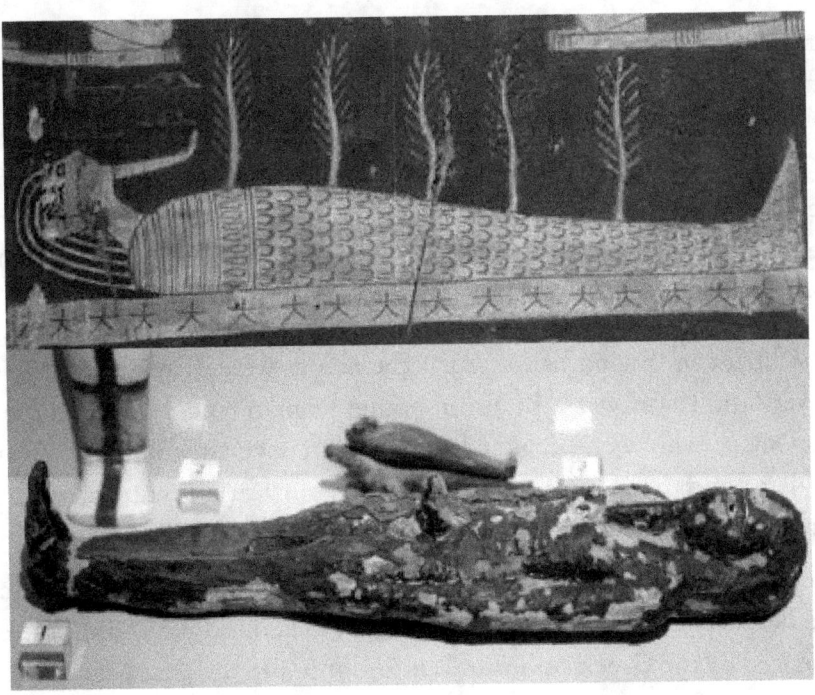

Egyptologists have debated the significance of these similarities, not just with Dumuzid, but with Tammuz, Adonis, and Attis, and have not come to a consensus.[259] The death of Osiris, along with his resurrection, his association with the grain sprouting ceremony, and his eternal youth date back to at least the Old Kingdom,[260] and many Egyptologists believe they may date back to the pre-dynastic era.[261]

If Osiris and Dumuzid do have a common ancestral story, it appears to have been very corrupted by one of the cultures during the early dynastic eras. This further complicates the issue for Assyriologists that would like to maintain the fiction that Dumuzid the Shepherd was a mythical version of Dumuzid the Fisherman, as Dumuzid the Fisherman lived during the time of the Egyptian Old Kingdom. Using the conventional timelines, the Old Kingdom was circa 2686 to 2181 BC, while the life of Dumuzid the Fisherman is guesstimated to be around 2600 BC.

If on the other hand the ULT is used, there is more than enough time for Dumuzid's story to have been corrupted into the Osiris myth, as the Inanna cult would have moved from Aratta to Uruk around the time that Lugal Banda became king, circa 9136 BC, while the Egyptian dynastic era would have begun circa 5510 BC. The long-timeline also allows more than enough time for the Dumuzid story to have spread up to the Phrygians by 6000 BC when they made the statue of the 'Mother of the Mountain.'

In the Etruscan version of the story, the heroes were Turan and Atunis. In this version, Turan was a beautiful young woman, and Atunis a beautiful young man, who were depicted as being in love. As the early Romans conquered and then assimilated the Etruscans, little else is known, other than their midsummer month was named after Turan, and she was sometimes depicted with wings, like Ishtar.[262] The oldest Etruscan artwork depicting these heroes dates to only around 300 BC, meaning they could have been influenced by the Greek Aphrodite and Adonis. On the next page is a sketch of the back of an engraved Etruscan mirror from between 500 to 300 BC, which depicts Attis (left), Turan (center), and Zipunu (right).

BROKEN TIMELINES - BOOKS 1-3: EGYPT, MESOPOTAMIA, THE INDO-EUROPEANS AND HARAPPANS

Dionysus, Disonuso, Diwonijo, and Bacchus

The most enigmatic Greek god, Dionysus, was steeped in Dumuzid-Tammuz lore. For the Greeks, he was always the foreign god, even though being part of the Greek pantheon since the Mycenaean era, circa 1500 to 1100 BC, when they called him Disonuso.[263] This foreign god was also worshiped by the Minoans under the name Diwonijo, although it is unclear when they started worshiping him. Below is a photo of the ancient Greek painter Amasis' rendition of Dionysus, Demeter, and Persephone, from circa 525 BC.

The Minoans built a major civilization in the Aegean long before the Greeks. Their civilization was devastated by the volcanic eruption of Thera sometime between 1650 and 1500 BC, however, dating systems all disagree on when.

Archaeologists working in Crete generally claim it was circa 1500 BC[264] due to the style of pottery being made at the time, carbon dating places it between 1627 and 1600 BC[265] by examining the remains of plants buried at the time. Egyptologists have found a layer of pumice they think is related to Thera at Tel el Dab'a that is dated to the reign of King Ahmose I, which places the Thera eruption circa 1540 BC.[266] Meanwhile ice core samples from Greenland show evidence of a large volcanic eruption circa 1642 BC,[267] and dendrochronology shows a disruption of the normal growth cycles of trees circa 1628 BC in both North America[268] and Europe.[269] Additionally Chinese records of the year 1618 BC imply a large volcanic eruption somewhere in the northern hemisphere.[270]

This eruption of Thera didn't destroy the Minoans but did cause a great deal of damage throughout the Aegean. The eruption caused tsunamis and ash-fall across the region damaging their economy and causing their civilization's decline. In the longer term, the decline of the Minoans ultimately allowed the rise of the Greeks. Like the history of other nearby cultures, the Minoans timeline is based on how it correlates with Egypt, however, unlike the Middle Eastern cultures, there is no complex written histories or invasions by other cultures before the Greeks invaded near the end of Minoan history.

The Minoan timeline was largely the creation of Arthur Evans, circa 1900 AD. Evans was the discoverer of the Minoan civilization and subsequently divided the civilization into three periods which he lined up with the periods of the three Egyptian Kingdoms, based on imported Egyptian pottery and artifacts. Archaeologists working in Crete have largely followed Evans' model, adjusting the Minoan timeline to keep it in sync with the contemporary view of Egyptian history. This means the history is currently viewed as falling between 3500 and 1100 BC, beginning a few hundred years before the unification of Egypt, and ending during the Greek dark age. If Minoan history is placed in the ULT, then it would span approximately 6000 to 1100 BC.

If Diwonijo was being worshiped throughout Minoan history, then he could plausibly be a direct precursor for Osiris, or he could have been adopted by the Minoans at some point from Osiris, however, there is no reason to assume he was. We have no stories surviving about Diwonijo or Disonuso, and are therefore limited to studying Dionysus and his Roman equivalent Bacchus, to understand this early Mediterranean version of Dumuzid. Unfortunately, as Dionysus was that mysterious 'foreign' god, he was tied to many cults, and there were many theories of his origin.

Evans himself suggested that the earliest phase of Minoan civilization looked like an Egyptian Early Dynastic colony, predating the Old Kingdom in Egypt. Below is a photograph of the massive megalithic stones of the Gournia palace walls from the earliest phase of Minoan civilization, which looks like the masonry in the Egyptian megalithic temples and Osireion.

The Greeks tried to integrate him into their pantheon several ways and sometimes listed him as an Olympian. He was said to the son of Zeus and the mortal Seleme, or in the Orphic tradition the son of Zeus and Persephone, the Queen of the Underworld. In the Eleusinian mysteries, he was called Iacchus, the husband of Demeter. As Demeter was another deity inherited from the Minoans, who called her Damate,[271] and she was a mother-goddess, a grain-goddess,[272] and an earth-goddess, this shows a clear Minoan parallel to the Phrygian Cybele-Attis,[273] and the Cypriot Aphrodite-Adonis relationships.

The Eleusinian Mysteries was an ancient Greek religion that was practiced in the city of Eleusis. Little is known about the origin of the religion, however, it was practiced during the entire pre-Christian Greco-Roman era, in Greece and then Rome. It is believed to have originated somewhere in Anatolia or the Minoan Civilization. The name of the town, Eleusis, is believed to be related to the Greek goddess Eileithyia, who was called Ereutija[274] during the Mycenaean era. This goddess was widely worshiped through the Aegean, under a variety of names including Elysia in Laconia and Messene.

Some have linked the name Elysia to the Greek concept of the island of the happy dead: the Elysian Fields.[275] The Elysian Fields, or Elysium, was a garden or land far to the west of Greece, described as a paradise without snow or storms. It was originally considered separate from the Underworld ruled by Hades and was where the gods went when they died. Later it became a place where anyone could go when they died, as long as the gods approved of the way they lived their life. Otherwise, they would be dragged to the fires of Hades' Underworld.

These two lands would later serve as the basis for the Christian heaven and hell concepts, neither of which have a basis in Judaism. In both classical and modern Judaism, the soul dies with the body, however, if deemed worthy will be resurrected at some point, when God gets around to it. Some exceptional Jews did get taken to heaven, such as Elijah and Enoch, however, they were alive when God took them, and were still alive when returned to the Earth. This understanding was clearly still present in the first group of Jewish Christians, as Jesus had to be resurrected before he could be taken up to heaven. However as Christianity spread across the Roman Empire, Heaven and Hades became the two fates waiting for everyone at the end of their lives.

In the Odyssey, circa 700 BC, Homer referred to the fair-haired Rhadamanthus ruling Elysium. Rhadamanthus' name is believed to be derived from the Greek word 'damázo' which means 'to overpower,' 'tame,' or 'conquer.' In the Greek legends of the ancient Minoan civilization, King Minos had a daughter named Ariadne, who was in charge of the labyrinth the Minotaur was kept in. In most versions of her story she married Dionysus,[276] however, according to Plutarch there was an alternate version of her story, where she was married to Rhadamanthus.[277] While we don't know what source Plutarch was using, he certainly would have known the more common Dionysus version, and so giving her this somewhat obscure husband seems odd unless he truly believed the Rhadamanthus version of the story was the original.

As both these gods were said to be married to Ariadne, and both were associated with the dead, it is plausible that these are two divergent versions of the Minoan Diwonijo. The story of Ariadne and Dionysus was certainly spread far enough that divergent version of Dionysus could have appeared, the Etruscans called them Areatha and Fufluns.[278] On the next page is a diagram of an Etruscan engraved mirror back depicting a Satyr (left), Areatha (center-left), Fufluns (center-right), and Fufluns' mother Semla (right).

The city of Eleusis was apparently originally called Saesara before Demeter visited the city, after which it was renamed Eleusis. This story does not make any sense unless the early Greeks considered Eleusis to be another name for Demeter. The story of the city's renaming is embedded within the overarching narrative of the Eleusinian Mysteries. While Demeter was looking for her daughter Persephone and happened to be disguised as an old lady, she was found by the daughters of King Keleos of Saesara. They took her back to the palace to be the nursemaid to the baby Prince Demophoon. King Keleos' wife Queen Metaneira became jealous of the growing relationship between her son Demophoon and his nursemaid Demeter, and insulted

Demeter, causing Demeter to remove her disguise, revealing herself to the Saesarian royal family. After that, King Keleos ordered the building of a shrine for Demeter in Saesara, and at some point the city's name was changed to Eleusis, to commemorate Demeter's visit.

It is unclear if this was ever a part of the mysteries, and seems like an unlikely chapter: 'Goddess stops in the middle of panicked quest to find daughter to nurse young prince.' This story is most likely something that was invented as theo-political propaganda, sometime in the Greek dark age, or, based on the archaic name, the earlier Mycenaean period.

Demeter's quest to rescue Persephone from the Underworld was a central theme of the Eleusinian Mysteries. In the Eleusinian Mysteries Persephone, who was also called Kore, meaning maiden in Greek, was abducted by Hades, ruler of the Underworld, which started Demeter's quest. Demeter was so distraught over the loss of her daughter that she caused a drought, which caused both the god and mortals to starve. The people and gods cried out to Zeus, ruler of the Greek pantheon, and he decided to intercede, sending Hermes to the Underworld to demand that Hades release Persephone.

Hades obeyed Zeus' commands, but first tricked Persephone into eating some pomegranate seeds. Apparently, it was the law of the Fates, called Moirai in Greek, that once someone ate the fruit of the Underworld they were forced to live there eternally. This forced Persephone to spend four or six months in the Underworld each year. The accounts differ on the number of seeds she ate, and the resulting number of months in the Underworld. Below is a painting of Hades abducting Persephone, believed to have bee painted by the ancient Greek painter Nikomachos circa 345 BC.

These mysteries can be considered an elaborate story designed to explain why the seasons come and go, however, it is clearly related to the Dumuzid epic in several ways. Demeter and Inanna are both mother and earth goddesses. Persephone and Eresh-Kigal were both the Queen of the Underworld. Both the Eleusinian Mysteries and the Sumerian epic *Inanna Descends to the Underworld* are focused on the tale of these two female protagonists, and not their husbands, Dionysus/Dumuzid or Gugalanna/Hades. In both cases when the god that interceded did so, he sent someone connected with sexual ambiguity down into the Underworld to do his bidding, Enki's gala priests, and Hermes, the father of Hermaphroditus, the hermaphrodite god.

There are obviously many differences too. In the Sumerian version, the woman that is forced to spend half the year in the Underworld is Geshtinanna, Inanna's sister-in-law, not the Queen of the underworld. In the Sumerian version, Gugalanna had died, and Eresh-Kigal was ruling the underworld, however, in the Eleusinian version Hades was alive and ruling the underworld. This point may indicate the Eleusinian version was drawn from a later Semitic version of the story where Nergal was co-ruling the Underworld with Eresh-Kigal.

The god that interceded was Zeus in the Eleusinian version, not An's equivalent Uranus, however, the Greeks really didn't have any interest in Uranus, and only some vague creation stories in which he was involved. However, Zeus' equivalent in the Sumerian pantheon was Enlil, Enki's Greek equivalent was Poseidon. The fact that the story was changed from Enki/Poseidon to Enlil/Zeus may date the adoption period.

Almost all of the gods in the story are found in the Mycenaean Greek period, Zeus as Diwe and Diwo, Poseidon as Posedao or Posedawone, Demeter as Sitotptinija, Persephone as Preswa, and Dionysus as Diwonuso. The only god that does not seem to date back to the Mycenaean Greek period is Hades. Additionally, a couple of these gods can be traced back to Minoans, namely Dionysus as Diwonijo, and Demeter as Damate, meaning aspects of this story may date back to the Minoans, and were certainly known to the Mycenaean Greeks.

Zeus is an archetypal Indo-European storm-god, related to Indra, Thor, Jupiter, Perun, and many others. He was worshiped by the Mycenaean Greeks and is believed to have entered the Aegean region with the earliest Greeks by 1500 BC.[279] On the other hand, the origin of Poseidon's name has been debated since the time of ancient Greece and is theorized to be Pre-Greek,[280] inherited from the cultures in the Aegean before the Greeks migrated into the region.

What is clear is that in the Mycenaean period, Poseidon was far more popular than Zeus. Zeus gained popularity in the Greek Dark Ages, and emerged as the head of the Olympians, ruling Olympus and serving as the supreme god for the Greeks until the Christian era. Persephone's name is also believed to be Pre-Greek in origin as well, as ancient Greeks had several different versions of her name across their territory.[281]

Hades name is of unknown origin. As with Poseidon and Persephone, Greeks argued the origin of Hades name through the classical period, and modern historians continue the debate. Plato devoted a section of his dialogue *Cratylus* to the etymology of Hades name, and modern linguists have proposed both Indo-European origins, and non-Greek origins. What is known is that in the time of Homer, circa 700 BC, he was known as Aides,[282] as well as other regional variations including Aidoneus (Ἀϊδωνεύς), Aidos (Ἄϊδος), Aidi (Ἄϊδι), and Aida (Ἄϊδα). Seeing the similarity between these names and the Cypriot Adonis is not difficult, however, Adonis was the youthful lover of Aphrodite, while Hades was the raper of Persephone, meaning that Hades could not be derived directly from Adonis.

The two gods could still both derive from contact with Phoenicians, as Adon simply meant 'lord' in Canaanite, and both were lords of something. In fact, both could be interpreted as Lords of the Dead, by the Canaanite era. Tammuz was the god that died for part of the year, and Nergal was married to the Queen of the Underworld. However, if Hades was an adaption of Adon it was clearly more corrupted than the Cypriot version. In the Greek version, it was Hades who raped the youthful Persephone, not the other way around, while in the Cypriot version Adonis was still the youthful lover of Aphrodite.

Gender role reversals aside, the correlations between the Rape of Persephone and *Nergal and Eresh-Kigal*, are difficult to ignore. In both cases, a youthful person is forced into a marriage by the ruler of the underworld. In one case the raper is the Queen of the Underworld, and in the other case, she becomes the Queen of the Underworld. In both Sumerian stories, the female characters are dominant, both Inanna and Eresh-Kigal are depicted as being both generally and sexually dominant in their relationships with their respective husbands. The Greek Aphrodite and Demeter goddesses were similarly depicted, as was the Phrygian Cybele, however, Persephone was the opposite, an adolescent girl abducted by Hades.

While many of the western stories of Aphrodite, Demeter, and Cybele might be based on adopted beliefs dating from the Sumerian period, the Rape of Persephone must have been inspired by the later subservient Eresh-Kigal from the Babylonian period. The Babylonian era version of *Nergal and Eresh-Kigal* is known to date to at least 1350 BC, and has been found as far west as Egypt, and so it is plausible that it could be the source for the Greek story.

The ancient Greeks themselves debated where the foreign god Dionysus had come from. In some Greek cults Dionysus was considered a Thracian and Phrygian god,[283] in others he was Asian, and in others he was Ethiopian. The Greek historian Pliny the Elder,[284] and the Roman historian Arrian,[285] both claimed the Dionysus had originated in India, Pliny claiming that he had founded the first Indian dynasty 6451 years before the conquest of Alexander. The ancient Greeks believed Dionysus' name was derived from the Greek words 'dios' and 'nysa.' Dios meant 'Zeus' and implied 'god' when embedded in the name of another god.[286] Nysa referred to the name of the mountain Dionysus was born on, and where he lived with the Nysiads.[287]

Unfortunately, the Greeks didn't know where Mount Nysa was. Hesychius of Alexandria, who lived around 500 AD, listed a number of locations that different ancient Greeks had suggested for Mount Nysa including Arabia, Babylon, Cilicia, Egypt, Ethiopia, India, Libya, Lydia, Macedonia, Naxos, the Red Sea, Syria, Thessaly, and Thrace. The Greeks that preferred the Indian origin, believed that Mount Nysa, was Mount Meru. Nysa becomes even more complicated than simply being a long lost mountain, with Pherecydes of Syros observation in the 6th century BC, that Nysa was derived from 'nusa' an archaic Greek word for 'tree.' These correlations with other Eurasian belief systems have led many scholars to associate Nysa with the axis-mundi world-mountain or world-tree concept.[204]

Dionysus and Demeter, as Diwonijo and Damate, are both Minoan gods that the earliest Greeks either adopted or synchronized with their existing gods. This means that the Dumuzid and Inanna or Tammuz and Ishtar story could have been adopted by the Minoans at any point in their history. As both Poseidon and Persephone are believed to be pre-Greek names as well, the core cast of characters from the Dumuzid tale are all present: Dumuzid and his wife Inanna, her sister/daughter Persephone, and Poseidon, the god that intercedes. Without Hades, Persephone could not have been raped, and so had to be the Queen of the Underworld in her own right.

The Greeks also incorporated the story of Eos and Tithonus into their pantheon, pictured above on a Greek vase from circa 470 BC. The Greeks inherited some odd stories from the Minoans, including one about the birth and death of Zeus in a cave on Crete. As Zeus is an Indo-European deity, and the Minoans are generally not considered to have been Indo-Europeans, this must have originally been a different god that became conflated with Zeus at some point after the Greeks arrived in the Aegean. This Zeus was known by the name Zeus Velchanos, and is said to have been born, and then later died, in Dictaean cave, today identified as Psychro Cave.[288] Zeus Velchanos was always depicted as a youth and was married to a great goddess in the Minoan religion, although it isn't clear which one.

Throughout Greek history Hades was commonly called Zeus by those wishing to avoid saying the name Hades, generally titled as Zeus Chthonios, Zeus Katachthonios, or Zeus Plousios. All of these Zeuses' titles referred to the abode of Hades. Clearly, the Greeks were using the word 'Zeus' as a synonym for 'god,' meaning Zeus Chthonios can be translated as 'Earthly god', Zeus Katachthonios means 'god under the Earth,' and Zeus Plousios means 'god bringing wealth.' If the Classical Greeks used the name Zeus when referring to Hades, it is plausible that Zeus Velchanos may have been the Minoan forerunner of Hades, married to the Queen of the Underworld, but still a youth, like the Babylonian Nergal.

This would imply that the big shift in the beliefs began sometime during the early Greek era when the sky-father god was interjected into the story, and Persephone went from being the Queen of the Underworld to a rape victim. In the Greek story about the rape of Persephone, it is, in fact, Zeus that advised Hades to abduct Persephone and rape her. In this context, this version of the story seems like a deliberate attack on the ancient goddesses of the region. Zeus not only had the Queen of the Underworld abducted and raped, but he also got to play the hero when the Earth-mother came crying and begging for the release of Persephone. A trifecta of theo-propaganda, in which the sky-father subjugated both of the ancient goddesses and got to play the compassionate hero who frees the maiden.

In the Eleusinian version of Dionysus, he was sometimes called Iacchus, although historians do not know why as the Eleusinian Mysteries were never written down. This name seems to be the source of the name of Bacchus, the Roman version of Dionysus. Both the Greek and Roman versions of this god's worship were focused on the drinking of a psychoactive wine that would put participants into an altered state of consciousness. After the Cult of Bacchus had spread to Rome circa 200 BC additional aspects were introduced, including ripping apart living animals and eating them raw, and poly-amorous orgies. In 186 BC[289] the Senate issued the legislation to reform the Bacchanalia, placing the priests of the cult under imperial authority. According to the Roman historian Livy writing 200 years later, the Senate needed to execute 7000 cult leaders to exert their authority over the Cult of Bacchus. Over the following two centuries Bacchus merged with the Roman god of wine Liber Pater.

Eos and Tothonus appear to be an Anatolian version of the story, adopted during the Greek dark ages or earlier. Eos was the Titaness of the dawn, descended from a Proto-Indo-European archetype called Hausos. Other goddesses derived from Hausos include the Vedic goddess Ushas, Baltic goddess Aušrinė, and Roman goddess Aurora. Eos' young lover was Tithonus, a prince of Troy long before the Battle of Troy. In Homer's version of the myth, Eos fell in love with Tithonus, and asked Zeus to grant him immortality, which Zeus did, however, she did not ask Zeus to keep Tithonus young, and so he aged but could not die. As described in the *Hymn to Aphrodite*:

> 'but when loathsome old age pressed full upon him, and he could not move nor lift his limbs, this seemed to her in her heart the best counsel: she laid him in a room and put to the shining doors. There he babbles endlessly, and no more has strength at all, such as once he had in his supple limbs.'[290]

This darker version of the story takes a different path from most, in which the Dumuzid character either remained eternally young or periodically died and resurrected, also remaining young. The core of this story does appear to derive from the ancient story, of an older more powerful female monarch or goddess, and her younger male spouse who was granted immortality. The fact that the Titaness was an Indo-European goddess implies that the Greeks may have carried the story into Greece, however the fact that they placed the hero in Troy, also indicates a possible Anatolian source for the story. Either way, this version appears to be Indo-European in origin.

Panthers and Lions

There is a common element across the varied Dumuzid-like myths: panthers and lions. These are not the panthers of today's world, but rather an extinct species that once apparently lived on the Mountain in the Steppes. The modern word panther is derived from the name of the mythical creature. According to Pliny the Elder, panthers emitted a scent that drew other animals to them, which they would then kill.[291] This sounds like an attempt to explain the strange behavior of animals infected by toxoplasma, which is a parasite most felines carry. When infected by toxoplasma most animals lose there natural fear of felines, some even become attracted to their natural predators. In the middle ages, the dragon was added to the panther myth as the only creature immune to the panther's scent. Below is a photograph of a Greek painting from circa 370 BC of Dionysus riding a Panther (center).

In the Greek myths of Dionysus, he rode a panther. Which is virtually identical to Pravati riding her mounts Dawon the lion and Manasthala the tiger. Parvati, whose name means 'mountain' has been described as the Indian version of Cybele[292] and Aphrodite.[293] Likewise, the chariots of Ishtar,[294] Cybele, Demeter, and another variant Rhea, were all pulled by lions. Inanna was depicted as standing on the back of lions, implying she rode them. In all the Mesopotamian depictions the lions were depicted as having no manes, which led to Greeks identifying them as panthers. Dumuzid's alter-ego Ishtaran was also depicted as being accompanied by lions, as was Zababa. These panthers or lions were sometimes also given the power of human speech and the ability to use tools, in the myths surrounding them, becoming the lion-man Guardians in the Garden-of-the-Gods in the Dumuzid saga. Below is a photograph of a Hindu statue of Pravati riding her mount Dawon.

This motif is also found in Egypt, where the lion-woman hybrid Sekhmet was the consort of Ptah. The Egyptian 'Fortress of the Smiths,' Memphis, was named after Ptah, which connects Semhket back with the Sumerian story of a garden in a Fortress of Smiths on a mountain in the steppes. She even had a partner guardian, Bastet, who was also still depicted as a fierce lion-woman in the Old Kingdom, however, she became a housecat-woman hybrid by the New Kingdom.[295]

This twin lion Guardian concept has been in China, since at least the Han Dynasty. Guardian Lions, also called lion-dogs have been common at the entrances to important buildings, such as temples and palaces throughout China. These Guardian Lions are believed to have been imported to China from India by Buddhist missionaries around 2000 years ago. Due to Chinese cultural influence over the past two thousand years, the Guardian Lions are now commonly seen in Cambodia, Japan, Korea, Laos, Myanmar, Nepal, Singapore, Sri Lanka, Thailand, Vietnam. Below is a photograph of a Lion Guardian in the Forbidden City, Beijing.

While the anthropomorphic lion-people may be more entertaining, the fact that there are often the depictions of gods with lions or panthers suggests that the Guardians may have originally been lion-tamers and not human-feline hybrids. Preposterous as riding a large cat might seem, the Panther myth explains the lion-men chimeras connected to the Dumuzid lore stories across several cultures.

Several extinct large cats once roamed the Eurasian continent, whether humans ever tamed or rode them is a different question. Saber-toothed cats and European Leopards became extinct around 27,000 to 28,000 years ago,[296] while the Eurasian cave lions became extinct circa 10,900 years ago.[297] The European leopards would have been virtually identical to the leopards that currently roam Africa and Southern Asia, which are slightly smaller than humans, and therefore could not serve as a mount, however, have been successfully raised in captivity, and can be trained to some extent. Saber-toothed cats were slightly larger than leopards, however still not large enough to ride. If any were ever tamed it is unlikely to ever be known.

The Eurasian cave lions were one of the largest felines we know of and were the size of the first horses humans rode. They also match the Panther myth in that they are believed to have had no mane. As for whether they were ever tamed or ridden we may never know, however, if the Panther myth of a rideable cat was based on a real animal, it was most likely a Eurasian cave lion. Below is a graph showing the relative size of a human and a Eurasian cave lion.

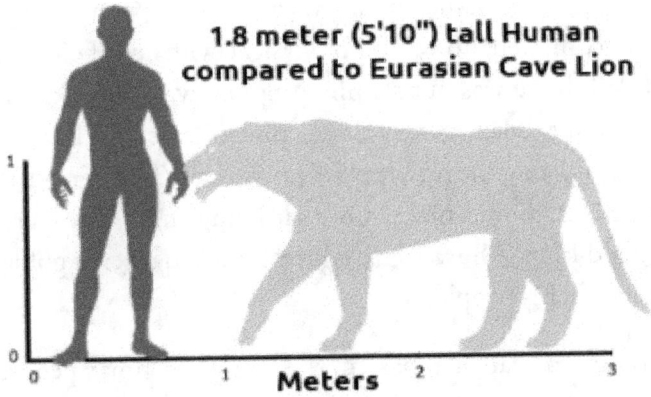

Yemo the Shepherd

Another archaic hero that has major correlations with King Dumuzid the Shepherd is the reconstructed Indo-European hero Yemo the founder twin. Yemo has been reconstructed as part of the Indo-European pantheon based on several similar heroes found in ancient Indo-European beliefs. These include the Hindu god Yama, the Zoroastrian King Jamshid, and the Germanic ice-giant Ymir.

The Zoroastrian and Hindu versions seem to preserve more of the original story, as the Indo-Iranian peoples became literate long before the Germanic tribes. The oldest Germanic poems that mention Ymir only date to the early 1200s AD. Meanwhile, Yama is first mentioned in Mandala 10 of the Rig Veda Samhita, which the conventional Indian timeline (CIT) dates to circa 1500 to 1200 BC. The Zoroastrian King Jamshid was first mentioned in Yasht 19, Vendidad 2, of the Avesta, where he was named Yima-Kshaeta in the Younger Avestan language. The Vendidad, and the Young Avestan sections of the Avesta, were likely compiled in Central Asia, sometime between 3700 and 900 BC, although there is a great deal of debate about the dating of the Avesta.

In the somewhat confusing Avestan story of Yima, he began life as a shepherd, yet is also listed as the fourth king of the Pishdadian Dynasty. This dynasty preceded the Kayanian dynasty, who were apparently in power when the Avesta was compiled, however, no physical evidence of either dynasty has been found. While he was out shepherding, he was approached by a being of light called Ahura Mazda, who asked Yima to teach his law to the people. Yima refused, and they negotiated a deal where Yima agreed to rule over and nourish the earth and make sure that living things prospered. In trade for being a good king, Ahura Mazda gave Yima a dagger, a golden seal, and immortality for all his people.

After three hundred years had passed, the land that Yima's people inhabited was full. This land was called Airyanem Vaejah, and its inhabitants were the Aryans, outside of it was the lands of the daevas who served Ahriman.

After three hundred years, Ahura Mazda returned to Yima and told him that the land was overpopulated, and so King Yima took the dagger and the golden seal and expanded the land of the Airyanem Vaejah. All of this is interpreted somewhat magically in the Zoroastrian religion, wherein the daevas are insubstantial demons, and Ahriman is the devil, however, the story itself seems somewhat ordinary other than the immortality, and beings of light that kept visiting the ancient Aryans.

The expanded Airyanem Vaejah was able to house the Aryans for six centuries before it became overpopulated again. And so once more King Yima took his dagger and his golden seal and expanded the Airyanem Vaejah. Again the expanded Airyanem Vaejah was able to house the Aryans for some time, but then began getting overpopulated around 900 years later, and so once more King Yima expanded the land. Soon afterward Ahura Mazda returned, with a contingent of yazatas, a word that is generally translated as angels. King Yima also brought along a council of immortal Aryans when meeting with Ahura Mazda. The beings of light warned the king and his council of immortals of the coming evil winters. Apparently, somewhere outside of the Airyanem Vaejah, Ahriman had done something that was causing the world's climate to change. Ahura Mazda warned Yima before the onset of the evil winters, and advised him to build an underground city described in the *Vendidad* 2:22-30:

> 22 'And Ahura Mazda spake unto Yima, saying: 'O fair Yima, son of Vivanghat! Upon the material world the evil winters are about to fall, that shall bring the fierce, deadly frost; upon the material world the evil winters are about to fall, that shall make snow-flakes fall thick, even an aredvi [fourteen fingers] deep on the highest tops of mountains.'

> 23 'And the beasts that live in the wilderness, and those that live on the tops of the mountains, and those that live in the bosom of the dale shall take shelter in underground abodes.'

> 24 'Before that winter, the country would bear plenty of grass for cattle, before the waters had flooded it. Now after the melting of the

snow, O Yima, a place wherein the footprint of a sheep may be seen will be a wonder in the world.'

25 'Therefore make thee a Vara, long as a riding-ground [2 miles] on every side of the square, and thither bring the seeds of sheep and oxen, of men, of dogs, of birds, and of red blazing fires. Therefore make thee a Vara, long as a riding-ground on every side of the square, to be an abode for man; a Vara, long as a riding-ground on every side of the square, for oxen and sheep.'

26 'There thou shalt make waters flow in a bed a hathra [1 mile] long; there thou shalt settle birds, on the green that never fades, with food that never fails. There thou shalt establish dwelling-places, consisting of a house with a balcony, a courtyard, and as gallery.'

27 'Thither thou shalt bring the seeds of men and women, of the greatest, best, and finest on this earth; thither thou shalt bring the seeds of every kind of cattle, of the greatest, best, and finest on this earth.'

28 'Thither thou shalt bring the seeds of every kind of tree, of the highest of size and sweetest of odour on this earth; thither thou shalt bring the seeds of every kind of fruit, the best of savour and sweetest of odour. All those seeds shalt thou bring, two of every kind, to be kept inexhaustible there, so long as those men shall stay in the Vara.'

29 'There shall be no humpbacked, none bulged forward there; no impotent, no lunatic; no malicious, no liar; no one spiteful, none jealous; no one with decayed tooth, no leprous to be pent up, nor any of the brands wherewith Angra Mainyu stamps the bodies of mortals.'

30 'In the largest part of the place thou shalt make nine streets, six in the middle part, three in the smallest. To the streets of the largest part thou shalt bring a thousand seeds of men and women; to the streets of the middle part, six hundred; to the streets of the smallest part, three

hundred. That Vara thou shalt seal up with thy golden seal, and thou shalt make a door, and a window self-shining within."

The *Vendidad* continues with King Yima building the described underground city, and then taking two thousand Aryans into the Vara and sealing the door before the evil winters covered the Airyanem Vaejah with snow covering the valleys as high as the peaks of the mountains. There are certainly some differences between this version of the story and many of the other Dumuzid like stories. For one, there are no female deities present. This is however due to the nature of the *Avesta* itself. Zarathustra was teaching a monotheistic religion, and therefore all gods, other than Ahura Mazda, were demoted to either yazatas or daevas. There are however several similarities to the Dumuzid stories. Both kings are also called 'the Shepherd,' both stories include an underground city, both stories involve immortality, and most distinctively, both stories are set at the onset of the Last Glacial Period. According to the *Sumerian King List* Dumuzid's reign was somewhere between 129,579 and 93,579 BC, while the Last Glacial Period is estimated to have begun 115,000 years ago.

Considering that both the Avestan Yima and Greek Tithonus descend from a Proto-Indo-European original, it seems that the followers of Zarathustra cut a lot from the story, including Eos, and possibly something going wrong with whatever immortality process Zeus/Ahura Mazda gave the Aryans. While the two stories are greatly divergent, the final resting place of both deities seems to be similar. The room where Eos left Tithonus was sealed with shining doors, while the Vara, which Yima never left, was described as being closed with a golden seal, which also turned on the 'self-shining window,' which has historically been interpreted as either a magical or an artificial light source, depending on the interpreter.

The Queen of Heaven

Throughout the Babylonian Dark Age, the worship of Inanna spread throughout the Semitic cultures of Mesopotamia under a variety of local names, including the Babylonian and Assyrian Ishtar, Canaanite Astarte, and Hebrew Asherah, as well as north into the Hittite civilization under the name of Aserdu. She was also known under the titles of Elat, meaning 'goddess,' and Qodesh, meaning 'holiness.' During the Second Egyptian Dark Age worship of the goddess spread into Egypt under the name of Qetesh, which was carried into Egypt by Canaanites starting in the 14th Dynasty. Below is a photo of a Sumerian-era seal impression depicting Inanna riding a lion.

This strongly implies that the Babylonian Dark Age happened before the 14th Dynasty, however, that is not the conventional view. Currently, the 14th Dynasty is placed between 1705 and 1690 BC CET, while the Babylonian Dark Age is placed between the fall of the Old Hittite Kingdom circa 1524 BC CET, and the foundation of the Middle Assyrian and New Hittite Kingdoms sometime before the Battle of Megiddo in 1457 BC.

In the ULT the two dark ages happened at the same time, with the 14th Dynasty happening between 2793 and 2533 BC, while the Babylonian Dark Age happened between 2965 BC and sometime before the Battle of Megiddo circa 1457 BC.

The holy city of this goddess was the city of Kadesh, also transliterated as Qadesh, located near the modern border of Syria and Lebanon. The earliest reference to this city is from the reign of King Ishi-Addu of Qatna, who was contemporary with the Assyrian Old Kingdom King Shamshi-Adad I, from circa 3158 to 3191 BC ULT (1785 to 1752 BC CMT). It is unclear when the city was renamed Kadesh, however, the older Akkadian name was recorded as Gizza.[216] The name was clearly named Kadesh at the end of the dark age as the King of Kadesh led two resistance movements against

Egyptian expansion, culminating in the Battle of Megiddo in 1457 BC, which led to the collapse of the Mitanni Empire, and the Battle of Kadesh in 1274 BC, which led to the collapse of the Hittite Empire.

In each culture, this goddess was known as the 'Queen of Heaven,' which is a clear descendant of Inanna's title 'Lady of Heaven.' In each culture, this Queen of Heaven was also married to the local highest god outside of Babylonia and Assyria where she was married to Tammuz. In Canaan she was married to El, in Israel she was married to Yahweh, in the Hittite Empire she was married to Elkunirsa, and in Egypt, she was married to Ptah. Above is a photograph of a New Kingdom relief of Qetesh riding a lion (center), accompanied by Ptah (left).

According to the Phoenician Historian Sanchuniathon's *Phoenician History* from the Egyptian New Kingdom era, the Canaanite Astarte was also the Greek Titaness Dione, whose name also translates as 'goddess.'[298] Dione appears to have been worshiped in the Mycenaean era under then name Di-u-ja in the Linear-B script. In *Phoenician History,* Dione was married to El, who the Greeks considered the Canaanite version of the Titan Cronos. This suggests that in the Mycenean pantheon Cronos' wife was Dione. In the later Greek pantheon of the Classical era, Cronus' wife was Rhea, an Earth and nature goddess, who was also depicted as riding a lion. Below is a photo of a Greek painting of Rhea riding a lion from circa 450 BC.

The Mycenean Greek civilization is generally dated to between 1600 and 1100 BC, however, some archaeologists have suggested the early Greeks may have been in Greece since 2500 BC or earlier. The Myceneans appeared in Greece during the Second Egyptian Dark Age and Babylonian Dark Age, showing up in the records of the New Hittite and New Egyptian Empires as a significant power from the beginning of the New Kingdom era. The Egyptians referred to the Greeks as Danaya, starting circa 1437 BC, during the reign of King Thutmose the third early in the New Kingdom era. The Hittites called the Greeks the Ahhiyawa, a reference to Achaea, in Greece, starting around 1400 BC as the New Kingdom emerged from the Babylonian Dark Age.

The fact that the worship of the Queen of Heaven spread as far as it did, integrating into many local religions during this dark age speaks volumes as to how long the dark age lasted. These Queens of Heaven and their respective husbands formed a widespread belief system throughout the Middle East, Egypt, and the Aegean, in which the lion-riding Queen of Heaven was married to the supreme god in each region, often supplanting older goddesses. The fact that Inanna's cult was limited to the Temples in Uruk and Nippur before the Akkadian era, and only started expanding in the Old Babylonian era, is well documented by Assyriologists.[299]

In the conventional timelines, the worship of Inanna the Queen of Heaven started spreading from Uruk circa 2334 BC during the rule of Sargon of Akkad. During the Old Babylonian Empire, between 1894 and 1595 BC, the worship of Ishtar the Queen of Heaven became widely practiced in Babylonia, where she was married to Tammuz. The worship of Astarte the Queen of Heaven spread to Canaan likely before 1752 BC, where she became the patron goddess of Kadesh as the wife of El. In Canaan, she was also known as Qodesh, which is the name that the Canaanite 14th Dynasty used when they introduced her worship to Egypt. Even though the Canaanite 14th Dynasty was only 15 years long, Qetesh became widely worshiped across Egypt as Ptah's wife, replacing Ptah's original consorts Bastet and Sekhmet. Sometime during the Old Hittite Empire, between 1664 and 1524 BC Aserdu was adopted by the Hittites, as the wife of Elkunirsa. Elkunirsa's name literally translates as 'El the Creator of Earth,'[300] implying the Hittites had adopted El along with Astarte from the Canaanites. Sometime before 1437 BC, the Mycenaean Greeks adopted Elat into their pantheon as Dione and had her married to the Titan Cronos. This timeline is possible but does not seem likely given how quickly certain events needed to take place, such as the Egyptians accepting Qetesh as Ptah's wife in only 15 years.

In the ULT, the worship of the Inanna the Queen of Heaven started spreading from Uruk circa 3885 BC during the rule of Sargon of Akkad. During the Old Babylonian Empire, between 3352 and 3038 BC, the worship of Ishtar the Queen of Heaven became widely practiced in Babylonia, where she was married to Tammuz. The worship of Astarte the Queen of Heaven spread to Canaan likely before 3191 BC, where she became the patron goddess of Kadesh as the wife of El. In Canaan, she was also known as Qodesh, which is the name that the Canaanite 14th Dynasty used when they introduced her worship to Egypt. During the 260-year-long Canaanite 14th Dynasty, Qetesh became widely worshiped across Egypt as Ptah's wife, replacing Ptah's original consorts Bastet and Sekhmet. Sometime during the Old Hittite Empire, between 3103 and 2965 BC, Aserdu and Elkunirsa were adopted by the Hittites, from the Canaanites. Sometime before 1437 BC, the Mycenaean Greeks adopted Elat into their pantheon as Dione and had her married to the Titan Cronos. The longer timeline of the ULT does seem to make more sense than the conventional timelines, as religions generally take centuries to become adopted by large portions of a nation's population.

Antediluvian Eridu

The first two kings listed on the *Sumerian King Lists* were Alulim and Alalngar who were listed as the kings of the antediluvian Eridu, between 266,379 to 237,579 BC and 237,579 to 201,579 BC respectively. This time period falls within a highly variable time in the Earth's climatic history. According to the analysis of ice-core samples from Antarctica, around 270,000 years ago, the world was in a glacial period. By 240,000 years ago the world had emerged from that glacial period, however, it sank back to a glacial period within 10,000 years, and then rose back out of that glacial period within another 10,000 years. The world remained in this state until around 200,000 years ago when the world sank into the Penultimate Glacial Period. Below is a graph showing the analysis of ice core samples from the European Project for Ice Coring in Antarctica (EPICA) and the Russian Vostok Station, covering the last 750,000 years.

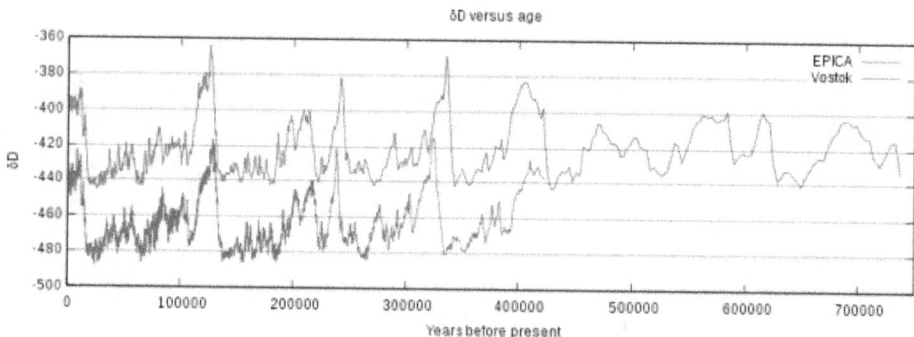

This rapidly fluctuating time period falls within one of the most chaotic periods of the last 800,000 years. The foundation of Eridu at circa 266,379 BC, roughly correlates with the depth of the glacial period of the era circa 270,000 years ago. The transition from Alulim to Alalngar at circa 237,579 BC, roughly corresponds to the height of the brief inter-glacial around 240,000 years ago. And finally, the fall of Eridu circa 201,579 BC, happened around the beginning of the Penultimate Glacial Period circa 200,000 years ago.

The name Eridu is generally translated as 'mighty place' or 'guidance place,' depending on the translator. The Sumerian logograms that spell out Eridu are NUN and KI. Like many Sumerian words, the logograms do not spell out the pronunciation of the word, meaning that the word was either adopted or inherited from another culture. These logograms can be translated as:

NUN: prince, noble, master, to rise up, great, fine, deep

KI: earth, place, area, location, ground, grain

This would mean that Eridu's original name could be translated as something vague like 'prince of the area,' or 'noble place,' or, conversely, as something specific, like 'Prince of Grain,' which is similar to the mythical Chinese King Hou Ji, whose name translates as 'Lord of Millet.' The origin of millet is a significant historical enigma, as the grain appears to have originated in multiple places on the Earth. In China the cultivation of foxtail-millet and broomcorn-millet has been traced back to between 21,000 to 17,500 BC,[301] while proso-millet was domesticated in Greece sometime before 3000 BC.[302] Little-millet was domesticated in South Asia by 3000 BC. Pearl-millet was domesticated in Mali by 2500 BC,[303] and finger-millet was domesticated in Ethiopia sometime before 2000 BC.[304] The cultivation of Asian varieties of millet had spread across the Eurasian steppes to Europe by 5000 BC,[305] while both East and West African varieties of millet had spread to India by 1800 BC.[306] Foxtail-millet (priyangu), barnyard-millet (anu) and black-finger-millet (syamaka) are all mentioned in the Yajur-Veda,[306] indicating that they were all being cultivated in Central Asia by 1800 BC ULT (1200 CIT).

The wide-spread range of wild millet varieties has been debated among palaeoethnobotanists, questioning whether the wide-spread range represents the wild progenitor of millet or represents feral forms of millet that escaped from domesticated production.[307] While there is currently no known evidence for the cultivation of millet prior to Chinese adoption circa 21,000 BC, it is clear that humans were cultivating grains by 200,000 years ago, as grain grinding stones have been found dating back to that time in Africa.[308] If millet was harvested in Eurasia prior to the onset of the Penultimate Glaciation, the crops would have failed drastically at the beginning of the glacial period, as millet is frost-sensitive and grows in soil that is 14 °C or warmer. Millet is a highly drought-resistant crop and therefore would have been one of the few crops that could have been grown in warmer climates during the arid glacial periods.

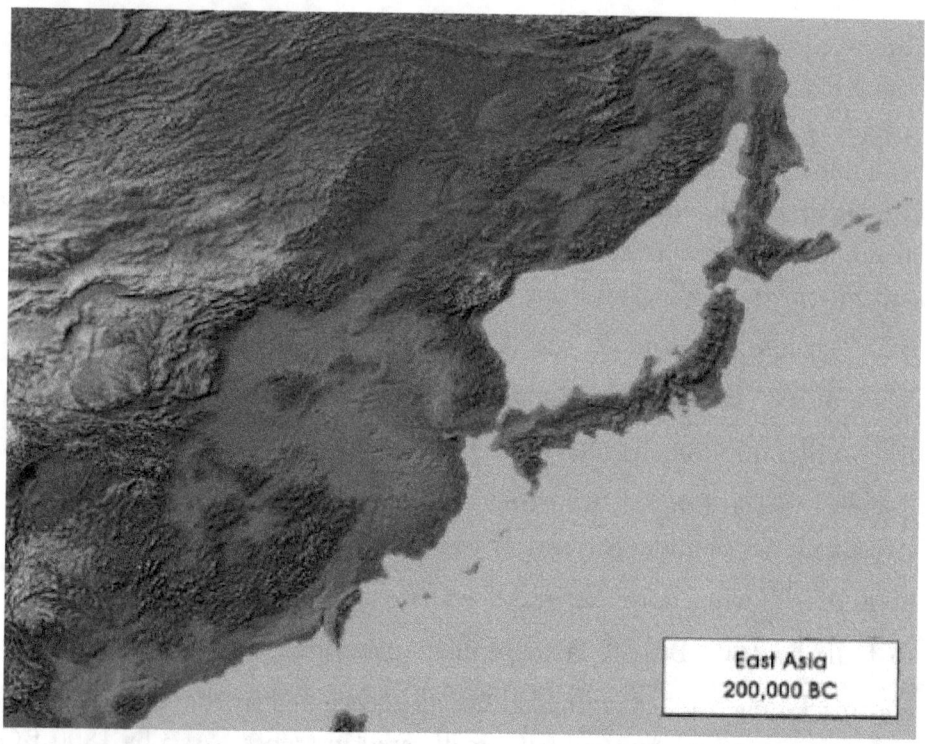

East Asia
200,000 BC

The names of the two kings Alulim and Alalngar translate as 'stag,' and 'pipe irrigator' respectively. These names are related to specific agricultural periods, stag implying animal husbandry, and pipe irrigator implying grain or vegetable cultivation. While there is no clear evidence of either animal husbandry or irrigated agriculture before the onset of the Penultimate Glaciation, there are the Dali-Man remains that were found along with ox remains dating back to 260,000 years ago.[221] The time-period of the

Dali-Man remains correspond with the time-period of Alulim recorded in the Sumerian King Lists, between 266,379 and 237,579 BC. The Dali-Man remains were found in Dali County, Shaanxi Province, China, implying that the land of Eridu may have been in China. The remains of Dali-Man have been described as being either early homo-sapiens or late homo-erectus, implying that the first modern-humans may have originated in the region.

Section 6: Indo-Aryan and Harappan Mythic Era

Like the Egyptian and Sumerian texts, the ancient Sanskrit and Avestan texts include references to ancient civilizations before their own, however, in both cases the ancients were said to have more advanced technology than one would expect. In the case of the Sanskrit epics, the current versions are believed to date to approximately 300 AD, although they are accepted as being copies of much older texts, dating to at least 500 BC, and possibly thousands of years earlier. Flying machines were common in fantasy stories from the period, appearing in the story of Icarus in Greece, Ahikar in Judea, and Bladud in Britain, and therefore it is plausible that the airplanes were a late addition to the epics to make the enemies of the heroes seem more powerful. Emperor Ravana's massive, seven-story high airplane is mentioned but does not play a role in the story.

Yima, Yama, Yami, and Ymir

The artificial lighting in the Avesta is harder to explain away, however, is sometimes dismissed as a late addition as it is in the Vendidad, which is the youngest section of the Avesta, written in the disputed Youngest Avestan dialect. As the origin of the Vendidad is unclear, some have dismissed the artificial lighting, and the entire story as Persian or Greek era fiction, however, the Greeks and Persians did not have artificial lighting, and it is not found in their fantasy stories, so this may be part of the original story. The story found in the Avesta appears to be a direct parallel of the Dumuzid saga from Sumer, and several related stories from across the world that involve the Underworld in the Mountain and the Queen of Heaven. In the Avestan version of the story, the Queen of Heaven wasn't mentioned, and King Yima the Shepherd was the focus, the parallel of King Dumuzid the Shepherd in the Sumerian story, and like the Dumuzid story, it was set over 115,000 years ago, at the onset of the current ice age.

By the Persian era he was called Jamshid, however, linguists believe the earliest version of the name is believed to have been Yemo. Both the Rigvedic Yama and the Germanic Ymir are also believed to be descended from Yemo. Both stories diverged greatly from the Avestan version. Yama, was the first man who died in the Rig-veda, and as a result, his name became the word meaning death, and he became the god of the dead. The Germanic version of Yemo evolved into the ice-giant Ymir, who was born in the ice rivers at the beginning of the world, and when he died there was a great flood. The Germanic myths about Ymir appear to have only been written down in the 13th century AD, and so this story had a long time to evolve after the Rig-veda and Vendidad were written. Nevertheless, Ymir sounds like a personification of the ice-age itself, or at last a glacial period.

As the dialect of the Vendidad is disputed, and therefore its age is unknown, the Rig-veda is the oldest acknowledged text with mentions Yama along with his twin Yami. While a great deal of literature was written in later periods about them, in the Rig-veda Samhita there is very little. Yama was the first mortal that died and became the lord of the Underworld. His name

Yama, as well as his twin's name Yami, both, translated as 'twin,' his being masculine, and hers being feminine. The nature of the two is unclear in the Vedas, as they appear as both siblings or as husband and wife depending on the text, however, it is generally believed by Hindus that they were twins in the metaphorical sense, as in identical and opposite, but not actually related. Yami later became associated with the Yamuna River, and therefore became a fertility-goddess, the opposite of Yama, the lord of the dead. This is something that can only be identified from the Classical Sanskrit period onward, and so it is unclear what their exact role was in the society of the Rigvedic Sanskrit period, however, they are found in the Old-Rigvedic sections of the Rig-veda, meaning they are some of the earliest people recorded in the Vedas.

In the Vendidad, the book in the Avesta that recounts the history of the Avestan-speaking people, tells the story of King Yima the Shepherd, however, due to disputes over the dialect, it is unclear when the book was written in relation to other Avestan and Sanskrit texts. Nevertheless, the story is strange and set before the onset of the last glacial period, or according to some interpretations, before the beginning of the current ice age. This view was discussed at length in his 1903 work 'The Arctic Homeland in the Vedas,' by Bal Gangadhar Tilak. Tilak had spent decades studying the Vedas and the Avesta, which he was considered a worldwide authority on. He was fluent in many languages but contemporary and ancient, and over collaborated with leading Zend and Sanskrit scholars in Britain, France, and Germany.

In 'The Arctic Homeland in the Vedas,' Tilak explored the geographic and astronomic references of the Vedas and Avesta and concluded that the Indo-Iranian peoples must have originated in a land in the Arctic Circle that sank into the sea between 10,000 and 8000 BC due to glacial melting, causing the Indo-Iranians to migrate south into the Eurasian continent. At the time, very little archaeological research had been done in Central Eurasia and the Steppes, however, the idea that the Indo-Iranians originated to the north was not new. The ancient Greeks recorded that the Iranian peoples lived in Ukraine, Southern Russia, and Central Asia through the Classical Era, however, there was no reference to them starting out farther north.

This idea that the Indo-Iranians stared out on a lost Arctic land was expanded to all Indo-European peoples and adopted by the Thule Society in Germany before World War 1, and then became entrenched in Nazi propaganda during World War 2, and subsequently became unpopular among academics. In the former Soviet Union research into Indo-Iranian origins continued incidentally, as a by-product of the archaeological digs in the Kurgans, and discovery of horse burials that matched the description of the setting of the Rig-veda. In the late 1800s Tilak's time, knowledge of the ice age was limited, and it was initially assumed the ice age had happened suddenly trapping the mammoths of Siberia in the ice they were found in.

The mass deaths of these mammoths is now identified as being caused by the last major cold-snap of the most recent glacial period, today called the Younger Dryas period, which is dated to between 10,900 and 9700 BC. Tilak dated the glacial period to between 10,000 and 8000 BC based on the early estimates of when the ice age was believed to have been, however, it is now recognized from several sources that the last glacial period happened over a very long period, beginning around 113,000 BC and ending around 9700 BC. Tilak's original research divided the era when the Avesta and Vedas into several periods based on the astronomical details in the texts.

> 10,000 to 8000 BC – Destruction of Arctic homeland and initial migration south into Eurasia.
>
> 8000 to 5000 BC – Pre-Orion Period – Gathic Hymns focused on the Sun (Ahura Mazda)
>
> 5000 to 3000 BC – Orion Period – The vernal equinox was in the constellation Orion. The Hymns still contained references to the Dawn, but now also had several references to Orion. Tilak also identified an attempt to reform the ancient Aryan calendar at this time, to correct for the succession of the equinoxes.
>
> 3000 to 1400 BC – Krittika Period – The vernal equinox was in the Hindu constellation Krittika, focused on the Pleiades, which is in the Western constellation Taurus. The Vedic Hymns from

this period make little sense astronomically as the composers no longer understood the astronomical basis of the original hymns.

1400 to 500 BC – Pre-Buddhist Period – The when the Sutras and associated philosophy was developed.

Tilak's astronomical interpretation of the Vedic texts has still not been challenged academically, although many do not like it for ideological reasons. It also happens to be generally in tune with the ULT, at least from the Pre-Orion period onward. Tilak's Pre-Orion period focused on the worship of the Sun and composition of the Gathic Hymns happening between 8000 and 5000 BC, corresponds roughly to the Old Avestan period of 6500 to 5500 BC, in the Bug-Dniester culture of Ukraine. Tilak's Orion Period of 5000 to 3000 BC, included most of the Rig-vedic Hymns, corresponds very closely to the Cucuteni-Trypillia and Sredny Stog culture of Romania, Moldova, and Ukraine, between 4800 and 3000 BC. Tilak did not have access to this information, as virtually no archaeological work was done in the Russian Empire, and yet, based on the astronomy, he predicted the Rig-vedic period exactly as is now known to have happened.

The story of the earlier glacial period destroying the original homeland of the Aryans is currently impossible to prove. Tilak himself did not try to set a date for it, beyond the contemporary scientific theories of the ice age, which are now known to simply be the Younger Dryas period at the end of the glacial period. Some have suggested that the story may have been set in the intermediate warm period between the Younger and Older Dryas periods, when the world warmed for a few centuries. This theory holds that when the world warmed between 14,670 and 12,890 BC, humans migrated north into the newly habitable lands of northern Siberia, and when the Younger Dryas set in, they were forced south to escape the cold. While this is a valid theory, and no doubt someone ventured north into the Siberia, it is unlikely the source of this story from the Vendidad, as the Vendidad's version is the story of a warm tropical land with water snakes, being destroyed by an ice age, and a technologically advanced people surviving in an underground city, which, whether it happened or not, is not the story of primitive hunters following animals into northern Siberia.

The Vendidad clearly describes the onset of a glacial period, which destroyed the homeland of the Aryan people. This real question is not if it is the description of the onset of a glacial period, but when the Vendidad was written. The latest the text could have been written in was the Classic Era of the Persian Empire, as after that time it was in the Avesta, and referenced extensively in Zend commentary. Naturally, it could be discounted as a Classical period fiction, however, it seems abstractly odd that the authors would describe the onset of a glacial period as destroying their original homeland in the arctic, even if there had never been an ice age. The fact that there was a glacial period, makes the Vendidad clearly worth deeper consideration than simply dismissing it as an odd piece of fiction that somehow became entrenched in a religion with much older texts, some of which really cannot be seen as dating to much after 6000 BC, based on the linguistic evidence. The fact that the Vendidad has always been treated as an authentic Avestan test within the Zend commentary, even the earliest commentaries, means it is likely not a Persian era forgery and represents an otherwise lost Avestan dialect.

In any event, it is at least 2500 years old, yet it describes the onset of a glacial period that must have happened 110,000 years earlier. According to the story recorded in the Vendidad, before the ice age began, the Aryans lived in a tropical land with water snakes, which was then covered in snows that filled the valleys and covered the mountains. The Aryans took refuge in a subterranean town called Vara, that King Yima had built in a mountain after being fore-warned of the coming ice age by Ahura Mazda, as described in the *Vendidad 2:22-30*:

> 22 'And Ahura Mazda spake unto Yima, saying: 'O fair Yima, son of Vivanghat! Upon the material world the evil winters are about to fall, that shall bring the fierce, deadly frost; upon the material world the evil winters are about to fall, that shall make snow-flakes fall thick, even an aredvi [fourteen fingers] deep on the highest tops of mountains.'

23 'And the beasts that live in the wilderness, and those that live on the tops of the mountains, and those that live in the bosom of the dale shall take shelter in underground abodes.'

24 'Before that winter, the country would bear plenty of grass for cattle, before the waters had flooded it. Now after the melting of the snow, O Yima, a place wherein the footprint of a sheep may be seen will be a wonder in the world.'

25 'Therefore make thee a Vara, long as a riding-ground [2 miles] on every side of the square, and thither bring the seeds of sheep and oxen, of men, of dogs, of birds, and of red blazing fires. Therefore make thee a Vara, long as a riding-ground on every side of the square, to be an abode for man; a Vara, long as a riding-ground on every side of the square, for oxen and sheep.'

26 'There thou shalt make waters flow in a bed a hathra [1 mile] long; there thou shalt settle birds, on the green that never fades, with food that never fails. There thou shalt establish dwelling-places, consisting of a house with a balcony, a courtyard, and as gallery.'

27 'Thither thou shalt bring the seeds of men and women, of the greatest, best, and finest on this earth; thither thou shalt bring the seeds of every kind of cattle, of the greatest, best, and finest on this earth.'

28 'Thither thou shalt bring the seeds of every kind of tree, of the highest of size and sweetest of odour on this earth; thither thou shalt bring the seeds of every kind of fruit, the best of savour and sweetest of odour. All those seeds shalt thou bring, two of every kind, to be kept inexhaustible there, so long as those men shall stay in the Vara.'

29 'There shall be no humpbacked, none bulged forward there; no impotent, no lunatic; no malicious, no liar; no one spiteful, none

jealous; no one with decayed tooth, no leprous to be pent up, nor any of the brands wherewith Angra Mainyu stamps the bodies of mortals.'

30 'In the largest part of the place thou shalt make nine streets, six in the middle part, three in the smallest. To the streets of the largest part thou shalt bring a thousand seeds of men and women; to the streets of the middle part, six hundred; to the streets of the smallest part, three hundred. That Vara thou shalt seal up with thy golden seal, and thou shalt make a door, and a window self-shining within."

The term 'self-shining window,' has always been interpreted in Zend commentaries as some kind of magical artificial light. Today, artificial lights are no longer seen as magical, however, for thousands of years, the self-shining light was as magical as the flying machine. The Magi, who were the priests of the Zoroastrian religion, is also the source of the English word magical, as they're ancient texts described how to build many magical devices before Alexander destroyed their archives. If these magical texts ever actually existed, and if they contained something other than nonsense, it is possible that they were describing technology. It is generally accepted that the Baghdad Batteries were built by Magi, which would mean that they maintained a rudimentary understanding of electricity as late as 50 AD, however, what these batteries were used for is still a matter of much debate.

The batteries themselves are even debated. They were discovered in the ruins of ancient Ctesiphon, in Iraq. Ctesiphon was the capital of the ancient Parthian Empire, and therefore they are assumed to be from the Parthian era, however, no one bothered carbon dating them, and they were plundered from National Museum of Iraq during the American-led 2003 Invasion of Iraq, so we may never know their true age unless more are unearthed. There were first proposed as batteries in 1938 by Wilhelm König, an assistant at the National Museum of Iraq in 1938. He noted several ancient Mesopotamian objects that had been plated with gold and suggested the batteries had been used for electroplating. Various experts had chimed in during the past century, either supporting or dismissing the idea. Generally, engineers supported the idea that these are batteries, while Assyriologists dismiss the idea that these are batteries, because... you know, 'they didn't know about electricity.'

Archaeologists have yet to propose an alternative idea of what these batteries were, other than some kind of weird jar for storing papyrus. No papyrus was found in the batteries, and no jars for storing papyrus have been found anywhere else like these. What was found in the batteries was acidic residue, and the lack of acid is the only thing that stops these batteries from giving off voltage. Multiple duplicates have been created which prove they do work for small scale power generation when acids which the Parthians had access to are added, such as lemon juice, or grape juice. But, you know... 'they didn't know about electricity,' so 'they're not batteries.' The close-minded circular logic of the cultist convicts to itself. If these aren't batteries, someone built something that just happens to work like a battery, around 2000 years ago, for unknown reasons.

The problem with interpreting these as batteries is that if they were, they did not develop into an electrical system like we have today 2000 years ago. Therefore, many reject the idea. Surely if they could build batteries, they would build hydroelectric dams and ... nuclear power plants? If in fact, all they had were batteries, they would have been of very little use. The modern electrical systems were built for lighting first and foremost. After houses were wired for lighting, other appliances that use electricity became practical. No one said, 'I've invented an electrical dishwasher, now let's build an electrical grid so I can start selling them. Without the invention of the light bulb, we most likely would still not have an electrical grid, and certainly would not have developed hydro-electric plants, nuclear technology, or the internet.

The galvanic cell, which is what the Baghdad batteries look like, was invested in the 1700s. It took a century of capitalist investment to drive the technology to the point where we were building street lighting grids for cities, and there is no reason to believe the Baghdad batteries were ever in the hands of capitalists. There was no patent office in the Parthian or Roman empires. The patent of the time was secrecy. To this day, historians aren't sure what Greek fire was, although it is widely described as a fluid that burnt virulently and was used to destroy enemy ships at sea. It has been suggested it could have been naphtha, or pigs lard, or several other things, however, we don't know, because the Greeks who created and sold it did not want anyone to know, and so they didn't write it down. If the Baghdad batteries were being used to electroplate gold onto silver or lead objects, surely whoever was doing it would not have told anyone. They were, after all, running a con, who advertised that.

This electroplating technology also explains the myth that the Magi could transmute other metals to gold, but the 'spell was broken' if the metals were melted down, and the metals would revert to their original form. This is exactly what would happen if they were electroplating other metals. If it was the Magi using these batteries, then their origin is less mysterious as if the Avesta is accurate, they had more advanced technologies at one point but had been wandering between nations for thousands of years. In the *Vendidad*, there are brief descriptions of the 15 lands they lived in after leaving the Vara. In each country, they found something that was undesirable and so left. These undesirable things included termites, cannibals, pedophiles, and atheists, and each time they moved on to another land, eventually settling in the land were Zoroaster met the beings of light, and sang the Gathas. This means before the Avestan speakers were in the Bug-Dniester region, circa 6500 to 5500 BC, they had already migrated through 15 lands. If their story of being trapped in/on a mountain surrounded by glaciers is accurate, then they would have likely been trapped until sometime after 20,000 BC, the Last Glacial Maximum, when the glaciers were at their greatest expanse. If Europe the glaciers initially retreated between 20,000 and 16,000 BC, while in Siberia the glaciers began retreating after 15,000 years ago. In either case, there was move than enough time to settle for some time in 15 nations before ultimately ending up in Ukraine by 6500 BC.

If this is, in fact, the story of an ancient civilization in the arctic being destroyed by the onset of the last glacial period, then the original story would have been set approximately 115,000 years ago, at approximately the same time as the life of King Dumuzid the Shepherd in the Sumerian king lists, who was recorded as having lived between 129,579 and 93,579 BC. The number of similarities between these two shepherd kings is striking, and difficult to dismiss. Both were reported to have lived in an underground community of some kind, specifically Ganzir and the Vara, although the Dumuzid story makes Ganzir sound more like a gulag than the Vara was in the Yima story. Comparing the Vedic version to the Sumerian, both Dumuzid and Yama became associated with death, and a lord of the Underworld, and both were married to (or twins with), a fertility goddess, specifically Yami (later Yamuna) and Inanna (later Ishtar).

While similar stories across a region are not unusual, as religious cults migrate between cultures and adopt the languages of their new cultures, these stories are hard to trace to an origin. The Sumerians and Steppes cultures do not seem to have been in contact. It is possible in the ULT that given enough time, the cult of Dumuzid could have expanded as far north as the Steppes, however, this still would not explain the glacial period, which was not part of the Dumuzid story. In the surviving Sumerian stories the land outside the mountain Ganzir is built in becomes a wasteland, but snow, for which a word did not exist in Sumerian, was not mentioned. Conversely, in the ULT the Sumerian civilization existed before the Avestan speaking Bug-Dniester culture, and therefore the Sumerian story could not be based on the Avestan one. If one only considers the conventional timelines, then the Bug-Dniester culture did predate the Sumerians, and could have been the source of the Sumerian story, but only if one accepted that it was an Avestan culture and that Indo-Iranian culture extended south into Mesopotamia from the dawn of Sumerian civilization, which there is no other evidence of. In any event, neither the Avestan nor Sumerian languages show any traces of the other, which one would expect if the cross-fertilization happened as recently as 5000 BC ULT (3000 BC CMT).

These appear to be two separate versions of the same story, set circa 115,000 years ago. In both stories, there is machinery in the underworld which seems out of place if these were always metaphors for the state of death. In both cases, the world outside the mountain became wasteland and remained that way for a very long time. In the case of the Avesta, some laws had punishments of up to one thousand years, for the family of the criminal. Clearly, they weren't in the Vara for just a few years or a few decades. The laws strictly controlled the birth rate, and violators were sent to the 'worst existence,' which sounds like extradition to the wastelands outside, however, the Dumuizd saga from Sumer offers another interpretation. In the Sumerian version of the story, on the top of the mountain was the garden of the gods, where those not forced to work in Ganzir lived freely.

This is similar to the paradise that was reported to have existed on a mountain in some Zoroastrian stories, according to early Greek interpretations of Zoroastrianism. The English word paradise was adopted via the Greek word for paradise from the Avestan term for a 'walled-garden,' however, the garden on the mountain does not appear in the Avesta. It seems the sections dealing with it were lost when Alexander burnt the Avestan archives, however, it seems unlikely that is was a completely unrelated mountain, and many Zend scholars have accepted that there was a walled garden on top of the mountains, and likely where the people of the Vara grew their food. Some have even suggested that the original story was probably just about a walled garden being built by Yima, and not the bunker-town described in the Vendidad, however, this is simply an opinion, not based on the existence of alternate versions of the story within the Avesta. If the Paradise was built on the top of the mountain the Vara was in, like the Garden of the Gods above Ganzir, then the 'worst existence' may have been working in the Vara, as life in Ganzir was described.

Nevertheless, while Neanderthal remains have been found north of the Arctic circle from the time period in question, so far no modern human remains have been found. Of course, as the ground is generally frozen year-round, and there is a general assumption that little or nothing will be found, there continues to be little archaeological research done in northern Russia.

The Rama Epics

Several Classical Sanskrit epics are set in the ancient Indus Valley Civilization, most notably, the Mahabharata and the Ramayana. The idea that Krishna was a Harappan has been generally accepted by Hindus since the civilization was discovered in the 1920s, as he lived in both the region and era of civilization. Hindus expected to find the ruins of a civilization in the region that dated from that time, and therefore there it was not surprising, however, Indologists are cautious about ascribing the Mahabharata to this civilization. There are a large number of similarities between the Harappan ruins and the described civilization in the Mahabharata, for instance, both civilizations appear to be river-based, using boats to carry the majority of their cargo.

Before the domestication of horses by the steppes peoples, the majority of cargo and transportation seems to have been done by boat, and as a result, almost all early civilizations were based along rivers of lakes. In India though, there was a beast of burden being used, the elephant. Asian elephants are more docile than their African cousins and have been used throughout recorded history as a beast of burden, as well as a war-machine. Armored elephants are reported as being what stopped Alexander the Great's invasion of India. In the Mahabharata, both cattle and elephants are being used, however in minor roles. The major animal being used is the horse, which the Harappans did not have. Not only are there no remains of horses found in the ruins of the civilization, but it is also difficult to imagine their usefulness as a means of transportation between cities surrounded by water. If the Harappans had horses, they no doubt would have built their civilization very differently, with roads crossing the dry inland regions of the subcontinent, instead, we find they built their cities in flood plains. If anything, the introduction of the horse to their civilization would have lead to such a transition that it could be interpreted by later archaeologists as a collapse, as the people would have suddenly had access to a much greater range of territory, and would have abandoned their flooded cities.

It is the existence of these horses that causes the authenticity of the Mahabharata to be questioned, however, there is no reason to assume these were part of the original story. If the Mahabharata was a Harappan story, then it was written or recited in the ancient language of the Harappans for thousands of years before the arrival of the Indo-Aryans. As it appears to have only been translated into Sanskrit during the Classical era, circa 500 BC, it is fair to assume that the horses would have been inserted into the story at that time. The Mahabharata is not intended to describe a group of primitive barbarians bashing each other with clubs, it is the backdrop for the Bhagavad Gita, what would have been viewed as the greatest philosophical doctrine by the scribes that took the time to translate it into Sanskrit. They likely described the ancient land with the same technologies they were familiar with so the reader would understand what was happening. These anachronistic horses would have been much like Shakespeare giving Caesar a clock, or writing that Cleopatra wanted to play billiards, things people in the 1700s would have understood, but not historically accurate.

The dating of the Ramayana is more problematic, as, while it is set in the region of the later Indus Valley Civilization, its dating has been debated for over a thousand years. The earliest non-Indian records of Rama, the Greek records of Indian-Dionysus and Roman records of Indian-Bacchus, both place his life circa 6600 BC, which places it before the Harappan 1 Phase in either the CHT or ULT. Naturally, with the ruins near Bhirrana carbon-dated to between 7380 and 6201 BC, both timelines will need to be updated, and to Rama's existence circa 6600 BC becomes an archaeological possibility. However, Hindus do generally not believe Rama lived around 6600 BC, instead they date his life to millions of years earlier. Conversely, Indologists that consider the Ramayana as being based on a real story that became mythologized generally suggest he lived maybe around 1200 BC, at that 'Mediterranean Iron Age' date that seems to underpin all of Indology.

Another aspect of the Rama story that results in people generally dismissing it as a fairy-tale is the existence of a large island called Lanka, which is simply the Sanskrit word for 'island.' This is not generally considered Sri Lanka, as is was described as being 1300 kilometers (100 yojanas) from

India. This would place it either in the Indian Ocean, south of the equator, East Africa, or Indonesia. Hindu commentary has generally treated it as a sunken continent since the 1700s, however, it is most likely a reference to the islands of Indonesia, as it is described as one of many large islands, one being 800 miles across. The following is the description of India and Lanka from Ramayana when Rama sent Hanuman to look for Sita:

> "To search for Sita in the southern region, Sugriva hand-picked the best of the vanaras. Nila son of Agni, Hanuman the son of Vayu, the supremely mighty Jambavan, and many other mighty vanaras were chosen to constitute this party. He appointed Angada, the son of Vali, and the prince regent himself as the commander of the vanara forces that constituted this search party.
>
> In his briefing, Sugriva specially mentioned those places which were difficult of access. He said: 'Start with the Vindhya mountains, and the plains of the rivers Narmada, Krishna Godavari, and Varada. Thoroughly search the regions of Mekhala, Utkala, Vidarbha, Vanga, Kalinga, Andhra, Cola, Pandya, and Kerala. Then proceed to the Malaya mountains, with the blessings of the sage Agastya whom you will see there.
>
> Proceed from there to the golden gate city of the Pandyas whose city walls are studded with precious stones. Between the city and the hermitage of Agastya is the Mahendra mountain which is full of gold, and which Agastya sank into the ocean. Indra himself visits this mountain every fortnight.
>
> Beyond this is the inaccessible island which is eight hundred miles wide: it is inaccessible to human beings. Search this island carefully. Surely that is the territory of the powerful Ravana who deserves to be killed. Before you leave that territory make sure that Sita is not there: do not leave anything in doubt.
>
> Eight hundred miles beyond that island in the ocean is the partly submerged island Puspitaka with its high mountains resembling

gold and silver. One hundred and twelve miles beyond Puspitaka is the mountain Suryavan, beyond that Vaidytua, and beyond that the mountain Kunjara where the sage Agastya has a hermitage which is eighty miles broad, and eighty miles high, made of gold and precious gems. There exists the abode of nagas known as Bhogavati. Search this dreadful place carefully. Search the mountain beyond this, known as Risabha.

Beyond that is the world of the Manes: do not go there. Wherever you go search for Sita carefully. Whoever returns first in a month and says Sita has been discovered will enjoy luxuries equal to mine, for he will be most dear to me.'"

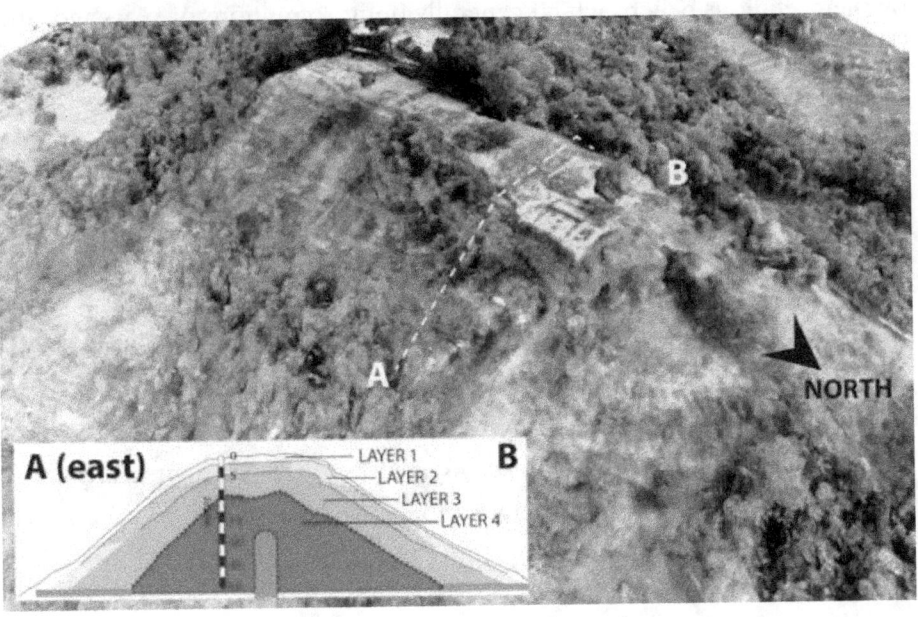

This description cannot be applied to Eastern Africa, or anything directly south of India, including the submerged plateaus near Madagascar, however, does apply to the islands of Southeast Asia. If this is a description of ancient Malaysia and Indonesia, then there should be ruins in the region that date to the period, and there are. At Gunung Padang, on the island of Java, is a megalithic site that has been carbon-dated to between 10,500 BC and 2800 BC. Only the top 10 meters have been excavated, and the site is known to go down to at least 15 meters, which researchers at the site have estimated could be 20,000 years old. The earlier dates are speculation, however, the upper levels do prove the site existed at the time of Ravena's apparent kingdom in the region. The site is extensive, covering an estimated 25 hectares (62 acres), and the east side has an estimated 100 stone terraces.[309]

Unfortunately, the historical accuracy of the Ramayana is very doubtful regardless of when it happened. It is a story with talking monkeys, talking bears, ancient airplanes, ancient horses in India, and what sounds like extra-terrestrials orbiting the Earth, Moon, and Sun in massive flying cities. Naturally, there has been little real interest in trying to determine when it happened by western Indologists, and Hindu Indologists are often guided by their religious beliefs, which generally point to millions of years ago, and therefore, nothing found to date in India or Pakistan would date to the correct time period. Research into the Ramayana is further hampered by the fact that there are dozens of different versions spread throughout South and Southeast Asia, and they are different. Each version of the story has the same central conflict between Rama and Ravana, however, Rama isn't always the hero, sometimes its Hanuman, the talking monkey, or sometimes even Ravana, Rama's enemy. In the Hanuman focused versions, he generally ends up married to a mermaid, who is sometimes Ravana's daughter. While it is a natural assumption that all versions of this story must descend from an original, this is not something that can be shown through any literary analysis, and in fact, each version seems as authentically ancient as any other. In the Philippines, even non-literate tribes have been shown to have a local version of the Rama epic.[310] Some major versions include:

- Ramayana: Indo-Aryan version of northern India
- Ramavataram: Tamil (Dravidian) version of southern India
- Ranganatha Ramayanam: Telugu (Dravidian) version of southern India
- Torave Ramayana: Kannada (Dravidian) version of southern India
- Yama Zatdaw: Burmese version
- Ramakien: Thai version
- Phra Lak Phra Lam: Laotian version

- Reamker: Cambodian version
- Hikayat Seri Rama: Malaysian version
- Ramakavaca: Balinese version of Indonesia
- Maharadia Lawana: Maranao version of the Philippines[311]
- Lam-Ang: Ilocano version of the Philippines

Rama and Ra

All of the varying versions of the Rama epic point to the core of the story being very old, much older than 1200 BC. There are also several striking parallels between the various versions of the Rama epic and the cult of Ra in the earliest phase of Egyptian history. Ra later became the Sun-god during the Middle Kingdom through his association with Amun, and again in the New Kingdom through his association with Atum, the Sun, as all of their cult centers were in On, later called Heliopolis by the Greeks. During the New Kingdom and then Late Period On (Heliopolis) rose to religious dominance as the center of Sun-worship in Egypt. This was the time when Sun-gods rose to prominence in the Middle East, and at one point included the Zoroastrian and Jewish Gods, before they began to diverge again.

However, thousands of years earlier Ra was not the Sun-god, but instead the central character in the early dynastic struggle between Ra and Apophis, a snake-god. In the earliest surviving texts from the 2nd dynasty, he was aided in his fight against Apophis by Set and Babi, a story that later became absorbed into the solar cult that developed. Ra was in ancient times called the King of the Three Worlds, the same title given to Ravana in many versions of the Rama epic. Several other animal-deities are also shared between the Ramayana variations as well as other early Sanskrit epics, and the earliest Egyptian and Sumerian religions, which support the idea that these are interconnected religions.

These animal-human icons are often disregarded as deified animal totems, however, this simple dismissal of the icon results in ignoring the existence of a widespread belief system in early times. If Hinduism had have died out a thousand years ago, and its statures and artwork were examined through the same lens, it would simply be dismissed as a bunch of deified animal totems, and there would be no reference to anything like Hinduism in modern scholarly work. Fortunately, it did not, and not only maintained some of the world's oldest literature, the Vedic Texts, but also a rich religion that is replete animalistic iconography. Hindus believe that the spirit can incarnate as animals or humans, and perhaps, this is a better lens through which to view the ancient animal-human icons. Regardless of the source of these icons, a large number of people, believed something, for a very long time, and it is the fact that they believed it that is important from a historical perspective, not whether the belief was valid from our perspective. This idea that it was simply primitive non-sense was used to dismiss it by early Christian scholars and is now also used by their atheist descendants.

The Monkey-God

Babi was Ra's main ally in the early Egyptian stories and was in every respect identical to Hanuman. In the past couple of centuries, several Orientalist and then Indologists have proposed that Hanuman was a Harappan deity, based on the etymology of his name. The orientalist F. E. Pargiter theorized that Hanuman was an early-Dravidian deity, and the name 'Hanuman' was a Sanskritization of the Old Tamil words *Aan-mandhi* meaning 'male monkey.' The Hindu scholar Ray Govindchandra influenced by Pargiter's opinion, suggested in 1976 that the early Indo-Aryans may have invented a Sanskrit etymology for the deity's name after they accepted Hanuman into their pantheon.[312] Below are two pictures, the left is an ancient Egyptian carving of Babi, and to the right is a traditional depiction of Hanuman.

The Egyptian name 'Babi,' translates as 'bull of the baboons,' and roughly means 'alpha-male of the baboons.'[313] There are several identical attributes to these gods. They both were always depicted as carrying a mace, and both were reported as flying in machines of some kind during the respective battles they fought in. Ra's flying machine was described as a flying barge in Egyptian records, while Ravana's flying machine was simply called an airplane (vimana). Ancient statues of Hanuman are found throughout Southeast Asia, where Hindu-based beliefs were common before Islam spread into the region.

Statues of a monkey-god, or monkey-people, have also been found in the region around Gimpie, Queensland, Australia, which cannot be a local development, as monkeys are not indigenous to Australia. Monkey-gods with identical iconography to Hanuman and Babi have been found in Mayan ruins in Copán, Honduras, pictured above. At the time of contact, the Spanish explorers recorded that in the Alta Verapaz region, the monkey-gods were known as *Hun-Ahan*, and *Hun-Chevan*, which is translated today as *Hun-Chowen* the *Popol Vuh*. The similarity of the names and iconography seems more than just coincidental and may indicate a trans-Pacific spread of an early Hindu belief system. Copán was the capital city of a major Mayan kingdom between 426 and 822 AD,[314] believed to have been known as Oxwitik at the time. It is unclear when Copán was originally settled, however, the settlement dates back to the Early Preclassic period, between 2500 and 1500 BC.

The Sha and the Enusha

The other major ally of Ra was Set, a strange-looking god, who was depicted either as a Set-headed human, or a Set-creature. Like other Egyptian gods, he was depicted either as an animal or as a human-animal hybrid, however, in the case of Set the animal is unknown. This creature was depicted in a tomb from the Naqada I phase of Egyptian prehistory, which in the ULT would date to between 6500 and 6000 BC, approximately 500 to 1000 years before the foundation of the 1st dynasty circa 5510 BC ULT.

It was subsequently depicted on the mace of the King Scorpion shortly before the foundation of the 1st dynasty, meaning this creature was clearly considered important around the time of the foundation of Egypt. The Egyptian name for the creature was Sha, which may have been an earlier name for Set. Below is a photo of Set and Nephthys from circa 1250 BC.

In India, a similarly named mysterious creature was also associated with the Rama story: Emusha, whose name was later changed to Varaha in the Sanskrit epics. Varaha means pig or boar in Sanskrit, and as a result, Varaha is depicted as a boar-headed-human in Hindu art, however, it is unclear what Enusha originally looked like. In some of the later pyramid texts, Set was depicted as a boar, meaning that there must have been some cross-fertilization between the later Egyptian and early-Hindu religions.

This also suggests that the earliest Egyptian version of the Ra story was another of the many renditions of the Rama story, however, this would place its origin before the Old Kingdom in Egypt, circa 4945 BC ULT, and likely before the oldest known depictions of a Sha from between 6500 and 6000 BC ULT. This dating would support the ancient Greek and Roman claims about the ancient Indian king lists which recorded Rama as ruling circa 6600 BC, however, it also means that the Hanuman and Emusha creatures were part of the story from its earliest versions. Below is a photo of a carving of Varaha from Mahabalipuram in Tamil Nadu, from the 7th-century.

The Werelions and Werejaguars

Narasimha is a werelion within the Vaishnavism branch of Hinduism, created by Vishnu so he could incarnate on the Earth. Narasimha was also known as the Great Protector as he incarnated on Earth to protect humanity. His name means 'lion-man' in Sanskrit however he was not found in the Vedas, which implies he was a Harappan god adopted by the Indo-Aryans after they arrived in South Asia. In Egypt, Bastet and Sekhmet were two virtually identical goddesses, one from Upper Egypt, and one from Lower Egypt, which were venerated since at least the 2nd dynasty. Both are believed to have been pre-dynastic, and likely local versions of the same early goddess as Upper and Lower Egypt spoke different languages and were separate nations before being unified circa 5510 BC ULT. To the south in Nubia, a virtually identical male lion-man god was known as Adepemek. Below are two photos, a photo of two Narasimhas at a temple in India to the left, and a photo of an ancient Egyptian carving of Bastet and Sekhmet to the right.

Bastet and Sekhmet ultimately became sisters in the Egyptian religion, the two protectors of Ra, and Adepemek was sometimes called their brother. In the Egyptian story, the werelions hunted and ultimately killed Apophis, the enemy of Ra, who was depicted by the Middle Kingdom as a giant-serpent that wanted to eat Ra, the Sun. Meanwhile in the early-Hindu story Narasimha, he incarnated on the Earth to stop a group of Nagas, which were snake-men, from stealing the Sun. Obviously, the stories sound like nonsense, but they are the same story, one in Ancient Egypt, likely dating to the pre-dynastic era, and the other in India, likely dating to the Indus Valley Civilization.

In Mesopotamia, these creatures were called Ugallu from at least the Old Babylonian and Old Assyrian eras through the ends of the Neo-Assyrian and Neo-Babylonian Empires. The name itself is Akkadian, meaning 'big day,' which indicates the being originated in the Akkadian civilization at the latest, however, he was generally associated with the Sumerian demon Lulal, the younger son of Inanna, which Ugallu back to Inanna's early husband Zababa, whose iconography included lions. As the Egyptian, Harappan, and Mesopotamian cultures were trading from the pre-Dynastic era of Egyptian history, it's possible the werelions of Egypt could have been adopted by the Mesopotamians and Indians at any point, if they originated in Egypt.

In ruins of the Olmec civilization of southern Mexico which have been dated to between 1600 to 1200 BC, multiple carvings of werejaguars have been found which are similar looking to the werelions of Eurasia, but are generally dismissed as a local development independent of what was happening in Eurasia. While this is possible, combined with the large number of other parallels found between Eurasian and Mesoamerican cultures, these werejaguar figures point to being part of a larger pattern of religious iconography that existed across the ancient world in the 2nd millennium BC. Below are pictures, of two Ugallu warriors, left, and an Olmec werejaguar figurine, right.

The Bird-Man

Garuda is the eagle-man god of the epics. His Vedic equivalent was Syena, and the two are generally seen as being the same god by Hindus. Syena is simply the Sanskrit word for 'eagle,' and therefore he is seen as being an eagle-god, however, the Vedas did not specify if this was simply an eagle or the eagles that were being worshiped, or an eagle-man-god, so the concept that Syena was an eagle-man-god could be an anachronism, and they may have simply been prayers to regular eagles in the Vedas. Garuda is believed to be derived from the Early Dravidian (or Old Tamil) word 'karug-u' meaning 'eagle,'[315] however, Garuda has always been depicted as being a bird-man hybrid, like Horus in Egypt, whose name translates as 'falcon.' In Egypt, the earliest representations of Horus depict him as a falcon, however, he became anthropomorphized over the course of the civilization. Below are two photographs showing the evolution of Horus in Egypt, the Narmer Palette from the beginning of the 1st Dynasty, circa 5510 BC ULT (3100 BC CET) to the left, and a carving of Horus from the Greek era, between 330 and 30 BC to the right.

These three deities could be dismissed as three random animal-totems that became deified at the beginning of civilization, however, their stories are intertwined with the Ra-Rama story, and therefore cannot simply be ignored. In early Egyptian stories of Ra, he was the father of Horus through Isis, however, in other early texts, this was Horus the Elder. In either case, he was later replaced by Osiris by the New Kingdom. In Hinduism, Garuda is not associated with Rama, however, the main focus of his story is the war against the nagas, like Narasimha. The Hindu story of Garuda fighting the nagas is well documented throughout Southeast Asia, as the region was home to many Hindu temples before the arrival of Islam. Below is a photo of a Balinese carving of Garuda fighting nagas, showing the common iconography with Chinese water-dragons (left), and a traditional Indian interpretation.

The Hindu story of Garuda fighting the nagas almost identical to the Sumerian story of the Anzu Bird fighting the snakes. The Anzu Bird was not depicted as a bird-man, but rather an ostrich or stork-like being, like the Bennu Bird in Egypt. The story of Lugal Banda and the Anzi Bird was set much earlier according to the Sumerian king list, circa 9124 BC ULT, which implies the story itself is much older than Rama but became merged with the Ra story in Egypt. Nevertheless, the iconography of the war against the nagas continued into the later epics, with the naga Ulupi fighting alongside Rama in the Ramayana, and Krishna defeating the naga Kaliya in the Mahabharata.

In the Assyrian Old Kingdom, the bird-man showed up as a replacement for the aquatic Abgal of earlier Mesopotamian civilizations, becoming the teachers of humanity. In the ULT this civilization existed between circa 3278 to 2965 BC, while in the conventional Mesopotamian timeline it existed between 1905 and 1517 BC. These bird-men continued through later eras of Assyrian civilization, not as gods, but as teachers and messengers from the gods. Above is an Assyrian seal from the Assyrian Middle Kingdom circa 1200 BC. These messengers passed into the later Middle Eastern religions, becoming the Jewish, Christian, and Islamic angels.

The Snake-People

The nagas and similar snake people appear in most of the Asian religions and are often aquatic. In the Indian epics, they are land-living snake-people, who were both described as enemies and allies of the heroes. They are described as living in tribes and kingdoms that are virtually identical to the human tribes and kingdoms, with equivalent weapons and technology. In the Southeast Asian versions of the Rama epic, such as the Thai Ramakien and Cambodian Reamker, the nagas were replaced by mermaids. In the Southeast Asian versions of the saga, Rama also wasn't always the focus of the story, sometimes it was focused on Rama's brother Laksmana, or Hanuman. In the Cambodian Reamker, there was a large focus on Hanuman and Sovann Maccha, the mermaid daughter of Ravana. Below is a photograph of a mural depicting Hanuman and Sovann Maccha at Wat Phra Kaew, in Bangkok.

These mermaids of Southeast Asian versions of the Rama epic were often described as water-dragons, not giant dragons, like their western mythological cousins, but human-sized water-dragons, a type of aquatic-reptilian-people. These water-dragons also appeared in the foundational myths of China as Fuxi and Nuwa, a brother and sister pair of water-dragons that either created humanity or taught humanity the arts of civilization, depending on the specific myth. Similar creatures were reported in Egypt, Greece, and Sumer, in each myth being amphibious teachers. In the Greek period of Egyptian history, Isis and Osiris were depicted almost identically to Fuxi and Nuwa, however, similar stories about them being teachers of civilization go back to the New Kingdom. In early Greek mythology, Cercrops was an identical amphibious teacher of civilization, and in Sumeria, there were several amphibious teachers, called Abgals, the most famous and iconic being Oannes.

This mythical war seems to have ultimately been lost by the water-dragons as the bird-people ultimately became the dominant set of gods in most cultures, later being demoted to angels in the west, while in most cultures mermaids and dragons were demoted all the way to fiction. This story of a group of snake-teachers being overthrown bird-men became the backdrop of Judaism, Christianity, and Islam, so this story, whatever it was originally about, seems to still be happening in the pan-human psyche.

The Elephant-Man

Another odd creature that shows up in Hindu iconography is Ganesha, who has a variety of local names throughout South and Southeast Asia. Throughout the region, he had always been depicted as a human-sized elephant-headed man. Again, there are elephants in India, and so it is not difficult to see this being developing from an animal-totem, as is generally assumed by non-Hindus, however, there are specific aspects of this story that try it into the epics. The Mahabharata was apparently written down by Ganesha as Vyasa dictated it, placing Ganesha, at least figuratively, in the Harappan civilization.

The elephant-headed man himself, is something that generally does not appear outside of South and Southeast Asia, the range of the Asian elephants, however, is depicted on the Oxford Palette, a caved stone tablet from the beginning of the dynastic history in Egypt, circa 5500 BC ULT. The Egyptians did not have elephants, or elephant-headed gods, so who was this carving representing? The creature arguably does not look like an elephant, however, it does have a trunk, which only elephants have, and therefore does seem like an attempt to depicts one, by someone that had never seen one. Below are pictures of the Oxford Palette from circa 5510 BC ULT, left, and one of the earliest surviving representations of Ganesha circa 500 AD, center, and a Ganesha-like statue discovered in Australia in 1906. The Ganesha-like creature in the Oxford Palette in the lower-left area.

The name Ganesha is another important factor, as it formed by combining the Sanskrit words *gana* meaning group, and *isha* meaning lord.[316] In this context the group is the Ganas, a group of phantoms or spirits that attend Shiva.[317] This means that the name Ganesha is not whatever he was called by the ancient Harappans, but an Indo-Aryan translation. If the original name was translated accurately into Sanskrit, then is had an identical meaning to the Sumerian Enlil, which translates as 'Lord of Phantoms.'[318] Enlil, later called Ellil by the Akkadians and Babylonians was never depicted as far as we know, and to it is unclear if he was also elephant-headed.

All of these elephant-people also seem reminiscent of the small white elephant from Buddhist beliefs, that artificially impregnated Siddhartha's mother, and then ten months later preformed the cesarean section to bring Siddhartha into the world. Of course, no one, other than some Buddhists, believe the Buddha was delivered by a small white elephant surgeon what came down from the sky, but, the point is that the belief in a small elephant-man persisted to at least the time of Siddhartha, circa 600 BC, and to our modern age, if one counts Ganesha, and it would be hard not to. Nevertheless, the Oxford Palette clearly depicts an upright-walking and clothed elephant-man circa 5500 BC ULT, so this icon has been around for a long time, and across a large area.

The Bull-Man

The various archaic belief systems across the region also all shared the icon of the bull-man. This bull-man is found on seals from both the Indus Valley and Sumer and was identically depicted. This Bull-man is identified as Enkidu in Sumerian stories, which would date his life, if he lived, to circa 7600 BC ULT in the Sumerian King List. Below are two seals depicting the Bull-man fighting with animals. The left image is from the Indus Valley, and the right is a depiction of Enkidu from the Akkadian Empire, circa 3885 to 3700 BC ULT.

This bull-man also shows up in several other cultures, most notably the Greek Minotaur story, which is itself set in the ancient Minoan Civilization. The Egyptians had several bovine deities, including including the Apis Bulls themselves, who were venerated much as cattle continue to be venerated in India today. The most prominent Egyptian Bull-man god of the Old Kingdom was Amen, also transliterated as Amon or Amun, the creator god who breathed life into the world, a story that was later incorporated into Jewish Torah, and continued to be believed by many Christians to this day. Ironically while both Jews and Christians have forgotten who the god was that breathed life into the world, they continue to say his name at the end of prayers and claim it means something different, and in completely unrelated to the original god from the story.

In the Middle East, and well as other regions of the world, the horned-god became synonymous with evil. This transition seems to have happened over a long period of time, with some horned-beings already seen as evil in the epics of India, and Bacchus, the last horned-gods in the Greco-Roman Civilization being officially restricted in 186 BC, and later banned with the rest of the old gods when Christianity became the state religion in the 4th century AD. In the Sanskrit epics, these horned beings were called rakshasas, and like the nagas, were depicted as living in generally human-like societies. One simple explanation for these 'peoples' were different and conflicting religions, one which venerated the bull, and another with venerated the snake, both of which were viewed as alien by the original authors of the epics. Whatever they were, like the nagas, some individuals fought on the side of the heroes, and others fought on the side of the enemies. In the Ramayana, the rakshasas served as an army for Ravana, while in the later Mahabharta individuals fought on both sides, and the most powerful warrior on the side of Arjuna and Krishna was a rakshasa called Ghatotkacha.

Unlike the nagas, the rakshasas were depicted as having many magical powers, although descriptions vary by the epic. Generally, rakshasas were illusionists, who could make themselves appear as giants, or look like humans. While this may be a later addition to the epics in the Classical era, it probably isn't as the ancient Sumerian Epic of Gilgamesh ascribes similar shape-changing abilities to Ninsun, the mother of King Gilgamesh. Ninsun, originally named Gula, was another cow-goddess, who also had the ability to appear in human form. While this may be a later mythical aspect added to the Gilgamesh story, it dates back to the Akkadian era in Mesopotamian history, circa 3885 to 3700 BC ULT, which would place it in the Harappan 3C Phase, at the same point in time as the seals that depict the Bull-man, which have been found in both the ruins of the Indus Valley Civilization and the Akkadian Empire.

Conclusion

The current dynastic timelines of Egypt and Mesopotamia are impossible. Believing in them means endorsing the idea the Hyksos were time-travelers, and that the Egyptians were technologically a thousand years behind their major trading partners in Mesopotamia during the Middle Kingdom. It also is not what the ancient Egyptians, Sumerians, and Akkadians actually recorded, so believing it means believing that modern Egyptologists and Assyriologists know more about ancient Egypt and Mesopotamia than the ancient Egyptians, Sumerians, and Akkadians themselves. Given that the ancient Egyptians, Sumerians, and Akkadians lived through it, and all Egyptologists have to go on is random bits of pottery and mostly ruined buildings, this seems like an incredible stretch of the imagination, granted no more than time-traveling Hyksos, but still a stretch. The fact that Egyptologists feel they don't need to explain these anachronisms because the history of Egypt is a political timeline, not subject to science, is insulting both to the intelligence and to the integrity of anyone that bothers looking into the history of these preeminent ancient cultures.

The idea that the ancient Egyptians built docks in the middle of the desert, and then dredged out mind-boggling amounts of sand to move the Nile to the docks, is beyond ridiculous. Maybe that's how Egyptologists would do it, but the existence of the pyramids proves the ancient Egyptians just weren't that stupid. The fact that they did dredge mind-boggling amounts of mud simply proves that the Nile water-levels were dropping rapidly at the end of the Old Kingdom. The fact that Egyptologists ignore the ancient Egyptian records of the pre-Dynastic era is probably for the best, imagine the nonsense they would have made up to explain the Osireion if they had to admit it is 15,000 years old! Wait... let me guess... time-travelers?

Unfortunately, the timeline of Egypt is the cornerstone of ancient history. As the Sumerian and later Mesopotamian civilizations were trading with the Egyptians, the Mesopotamian timeline is also broken as the dates of certain Egyptians Kings are known to have lived at the same time as certain Mesopotamian Kings. This means that the bulk of the recorded history of

Sumer has to be ignored by Assyriologists, as it just doesn't fit into the Egyptian timeline. As the Harappan history is then dated according to when they were trading with the Mesopotamians, and Indologists also fall subject to the inventive nonsense of Egyptologists. This means that Indologists have to accept the impossible fact that the bronze age Harappan civilization existed next to the iron age Ganges civilization for over 500 years, and never noticed they were there. These broken timelines then fan out further pulling the Minoans and Greeks, Iranians, and Chinese into this confusing mess.

Egyptologists haven't just stolen the real history of Egypt from us, they've stolen the real history of the world from us.

References

Section 1 – Dynastic Egypt

1 Toby Wilkinson (2010) "Timeline," *The Rise and Fall of Ancient Egypt*

2 Georg Friedrich Unger (1867) *Chronologie des Manetho*

3 W. M. Flinders Petrie (1906) *Researches in Sinai*, Chapter 12

4 Christopher Bronk Ramsey, et al. (2010) "Radiocarbon-Based timeline for Dynastic Egypt," *Science*, Volume 328, Number 5985, Pages 1554-1557

5 W. M. Flinders Petrie (1906) *Researches In Sinai*, Pages 166-167

6 Lisa L. Ely, et al. (October 15, 1993) "A 5000-Year Record of Extreme Floods and Climate Change in the Southwestern United States," *Science*, New Series, Volume 262, Number 5132, Pages 410-412

7 G. A. Zielinski, et al. (1994) *Nature*, Volume 264, Page 948

8 T. Blunier, et al. (1995) *Nature*, Volume 374, Page 47

9 L. G. Thompson, et al. (July 7, 1995) "Late Glacial Stage and Holocene Tropical IceCore Records from Huascaran, Peru," *Science*, Volume 269, Pages 46-50.

10 Selim Hassan (1944) "Excavations at Giza," *Antiquity*, Volume 18, Issue 70

11 Lauren Said-Moorhouse (September 3, 2018) "Archaeologists unearth village in Egypt older than the pharaohs," *CNN.com*

12 Reuters in Cairo (November 23, 2016) "Egypt unearths 7,000-year-old lost city," *The Guardian*

13 *Ludlow Bull, et al.* (1936) "James Henry Breasted 1865-1935," *Journal of the American Oriental Society*, Volume 56, Pages 113-120

14 Robert M. Schoch (2003) *Voyages of the Pyramid Builders*

15 M. Friedrich, et al. (2004) "The 12,460-year Hohenheim oak and pine tree-ring chronology from central Europe - A unique annual record for radiocarbon calibration and paleoenvironment reconstructions," *Radiocarbon*, 46 (3): 1111-22

BROKEN TIMELINES - BOOKS 1-3: EGYPT, MESOPOTAMIA, THE INDO-EUROPEANS AND HARAPPANS

16 Kimiaki Masuda (27 July 2012) "A signature of cosmic-ray increase in AD 774-775 from tree rings in Japan," *Nature*, Volume 486, Pages 240-

17 F. Y. Wang, et al. (14 Nov 2017) "A rapid cosmic-ray increase in BC 3372-3371 from ancient buried tree rings in China," *Nature Communications*, 8: 1487

18 Fusa Miyake (Jan 31, 2017) "Large 14C excursion in 5480 BC indicates an abnormal sun in the mid-Holocene," *Proceedings of the National Academy of Sciences*, 114 (5) 881-884

19 Felix Höflmayer (July 2016) Radiocarbon Dating and Egyptian timeline - From the 'Curve of Knowns' to Bayesian Modeling, Page 2

Section 2 – Dynastic Mesopotamia

20 Donald B. Redford, editor (2001) "Egyptian King List," *The Oxford Encyclopedia of Ancient Egypt*, Volume 2. Pages 626-628

21 James Mellaart (1979) "Egyptian and Near Eastern timeline: A dilemma?" *Antiquity*, 53(207), Pages 6-18

22 Thomas Schneider (2002) *Lexikon der Pharaonen*

23 Richard Caplice (1980) *Introduction to Akkadian*

24 Lisa L. Ely, et al. (October 15, 1993) "A 5000-Year Record of Extreme Floods and Climate Change in the Southwestern United States," *Science*, New Series, Volume 262, Number 5132, Pages 410-412

25 G. A. Zielinski, et al. (1994) *Nature*, Volume 264, Page 948

26 T. Blunier, et al. (1995) *Nature*, Volume 374, Page 47

27 L. G. Thompson, et al. (July 7, 1995) "Late Glacial Stage and Holocene Tropical IceCore Records from Huascaran, Peru," *Science*, Volume 269, Pages 46-50

28 Robert MacHenry (1992) The new encyclopaedia Britannica: in 32 vol. Macropaedia, India - Ireland, Volume 21. *Encyclopedia Britannica.* Page 36

29 Thomas Schneider (2003) "Kassitisch und Hurro-Urartäisch. Ein Diskussionsbeitrag zu möglichen lexikalischen Isoglossen," *Altorientalische Forschungen* (30): 372-381

30 E. D. Phillips (1963) "The Peoples of the Highland: Vanished Cultures of Luristan, Mannai and Urartu," *Vanished Civilizations of the Ancient World*. Page 241

31 Wozy z Bronocic (2009) *Strona oficjalna Muzeum Archeologicznego z Krakowie*

32 Kim Ryholt (1997) *The Political Situation in Egypt during the Second Intermediate Period*

33 Donald Redford (1992) *Egypt, Canaan, and Israel in Ancient Times*, Page 71

34 Darrell D. Baker (2008) *The Encyclopedia of the Pharaohs: Volume I - Predynastic to the Twentieth Dynasty 3300-1069 BC*. Page 174

35 Flinders Petrie (1917) *Scarabs and cylinders with names: illustrated by the Egyptian collection in University College, London*

36 David Rohl (2007) *Lords of Avaris*, Pages 494-6

37 Herodotus (c. 450 BC) *Histories*, II, 49

38 Euripides (c. 425 BC) *Bacchae*, 171

39 Diodorus Siculus (c. 20 AD) *Bibliotheca Historica* I, 23

Section 3 – Historic Indo-Europeans and Harappans

40 Gavin Flood (1996) *An Introduction to Hinduism*. Pages 35-39

41 Frits Staal (2009) *Discovering the Vedas: Origins, Mantras, Rituals, Insights*. Pages 136-137

42 Alex Wayman (1997) *Untying the Knots in Buddhism*. Pages 52-53

43 A Bhattacharya (2006) *Hindu Dharma: Introduction to Scriptures and Theology*. Pages 8-14

44 Michael Witzel (1997) "The Development of the Vedic Canon and its Schools: The Social and Political Milieu," in *Inside the Texts, Beyond the Texts. New Approaches to the Study of the Vedas*. Pages 284-285

45 Dilip K. Chakrabarti (1992) *The Early use of Iron In India*.

46 Constance Jones (2007) *Encyclopedia of Hinduism*. Page 404

BROKEN TIMELINES - BOOKS 1-3: EGYPT, MESOPOTAMIA, THE INDO-EUROPEANS AND HARAPPANS

47 E. Photos (1989) "The Question of Meteoritic versus Smelted Nickel-Rich Iron: Archaeological Evidence and Experimental Results," in *World Archaeology*. 20 (3): 403–421.

48 R. F. Tylecote (1992) *A History of Metallurgy*. Page 3

49 Richard Cowen (April 1999) "Chapter 5: The Age of Iron," in *Essays on Geology, History, and People*.

50 Akinori Useugi, editor (2018) "Iron Age in South Asia," in *South Asian Archaeology*, Series 2

51 Rakesh Tewari (2003) "The origins of Iron Working in India: New evidence from the Central Ganga plain and the Eastern Vindhyas," in *Antiquity*. 77 (297): 536–545.

52 Mariya Ivanova (2007) "The Chronology of the "Maikop Culture" in the North Caucasus: Changing Perspectives," in the *Armenian Journal of Near Eastern Studies*. II: 7–39.

53 W. Haak, et al. (2015) "Massive migration from the steppe was a source for Indo-European languages in Europe," *Nature*. 522 (7555): 207–211.

54 Eppie R. Jones, et al. (2015) "Upper Palaeolithic genomes reveal deep roots of modern Eurasians," in *Nature Communications*. 6: 8912.

55 Iain Mathieson (December 24, 2015) "Genome-wide patterns of selection in 230 ancient Eurasians," *Nature*. 528 (7583): 499–503

56 Sandra Wilde (2014) "Direct evidence for positive selection of skin, hair, and eye pigmentation in Europeans during the last 5,000 y," in *PNAS*. 111 (13): 4832–4837.

57 Rene J. Herrera (2018) *Ancestral DNA, Human Origins, and Migrations*. Page 518.

58 Iain Mathieson, et al. (30 May 2017) *The Genomic History Of Southeastern Europe*

59 David A. Anthony (2007) *The horse, the wheel, and language: how Bronze-Age riders from the Eurasian steppes shaped the modern world*

60 Benjamin Fortson IV (2011) *Indo-European Language and Culture: An Introduction*, Second Edition.

61 Martin Litchfield West (2013) *Hellenica: Volume III: Philosophy, Music and Metre*

62 Michael Stausberg, et al. (2015) *The Wiley-Blackwell Companion to Zoroastrianism*

63 Solomon Alexander Nigosian (1993) *The Zoroastrian Faith: Tradition and Modern Research*

64 Johan Schalin (2009) *Lexicon of Early Indo-European Loanwords Preserved in Finnish*

65 David W. Anthony (2007) *The Horse, the Wheel, and Language*. Pages 371-411

66 David W. Anthony (2007) *The Horse, the Wheel, and Language*. Pages 140, 147-151

67 I. Mathieson (2018) "The Genomic History Of Southeastern Europe," *Nature*. 555: 197-203.

68 Hristivoje Pavlović (23 August 2007) "Tajne Lepenskog Vira IV - Zapanjujuća veština obrade kamena," in *Politika*

69 Marco Merlini (2009) *Introduction to the Danube script*

70 Lisa L. Ely, et al. (October 15, 1993) "A 5000-Year Record of Extreme Floods and Climate Change in the Southwestern United States," *Science*, New Series, Volume 262, Number 5132, Pages 410-412

71 G. A. Zielinski, et al. (1994) *Nature*, Volume 264, Page 948

72 T. Blunier, et al. (1995) *Nature*, Volume 374, Page 47

73 L. G. Thompson, et al. (July 7, 1995) "Late Glacial Stage and Holocene Tropical IceCore Records from Huascaran, Peru," *Science*, Volume 269, Pages 46-50

74 Nils-Axel Mörner (1995) "The Baltic Ice Lake-Yoldia Sea transition," in *Quaternary International*. 27: 95–98.

75 Strasser F. Thomas, et al. (2010) "Stone Age seafaring in the Mediterranean," *Hesperia (The Journal of the American School of Classical Studies at Athens)*, volume 79, pages 145-190

76 Iravatham Mahadevan (1998) "Ancient Indus Valley Script" Interview by Omar Khan

77 Philip Lutgendorf (2007) *Hanuman's Tale: The Messages of a Divine Monkey.* Page 40

78 Robert Caldwell (1996) *A Comparative Grammar of the Dravidian Or South-Indian Family of Languages*, Third Edition, Page 591

79 Gauri Mahulikar (2001) *Effect of Ramayana on various cultures and civilisations*

80 Kisari Mohan Ganguli, translator (1893) Mahabharata 2.14.50

81 Vettam Mani (2010) *Puranic Encyclopaedia*, 9th Reprint, Page 89

82 Kisari Mohan Ganguli, translator (1893) *Mahabharata*, Book 16

83 S. Kathiroli (2004) "Recent Marine Archaeological Finds in Khambhat, Gujarat," *Journal of Indian Ocean Archaeology*, 2004 Pages 141-149

84 Pliny the Elder (79 AD) *Naturalis Historia*, 6.59-60

85 Arrian of Nicomedia (circa 150 AD) *Indica*, 9.9

86 Monier Monier Williams (1899) *Sanskrit English Dictionary with Etymology*, Page 877, ???

87 S. M. Sullivan (2011) *Indus Script Dictionary*, page viii

88 T. S. Subramanian (2006) "Significance of Mayiladuthurai find" in *The Hindu*, May 1, 2006

89 Nivedita Khandekar (2012) "Indus Valley 2,000 years older than thought," *Hindustan Times*, November 4, 2012

90 Jhimli Mukherjee Pandey (2016) "Archeologists confirm Indian civilization is 8000 years old," *Times of India*, May 29, 2016

Section 4 – Pre-Dynastic Egypt

91 Wolfgang Helck (1992) "Anmerkungen zum Turiner Königspapyrus," *Studien zur Altägyptischen Kultur* 19: 151–216.

92 Pierre M.Vermeerscha and WimVan Neer (2015) *Quaternary Science Reviews*, Volume 130, Pages 155-167

93 Facts On File, Incorporated (2009) *Encyclopedia of the Peoples of Africa and the Middle East*. Page 777

94 Strabo (7 BC) *Geographica*, 17.1.42

95 Edouard Naville (1914) "Excavations at Abydos: The Great Pool and the Tomb of Osiris," *The Journal of Egyptian Archaeology*, Volume 1

96 J. S. Westerman (Jan 2008) "An Archaeological Analysis of the Osireion." *Third International Conference on the Geology of the Tethys, Aswan, Egypt*

97 Bertha Porter and Rosalind Moss (1974) *Topographical Bibliography of Ancient Egyptian Hieroglyphic Texts, Statues, Reliefs and Paintings Volume III: Memphis, Part I Abu Rawash to Abusir*. 2nd edition

98 Selim Hassan (1949) *The Sphinx: Its history in the light of recent excavations*

99 Alice Leplongeon (2017) "Technological variability in the Late Palaeolithic lithic industries of the Egyptian Nile Valley: The case of the Silsilian and Afian industries." *PLoS ONE* 12(12): e0188824.

100 Clare M. Boston (2007) "An examination of the Geochemical properties of late devensian glacigenic sediments in Eastern England, Durham theses," *Durham E-Theses Online*

101 Fred Wendorf and Romuald Schild (November 26, 2000) *Late Neolithic megalithic structures at Nabta Playa (Sahara), southwestern Egypt*

102 G. A. Brophy and P. A. Rosen (2005) "Satellite Imagery Measures of the Astronomically Aligned Megaliths at Nabta Playa," *Mediterranean Archaeology and Archaeometry*, 5 (1): 15–24.

Section 5 – Pre-Dynastic Mesopotamia

103 Kurt Lambeck, et al. (October 28, 2014) "Sea level and global ice volumes from the Last Glacial Maximum to the Holocene," *Proceedings of the National Academy of Sciences*, 111 (43) 15296-15303

104 Vivien Gornitz (2009) *Encyclopedia of paleoclimatology and ancient environments*. Page 890 (Table S1)

105 T. M. Cronin (2012) "Rapid sea-level rise," *Quaternary Science Reviews*, 56:11-30

106 P. Blanchon (2011) "Meltwater Pulses," *Encyclopedia of Modern Coral Reefs: Structure, form and process*. Springer-Verlag Earth Science Series, Page 683-690

107 Bryan Sykes (2001) *The Seven Daughters of Eve*

108 Doron M. Behar, et al. (May 2004) "MtDNA evidence for a genetic bottleneck in the early history of the Ashkenazi Jewish population," *European Journal of Human Genetics*, 12(5):355-64

109 Lucia Simoni, et al. (2000) "Geographic Patterns of mtDNA Diversity in Europe," *American Journal of Human Genetics*, Volume 66, Pages. 262-278

110 Vincent Dubut (2003) "mtDNA polymorphisms in five French groups: importance of regional sampling," *European Journal of Human Genetics*, 12: 293–300

111 Amy Non (2010) *Analyses of genetic data within an interdisciplinary framework to investigate recent human evolutionary history and complex disease*

112 W. G. Waddell, translator (1940) *Fragments of Manetho. Aegyptica Book 1*. Editor's Note 2.

113 Anne Goddeeris (2002) *Economy and Society in Northern Babylonia in the Early Old Babylonian Period*

114 Archibald Henry Sayce (1911) "Sippara," *Encyclopædia Britannica*, 25, 11th Edition, Page 151

115 John MacGinnis (2002) "The use of writing boards in the Neo-Babylonian temple administration at Sippar," *Iraq*, 64, 217-236

116 Maximillien de Lafayette (2017) "Vol.1. Etymology, Philology And Comparative Dictionary Of Synonyms," *22 Dead And Ancient Languages*, Page 79

117 Manfried Dietrich (2003) *The Babylonian Correspondence of Sar-gon and Sennacherib*

118 David Woods (1965) *A history of tactical communications techniques*

119 Andrew R. George (1992) "Babylonian topographical texts," *Orientalia Lovaniensia Analecta*, 40, xviii, Page 261

120 Kelley Coblentz Bautch (25 September 2003) *A Study of the Geography of 1 Enoch 17-19: "no One Has Seen what I Have Seen."* pages 62–.

121 Revelation 21:1-4

122 Lihui Yang (2005) *Handbook of Chinese Mythology.* Pages 160-164

123 George Nathaniel Curzon (1968) *The Hindu World: An Encyclopedic Survey of Hinduism*, Page 184

124 Robert E. Buswell (2004) *Encyclopedia of Buddhism: A-L.* Pages 407-408

125 R Soekmono (1973) *Pengantar Sejarah Kebudayaan Indonesia*, Page 119

126 Wilfred G. Lambert (1967) "Enmeduranki and Related Material," *Journal of Cuneiform Studies.* Vol. 21, Special Volume Honoring Professor Albrecht Goetze, pages 126-138

127 J. J. Collins (1998) *The apocalyptic imagination: an introduction to Jewish apocalyptic literature.* Pages 44-47

128 Victor Hamilton (1990) "The Book of Genesis" *The New International Commentary on the Old Testament.* Pages 257-258

129 Mark Rose (September 3, 1998) Archaeology Magazine

130 Rig Veda, Book 4, Hymn 47, Verse 24

131 Ralph L. Roys (1967) *The Book of Chilam Balam of Chumayel.* Page 100

132 N. R. Nowaczyk et al. (2012) "Dynamics of the Laschamp geomagnetic excursion from Black Sea sediments," *Earth and Planetary Science Letters*, Volume 351-352, Pages 54-69

133 N. Bonhommet and J. Zähringer (1969) "Paleomagnetism and potassium argon age determinations of the Laschamp geomagnetic polarity event," Earth and Planetary Science Letters, Volume 6, Pages 43-4

134 Jeremy Black and Anthony Green (1992) *Gods, Demons and Symbols of Ancient Mesopotamia: An Illustrated Dictionary*, Page 180-187

135 Alberto R. W. Green (2003) *The Storm-God in the Ancient Near East*

136 Michael Staubwasser, et al. (September 11, 2018) "Impact of climate change on the transition of Neanderthals to modern humans in Europe," *Proceedings of the National Academy of Sciences.* 115 (37) 9116-9121

137 Jason Daley (August 29, 2018) "Climate Change Likely Iced Neanderthals Out Of Existence"

138 D. M. Behar, et al. (April 2012) "A "Copernican" reassessment of the human mitochondrial DNA tree from its root," *American Journal of Human Genetics.* 90 (4): 675-84

139 J. M. Larruga, et al. (May 2017) "Carriers of mitochondrial DNA macrohaplogroup R colonized Eurasia and Australasia from a southeast Asia core area," *BMC Evolutionary Biology.* 17 (1): 115

140 R. Rodríguez-Varela, et al. (November 2017) "Genomic Analyses of Pre-European Conquest Human Remains from the Canary Islands Reveal Close Affinity to Modern North Africans," *Current Biology.* 27 (21): 3396–3402.e5

141 M. Karmin (2005) "Human mitochondrial DNA haplogroup R in India," *University of Tartu.*

142 B. Sykes (2001) *The Seven Daughters of Eve*

143 Robert E. Krebs and Carolyn A. Krebs (2003) *Groundbreaking Scientific Experiments, Inventions & Discoveries of the Ancient World*

144 BGI Shenzhen (June 5, 2014) "The Sheep Genome: Study shows how sheep first separated from goats," *phys.org*

145 Rachel Lentz (September 22, 2016) "Past climate swings orchestrated early human migration waves out of Africa," *phys.org*

146 Martin Kuhlwilm, et al (25 February 2016) "Ancient gene flow from early modern humans into Eastern Neanderthals," *Nature.* 530, Pages 429-33

147 S. Sankararaman, et al. (2014) "The landscape of Neandertal ancestry in present-day humans," *Nature.* 507 (7492) Pages 354-57

148 Mait Metspalu, et al. (August 2004) "Most of the extant mtDNA boundaries in south and southwest Asia were likely shaped during the initial settlement of Eurasia by anatomically modern humans," *BMC Genetics.* 5: 26

149 Suvendu Maji, et al. (2008) "Distribution of Mitochondrial DNA Macrohaplogroup N in India with Special Reference to Haplogroup R and its Sub-Haplogroup U," *International Journal of Human Genetics*. 8 (1-2): 85-96

150 Jose M Larruga (23 May 2017) "Carriers of mitochondrial DNA macrohaplogroup R colonized Eurasia and Australasia from a southeast Asia core area." *BMC Evolutionary Biology*. 17

151 A. Robock, et al. (2009) "Did the Toba Volcanic Eruption of ~74k BP Produce Widespread Glaciation?" *Journal of Geophysical Research*. 114: D10107

152 S. C. Jones (2007) "The Toba Supervolcanic Eruption: Tephra-Fall Deposits in India and Paleoanthropological Implications," *The Evolution and History of Human Populations in South Asia*. Page 173-200

153 Pedro Soares (2009) "Correcting for Purifying Selection: An Improved Human Mitochondrial Molecular Clock," *The American Journal of Human Genetics*. 84 (6): 740-59

154 Chris Clarkson, et al. (2017) "Human occupation of northern Australia by 65,000 years ago," *Nature*. 547 (7663): 306-310

155 A. Cooper and C. B. Stringer (2013) "Did the Denisovans Cross Wallace's Line?" *Science*. 342 (6156): 321-23

156 B. Malyarchuk, et al. (2008) "Mitochondrial DNA Phylogeny in Eastern and Western Slavs," *Molecular Biology and Evolution*. 25 (8): 1651-8

157 A. Achilli, et al. (November 2004) "The molecular dissection of mtDNA haplogroup H confirms that the Franco-Cantabrian glacial refuge was a major source for the European gene pool," *American Journal of Human Genetics*. 75 (5): 910-8

158 Agnar Helgason, et al. (2001) "MtDNA and the Islands of the North Atlantic: Estimating the Proportions of Norse and Gaelic Ancestry," *The American Journal of Human Genetics*. 68 (3): 723-37

159 Malliya Gounder Palanichamy, et al. (2004) "Phylogeny of Mitochondrial DNA Macrohaplogroup N in India, Based on Complete Sequencing: Implications for the Peopling of South Asia," *The American Journal of Human Genetics*. 75 (6): 966-78.

160 Lluís Quintana-Murci, et al. (2004) "Where West Meets East: The Complex mtDNA Landscape of the Southwest and Central Asian Corridor," *The American Journal of Human Genetics*. 74 (5): 827-45

161 Khaled K. Abu-Amero, et al. (2008) "Mitochondrial DNA structure in the Arabian Peninsula," *BMC Evolutionary Biology*. 8: 45.

162 Gyaneshwer Chaubey, et al. (2008) "Phylogeography of mtDNA haplogroup R7 in the Indian peninsula," *BMC Evolutionary Biology*. 8: 227

163 Kumarasamy Thangaraj, et al. (2009) "Deep Rooting In-Situ Expansion of mtDNA Haplogroup R8 in South Asia," *PLoS ONE*. 4 (8): e6545

164 Clarissa Scholes, et al. (2011) "Genetic diversity and evidence for population admixture in Batak Negritos from Palawan," *American Journal of Physical Anthropology*. 146 (1): 62-72.

165 Miroslava Derenko, et al. (2007) "Phylogeographic Analysis of Mitochondrial DNA in Northern Asian Populations," *The American Journal of Human Genetics*. 81 (5): 1025-41

166 M. Tanaka, et al. (2004) "Mitochondrial Genome Variation in Eastern Asia and the Peopling of Japan," *Genome Research*. 14 (10a): 1832–50

167 Yong-Gang Yao, et al. (March 2002) "Phylogeographic Differentiation of Mitochondrial DNA in Han Chinese," *American Journal of Human Genetics*. 70(3): 635-651

168 K. A. Tabbada, et al. (2009) "Philippine Mitochondrial DNA Diversity: A Populated Viaduct between Taiwan and Indonesia?" *Molecular Biology and Evolution*. 27 (1): 21-31

169 M. J. Pierson, et al. (2006) "Deciphering Past Human Population Movements in Oceania: Provably Optimal Trees of 127 mtDNA Genomes," *Molecular Biology and Evolution*. 23 (10): 1966–75

170 Catherine Hill, et al. (2006) "Phylogeography and Ethnogenesis of Aboriginal Southeast Asians," *Molecular Biology and Evolution*. 23 (12): 2480-91

171 S. Mona, et al. (2009) "Genetic Admixture History of Eastern Indonesia as Revealed by Y-Chromosome and Mitochondrial DNA Analysis," *Molecular Biology and Evolution*. 26 (8): 1865-77

172 Min-Sheng Peng, et al. (2010) "Tracing the Austronesian Footprint in Mainland Southeast Asia: A Perspective from Mitochondrial DNA," *Molecular Biology and Evolution*. 27 (10): 2417-2430

173 Catherine Hill, et al. (2007) "A Mitochondrial Stratigraphy for Island Southeast Asia," *The American Journal of Human Genetics*. 80 (1): 29-43

174 Simona Fornarino, et al. (2009) "Mitochondrial and Y-chromosome diversity of the Tharus (Nepal): A reservoir of genetic variation," *BMC Evolutionary Biology*. 9: 154

175 J. Friedlaender, et al. (2005) "Expanding Southwest Pacific Mitochondrial Haplogroups P and Q," *Molecular Biology and Evolution*. 22 (6): 1506-17

176 Georgi Hudjashov, et al. (2007) "Revealing the prehistoric settlement of Australia by Y chromosome and mtDNA analysis," *Proceedings of the National Academy of Sciences*. 104 (21): 8726-30

177 M. Kayser, et al. (2006) "Melanesian and Asian Origins of Polynesians: MtDNA and Y Chromosome Gradients Across the Pacific," *Molecular Biology and Evolution*. 23 (11): 2234-44

178 K. A. Hallin, et al. (2012) "Paleoclimate during Neandertal and anatomically modern human occupation at Amud and Qafzeh, Israel: the stable isotope data," *Journal of Human Evolution*, 62(1), 59-73

179 S. Sankararaman, et al. (2012) "The Date of Interbreeding between Neandertals and Modern Humans," *PLoS Genetics*. 8 (10): e1002947

180 Matthew Warren (22 August 2018) "Mum's a Neanderthal, Dad's a Denisovan: First discovery of an ancient-human hybrid - Genetic analysis uncovers a direct descendant of two different groups of early humans," *Nature*. 560 (7719): 417-418

181 Qiaomei Fu, et al. (2014) "Genome sequence of a 45,000-year-old modern human from western Siberia," *Nature*, Volume 514, Pages 445-449

182 Q. Ding, et al. (2014) "Neanderthal Introgression at Chromosome 3p21.31 was Under Positive Natural Selection in East Asians," *Molecular Biology and Evolution*. 31 (3): 683-95

183 Lukas Bicke, et al. (October 2015) "The timing of the penultimate glaciation in the northern Alpine Foreland: new insights from luminescence dating," *Proceedings of the Geologists' Association*, Volume 126, Issues 4-5, Pages 536-550

184 D. Dahl-Jensen, et al. (2013) "Eemian interglacial reconstructed from a Greenland folded ice core," *Nature*. 493 (7433): 489-94

185 William W. Hallo and William Kelly Simpson (1974) *The Ancient Near East: A History*, Page 32

186 W. F. Albright and T. O. Lambdin (1971) "The Evidence of Language," *The Cambridge Ancient History I*, Part 1, Page 150

187 Vaughn E. Crawford (1960) "The Location of Bad-Tibira," *Iraq* 22, Page 198

188 Ferris J. Stephens (1932) "A Newly Discovered Inscription of Libit-Ishtar," *Journal of the American Oriental Society*. 52.2 Page 183

189 Th. van Kolfschoten (2000) "The Eemian mammal fauna of central Europe," *Netherlands Journal of Geosciences*. 79 (2/3): 269-281

190 Liora Kolska Horwitz and Eitan Tchernov (1990) "Cultural and Environmental Implications of Hippopotamus Bone Remains in Archaeological Contexts in the Levant," *Bulletin of the American Schools of Oriental Research*. 280 (280): 67-76

191 Jeremy Black and Anthony Green (1992) *Gods, Demons and Symbols of Ancient Mesopotamia: An Illustrated Dictionary*. Page 73-77

192 Monica S. Cyrino (2010) *Aphrodite, Gods and Heroes of the Ancient World*. Page 95-97

193 Matthew Dillon (2003) "'Woe for Adonis' – but in Spring, not Summer," Hermes 131 (1), Pages 1-9

194 K. A. Raymoure (2014) "Possible evidence of human sacrifice at Minoan Chania," *Archaeology News Network*

195 J. G. Frazer (1906) "Adonis, Attis and Osiris," *Studies in the History of Oriental Religion*, Page 356

196 Samuel Noah Kramer (1961) *Sumerian Mythology: A Study of Spiritual and Literary Achievement in the Third Millennium B.C.*: Revised Edition

197 John Byron (2011) *Cain and Abel in text and tradition: Jewish and Christian interpretations of the first sibling rivalry*. Page 98

198 K. Aterman (5 March, 1999) "From Horus the child to Hephaestus who limps: a romp through history," *American Journal Medical Genetics*. 83(1):53-63

199 T. Abusch (2000) "Ištar." *Nin* 1: 23-7

200 Gwendolyn Leick (1998) *A Dictionary of Ancient Near Eastern Mythology*, Page 86-87

201 Kim Plofker (2007) *Mathematics in India*. Page 17

202 Peter Roger Moorey (1999) *Ancient mesopotamian materials and industries: the archaeological evidence*. Pages 86-87

203 D. O. Edzard (1957-71) "Geštinanna," *Reallexikon der Assyriologie und Vorderasiatischen Archäologie*. 3, Pages 299-301

204 Samuel Noah Kramer (1964) *The Sumerians: Their History, Culture and Character*. Page 293

205 L. R. Bailey (1968) "Israelite 'Ēl šadday and Amorite Bêl šadê," *Journal of Biblical Literature*. 87, 434-38

206 F. Wiggermann (1998-2001) "Nin-ĝišzida," *Reallexikon der Assyriologie und vorderasiatischen Archäologie*. 9, Pages 368-373

207 Genesis Chapter 3

208 Ezekiel Chapters 9-10

209 Stephen L. Harris (1985) *Understanding the Bible*

210 Archibald Henry Sayce (1899) "Kenites," *A Dictionary of the Bible*. II. Page 834

211 Louis Ginzberg (1909) *The Legends of the Jews Vol I: The Ten Generations - The Birth of Cain*

212 Gerard P. Luttikhuizen, editor (2003) *Eve's Children: The Biblical Stories Retold and Interpreted in Jewish and Christian traditions*, Volume 5, Page vii

213 Dianne Bergant and Robert J. Karris (1992) "Genesis," *The Collegeville Bible Commentary: Old Testament*. Pages 46-47

214 Martin Kuhlwilm, et al. (25 February 2016) "Ancient gene flow from early modern humans into Eastern Neanderthals," *Nature*. 530, Pages 429-33

215 C. Lalueza-Fox (2007) "A Melanocortin 1 Receptor Allele Suggests Varying Pigmentation Among Neanderthals," *Science*. 318 (5855): 1453-55

216 Matthias Meyer, et al. (24 March 2016) "Nuclear DNA sequences from the Middle Pleistocene Sima de los Huesos hominins," *Nature*. 531, pages 504-507

217 E. Indriati, et al. (2011) "The Age of the 20 Meter Solo River Terrace, Java, Indonesia and the Survival of Homo erectus in Asia," *PLoS ONE* 6(6): e21562.

218 D Mania and U Mania (1988) "Deliberate engravings on bone artefacts of Homo Erectus," *Rock Art Research*. 5, 91-97

219 I. Hershkovitz, et al. (April 2011) "Middle pleistocene dental remains from Qesem Cave (Israel)," *American Journal of Physical Anthropology*, 144 (4)

220 Ewan Callaway (7 June 2017) "Oldest Homo sapiens fossil claim rewrites our species' history," *Nature*.

221 J. L. Xiao, et al. (2002) "Age of the Fossil Dali Man in North-Central China deduced from Chronostratigraphy of the Loess-paleosol Sequence," *Quaternary Science Reviews*. 21 (20): 2191-2198

222 Ankita Mehta (26 January 2018) "A 177,000-year-old jawbone fossil discovered in Israel is oldest human remains found outside Africa," International Business Times

223 Simon J. Armitage (January 2011) "The southern route "out of Africa": evidence for an early expansion of modern humans into Arabia," *Science*. 331 (6016): 453-6

224 Christopher J. Bae, et al. (8 December 2017) "On the origin of modern humans: Asian perspectives," *Science*. 358 (6368)

225 J. I. Rose, et al. (2011) "The Nubian Complex of Dhofar, Oman: an African middle stone age industry in Southern Arabia," *PLoS ONE*. 6 (11): e28239

226 Ning Yu, et al. (May 2002) "Larger Genetic Differences Within Africans Than Between Africans and Eurasians," *Genetics*. 161 (1): 269-274.

227 G. Coop, et al. (June 2009) "The role of geography in human adaptation," *PLoS Genetics*. 5 (6): e1000500.

228 Deepti Gurdasani, et al. (July 2015) "The African Genome Variation Project shapes medical genetics in Africa," *Nature*. 517 (7534): 327-332

229 Ewan Callaway (26 April, 2017) "Controversial study claims humans reached Americas 100,000 years earlier than thought," *Nature*

230 William Hansen (2005) *Classical Mythology: A Guide to the Mythical World of the Greeks and Romans*, Page 182

231 C. E. Barret (2007) "Was dust their food and clay their bread?: Grave goods, the Mesopotamian afterlife, and the liminal role of Inana/Ištar," *Journal of Ancient Near Eastern Religions*, 7 (1): 7-65

232 M. Choksi (2014) "Ancient Mesopotamian Beliefs in the Afterlife," *Ancient History Encyclopedia*

233 Maciej M. Munnich (2013) *The God Resheph in the Ancient Near East*. Pages 62-63

234 Charles Penglase (1994) *Greek Myths and Mesopotamia: Parallels and Influence in the Homeric Hymns and Hesiod*. Page 157-9

235 Jeremy Black and Anthony Green (1992) *Gods, Demons and Symbols of Ancient Mesopotamia: An Illustrated Dictionary*, Page 141

236 Diane Wolkstein (1983) "Sumerian Goddess," *The New York Review of Books*

237 Diane Wolkstein and Samuel Noah Kramer (1983) *Inanna: Queen of Heaven and Earth: Her Stories and Hymns from Sumer*, Page 56

238 Jeremy Black, et al. (2003-2006) "Inana's descent to the netherworld," *Electronic Text Corpus of Sumerian Literature*

239 Jean Bottéro and H. Petschow (1972-1975) "Homosexualität," *Reallexikon der Assyriologie und Vorderasiatischen Archäologie*, 4:459b-468b

240 Gwendolyn Leick (1994) *Sex and Eroticism in Mesopotamian Literature*

241 Luther H. Martin (1987) *Hellenistic Religions: An Introduction*. Page 83

242 Maarten J. Vermaseren (1977) *Cybele and Attis: the myth and the cult*, translated by A. M. H. Lemmers, Page 115

243 James Frazer (1906–15) *The Golden Bough*, Chapter 34

244 John A. Halloran (December 10, 2006) *Sumerian Lexicon Version 3.0*, gal5-lá

245 Diane Wolkstein and Samuel Noah Kramer (1983) *Inanna: Queen of Heaven and Earth: Her Stories and Hymns from Sumer*, Page 74-78

BROKEN TIMELINES - BOOKS 1-3: EGYPT, MESOPOTAMIA, THE INDO-EUROPEANS AND HARAPPANS

246 Steve Tinney (April 2018) "Dumuzi's Dream" Revisited," *Journal of Near Eastern Studies*, 77 (1): 85-89

247 Charles Penglase (1994) *Greek Myths and Mesopotamia: Parallels and Influence in the Homeric Hymns and Hesiod*. Page 84

248 S. Dalley (2000) *Myths from Mesopotamia: Creation, the Flood, Gilgamesh, and Others*, Page 164

249 Tikva Frymer-Kensky (1993) *In the Wake of the Goddesses: Women, Culture and the Biblical Transformation of Pagan Myth*

250 Gregory Shushan (2009) *Conceptions of the Afterlife in Early Civilizations: Universalism, Constructivism, and near Death Experience*, Page 78

251 M. L. West (1997) *The East Face of Helicon: West Asiatic Elements in Greek Poetry and Myth*, Page 57

252 R. S. P. Beekes (2009) *Etymological Dictionary of Greek*. Page 794

253 S. A. Takács (1996) "Cybele, Attis and related cults," *Essays in memory of M.J. Vermaseren*. Page 376

254 N. H. Ramage and A. Ramage (1996) *Roman Art, Upper Saddle River*, figure 1.39

255 John Gwyn Griffiths (1980) The Origins of Osiris and His Cult, Page 158-162, 185

256 Tryggve N. D. Mettinger (2001) *The Riddle of Resurrection: "Dying and Rising Gods,"* Pages 15-18, 40-41

257 Rosalie David (2002) *Religion and Magic in Ancient Egypt*. Page 157

258 Plutarch (c. 100 AD) *Isis and Osiris*, translated by Frank Cole Babitt (1936) Volume 5:39

259 Donald B. Redford, editor (2003) *The Oxford Guide: Essential Guide to Egyptian Mythology*, Pages 302-307

260 Geraldine Pinch (2004) *Egyptian Mythology: A Guide to the Gods, Goddesses, and Traditions of Ancient Egypt*. Page 178-9

261 John Gwyn Griffiths (1980) *The Origins of Osiris and His Cult*. Page 44

262 Herman te Velde (1967) *Seth, God of Confusion*. Page 76-80

263 K. A. Raymoure (November 2, 2012) "Khania Linear B Transliterations" Minoan Linear A & Mycenaean Linear B. *Deaditerranean*.

264 Barbara J. Sivertsen, (2009) "The Minoan Eruption," *The Parting of the Sea: How Volcanoes, Earthquakes, and Plagues Shaped the Story of the Exodus*. Page 25.

265 Walter L. Friedrich, et al. (2006) "Santorini Eruption Radiocarbon Dated to 1627–1600 B.C." *American Association for the Advancement of Science*. 312 (5773): 548

266 Louise Schofield (2007) *The Mycenaeans*. Page 69

267 Bo M. Vinther, et al. (2006) "A synchronized dating of three Greenland ice cores throughout the Holocene," *Journal of Geophysical Research*. 111 (D13).

268 M. G. L. Baillie (1989) "Irish Tree Rings and an Event in 1628 BC," *The Thera Foundation*

269 H. Grudd, et al. (2000) "Swedish tree rings provide new evidence in support of a major, widespread environmental disruption in 1628 BC," *Geophysical Research Letters*. 27 (18): 2957-60

270 K. P. Foster, et al. (1996) "Texts, Storms, and the Thera Eruption," *Journal of Near Eastern Studies*. 55 (1): 1-14

271 Y. Duhoux (1994–1995) "LA > B da-ma-te = Déméter? Sur la langue du linéaire A," Minos 29/30 (1994-1995): 289-294

272 K. A. Raymoure (November 2, 2012) Inscription MY Oi 701. "si-to-po-ti-ni-ja". *Deaditerranean*

273 Martin Nilsson (1967) *Die Geschichte der Griechische Religion*. Page 444

274 K. A. Raymoure (November 2, 2012) "e-re-u-ti-ja," Minoan Linear A & Mycenaean Linear B. *Deaditerranean*.

275 Hesiod (c. 700 BC) *Works and days*. 166ff.

276 Mary Renault (1962) *The Bull from the Sea*

277 Plutarch (c. 100 AD) *Life of Theseus* 20

BROKEN TIMELINES - BOOKS 1-3: EGYPT, MESOPOTAMIA, THE INDO-EUROPEANS AND HARAPPANS

278 Larissa Bonfante and Judith Swaddling (2006) *Etruscan Myths (The Legendary Past)*, Page 41, Figure 25

279 Oliver Dickinson (December 1999) "Invasion, Migration and the Shaft Graves," *Bulletin of the Institute of Classical Studies*. 43 (1): 97-107

280 R. S. P. Beekes (2009) *Etymological Dictionary of Greek*, Page 337

281 Martin Nilsson (1967) *Die Geschichte der Griechische Religion*. Page 474

282 Anatole Bailly (1963) " Ἀιδης" *Dictionnaire Grec - Grançais*, 26th Edition.

283 Thomas McEvilley (2002) *The Shape of Ancient Thought*. Pages 118-121

284 Pliny the Elder (79 AD) *Naturalis Historia*, 6.59-60

285 Arrian of Nicomedia (c. 150 AD) *Indica*, 9.9

286 Michael Janda (2010) *Die Musik nach dem Chaos*. Pages 16-44

287 Homer (c. 750 BC) *Hymn 26 to Dionysus*. 2 ff

288 William Smith, editor (1873) *A Dictionary of Greek and Roman biography and mythology*

289 Basilio Perri (17 February 2014) *The so called Senatus Consultum de Bacchanalibus detailed analysis of the language*. Pages 3-.

290 Unknown Author (c 650 BC) *Homeric Hymn to Aphrodite*, 218 ff

291 Pliny the Elder (79 AD) *Natural History*, Book 8, 23

292 Edward Balfour (1885) "Parvati" *The Cyclopaedia of India and of Eastern and Southern Asia*, Page 153

293 Edmund Ronald Leach (2001) *The Essential Edmund Leach: Culture and human nature*, Page 85

294 Jana Garai (1973) *The Book of Symbols*

295 Geraldine Pinch (2002) *Egyptian Mythology: A Guide to the Gods, Goddesses, and Traditions of Ancient Egypt*, Page 115

296 Jelle W. F. Reumer, et al. (2003) "Late Pleistocene survival of the saber-toothed cat Homotherium in northwestern Europe," *Journal of Vertebrate Paleontology*. 23: 260

297 R. Barnett, et al. (2009) "Phylogeography of lions (Panthera leo ssp.) reveals three distinct taxa and a late Pleistocene reduction in genetic diversity," *Molecular Ecology*. 18 (8): 1668-1677

298 A. B. Lloyd (1993) *Herodotus*, Page 162

299 Saul M. Olyan (1988) *Asherah and the cult of Yahweh in Israel*, Page 79

300 Herbert Donner and Wolfgang Röllig (1962-1964) *Kanaanäische und aramäische Inschriften*.

301 Li Liu (2015) "A Long Process Towards Agriculture in the Middle Yellow River Valley, China: Evidence from Macro-and Micro-Botanical Remains," *Journal of Indo-Pacific Archaeology* 35 (2015): 3-14

302 Mark Nesbitt, et al. (January 1988) "Some Recent Discoveries of Millet (Panicum miliaceum L. and Setaria italica (L.) P. Beauv.) at Excavations in Turkey and Iran," *Anatolian Studies* (38): 85-97

303 Katie Manning, et al. (2011) "4500-Year old domesticated pearl millet (Pennisetum glaucum) from the Tilemsi Valley, Mali: new insights into an alternative cereal domestication pathway," *Journal of Archaeological Science*. 38: 312-32

304 J. M. M. Engels, et al. (1991) *Plant Genetic Resources of Ethiopia*

305 A. Lawler (2009) "Bridging East and West: Millet on the move," *Science*. 325: 942-943

306 Mira Roy (2009) "Agriculture in the Vedic Period," *Indian Journal of History of Science*, 44 (4): 497-520

307 Daniel Zohary and Maria Hopf (2000) *Domestication of plants in the Old World*, third edition, Page 83

308 R. Fullagar (2006) "Starch grains, stone tools and modern hominin behaviour." *An Archaeological Life: Papers in Honour of Jay Hall (Aboriginal and Torres Strait Islander Studies Unit Research Report Series 7)*. Pages 191-202

Section 6 – Harappan Mythic Era

309 Zulhidayat Siregar (June 28, 2012) "Tim Terpadu Riset Mandiri: Gunung Padang Truly Extraordinary," *Kantor Berita Politik RMOL*

BROKEN TIMELINES - BOOKS 1-3: EGYPT, MESOPOTAMIA, THE INDO-EUROPEANS AND HARAPPANS

310 E. Arsenio Manuel (1963) "A Survey of Philippine Folk Epics," Asian Folklore Studies, Volume 22, Pages 1-76

311 Mellie Leandicho Lopez (2008) A Handbook of Philippine Folklore

312 Philip Lutgendorf (2007) Hanuman's Tale: The Messages of a Divine Monkey. Page 40

313 George Hart (2005) The Routledge Dictionary of Egyptian Gods and Goddesses, Second Edition, Page 44

314 Robert J. Sharer and Loa P. Traxler (2006) The Ancient Maya (6th edition), Page 333.

315 Robert Caldwell (1996) A Comparative Grammar of the Dravidian or South-Indian Family of Languages, Third Edition, Page 591

316 A. K. Narain (1991) "Gaṇeśa: A Protohistory of the Idea and the Icon" in Robert Brown, editor: Ganesh: Studies of an Asian God, Page 21-22

317 Anna L. Dallapiccola (2002) Dictionary of Hindu Lore and Legend

318 P. Michalowski (1989) "The Lamentation over the Destruction of Sumer and Ur," Mesopotamian Civilizations, Volume 1

Available Formats

AVAILABLE DIGITALLY:

Broken Timelines Book 1: Egypt

Broken Timelines Book 2: Mesopotamia

Broken Timelines Book 3: The Indo-Europeans and Harappans

AVAILABLE IN PRINT:

Broken Timelines Book 1: Egypt

Broken Timelines Book 2: Mesopotamia

Broken Timelines Book 3: The Indo-Europeans and Harappans

Broken Timelines Books 1-3: Egypt, Mesopotamia, the Indo-Europeans and Harappans

www.ingramcontent.com/pod-product-compliance
Lightning Source LLC
Chambersburg PA
CBHW070748230426
43665CB00017B/2289